Sexual Issues

Understanding and advising in a Christian context

Edited by
Joanne Marie Greer
Brendan Geary

kevin mayhew

First published in Great Britain in 2010 by Kevin Mayhew Ltd
Buxhall, Stowmarket, Suffolk IP14 3BW
Tel: +44 (0) 1449 737978 Fax: +44 (0) 1449 737834
E-mail: info@kevinmayhewltd.com

www.kevinmayhew.com

9 8 7 6 5 4 3 2 1 0

ISBN 978 1 84867 252 9
Catalogue No. 1501218

Cover design by Rob Mortonson
© Image copyright Elena Ray. Used under licence from Shutterstock Inc.
Edited by Alison Evans
Typeset by Richard Weaver
Proof read by Rebecca Henning

Printed and bound in Great Britain

Contents

Part III: Contemporary issues in human sexuality

Part IV: Theoretical perspectives

Introduction

Brendan Geary and Joanne Marie Greer

This book intends to provide information and advice to priests, ministers, preachers, teachers, managers, pastoral workers, counsellors, people in training for ministry, and others in positions of leadership. Many may have to deal with one or more of the sexual issues raised in the book. They may not have specialist training in psychology or the social sciences, but would like to be better informed when considering these areas of difficulty. The book may also be useful to lay Christian persons experiencing sexual conflicts themselves, or who are perplexed by the sexual behaviour of significant others.

The book takes up a range of sexual issues that people may encounter in the course of their lives. Sex and sexuality are at the core of what it means to be a human being. At the most basic level, they relate to our ability to reproduce and continue our species; at a deeper level of meaning it is often in the area of sexuality and human relatedness that the deepest parts of ourselves are encountered and revealed – it is also often in the area of sexuality that we see how our humanity can be distorted, or that we can behave in a manner that is demeaning or abusive of others.

To our knowledge, every human society and every faith tradition has developed ways of dealing with and regulating human sexuality. There are traditions related to birth, coming of age, marriage, and having children. Each society has developed understandings and laws concerning the acceptable context, time, place and gender with which members of the group can have sexual intercourse. There are traditions of courtship, what are considered appropriate displays of affection or levels of nudity. There are communication patterns and roles assigned to men and women. Within the Christian tradition there are teachings related to marriage, premarital sex, sexual behaviour outside of marriage, homosexuality, masturbation, child-bearing, contraception and acceptable levels of sexual difference. While these may vary between different churches, and there can be a variety of opinions within churches, there still exists a core shared tradition for working through any of these issues that is the common inheritance of all people who call themselves Christian. All of us, for example, look to the scriptures of the Old and New Testaments as sources of teaching and wisdom in this area, although there are different approaches to the authority of scripture and different ways of working with the biblical material.

We live, relate as sexual beings, reflect theologically and involve ourselves in work or ministry in a particular historical context. The context in which we live has been affected by some significant developments that occurred in the last century. First and foremost, perhaps, was the revolution in thinking brought about by psychology and psychiatry, in particular the writings of Sigmund Freud. Freud spoke about topics that, until then, had been taboo in most societies; sexual development in childhood, incest, homosexuality, masturbation, sexual perversions. He also suggested that many people repressed their sexual desires and that this anxiety could give rise to other problematic behaviours.

Freud's theoretical writings, and the applied process of psychoanalysis which he used to help his clients, were highly controversial but also influential. So, too, was the research conducted by Alfred Kinsey in the United States, which was based on detailed interviews with thousands of people who were willing to disclose details about their sexual behaviour.[1] This landmark study marks the beginning of empirical research into human sexual behaviour, which, for the first time, provided researchers, teachers, counsellors, psychiatrists, psychologists, priests and theologians with actual data based on human

---

1. Kinsey, A. C., Pomeroy, W. B. , & Martin, C. (1948). *Sexual behavior in the human male,* and Kinsey, A. C., Pomeroy, W. B. , Martin, C. E., & Gebherd, P. H. (1953). *Sexual behavior in the human female,* both Philadelphia: Saunders.

experience. Later the work on marriage by Masters and Johnson would further develop this empirical approach through their studies of human sexual response.[2]

The sixties are considered a cultural watershed for many reasons, not least of which was the 'sexual revolution'. The 'Lady Chatterley' trial, which significantly curtailed the power of censorship to ban books in the United Kingdom, led to a much greater openness on the subject of human sexuality. The legal availability of oral contraception for women and condoms for men, in the general context of the challenge to authority that characterised that decade, led to sexual experimentation and greater sexual freedom. The women's movement and the gay liberation movement, with the subsequent decriminalising of homosexual acts and promotion of the rights of women and sexual minorities, continued this line of 'liberal' development in the public sphere.

With greater freedom came different problems: the arrival of AIDS and HIV, media exposure of child sexual abuse in homes, institutions and the Churches, and exposure of the previously hidden incidence of rape and sexual violence toward women. The resulting heightened awareness and openness made it timely to re-examine issues related to sexuality. Over the last fifty years all of the major Churches have gradually crafted responses to these changes in society; some have adjusted their teaching on sexuality, for example, the American Episcopal Church, which now accepts gay partnerships and recently voted to ordain gay bishops. Other Churches, like the Roman Catholic Church, and the Evangelical wing of the Church of England, have steadfastly held to the traditional line, arguing that they are promoting a 'yes' to life by teaching that sexual behaviour's proper place is solely within a heterosexual marriage. They see greater liberalism in the area of sexual morality as dishonouring God and often resulting in promiscuity, sexual exploitation and behaviours that do not reflect the dignity of being human. However, even some

2. Masters, W. & Johnson, V. (1966). *Human sexual response*. Boston: Little Brown.

of the most traditional Churches have modified their views of the purpose of heterosexual marriage, from solely procreation to also the creation of a community of mutual love, companionship, and support.

This complex ongoing dialogue is the context within which this book has been written. The editors hope to provide a range of chapters which is not exhaustive, but which is reasonably comprehensive, covering topics related to sexual development, and focusing on specific issues that confront Christians today. The book has been divided into four sections. The first section deals with sexual development in childhood and adolescence. Mary Ross' chapter outlines the normal path of sexual development and makes use of the stages outlined by Freud to explain how the lines laid down in infancy and childhood provide a template for adult sexuality. This chapter began its life as a series of workshop presentations, and the editors have tried to preserve Mary's lively style in preparing this chapter. Mary makes use of her extensive experience as an educational psychologist who specialises in working with children and adolescents. This is shown also in the second chapter that offers some perspectives on the issue of child sexual abuse. One of the editors, Joanne Marie Greer, has developed this chapter further by using her own experience as a psychologist and psychoanalyst to share information that will be of practical use to those who work with children and want to be alert to any signs of possible abuse.

The second section is concerned with aspects of adult sexuality. The first chapter deals with the sensitive topic of masturbation. This topic is often dealt with in the context of adolescent sexual development, which is only part of the story. The editors, who wrote this chapter, wanted to share the data that is available from researchers in order to put this topic in the context of adult sexual behaviour. They reflect on the history of the subject and provide data that suggests that, rather than being solely a manifestation of loneliness, sexual frustration or inadequacy (or self-centredness), masturbation appears to be a part of normal adult sexuality for many men and women. Issues relating to guilt and religious convictions are also discussed and recommendations have been provided for pastors and spiritual directors.

One of the significant changes in adult behaviour in the last forty years or so has been the number of couples who live together either before marrying or without any desire to marry. This has traditionally been forbidden by Churches and disapproved of by society. Kevin Kelly, a moral theologian, asks in his chapter if it is time to re-evaluate this behaviour in the light of the pastoral reality that confronts clergy of all denominations. This is followed by Joanne Marie Greer's chapter on an under-researched topic: delays and aberrations in psychosexual development. People who have read Ian McEwan's book, *On Chesil Beach*, will be aware of the devastating consequences of sexual naïveté or fears. Joanne Marie Greer sensitively explores this under-discussed topic and sheds light on issues of ignorance, underdevelopment, fear, anxiety and naïveté, with particular reference to applicants for ministry. Alison Moore's chapter deals with sexual concerns in marriage. Alison discusses issues related to healthy sexual relating within marriage and discusses ways of helping people when sexual problems emerge in the marriage.

The topic of homosexuality is dealt with in chapter 7. Ashley Wilson has tried to avoid going down well-travelled roads, where strongly held positions are often encountered, and instead invites the readers to engage their empathy to imagine the world from the perspective of gay men and women who want to live Christian lives as part of a Church community. He shows ways that this is made difficult for them, but also acknowledges that responding to men and women with a homosexual orientation has made severe demands of the Churches, as they struggle to be inclusive and compassionate, but stay faithful to any teaching on homosexuality that is part of the tradition of their Church. He also addresses the issue of married men (and women) who 'come out' to their spouses, the hurt, misunderstanding and pain involved in this choice, and the need for pastoral care of the spouse who has to deal with the consequences of this revelation and possible break-up of the relationship.

In chapter 8 Joanne Marie Greer discusses the complex and often disturbing issue of sexual perversions. She discusses the possible origins of these behaviours, and also describes the different kinds of disorders or perversions of normal sexuality that a pastor, confessor, employer, head teacher or mental-health professional might encounter as part of their work. Making use of clinical examples (which have been disguised to protect the anonymity of the clients involved) she discusses ways that perversions can manifest themselves in human behaviour. She also offers a theoretical perspective to help readers have a more empathic understanding of what can lead to the development of these perplexing behaviours.

In the last chapter in this section Jocelyn Bryan discusses the issue of sexuality and ageing. She notes that sexual researchers often do not collect data from people over 60 or 65 and opens up the topic of sexuality in the later years. Most people do not find it easy to discuss sexual topics, particularly when it involves their own bodies or relationships. This can be particularly difficult for older people, when there are cultural assumptions that older people are not – or should not be – sexually active. Jocelyn discusses the research that is currently available and shares stories about the experiences of older people which show that this can be a rich time when sexuality may continue as before, or change, in subtle or dramatic ways. Whatever the case, people do not stop being sexual beings as a result of the length of years. Her chapter invites people involved in pastoral care of older people to be more sensitive and aware of this aspect of human relating.

In the third section of the book we have drawn on a range of authors from different backgrounds to discuss a number of contemporary issues which we feel merit inclusion in a volume such as this. The first revisits the important subject of child sexual abuse in church settings, but from the perspective of a parish that has been wounded through the abusive behaviour of a priest or a member of the congregation.[3] The four authors, Tony Robinson, Gerard Fieldhouse-Byrne, Andrew Peden and Gerardine Taylor-Robinson, have drawn on their experience as psychologists, and as a priest who has worked with a parish in the aftermath of an abuse case, to discuss ways that the whole community; victim, perpetrator, clergy and community, can be helped to experience healing and hope after this devastating experience. This chapter should be particularly useful to any professional or clergyperson who is asked to work with a parish that has experienced abuse from a member of the clergy or a parishioner.

Ed Hone and Brendan Geary focus on the growing concern with Internet sex in chapter 11. Rather than focus solely on the issues of addiction and compulsivity, or the disturbing issue of Internet child pornography, Brendan and Ed have chosen to focus on the great majority of users (around 90%) who do not appear to be addicted, but whose use may be a source of problems for themselves or their families. The chapter contains a section showing how people's guilt or discomfort over use of the Internet for sexual purposes can create opportunities for significant pastoral conversations that may not have happened before this relatively recent development. They recommend that pastors and other leaders try to become more familiar with the issues involved in order to respond sensitively to anyone who feels a need to talk about this behaviour and its inherent dangers.

Jocelyn Bryan has written a chapter on contemporary issues in gender identity. This is a highly complex topic and Jocelyn presents the most recent research in this area. She also discusses issues related to gender and sexual identity, sexual orientation, and the topic of transgender individuals. Responding to people who have chosen surgery to change their gender is a challenge to many Churches. Jocelyn's

---

3. A more detailed discussion of the issue of child sexual abuse, focusing on the nature of abuse, effects on victims, and approaches to treatment, can be found in *The Christian handbook of abuse, addiction and difficult behaviour* (Suffolk: Kevin Mayhew). Some sections of the chapter from this book have been summarised for inclusion in the current chapter.

chapter presents helpful information for people who are interested in the issue of gender and the Churches, and wish to understand better some of the complex issues involved for those who do not feel comfortable in their own bodies.

In the last chapter in this section Brendan Geary and Alison Moore discuss the issue of sexuality in ministerial relationships. Alison works as a counsellor with clergy and their families, and Brendan currently works in formation of people who are preparing for priesthood. They make use of their experiences to discuss ways that our sexuality is alive and present in our ministerial interactions. They also discuss ways that people can misread signals or behave in immature, inappropriate or unhealthy ways that can lead to harm of others and compromising situations for priests and ministers. Fundamentally this chapter is a plea for ongoing self-awareness (and supervision) on the part of ministers and the need for healthy boundaries – not barriers – for those involved in pastoral work.

The final section of the book deals with theoretical perspectives. The first chapter in this section explores the topic of sexuality and spirituality. In the past these two areas of life were often seen as separate, if not antithetical. In recent years there has been a growth of writing and research that views sexuality and spirituality as closely related dimensions of our humanity. Chris Cook discusses some of the sources of different ways of looking at sexuality and spirituality and proposes a way that they can be brought together in a dynamic and healthy way.

This book has been written for people who come from a Christian background, and, as such, we felt it was appropriate to include a chapter on sexuality and the process of theological reflection. Charles Gay, the author, shows how ways of thinking about sexuality have undergone a paradigm shift, and that this has led to uncertainty, the taking of opposing positions, retrenchment by some, and the development of new insights and perspectives by others. He highlights the move in moral thinking from a static view of human nature, to a dynamic view of the human person. He also shows that moral thinking currently gives greater emphasis to persons rather than acts, and that the human, lived experience of believing Christians is now regarded as an important source of moral thinking. He also mentions that some writers have chosen to approach issues of sexuality from the perspectives of justice, compassion and human rights rather than from a consideration of sexual acts in the abstract.

In the concluding chapter the editors share their reflections on the place of sexuality within the Christian tradition. They suggest that the Christian vocation requires 'continence' in all sexual relationships, reflecting the Christian virtues of love, care, concern, generosity, sacrifice and discipline. This is part of the consistent teaching of the Churches, in fidelity to the Gospel message of Jesus. The chapter ends with a plea to avoid being overly preoccupied with sex *per se*, but rather to place sexuality within the context of our first call as Christians to love God and our neighbours.

This book is concerned with a number of – but not all – sexual issues. We have not, for example, included chapters on abortion or contraception. This is partly as these topics have been dealt with comprehensively elsewhere. We have also not dedicated chapters to the issue of celibacy and the priesthood, or clerical sexual abuse. There has been extensive discussion of all these topics from a variety of perspectives, and we instead turned our attention to issues we felt were important and timely but perhaps neglected in comparison. In this volume we do address the abuse crisis from a different perspective – rebuilding the Christian community of the violated parish, with recommendations for priests or ministers who are asked to step into a parish where abuse has taken place. The topic of sexual abuse in general is also dealt with in the second chapter.

The contributing authors come from different backgrounds, and this is reflected, inevitably, in their writing styles. As editors, we have tried to respect the different styles of the authors, while providing a text that is clear, stimulating, practical, and accessible to non-specialist readers. As far as possible, we have encouraged authors to share up-to-date research on sexual topics, where it is available, and to provide anecdotes that illustrate the points they wish to make. Some chapters offer practical advice, or lists of 'do's' and 'don'ts', however, this approach did not lend itself to all of the topics included in the book.

We would like to thank the authors who found time to write despite their various commitments, and who responded generously and thoughtfully to proposed changes to their texts. All of the authors share a commitment to the Gospel, though they write from the varying perspectives of different Christian Churches. While some readers might not find themselves in agreement with all of the positions taken by the various authors, we hope that each chapter will provide valuable information and perspectives, and food for thought. This volume is purposefully ecumenical in its vision, and we hope it will contribute to discussion of these sensitive topics in a spirit of ecumenical listening and sharing. Margaret O'Gara, Professor of Theology at St. Michael's University in Toronto, has written about the 'ecumenical gift exchange', suggesting that in a spirit of openness, all of the Churches can learn from each other and find common ground.[4] The current volume is offered to its readers in that spirit.

We would like to thank our families, colleagues and students, who have listened to us as we talked about and worked on this book over the past year, and whose patience and encouragement have supported us through the work of editing and writing. We hope that the various chapters will lead to informed practice and compassionate pastoral presence to those who encounter difficulty or require understanding in the sexual aspect of their lives.

---

4. O'Gara, M. (1998). *The Ecumenical gift exchange*. MN: The Liturgical Press.

PART I

Sexual development in childhood and adolescence

ONE

Sexual development in childhood and adolescence

Mary Ross

All of us have been in the womb, a sexual organ, of somebody we call Mother. We have come from that point to where we are today and throughout our entire lives we have been sexual beings in the true sense of that word. I want to talk about what is normal in sexual development from babyhood right through to adolescence, and then I want to look at two related issues, that are intertwined. One issue I want to look at is if something goes wrong, if there is a block in development, from whatever source, external or internal. Another issue I will look at is taking account of today's world where children are growing up. For example, there was a story in the media while I was preparing this paper about a 13-year-old boy who looks eight, and yet has become a father. He is reported as saying that he will be a good father. We will look at the circumstances that allowed that to happen both from his own body's point of view and also from the perspective of changes in society.

I would like to refer to the learning theory of Brunner, who suggested that what a person learns at one stage he or she keeps revisiting at later stages of life. I believe that is more than true about sexuality. I want to try to use examples from my experience of working with children or young people and their parents, to illustrate how various things just keep coming up over and over and hitting us. People who have already experienced midlife will be aware of this. We revisit something we experienced at a younger age, and we are either stuck in the same spot or it now has quite a different meaning for us.

Beginnings

Until Freud came along at the turn of the twentieth century, people in the Western world were accustomed to thinking of small children as asexual. Even today some people have difficulties if Freud's sexual theories about small children are mentioned. It is fair to say that some of Freud's naming or describing of things can sound very peculiar. But anyone who has observed babies, one- to five-year-olds, will know that he was talking about what he observed. Some people have said that he didn't observe babies because he worked with adults, but in actual fact he was a daddy as well, of two girls and two boys.

What is the first thing that's said when a baby is born? 'It's a girl,' or 'It's a boy.' We know the answer to this right away because of the information we get from looking at the genitals. Until 10 to 15 years ago, when any of us had to study children we were told that the brain of a baby when it was born was intact, fully developed. It just grew, and by osmosis gained a pool of knowledge. Now we know that that is not true. There are two holes in the brain, in the sense that nerve endings have not joined up across the synapses. The two crucial ages are during those first two to three years of life, and then in adolescence[1]. We used to think babies didn't see for about six weeks. That's nonsense, unless there is some defect in their eyes or in the part of the brain that is affecting their eyes. They can see and they have a fixed face – more fixed than any of us because they have a lot invested in what they look at.

They are like ET, the film character. ET lands on the planet and has to figure out who these beings are and how they behave. The neck goes up and there is this absolute focus on figuring out what it is they are doing, how they feel, how they get fed etc. The baby is absolutely fixed on its mother. Now, if you look at a picture of a

---

1. Gerhardt, S. (2004). *Why love matters: How affection shapes a baby's brain.* London: Routledge, Strauch, B. (2003). *Why are they so weird? What's really going on inside a teenager's brain.* London: Bloomsbury.

mother and baby, how many orifices can you see? There are the ears, the eyes, nostrils, and mouth. The mouth is the most significant at the early stage and those who have had their own babies will know everything goes in the mouth – everything. I love standing behind a mother or a father in church who is holding a relatively young baby around three to five months. The adults are trying to pay attention to what is going on in the church, and, at the same time, trying to extract fingers from mouth, ears and nostrils. The baby is exploring territory, but the territory is the various orifices, and primarily the mouth. It is trying to stick its fist down the mother or father's mouth, or that of anybody else who is willing to hold the baby. This concern with orifices is very important; this is what Freud was talking about. Freud was saying that this 'orifice play' is sexualised behaviour that the child is going to revisit when a bit older. For example, if an adult gives someone an erotic kiss, he or she is certainly using the mouth as a sexual organ. (The reality, of course, is that the age of revisiting is arriving much younger in today's world.)

Freud suggested that children have the same sort of emotional lives as adults; they can be angry, they can rage, they can love, and they can be sad with same range of intensity as adults – and they are sexual beings. When he applied his thinking to sexuality in children it caused a strong reaction. The Catholic Church, for example, went so far as to put his works on the Index of Forbidden Books.

What Freud meant was that from the moment they are born babies can use their bodies in a way that gives them bodily pleasure, as we hope it will later give them pleasure with a partner when they have reached an appropriate age. That is what he was talking about, but he was writing and speaking in German. He was translated badly and it came out sounding rather strange in English. Remember that sexuality involves emotions; you love somebody, you hate somebody, you withdraw affection, you feel affection. Emotional learning comes from being in a very close, bodily relationship.

Touch

I have absolutely no problem at all with parents putting their young children into nurseries – I have a major problem if they haven't checked out that there will be good one-to-one contact for a major part of the day when their baby is in that nursery. Is there going to be enough lifting, holding, talking, and talking in grown-up language? They have to learn, so a caregiver must talk normally to very young babies so that they are getting the rhythm of speech that they will one day be able to use themselves. They must be held, bounced, tickled, etc., to learn about their own bodies and those of others.

The young baby in a suitable caregiving environment is not only learning language and movement skills but also being socialised. The social brain is absolutely vital in our sexuality. If we had a good social brain would we rape anybody, would we abuse anybody, would we demean them sexually in any way at all? Bruce Perry provides a good illustration of this when he describes Leon, a sixteen-year-old adolescent who was deprived of appropriate nurturance as a baby. He raped and then stabbed two teenage girls to death. His mother, Maria, was an immigrant in the United States who had received assistance from her extended family in Mexico when she was raising her first son, Frank. Her husband had then come to Washington DC for work. Maria had no family support and did not know how to respond to a crying baby. Perry writes:

> When Maria had taken Frank out for walks, Leon had wailed in his crib at first. But he'd soon learned that crying would bring no aid, so he stopped. He lay there, alone and uncared for, with no one to talk to him and no one to praise him for learning to turn over or crawl (and not much room to explore anyway). For most of the day he heard no language, saw no new sights, and received no attention.[2]

2. Perry, B. D., & Szalavitz, M. (2006). *The boy who was raised as a dog.* New York: Perseus Books, p.112.

With a good social environment the baby is learning good touch as opposed to bad touch. If everybody learned to touch properly then no one would ever grow up to abuse a child physically or sexually. An important way of sharing good touch with a baby is through massage. It's a shame we have to teach young mothers baby massage; you would think it would be natural. But people are busy and they do not know that taking up a baby and just stroking it in a very slow rhythmical way is part of its ongoing development, including its sexual development.

When couples are having problems in their sexual lives and go to some expert for advice, often the first thing they are told is to massage each other. They are learning to return to what the baby had as a natural pleasure. What is vital is just good rhythmical, soft touch. Also, when you see children who are out of control, and might have to grab them because they are being a danger to themselves or somebody else, one of the things that can help (once you have got them calmed down) is to very slowly – just very slowly – massage them. One of the exercises I have done with groups in the past is to get people just to stand in a big circle, not facing in but facing around the room, and massaging one another's shoulders. Each person is massaged just so gently. It is interesting to see what happens. Now there are some people who are not living in their bodies, and that exercise feels like a violation to them, so you have to be very careful about deciding to do this. You also have to be very careful with children because they may have had a very bad experience of touch.

When there is a good experience of cheek-to-cheek touch between a parent and their child – just holding the child against them, feeling the rhythm very gently and possibly eventually stroking the head – you have one foundation of good, healthy sexual development of the child, and not only in Freud's terms. Anybody who has had to hold a baby or a young child will know that you are preparing them to be happy about touch, to find touch a welcoming thing and to receive touch from others. Having said that, you will continue to try to extract their fingers from up your nostrils because it gets sore, or in your ears, or especially when they then stick their fingers in their mouths, since that is where they like to put everything! It is all part of the learning about their own bodies.

We have to be kind to parents who are not comfortable with touch. You cannot blame them for it and we must be careful about laying all the blame at the doors of mothers, particularly fastidious mothers.

Sue Gerhardt's book, *Why Love Matters,* contains a wealth of information about the importance of those first three years of life. What is not learned properly in the first three years is not irretrievable, but it becomes harder at a later point in life. Counsellors know that there are some people who just cannot be helped. I am thinking of a woman with whom I am working at the moment. She is in her late thirties and something has gone quite awry for her. She was musing with me last week about men who were drilling outside her house. She said, 'It's just like I feel violated.' I noticed how often she said this word because at some later stage I think she is going to have to deal with an experience of being violated in childhood. Something has gone really quite awry, and I wonder what is ever going to make her feel happy about her existence on this planet.

Breastfeeding and living with the mess

I have had to do a lot of home visits over the years. Sometimes walking into an unbelievably tidy house would immediately shed light on the symptoms that a child or young person might be producing. Then my heart would sink, as the parents often did not like any mess at all, and could not allow their child a space to paint and do all the messy things involved in normal learning.

Consider the situation where breastfeeding is being forced on a mother, possibly by a really active health visitor who says that this is the right thing to do, but the mother does not like the process. I can actually feel her whole body pulling back at the thought of it, and the baby feels that too. The baby feels the rejection but doesn't know what it means. It knows that it is trying to get a good bond here, and that it is not succeeding. It doesn't know any of those words because it is only learning through its skin. This tells us again about the importance of touch. The baby and breast are touching, and the baby is learning that this is good and pleasurable, or bad and rejecting.

Some women would say at the beginning that breastfeeding is not for them, but they could hold the baby close and help it to use a bottle. It's the closeness that is important. Unfortunately some mothers and fathers don't understand this. They see all the grunge that comes out of the various orifices. There are some that do not like it, but what matters to the baby is that there is someone who can cope with it. What is important is that the baby isn't made to feel dirty. We will come back to this sense of dirtiness when we look at shame.

Comfort

Harlow[3] did an important series of experiments in the 1960s with baby monkeys. (Unfortunately in those days we felt we could frighten baby monkeys in the name of scientific research.) He produced two models of mother monkeys. One was made of wire netting with a teat and a bottle that the baby could feed from, and the other was made from the same wire netting, but was also covered in terry towelling. The monkeys always went to the terry towelling. Contrary to what people expected, they did not go to suckle, but to be comforted.

In many dire situations children of a variety of ages will come for a hug. Sadly, as I often say to teachers, we have produced a society today where we are producing robots, 'the untouchables'. Staff will say to me that they are not allowed to touch a child. I tell them that they are ruining the children because they need healthy touch and

3. http://en.wikipedia.org/wiki/Harry_Harlow, retrieved 12 November 2009.

good touch. I used to be a mathematics teacher before I became a psychologist. In my class I would have to help one or two children, and I would automatically touch them gently. Just the lightest touch, but you are in contact with them. That is very important for children. Some would draw back, but that was often because they had been hit at home, and they were expecting to be hit. You wonder how we can do this to children. Think of adult sexual beings who can enjoy all aspects of sexuality; good friendship, good contact physically, etc. We are ruining this for a child if it starts out frightened to actually be touched in any way at all, because it could be harmful or demeaning.

Freud's stages of psychosexual development[4]

So what was Freud talking about? The first stage, which is during the first year of life, he dubbed the oral stage. What did he mean by the oral stage? He meant the mouth. In the clinic where I work we have bottles lying around in all of our play therapy rooms – whether it is with very young children or adolescents. You can actually see adolescents in play therapy sitting there sucking from a bottle. They have to relearn, or learn for the first time, what it is like to be 'hooked on' as opposed to being in charge of your own feeding.

Freud said that people can get stuck at this stage. What did he mean by that? If you continue to emphasise oral behaviour as your primary source of pleasure you might become involved in smoking, over-eating etc. The need to suck is activated when we are anxious. In other words, we are 'suckers' – literally – and if you are anxious you want to suck. Some of us buy 'sucky' sweets when anxious. It's something going into your mouth that is important, and so you will see people sucking on empty pipes, just to have that sense that they

---

4. There is a wonderful book by Anna Freud, Sigmund Freud's daughter, where she took her father's language and simplified it to make it more comprehensible and accessible. Freud, A. (1931 / 1974). *Introduction to psychoanalysis: Lectures for child analysts and teachers 1922 – 1935.* London: The Hogarth Press.

can suck. Most of us as adults keep that sucking behaviour to appropriate places and objects most of the time. If as a clergyperson you took a pipe up into the pulpit with you, it would not be looked upon kindly. But you might be nervous, and might take your pipe with you. Some people would just have it in their pocket so that they know that it is there. It's a kind of internal pipe.

The stage of primarily oral pleasure comes to a close with weaning. Whether you have been breastfeeding or you have been feeding through a bottle you have to wean the child. Some people think that you only wean breastfed babies, but you have to wean them from that teat whether it is on the breast or on the bottle. This is important so that later they can move on to use a spoon. At each stage something is relinquished so that something new can happen.

Freud's second stage is known as the anal stage, which involves the stage where infants learn how to control their sphincter. In toileting you have two sphincters, which means that the child has two muscles that it has to learn to control. During workshops I often ask people to try and pull in their anal sphincters. People realise immediately that it pulls in the tummy as well. The infant has to learn this without knowing that the tummy muscle is there. Think of the developmental activity involved and the jump they have to make. I ask people to try and imagine that they were about to pee and wanted to avoid embarrassment. As adults we have often forgotten how hard it is to actually do this because we know immediately if we are managing it or not managing it.

Infants don't know that these muscles are there. They just see the watery stuff that keeps coming out and they love it, small boys in particular. How many people have witnessed this when they see a baby's nappy being changed? Just before the new nappy is being fastened the baby may spray right over everything. They reach down to handle the faeces while the caregiver is trying to clean them up. An older infant may 'fingerpaint' on the wall with faeces. Most babies love the mess unless they are told it's dirty – or worse – that *they* are dirty, because they automatically go to play with it if they get a chance.

R. D. Laing, the famous psychiatrist (who worked for a time in the clinic where I worked in Glasgow), developed a place for really distressed and disturbed adults who were fairly stuck at another bit of their early life. One of them, Mary Barnes, a woman who was very 'faecally oriented' (as we would say) became a wonderful finger painter and changed career when she was well enough. She was an amazing woman and her exhibitions of paintings done in oils are incredible. In Freud's language that could be seen as sublimating her love of getting her hands in messy, messy stuff. She transformed (sublimated) it into legitimised stuff that has made her a lot of money because her paintings can sell incredibly well. However it took years of therapy to get her to that point.

If you get stuck for whatever reason at that toilet-training stage, it could be that you become obsessed with excessive orderliness, or conversely you grow up to be an incredibly messy person. We rather unkindly call excessively orderly persons 'anally retentive', i.e., they cannot let go in a smooth natural way but cling to order. For them, there must not be a speck in view or anything even slightly out of place (some people need to rearrange things that are not orderly as it upsets them – even when it is not their property or their place). On the other hand if they haven't learned to leave the messy bit behind and move on to the next stage they can stay unbelievably messy, in a rather extreme way. I am thinking of a programme I saw recently which was looking at MENSA and those who are members of this organisation that comprises people with high levels of IQ. We were introduced to one man who was absolutely brilliant, but in his bedroom everything, including his clothing, was on the floor.

Again, to move on developmentally something must be given up. In this case, what is given up is freedom. The child who by nature wants to be in control of when and where to urinate and defecate must submit to the parent's rules. Children who delight in messes must start to keep themselves clean and pick up their messes.

Freud described the next stage as the phallic stage, which is where some people would say that sexuality begins. This is where children become unbelievably interested in their genitalia and, to the embarrassment of their parents, other people's genitalia – especially brothers and sisters, and sometimes mums and dads if they get a chance. Because they don't know what genitals are, they become ET again and want to investigate what this is all about. Of course what they find is that there are differences between boys and girls, and that the genital area is unbelievably pleasurable when touched. We have a word for that – masturbation – and many a child at that point is made to feel ashamed of natural impulses. Remember that they may have been made to feel ashamed before if they have been told they are dirty for wanting to play with their excrement, and now if they are also masturbating then they are told that's dirty. What is worse, their hand might get smacked as well, and that really affects them as they are being punished as well for their curiosity and experience of pleasure. Small children can become quite proud of their genitals. For boys it's rather obvious that they might be very proud of that little instrument, but girls can also be proud in the way they walk, as they get some sense from parents that they have 'things inside them to make babies'. They can be quite proud of that.

If children are not responded to properly for their normal interest in their genitalia they can have sexual dysfunctions or even sexual deviancy later on. There can also be other psychological impairments. They can for example be very vain as a compensation for having been humiliated. Note that we sometimes use the word 'cocky' to describe someone like this, 'cock' being a slang word for the penis.

It is at this stage that young children first sense the relational aspects of sexuality. They are often aware of their own physical attractiveness and may be flirtatious or innocently seductive with either or both parents, or with other adults. This is Freud's famous 'Oedipus complex'. The parents' responses are crucial. If an adult is actually seduced, either literally or metaphorically, a developmental disaster occurs. The necessary response is a kindly firmness and enforcement of boundaries between adult and child. Freud speaks of the disappointment the child experiences when the parent enforces rules even in the face of the child's attempts to manipulate.

Accepting this disappointment opens the way for the next developmental stage, which Freud calls 'latency'. When I was training to be a secondary teacher it was just at the end of a Scottish tradition when you also had to do a term in primary school. It was an amazing experience, and I wish that every secondary teacher still got that opportunity. You learn that children in the primary-age group are avid for knowledge of rules. They are avid for learning in general, even if they are not getting support at home to encourage them. Freud's idea about this age group was that there isn't any major change in the sexual aspect of development. Nothing new happens until puberty. They are not distracted by either the pleasurable or the relational aspects of sexuality and they can get on with the learning process. Interest in the body is, to some extent, put to the side, but it is used in sport and other activities. Children become very interested in games; either mental games, board games or physical games. They are using their body externally as opposed to touching it all the time. At this stage it would be abnormal for a child to masturbate openly or excessively, or to try to touch the genitals of others. This would be an alert that something has gone amiss.

Lastly, in adolescence comes the 'genital' stage, by which Freud means that there is not only a refocusing on the genitalia *per se* but also an intense interest in all that goes with becoming and moving towards being a full adult sexual being with all its possibilities. The genital stage recaps the phallic stage, but adds the use of the genitalia *relationally*, to enrich partnership with another human being.

Erik Erikson, who is perhaps best known for his stages of psycho-social development, extended Freud's developmental ideas beyond young adulthood. Erikson proposed that we never stop developing, that we are developing from the minute we are conceived to the moment we draw our last breath.

Looking at today's world

From the minute that they are born today's children are growing up in a highly sexualised world. We are breathing sexuality – and not always the nicest kind – through our pores from a very young age. It might be the music that they hear from a very young age that they might not understand. However, they are getting a beat that is not the appropriate beat for them at that age. There is a retired psychiatrist in Edinburgh who goes round the world watching and filming parents with very, very young babies, even ten minutes old. He has shown how a baby initiates the behaviour that leads to imitation as opposed to what we thought in the past, that they imitate us. No, we imitate them. The baby *pulls a face* and we *pull the same face* back at them. He has listened to lullabies in all different languages, and he has worked with musicians in Edinburgh who then break down the music. They have discovered that they are all the same. The words are all different but they all use the same rhythm. It is a natural thing and if the baby learns this natural rhythm it will be all right. I don't mean to demean young parents but if the young parents are still into heavy metal, then that's what the baby will pick up through the vibrations, and this will disorder them in a certain sense.

Another aspect of inappropriate sexualisation is in the area of dress. I recently picked up a magazine with an article entitled 'Decisions, Decisions: Lily aged 5'. Lily is dressed in a bikini in a fabulous clothes store. Think of yourself when you were five being dressed like this little girl. Her face communicates a certain seductiveness and desire. Would most adults want this for their daughter or grandchild, their little niece or grand-niece? Lily strikes me as screwed-up already. She is dressed in a store in public – not even in a private home – in a kind of bikini. I think that this is wrong and I do not feel that I am being an old 'fuddy duddy' in saying it. To put a child dressed like that into a public space like a shop or a magazine is, in effect, to put them into the public arena. Some may think I am exaggerating, but once when I was talking about this to a large group of primary teachers a teacher came up at the break time and told me the following story:

> We love the poet Robbie Burns in Scotland and this young teacher had decided that she would have a little Burns event in the classroom since it was close to 23 January when we celebrate Burns' night. She told all the children to tell their parents about this so that they could wear something tartan the following Friday. When the Friday came she had lots of things prepared and as they came in they were all wearing various clothes with tartan designs; kilts, ties, ribbons or whatever. However one girl arrived wearing a black boob tube, a very short skirt and black fishnet tights. The teacher wondered what to do because she was embarrassed for the child and didn't know why this had happened. On the Monday morning the child's mother came in and apologised for sending her daughter in the way she did. She explained that her daughter had come home and said that the teacher wanted them to dress as tarts.

Now where is the mistake here? Why was that mother hearing that they were to come in dressed as tarts – which she did very well? Why did she not ask why anyone might tell her to dress her child as a tart – and then think it was OK? She was not apologising for having done it but because she had got the wrong message. Not all of our children are being brought up in such a standards-free world, but some of them are.

Body image and the sexualisation of children

Concern about body image is creeping down and is becoming a dilemma in young children. We have quite young children wanting to alter their image. One of the ways that they can do it is through the tanning salons. The problem with the tanning salons – apart from what might be going on in their heads that makes them feel that they have to look different from how they actually are – is that they believe they are not attractive if they are pale. Now the skin-cancer risk is getting very high because some of these very young people are going into these salons that are illegal for children. In some you can just put money in a slot and there is nobody supervising. Some children were badly burned recently as they stayed in too long and got third-degree burns. The real issue, though, is their motivation for doing this. Why do they feel they have to augment themselves in this way? Some might say kids have always done that, particularly girls with make-up, but it seems to me that these stories indicate that we have moved from a certain level of vanity to a sense of lack of self-worth related to poor body image, which is, to some extent, a product of our culture and society.

We have always had the opportunity to enhance ourselves through make-up, and teenagers were always renowned as fashion kings and queens. However, children are now becoming fashion kings and queens at two and three years of age and parents are allowing them to make choices that are not appropriate for their stage of development. The 'No' word can generate a great deal of resistance. Some of them are not expecting any limitation and we are, in fact, destroying them from a very young age by that very fact. Some parents allow them to dress in a very provocative way, or even facilitate this. The case of JonBenét Ramsey[5] will come to mind. She was murdered in a context of beauty competitions. It wasn't the child winning those competitions; it was her parents. There are talent competitions for

5. http://www.trutv.com/library/crime/notorious_murders/famous/ramsey/index_1.html

children as young as three, wearing full make-up etc. It is bit like child majorettes, although there is just a bit more concern in the world of children's beauty pageants because some of the songs they are singing and the actions that they are using are highly sexualised.

Some major companies need to be more responsible. I remember an advertisement for children's clothes from about two years ago. There were young kids of about four or five and one of the boys was moving his hips in a highly sexualised way. It is interesting if you watch footballers when they 'score' a goal. Now they don't simply score the goal, but have to go on to display themselves. What a lot of them do is a sexualised action. Of course, unconsciously some of them think they have just done a sexual thing because it's orificial. They put something in that hole which happens to be a ball net. One of the things they also do, which is really reasonably harmless, is put their shirts over their heads, which is what eighteen-month to two-year-olds do. Children know that they get a reaction if they pick up their skirts or they pull down their trousers. They also know it is naughty.

Last week a little two-year-old girl in the parish where I live pulled up her skirt so that you could see something of her bellybutton. She was giggling away to herself. That is normal activity for a child of that age. But it is serious if you are still doing it at 55 in public, as you may be arrested for indecent exposure. The problem for me about all of this is that we are encouraging the ongoing naughtiness of children in a way that is going to cause them trouble later on. In a certain sense, we need to learn to keep the 'naughty bits' in our heads. We might do funny things in private, but if we do them in public it will not be acceptable.

Paedophiles should never do what they are doing. *Never.* That is the bottom line. However, sometimes you cannot blame them entirely for what actually happens because of the way – particularly with girls – some of us dress children from a very young age. They look inviting, and they love to bond with others. We need to have the courage to challenge some parents. They may want to help their children look a little more attractive, but it may be done at the expense of dignity and appropriate modesty. Such clothing makes the child alluring to some adults, and we need to take some responsibility for the dangers we are creating for our children.

Recently two young girls passed me who were wearing lipstick. One of the latest fashions is to wear long jumpers that come down to the top of the legs with the girls wearing only tights. As they walked behind me I could see all these heads turning. They wore high heels that affected the way they walked as well. All you could see was a backside, a fringe under the backside, and then legs. Now I am not saying they shouldn't do that, but they need to know the effect this may have on some people, and that this might get them into possible harm. I do not want to dampen them down, but it is part of their education to be aware of the effect of their choice of dress on others.

One of the negative consequences of improved health and nutrition is the lowering of the age of puberty. You cannot start puberty unless your body weight and your body mass are at a certain level. Children are reaching puberty at a very young age and some girls are menstruating around about eight now, not the majority, but a sizeable number. If they are menstruating at eight they have got years of fertility ahead of them at an age when they lack the emotional maturity to handle sexual relations. Girls and boys can have bodies that are ready to do certain things that they are not intellectually or emotionally prepared for. They are not ready for the consequences of sexual behaviour, as we have seen from the newspaper story of the 13-year-old boy who, it was reported, had just become a daddy.[6] We have boys in court of nine, ten and eleven who are charged with rape. That would not have been humanly or physically possible about 20–25 years ago.

6. Bingham, J. (18th May, 2009). Alfie Patten, 13, is not baby's father, test shows. *The Telegraph.* Retrieved on 25th May, 2009, from: http://www.telegraph.co.uk/news/uknews/5345999/Alfie-Patten-13-is-not-babys-father-test-shows.html

Some young people grow very tall very quickly, and when there is a rape case against a man for raping a young girl he will often say that she told him she was 18. She may be thirteen or fourteen but she has got the body, stance and sophistication of an 18-year-old with the clothes and make-up and lingo that correspond to what we would expect of an 18-year-old. Developments in computers and mobile phones mean that sexual activity is often filmed, sometimes with agreement, and broadcast abroad. These developments are also having an impact on the worlds of children and adolescents.

Teenagers and post-adolescents

Sister Marie Hilda,[7] who founded the clinic where I work, went down to London in 1929 to learn how to engage in therapy with children. As well as setting up the clinic, she went around in the evenings and at the weekends talking to groups of people who would have to work with teenagers. The word adolescence comes from the Latin word meaning 'to ripen', which is what Freud was trying to say. In other words, what has been there all along now blossoms. Sr Marie Hilda said that adolescence is about the body changing, the mind changing, the heart changing and the soul changing. She called adolescence the period of three converging ages; the age of physical development, the age of mental conflicts, and the age of sex consciousness. It is also the age of independence and the age of idealism. (If you want to raise money for charity go to 12- and 13-year-olds as they are starting their adolescence. They will give you their all and they will raise money by whatever means you ask, for a good cause.)

Early or primitive societies, some of which still exist, have very clear rites of passage from childhood to adulthood, and they do not really have a proper adolescence. (They do not have any adolescence at all.) What happens is that you get invited into the adult group, and it is puberty that does it for you. In the Kota tribe in Congo,

7. Misiak, H. and Staudt, V. M. (1954). *Catholics in psychology.* McGraw Hill.

once the boys are pubertile their faces are covered in a blue inky material that marks them out in the tribe as being ready to learn how to be adult, and how to take the adult male role, which is very important.[8] As we know, there are certain behaviours associated with this transition in our own culture. We have all been through teenage life, and if you have had teenagers at home then you will know that you can certainly recognise when there is a teenager in the house. For the young women it is the face, the walk and the obstreperous attitude. They don't want to go with the flow or fulfil adult expectations.[9]

Sr Marie Hilda was looking primarily at the first three: physical development, sexual development, and mental conflict, which we now know is partly caused by the expectations put on them by adults. The adolescent's neural wires are still in the process of being joined up. Hence they feel that they are just constant failures in their parents' or teachers' eyes over certain things; not getting their stuff in on time, not getting their homework done, leaving their room untidy, etc. They are not quite at the point where everything they want to happen can happen in the way they might want. It may appear that the adolescent cannot hold a single train of thought and then suddenly, almost overnight, often round about sixteen years of age, it will all suddenly make sense for the young person.

When I first taught this material I suggested that adolescence could last from ten through to twenty-five years of age. Now it's from about eight years through to twenty-five years and increasing at the other end. Sr Marie Hilda called this the age of independence, which involves financial independence. A lot of young people today are still dependent upon their parents for money. Even if they are living in a flat they bring their dirty washing back home, they are often getting their food made for them, and maybe getting money

8. http://hrsbstaff.ednet.ns.ca/waymac/Sociology/A%20Term%201/2.%20Culture/Rituals.htm
9. Strauch, B. (2003). *Why are they so weird? What's really going on inside a teenager's brain.* Bloomsbury.

handed to them as well, especially if they are not managing their rent. So they are not actually independent yet. Independent means that you can stand alone and create your own new life around you. Many young people today simply cannot afford to be independent; it is as simple as that.

Physical development

Let's look at the physical changes first of all. Their size changes.[10] First and foremost we see growth spurts and this sometimes happens over holidays. Their shape changes, and their strength too, and this is often not thought about by adults. You will get a bigger brother or sister horseplaying with a younger sibling on Tuesday, and on Wednesday the child is crying because of being hit harder than yesterday. They did not mean to hit them and the mother or father will nearly always say, 'You just don't know your own strength'. If they were wise enough they would say, 'I know you don't know your own strength, because you cannot see your muscles and you don't know that they have become stronger. If you push that way then somebody will fall, whereas they never fell before.' Adolescents really come in for a rough time from adults. A mother came to see me last year and she brought her son. He didn't know his own strength and he got into trouble for hurting another boy at school.

Adolescent sexual development

As young people grow up a bit the dreaded secondary sex characteristics appear. In today's world adolescent development is starting much earlier. It is because we have fed them too much of a certain kind of food at a young age. It is only when we have got a certain amount of extra bulk to body mass and shape that the hormones can be released via the brain. That's what starts puberty off, and hence we have pubertal children aged eight, nine and ten. Some still delay

10. Konner, M. (1991 / 1993). *Childhood.* Little Brown and Co.

until what we would call a normal age and some are still delayed beyond it, but we have pubertal children very young now, when they are in no way equipped in mind, heart and soul to deal with these changes in their bodies. As one result you get children becoming parents.

A priest once contacted me and asked me to visit a family in his parish, where they had just found out that their 13-year-old boy was about to become a father. The parents told me that the girl was 16 and she was going to deliver the child very soon. The mother knew her son was full of life, but she insisted he be in by 9pm. I said that time wasn't the issue as sexual intercourse doesn't take long! I said I presumed he had not been dragged kicking and screaming to his fate. I don't think anybody felt abused in this relationship. What interested me was the difference between his father and mother. I asked his mother what her concern was, and she told me that he needed trainers, and wondered if she should give him the money for the trainers or should she put it in the bank for the baby. She really was in a state about this. I looked at her husband who had been sitting quite quietly and said, 'What is your worry?' He was concerned in case the Child Support Agency would be looking for his son when he is 16. I didn't know the answer but said I would find out. I phoned back later to tell him that in Scots law they could pursue him immediately because he is going to be the father of the child.

What fascinated me was that mother said that she would have her own two boys coming in at nine o'clock at night, and she would want them to have their bath. But what if the younger son – who was now a father – wanted to bathe the baby? What should she do? What she was asking was, 'Do I have a boy or do I have a man in this house?' Do I have my wee boy who should not be leaving school for three years, or is it the daddy of this baby that I have got in the house? We have to hold on to all that for parents, and help them sort it out.

These two quite different concerns were from two parents who had thought they had been very, very protective of this boy and then found they were about to become grandparents within about three months. Technically in Scots law the boy is a child and the prospective mother of this baby is an adult, and gender does not come into it. The father was worried if the boy would get into trouble for under-aged sexual behaviour. I said that on the contrary if they wanted they could get the girl charged for having sex with a minor. Now of course they didn't want to do that. In Scots law you are formally an adult at 16 unless you are in care. It is different in English law but in Scots law the minute you hit your sixteenth birthday you are adult, and you are free to marry without parental consent. As for the mother's original concern, I had no idea how to advise them about certain practicalities like whether or not she should buy her son a pair of shoes.

Sexuality and shame

I want to quote a small piece from a book on shame by Stephen Pattison, who is an Anglican minister and theologian. At the beginning he does something that not many people would be willing to do, which is talk about his own experience. This is a sobering little passage.

> When I was an ordination candidate of about 16 years of age I went to see the Diocesan Director of Ordinands to make my confession, a practice that he had recommended to me as part of my spiritual life. Towards the end of the confession when I had read out all the sins I could remember, he asked me directly whether I had been having any sexual thoughts or experiences.[11]

Let me comment that you should never ever ask anything like that directly, and certainly not within that kind of context. I know one or two people who have gone to prison for the very fact of just asking

11. Pattison, S. (2000). *Shame: Therapy, theory, theology.* Cambridge, p. 71.

questions like this when it wasn't volunteered. Returning to Pattison, he continues, 'Actually I had been having little else for a number of years', – just like the rest of the adult population. Pattison then goes on to write about the effect this experience had on him:

> Not having heard the adage, 'Ninety-eight per cent of adolescent boys masturbate, the other two per cent are liars', I felt desperately ashamed and guilty about my apparently uncontrollable physical urges. My confessor pressed his question again. My face went redder and redder, the world seemed to sway and the earth felt as though it was disappearing from beneath my knees. I managed to stumble out, 'No, nothing like that.' The priest looked at me doubtfully – he knew I was lying. Then he gave me absolution and penance. I fled as rapidly as I could from the church.[12]

One of the main features of the experience of shame is a sense of uncontrollable exposure. It is very important that we do not question or probe if we suspect there is something sexual around, particularly with an adult, that may have come from the normal experiences of growing up or, unfortunately, experiences that they shouldn't have had. I know of a situation where a young girl was questioned within our own church, and the priest was put in prison because the courts viewed the questioning as sexually, but not physically, invasive. We all have to be careful about intrusiveness. It is our place to create a sacred space where people can trust somebody so that they can eventually talk about whatever is worrying them, on their own initiative.

I remember working with a religious sister who came to see me primarily because of current difficulties regarding her career etc., but also about the death of her father that occurred when she was just a young teenager. Eventually one day she came in and was trying to say something. She kept opening her mouth like a goldfish, and

12. Pattison, S. (2000). *Shame: Therapy, theory, theology*. Cambridge. p. 71.

eventually I said to her, 'It sounds, [there was no sound] as if there is something that is unutterable.' Now that is all I said. If she had gone on with her performance I would have done that for weeks, but on that particular occasion, by putting it that way, she was able to say that she had been involved sexually with a sister of another religious community, and was unable to talk about it.

It emerged further down the line that she was the third child in quite a large Catholic family. The important thing was that when she was a teenager an older sister had sexually abused her. It may have been exploratory and to do with curiosity, but they were teenagers at the time and she experienced it as a violation in some degree. She held a lot of anger towards that sister. I hope this illustrates the point I am making that sometimes people need to talk, but do not know how to do so. It is not our job to question people the way that Stephen Pattison was questioned in a confessional atmosphere. Actually, if somebody has not been confessing anything sexual either in a sacramental way or in a counselling relationship and the priest or counsellor is asking about aspects of sexuality, then that is their problem and not the problem of the person who is being questioned.

Puberty, menstruation and loss

There is a big difference between boys and girls in relationship to puberty in that the girls have (unless there is some difficulty for them) to menstruate. It is a bit of a mystery to a male, but for women it is often a difficult part of life to cope with during adult years. It is important to be aware that not all women are the same and that women experience menstruation in different ways. There are two beautiful writings about this stage of development; one is Simone de Beauvoir's book, *Memoirs of a Dutiful Daughter* [13] and the other is *The Diary of Anne Frank,* [14] which is very, very beautiful in its

---

13. De Beauvoir, S. (1958 / 1963). *Memoirs of a dutiful daughter.* Penguin Books.
14. Frank, A. (1952). *The diary of a young girl.* Doubleday.

awareness. We read of the growing awareness of a very young woman (13 to 15 years of age at that time) in her appreciation of menstruation. She writes about what it meant to her and also about her falling in love with one of the boys in the house and the yearning, the real yearning she experienced, which jumps out of the pages at you.

Simone de Beauvoir has a lovely bit in her memoir about the actual experience of her first period:

> Worried, and somehow feeling guilty, I had to take my mother into my confidence: she explained to me that I had now become a 'big girl' and bundled me up in a very inconvenient manner. I felt a strong sense of relief when I learned that it had happened through no fault of my own; and as always when something happened to me, I even felt my heart swell with a sort of pride.

She then reflects on the physical aspects of adolescent change:

> I found this physical side of growing up (menstruation) very irksome and a real limit to my freedom. I wished very much that I was a boy as I felt that they got out of it all so lightly. It still irks me that the beginning of menstruation was, for me at least, an occasion of alienation from my mother.

She is a beautiful writer, and writes very simply, and not in a harrowing or theoretical way, about a girl's experience of adolescence. She continues:

> There was only one thing that sometimes cast a shadow on this happy state (i.e. childhood): I knew that one day this period of my life would come to an end. It seemed unbelievable . . . But my distress had a more profound significance. In that sad corridor I realised vaguely that my childhood was coming to an end.

One of the main marks of adolescence is that the adolescent, at different stages, is often aware that something has come to an end, as opposed to their growing into a new future. The kind of thing that they see as coming to an end is security. Even though they might have risked their own safety in all sorts of situations, they felt secure in the world of childhood. They probably never told anybody that they felt secure at that time, but now they have a sense that they are going to lose a fun-loving part of themselves.

A number of years ago I did research with 300 young people. When I asked them what they thought about being adults, to becoming a man or woman they said, 'No fun and too much responsibility.' I said to the teachers who were in the two schools where I was working, 'What a picture we give them of adulthood, which is the next stage they are about to reach.' We need to show them that being an adult is all right and that you can still have fun. De Beauvoir reflects this when she writes:

> My body was changing, and my life was changing too: my past was being left behind . . . I had always been sorry for the 'grown-up's' monotonous existence: when I realised that, within a short period of time it would be my fate too, I was filled with panic.

Yes there are a lot of responsibilities, and a lot of worries, which there should be since we care for other people and we have to be employed, care for houses, etc., but if there is no fun, then what message are we giving to young people?

The key issue is that the pubertal changes which mark the beginning of adolescence also mark an ending, as they are leaving childhood behind and are moving into what they perceive as the boring world of their parents and teachers, and everyone else who carries worries and responsibilities, a world where they do not expect to have fun. I suspect that that is one of the reasons why some of them go kind of crazy in their behaviour. It is as if they think that they have to get it all in before they get to sixteen or eighteen in case they don't have a chance later on. That is not true, but it is a big worry for quite a lot of them.

The age of mental and emotional conflicts

Adolescents have to cope with their sizes changing, their shapes changing, and their strength changing. Their secondary sex characteristics are appearing, and they develop logical and analytical thinking and the use of the critical pathways in the brain. They have to develop abstract thinking so that they can cope with concepts and ideas, and they have to develop in their spiritual life and their religious life. Many, of course, give up the religion that is practised by their parents, much to their parents' chagrin, and either abandon the practice of religion or take up another one that appeals to them better. This, of course, causes angst in the family.

Adolescents have to cope with mood swings too. I remember a mother telling me about her daughter and saying, 'I could have wrung her neck. She was really, really upset when she went out in the morning and I spent the whole day worrying about her. Then when she came home in the afternoon she was great.' This scenario will be familiar to many adults, who feel they have wasted their time in worry, only to find that their children are fine. Anyone familiar with mathematics will know what a sine curve looks like: it just goes up and down like a wave, and the distances between the high and low points are all the same. Those distances are what an adolescent is going through emotionally. You don't know how they are going to be when they walk through the door, and you don't know how long they are going to stay that way.

Sexual orientation and identity

Adolescents experience an intensity of relationships. Think what it is like for a young girl who is surrounded by her female friends and then suddenly finds herself attracted to a boy. Leaving her group can leave mayhem behind.

What if you are a girl and you go off with a girl? What does that mean? The whole topic of homosexuality and emerging sexuality is difficult for boys also. I remember on one occasion being asked to talk about adolescent boys and their awareness of homosexuality to a group of men who belonged to a Quest group.[15] Quest was an organisation that was started by Catholics but that has now opened its arms to many other, particularly Christian, denominations. Just before this talk I had been at a rather large hospital talking to the heads of all the departments about how to deal with adolescents and about the way that adolescents experience their bodies. The first shock I got when I met the Quest group was that I recognised some of the men from the previous talk. The second shock I got was the amazing variety of men in this group who were homosexual. I had read West's book, *Homosexuality*, that was written in 1960.[16] West said that there is no such a thing as a homosexual but rather there is a dimension of homosexuality (as there is with lesbianism). What struck me was that there were some men at the back of the room who did not like the fact that there was a woman in the room, and at the other end of the spectrum you had the ones with the cravats, with a bit of make-up on and who were very comfortable that way, and everything in between.

At the break time before the questions this group of doctors gathered around me and they asked me if I was surprised to see them. I said that I was, as I had not been expecting to see them there. One of them told me that he was married with three children, but that he was leaving his wife because he knew that he was definitely homosexual, and that was how he wanted to be. I asked if his wife knew, and he told me that she didn't at that point, but that he was getting help from others who had decided to make this choice. It was the variety of people that really struck me. In my head I had thought I would

15. Quest is group for lesbian and gay Catholics which meets regularly for Mass, discussion and social events. http://www.questgaycatholic.org.uk/home.asp
16. West, D. J. (1960). *Homosexuality*. Penguin.

know what a homosexual would look like. In our clinic we met a small number of boys who were very 'camp', but at that Quest meeting there was every variety of self-presentation. What heartened me was that they all had a place. There was a couple there also (a man and a woman), and I was taken aside and told that they were not Catholic but they were married and had decided that they really wanted the woman to go with a woman and the man to go with a man. What was wonderful about this whole experience for me was there was a place to take all of that and not to be criticised, and to have time to work all these things out. We have to allow young people to work this out for themselves in their own time.

One of the big fears for boys is to be called a 'poof' publicly in the playground. It may be because of their demeanour – they may be very slim, very pale-faced, and perhaps look a bit weak physically. There are others who have close male friends who may be only 12 or 13 years of age and somebody can turn around and call them a poof or ask if they are queer. It is like a dagger to them because, in fact, they are not anything yet and are just trying to develop their friendships.

What we found in the clinic where I work was there were two peaks for this kind of angst; one around 13 years of age and another very different kind of peak around about 18 or 19 years of age, when they are free from school, are beginning to enter the young adult world, and are trying to cope with their appearance. They find they have got an attraction to the same sex and they need a lot of support with how to deal with that.

I remember a priest in a religious order who phoned me up one day. He said he had been seeing a young fellow who was around nineteen or twenty at the time, who was thinking of the priesthood and who had just told him he was gay and the priest wanted me to see him. I had to think about his request to try to work out what he was thinking. I asked why he couldn't see the young man himself and he replied that it was because he was gay. I then said that he might or might not be gay, and he might be trying to figure it out, but that he had trusted this priest with this information and that it would be very wrong if he didn't go to see him as it would give the message that being gay meant there was something wrong with him. Does being gay not fit in with the priesthood? Here we find the shame factor coming in again; the young man had exposed himself by saying that he was gay. We have to give people time to figure out who and what they actually are.

The Self Profile

Many years ago when I was the director of our adolescent unit a psychologist came over from the United States who was very expert on adolescents. I thought it would be a great experience for our staff to have the opportunity to do a workshop with him. This is one of the exercises that he developed which I would invite you to take time to do yourself. This exercise invites you to think of yourself somewhere between the ages of twelve and twenty. You are asked to choose an age, for example, twelve, fifteen or eighteen, and then go through these questions of yourself at that age. The second part of the task is to take one of your parents and think what it was like for them at that age. This exercise can be used in groups where people can be asked to share in pairs, only, of course, in so far as they are comfortable.

The Self Profile

Task: You are to put yourself back in time to a period in your life when you were between 12 and 20 years of age, and create a picture of yourself with respect to the following issues:

1. Self-concept
- How I felt about myself in general?
- My feelings concerning my masculinity/femininity?
- My values and the things that were important to me?
- How I handled my emotional life?
- My intellectual abilities?
- My physical skills, e.g., in sports, dancing art?
- My ability to make and keep friends of both sexes?

2. Body image
- My physical features – body build, other bodily characteristics?
- My male/female image?
- What I found a problem about my body?
- My attitudes and feelings towards my physical development?
- Experiences of body exploration and experimentation with self?
- My attitude toward the body of the opposite sex?

3. Sexuality
- What did I know/not know about sex?
- How did I deal with my sexual feelings?
- In what ways could I express feelings of warmth, closeness, tenderness, affection?

When this is used as part of a training programme people can be asked to share with the whole group anything that has struck them. We need to remember that sexuality is quite a private area of our lives (although unfortunately for adolescents it is quite public as well) so people need to feel safe and know that they will not be pressurised into sharing anything they don't wish to. It is really a very helpful questionnaire as it deals with everything from feelings to body image. You can also give it to someone as an exercise in personal reflection, with the option of sharing if they wish to do so. We all experience ourselves differently, and our experiences change at different stages of our lives, though what happens in our childhood and adolescence clearly is very formative of attitudes and behaviours in later life.

Conclusion

I have tried to give a smattering of the beginnings of looking at the importance of sexuality throughout life, and not forgetting that sexuality didn't begin when we emerged from adolescence. It started right at the beginning of our lives and although little one-month-olds were not having sexual intercourse that does not mean that they were not having the pleasurable experiences that are part of what becomes more adult sexual behaviour, like sucking, holding, being touched, touching, or finding little orifices and figuring out what they are. All of that is part of adult sexuality. This all becomes part of their body memories, and remember that this is the way the body works as they haven't got any other form of memory yet. These memories are stored in the body. What they are putting in is pleasure and pain, and they know if something is pleasurable or whether it is painful. In adolescence and in later life they will call on those bodily memories and their adult sexual identity will be built on what they experienced in childhood.

Reading list

De Beauvoir, Simone. (1958). *Memoirs of a dutiful daughter.* Penguin Books (1963).

Di Ceglie, Domenico. (2000). *Gender identity disorder in young people: Advances in psychiatric treatment. Vol 6,* pp. 458 – 466. Royal College of Psychiatrists: http://apt.rcpsych.org/cgi/content/full/6/6/458

Frank, Anne. (1952). *The diary of a young girl.* Doubleday.

Freud, Anna. (1931). *Introduction to psychoanalysis for teachers.* George Allen and Unwin.

Gerhardt, Sue. (2004). *Why love matters: How affection shapes a baby's brain.* Brunner-Routledge.

Konner, Melvin. (1991 / 1993). *Childhood.* Little Brown and Co.

Pattison, Stephen. (2000). *Shame: Theory, therapy, theology.* Cambridge University Press.

Strauch, Barbara. (2003). *Why are they so weird? What's really going on inside a teenager's brain.* Bloomsbury.

TWO

Learning to navigate the minefield of child sexual abuse

Part I: A sample of cases

Mary Ross

Professor Fred Stone, a psychiatrist who worked with us at our clinic for many years and who died in July 2009, said that there were probably a lot of cases of child abuse that we missed. In my metaphor from the previous chapter, we were not being as curious as ET in relationship to the symptoms the children were showing. We were not being sufficiently curious, because we were not thinking that they might have been sexually abused.

In 1931, the same year that our clinic was opened, Anna Freud made one short reference to child abuse in her lectures to teachers.

> It is true that in juvenile courts and children's clinics there are cases in which boys have actually played the part of the father towards the mother as completely as was possible considering their physical development or in which a little girl has been used by her own father in the sexual relation but in all such cases it has never been the strength and energy of a child that has effected this abnormal accomplishment of his [normal childhood] emotional wishes but the abnormal desires of the adults . . . the satisfaction of their own lusts.[1]

Clearly, some teachers were aware of this as early as the 1930s, but the insight was not widespread throughout the country. Perhaps the important thing to bear in mind is that child abuse has been around

---

1. Freud, A. (1931 / 1974). *Introduction to psychoanalysis: Lectures for child analysts and teachers 1922–1935*. London: The Hogarth Press.

as long as children have been around. Child abuse was never spoken about and I am sure we missed many, many cases of it. I also suspect that many of the people reading this chapter will have people coming to them for counselling who have either personally been sexually abused as a child or know of somebody else – perhaps in their own family – who has been abused.

I just want to give you a few examples of child abuse and alert you to things that you need to look out for. I also want to offer some examples of what it might be that makes an adult either recall it or enable them to start talking about it. I was actually given the privilege – and it was a privilege – to be involved in the first case in Scotland where I was asked to help the police and social workers trying to uncover evidence against a well-known paedophile who had been involved with a lot of primary-age boys. Each victim had his own little team of police officers to work with him. The police were really pleased to see me, but when I saw the room where the interviews would take place I asked if they had any drawing material as well. This took them by surprise, but I said that from what I knew of the case it would be crucial to find out what the sleeping arrangements were in this man's house and the best way to handle that would be to get the children to draw it out, or if they were reluctant to do that, the listener could draw it out as the child talked about it.

I was put in a room the size of a cupboard with a monitor where I could see what was happening in the interview room and could direct at times if they were getting stuck. (The detective sergeant in charge was in with me and he would go and slip notes under the door.) I asked if we could video the sessions, and we were given permission to do this as a test case, which was wonderful because the police could look at the video themselves later and monitor their own way of working. Much more importantly they could monitor the reaction of children. These children were all from different families and none of them had fathers around. The perpetrator had targeted single mums. He would get friendly with the mother and then offer to take the boys on holiday. The problem the police had was that they couldn't get the eldest boy to break down and tell the police what had happened. The police were simply not getting anywhere. The perpetrator had been arrested and was in one of our biggest prisons, but the boy didn't know that. I said that in my opinion telling the boy this was the only way there would be a breakthrough. Why? Because this boy loved this man, which is what we sometimes cannot understand. The policeman who worked with the boy was wonderful, and would have made a natural therapist. He used tentative, hesitant language and got a lot of information, but none of the details that were needed to proceed with a prosecution. I can still remember the boy's reaction when the police told him that this man was in prison. I could hardly contain my own reaction to the boy's grief. He broke down sobbing real heartfelt sobs because his love object was in prison.

It taught me a lot about how we can underestimate the importance, to a child who has been abused, of the love they may feel for the abuser. We perhaps assume that the only logical emotions for the child to feel toward the abuser are hatred, disgust, or fear. But it is possible that they hold that person in great affection and we cannot take that away from them. We can tell them that this should not have happened, but we must not dismiss that affection because it is within them. Maybe the love will turn to something else later in life but we have to own the love for them, even if we cannot own it for ourselves. We wanted prison as a permanent solution for this man's offences, but the boy loved him and, in fact, all the wee boys loved him. Through the older boy's breaking down we were able eventually to get the details to put this man away for quite a long time. Sadly, it didn't stop there for the boys. Their friend had been taken away and that is where we, as a society, are not good at follow-up work in supporting children like these. The people who should be helping them are seen as the villains for taking away the person they loved.

Some time ago I was asked to speak to a group of counsellors in Scotland about how to work with adults who had been sexually abused, particularly in relationship to the Christian Church. I want to mention some of the points I made because these comments have come from people who came to our centre. Some say to themselves; 'I must be bad if I enjoy the [sexual] feelings. I still need the person who did this. What do I do about that?' One of the very difficult areas in sexual abuse is the victims can, and often do, enjoy all the physical aspects unless the abuse has been very aggressive. They may find themselves feeling guilt because this has happened over time and in a loving way, but it was also totally inappropriate. Whoever it is – boy or girl – they will need to be helped to acknowledge both the pleasure and the guilt. That is because they are talking about their bodies and it is as if they had masturbated; they would enjoy that, and in a similar way a sexual relationship with an older person can lead to pleasurable physical sensations. But they might also be talking about the emotional feelings that they had as well as the physical ones, where they enjoyed the attention, as well as the touching. We run a project in the adolescent unit (which is part of the clinic where I work) that was originally called the Vulnerable Young Women's Project. This was for young girls under the age of 16 who would have been known as prostitutes. Eventually we got the police to stop arguing with the social-work department and labelled their situation as sexual abuse, even though they were offering themselves to the men. They were earning money, often for drugs, for themselves or older sisters. We learned a lot from these girls. They did not know most of their clients, but many had been in long-term relationships with adult men in the past and we have had to accept that they might need a lot of help about how to cope with what we would never think of as loss. However, they were experiencing bereavement if their men had been taken away.

One 17-year-old girl came to us who had been very badly abused by a priest. I would say his behaviour was highly disturbed in a number of ways, because he would dress her up as if she were Our Lady (Mary, the mother of Jesus) and then abuse her. It caused multiple injuries for her as it wasn't just the physical boundary that was crossed, but also the faith and liturgical boundaries. She was referred to our unit by very angry parents. They were angry against the Church but they wanted her still to go to church because that was part and parcel of being Catholic. They thought that going to church would help her, but they failed to understand that she now experienced and understood church differently from them. Church was a negative and painful place for her.

I remember a 40-year-old female who had been abused in her own family as a child. She asked how you could continue to believe in anything, particularly in faith terms, when these things had happened. If your own family could abuse you then how on earth could you be expected to have a faith dimension to your life? It is a little bit like people asking how God could let this happen, when there is a tragedy, but especially when it happens in your own home, in a sense, within your own self.

I can think of another young woman I worked with. It was very difficult for her to begin to think about forgiveness, as those who abused her knew what they were doing. She had been abused by her mother and her older brother, as had her three younger siblings. It was a major court case in Scotland. At the time we were being asked (through a consultation by the Government in Scotland) to look at what would help child witnesses. We had an amazing experience where their assigned psychologist in our unit and myself worked with the four children while they drew and wrote out comments. We also sent all this material to the court, and they were amazed because it was the only time that children had actually returned their own comments and experiences of what it is like to be in court and not be believed about their mother's and brother's behaviour and their abuse. There is often difficulty in believing women would actually abuse, particularly in a sexual way, but that mother told us that she abused the children, even though it was the older brother who was the focus of the trial. She talked about her abuse of them all as babies. She was very ashamed, but fortunately did talk about it. She was involved in digital penetration when they were babies, from which she derived pleasure. If you think back to the early oral and anal developmental stages and how some people can be stuck back at those stages, that may help to explain what gave her pleasure. However, what is disturbing is the fact that she had thought of doing that to a very young child. She did it in turn to all of them as that is what gave her erotic feelings. It was only later in life when she started to think about this, that she realised it had been painful for the children because they were so small. We can hardly believe it but this gives some people pleasure. These startling experiences keep us working to see the world as ET might have. Practically speaking, they also alert us to be careful about who should be allowed to tend children in a parent's absence.

A 14-year-old girl who was abused by her maternal grandfather said, 'My head is f***** up because I still love him. How can I love and hate him at the same time?' We can see this young girl trying to hold her emotions in balance. She was actively engaged in working through her trauma. In the manner of Brunner's theory, she was revisiting her sexual abuse issues as she continued to develop. That is the dilemma if you have been sexually abused and you liked the person who was your abuser. You are left with that balancing act which is very difficult to resolve definitively.

A 20-year-old male who suffered organised abuse from a ring of abusers said, 'I would like to go back to Mass, I would like to talk to someone but maybe they are involved as well.' Now it wasn't people in a church that had been involved in his abuse, but he was afraid of returning to church as it is men who preside at Mass, and he had been abused by adult males. He wondered if he could trust any men because of what had happened to him. These kinds of comments bring up a lot of the issues that we really have to deal with.

One of the things that you have to be aware of is what effect subsequent events, such as the offender's parole, may have on the victim. Another important factor is how close and permanent was the family relationship between the abused child and the abuser. If it was very, very close it is quite hard to enable victims to move out of the double bind that they are in, even though they may fight to do so. I saw a 13-year-old girl last year who was abused by her maternal grandfather. He was just about to get out of jail and she had put an embargo on any of her family being with him ever – not to protect them, but to punish him. Even though he had served jail time for his offences, and even though her mother was still her grandfather's daughter. So here was this girl apparently causing mayhem in the family home about who would be able to see this man again. She was adamant that she would never talk to any family member who talked to her grandfather, and that included her own mother.

The duration of the abuse is an important factor. As an example of short-term abuse, we worked with a girl who was referred to us by a GP who phoned up to say that this girl had been the victim of a stranger rape. It was an isolated incident, but was very aggressive. This young girl's fear was of having to see this man in court again – not what was actually happening to her at the time and, at a later stage, in her body. As an example of long-term abuse, consider a father who has kept his daughter in a state of fear and had children by her. You wonder how that can go unnoticed by the extended family and the community, though the mother knew. What would the victim's understanding of family life be if that had been her long-term experience? Where would a therapist or pastoral helper go with all of that? The severity and degree of abuse and what the abuse meant to the child at the time have to be taken into account. Sometimes some children have been very physically damaged because of the abuse and one of the things that might have to be revisited is whether they themselves – particularly if they are girls – would be able to have children in the future. The degree of force used and the presence of terror because of threats etc. are extremely important factors.

One of the things that we need to look at is why, many years later, an adult suddenly starts talking about sexual abuse in their past life. What would instigate that? Now in Scotland, as in many parts of the world, the bishops or the leaders of many churches have now become involved in this whole area. They are concerned for the future of children that may otherwise be abused or who may grow up with difficulties, as well as concerns about compensation issues when the abuse is in a church context. I was the coordinator of a group of advisers on this issue for an interim period until the bishops found a full-time person to do the job. On one occasion we got a call from a priest in a very, very idyllic, tiny part of Scotland. He said that three sisters, all adult women, had come to him because of something that had made the eldest talk about the abuse she had experienced. It made her go to the other two to ask if anything had happened to them, which it had, though none of them had ever spoken about it. What provoked this conversation was an incident that had occurred at a very big family occasion where the relative who had been the abuser, but not the immediate family, was present. The eldest sister saw him lift a three-year-old onto his lap. Probably nobody else noticed it. It completely rocked the woman who saw it, and that was the stimulus to talk to her sisters and then to the priest. They wondered what to do and the priest said that he would call the advisers. Two of us went and met with them. It was quite a revelation that they had kept all this from one another and from anybody else for this length of time, but I was so glad that they were able now to talk about it. It had been quite serious abuse and this person had been free to roam for all the intervening years. They didn't know if anybody else had been affected, but they wanted to make sure that nobody else would be abused and that was their reason for going to the police. There was one policeman in the area and I said that they didn't need to go to that policeman as they felt that people were too close in this rural area. I recommended that they go to the city and speak to the police there, which is what they did. It was an agony for them, particularly dealing with the public exposure that later came about.

Now that brings me to another important issue: shame.[2] A point of the Adam and Eve story is shame, which is about being exposed. Let me share a personal example that does not seem in any way related to sexuality (although since I am a sexual being, it *is* related). My father died when I was six from the effects of the war and I remember as a primary 7 child (11 years of age) going to a big birthday party of one of the other girls in the class. Everybody else had their daddies come to collect them and I can still remember the feeling I had – it was like a cold shower. I felt ashamed about not having a daddy. Now I couldn't feel guilty because I had not done any wrong, but I felt ashamed because I was exposed by the fact that another daddy kindly, as it had been arranged, took me back home after the party. It was the fact that now everybody knew I didn't have a daddy that caused me to feel ashamed. That is the point of the Adam and Eve story. In sexual terms it is no wonder people cannot talk about abuse. They are going to get exposed as having been in an abusive relationship. Similarly, in cases of domestic abuse; a lot of women will not come forward and talk about what has happened to them because they will be exposed as having taken it, and will be seen as weak. I have to tell you that we also have men that are abused in Scotland, but mainly it is the other way round. Why do they not tell people? Why do they say, 'I walked into a door,' or, 'I walked into a lamp post'? Why do they not say, 'He battered me'? Because they are

2. Pattison, S. (2000). *Shame: Theory, therapy, theology.* Cambridge University Press.

ashamed. I think we cannot underestimate the shame that people experience when they have to expose to another that they have been so devalued as to have been abused, physically or sexually, no matter how kind that listener may be.

Another reason people don't want to be exposed is because it could precipitate change that they are not ready for, so they avoid being discovered. It can also be that they are irrationally scared that they will be abused again by the listener. I do have knowledge of a woman who is now in her thirties who was sexually abused by her step-father and then went to a counsellor many years later. She must have said something along the lines that she felt that she wasn't beautiful anymore because of what happened to her. To 'help' her he said, 'Oh no, you are very beautiful and I will show you how beautiful you are.' He made her open her blouse up and he caressed her breasts. (She has had a large financial compensation award for that behaviour.) I think as the adults who try to help people we need to be aware that not everybody will trust us because of the experiences they have had in the past. We have to go a long way to earn that trust, particularly if we are of the same gender or if we are in the same line of business as the person who originally abused them. We just have to be very, very aware that there could be natural and healthy mistrust in people whom we try to help.

Sometimes we have to leave things the way they are because there are people who just cannot take the help that is being offered to them. It is too much for them to face up to things that they are not ready to deal with. An important helping skill is knowing how far to go, what insights the person can tolerate today, next week, next year, or ever. Otherwise, misplaced zeal to root out offenders can lead to additional psychological damage to victims.

Part II: Identification of possible victims

Joanne Marie Greer

Anna Freud is responsible for proposing the concept of 'Developmental Lines'.[3] These are simply the various trajectories of development that are going on simultaneously. There are certain normative benchmarks for each developmental line at each age. School teachers, coaches, religious educators, paediatricians, and other caregivers are in the best position to notice anomalies of development. Here are some signs and symptoms that are often observed in physically or sexually abused children. Of course, some of these may signal other difficulties, but taken as a whole they indicate a child who needs follow-up by psychological staff.

Developmental lines

1. The Cognitive Developmental Line

- Even when assessed to have adequate IQ, there is failure of initiative – chronically missing work, uncompleted tasks. The child is simply not available for instruction. The probable explanation: the child is receiving random negative reinforcement from the abuser because sometimes the child is hit or penetrated, and sometimes he/she is not. Experimental psychology has demonstrated that random negative reinforcement is the most powerful strategy for extinguishing ALL behaviour. For example, laboratory animals treated this way will simply retreat into a corner of the cage and stop moving at all. Initiative is impossible.

- Child is in a survival mode, and therefore not interested in information extraneous to survival, such as maths.

---

3. Freud, A. (1963). The concept of developmental lines. *Psychoanalytic Study of the Child, 18*: 245-265.

2. The Social Developmental Line

- Development of autonomy is difficult – the child cannot work independently in the classroom; must be coached through a task step-by-step.

- Socially stunted in peer relations – the child is alone at lunch hour and on the playground. Does not seek to join games and is not chosen for teams. Not invited by other children for parties, etc.

- Abused children usually come from secretive families, and are cautioned against open relations with other adults. The teacher or caregiver should be suspicious if parents will never attend conferences, if the child balks at tasks involving revealing family information, such as drawing or writing about family, or if no other children ever visit in the child's home.

3. The Emotional Developmental Line

- Child lacks trust in teachers and caregivers, or paradoxically clings to them.

- Child is timid, startles easily.

4. The Physical Developmental Line

- Stunting of growth common in abused children, partly because anxiety interferes with eating.

- 'Failure to Thrive' syndrome may occur in infants and young children. In effect, the child attempts suicide by eating very little. One case I knew of was a four-year-old who would take only apple juice. Diagnosis is made by admission to hospital for a period of time. If normal eating is resumed in hospital and reverses on return home, removal from the home may be necessary.

- Unexplainable bruises and healed marks are observed, or the child dressed in an unusually covered-up fashion.

- The child exhibits bodily tension and takes a fearful stance toward adults.

- In the anal-sexually abused child, the physician or nurse observes a slack, thickened anal aperture; vaginal abuse also has characteristic signs; venereal disease may be present.

- The seduced child is often precocious sexually and is seductive toward adults. If challenged, the family may blame the learned behaviour on television viewing.

- The physically abused child may identify with the aggressor and be a bully on the playground.

Pseudo-incest and 'soft' abuse

There are child-adult transactions that fall short of violating the law, and yet violate common sense, and constitute a developmental interference. Here are some examples, but by no means a complete list:

- a father who kisses his daughter erotically on the mouth

- a parent of an adolescent walks about the house semi-nude, or leaves the door open when bathing or using the toilet

- a parent enters the bathroom to converse with an adolescent while the child is bathing or using the toilet

- the bizarre fundraising custom in parts of the USA of dressing young boys in bras and panties to parade across a stage for the amusement of adult men. (I actually viewed photographs of such an event in an album shown me by the adult leaders of a scout troop I was considering for one of my sons.)

- the tragic cases of JonBenét Ramsey and other very young girls who are erotically exploited by being 'dolled up' and displayed to adult voyeurs

- physical education teachers who require their charges to shower in the nude while the adults watch

- health-care workers who exploit innocents by touching and probing their bodies in ways unnecessary to proper diagnosis and treatment

- parents who carry on sexual intercourse within hearing and view of their children, especially if there is any chance that the parental interactions seem to be violent.

Empirical research on signs and symptoms of child abuse

A remarkable two-volume work, *Instinctual Stimulation of Children: From Common Practice to Child Abuse,*[4] contains not only theory but also case reports on a large number of children, and makes some statistical significance tests for differences in signs and symptoms between groups of children exposed/not exposed to various types of developmental interferences. A short summary of some of Weil's findings appears in Table 1. This work is highly recommended for the library of any clinic or other enterprise concerned with child abuse.

How are child victims identified to the authorities?

One important source of case finding is reports from neighbours who overhear, or even witness, abuse. Another source is health-care workers, either in hospital emergency rooms,[5] or during mandated physical examinations for school entry or sports participation. As noted above, teachers, church staff, and day-care workers may make observations that raise questions. It is very rare for a child to report unless a younger sibling is suddenly at risk. In incest cases, the child often takes the view, 'better the devil you know than the devil you don't know'. The abuser or another family member may have cautioned them that the family will lose their home or income if the abuse is revealed to authorities. When the child is abused by a non-family member, the child's silence is often ensured by threats against the safety of the child's loved ones.

4. Weil, J. L. (1989). *Instinctual stimulation of children: From common practice to child abuse.* International Universities Press: New York.
5. For example, see this excellent resource for health-care workers: McNeese, M. C., Hebeler, J. R. (1977). *The abused child: A clinical approach to identification and management. (CIBA Clinical Symposia,* Vol. 29, No. 5). Summit, NJ: CIBA Pharmaceutical Company, Division of CIBA-GEIGY Corporation.

Table 1: Correlations between exposure to experiences and symptoms.
Summarised from *Instinctual stimulation of children:*
From common practice to child abuse

Experience	Associated symptoms	Statistics
Cluster 1: Exposure to beatings Corporal punishment with belt, strap, or utensil; prolonged or violent hitting; kicking; parent hitting out of control; extremely painful punishments (tearing skin, sticking with pins, burns, blows which leave temporary or permanent imprint).	Setting fires; dreams of firemen, fire hoses, fire stations, fire extinguishers, fire alarms; playing with matches, dreams of burns or fiery substances such as lava. Also, **freezing of affect:** laughter during punishment; pleasure when others are being hurt or unhappy; inappropriate clowning, silliness, nonsense talk.	Difference between exposed and non-exposed children, $n = 100$, chi square[6] $p < .0018$
Cluster 2: Exposure to erotic contact with adult body Share adult bed with purpose of inducing child's sleep, at least weekly; child sleeps all night with adult at least once weekly.	Separation hysterics: noisy, fearful or agitated in relation to separation, including school phobia; may also have nausea, headaches, or other psychosomatic symptoms.	54% children sharing bed with adults display separation hysterics, as compared to 29% of non-exposed children.
Cluster 3: Exposure to anal stimulation Child subjected to enemas and/or suppositories on repeated occasions; child observes adult administering enemas; child has had anal rashes, anal fistulas, or pinworms; child's anus or rectum manipulated by adult on repeated occasions; child's rectum or anus contacted by adult or adolescent genitals.	Preoccupation with faeces, soiling, playing with faeces, eating faeces. Dreaming or irrational symptoms involving: brown, black, dirty, smelly substances, dirty, animals and insects, pimples, boils, garbage, refuse. Anal itching; anal poking; anal sex play and masturbation; psychogenic faecal withholding; psychogenic diarrhoea.	83% of children exposed to anal stimulation display 'excremental' symptoms, as compared to 52% of non-exposed children.

6. Chi Square is a statistical test that compares the expected proportions to the actual proportions of persons having or not having a specific characteristic. In this specific case, if there were no relationship between Exposure to Beatings and the listed Symptoms, then roughly equal numbers of Exposed Children and Non-Exposed Children would display the listed Symptoms, and Chi Square would be *non-significant*. Since Chi Square is *highly significant*, this means there is a *strong* relationship between Exposure to Beatings and the listed Symptoms.

Protections for reporters of child abuse

These obviously differ from country to country, even within the developed world. Anonymous reporting should be permitted, with the caveat that such reporting occasionally may be a malicious falsehood. But one would hope that repeated anonymous reports would rouse the authorities to action. In many jurisdictions, various professionals such as physicians, nurses, therapists, and teachers are legally required to report suspected abuse. However, responses to such reports can be disappointing, as publicly employed social workers are often overwhelmed with casework already. In situations of imminent danger, reports to the police tend to elicit a more rapid response, but the reporter probably cannot maintain anonymity.

Conclusion

This short chapter attempts to briefly orient the reader to the complex world of child abuse. The subject is so repugnant to psychologically normal persons that it is difficult to promote the public knowledge and create the social structures to protect children properly. The authors hope that the readers will be moved to inform themselves further as their responsibilities require, and to wholeheartedly support development of programmes and policies intended to protect children from exploitation.

For Christians, it is extremely important that church institutions be safe havens for children. This has not been the case in the past. Church authorities have been forced by painful events to take more seriously the task of protecting children. This involves a re-thinking of the privileged position of clergy vis-à-vis those in their care. It also involves a re-examination of the selection process for ministerial candidates, to eliminate candidates with predatory tendencies.

PART II

Sexuality in adulthood

THREE

Masturbation: A sensitive pastoral issue

Brendan Geary and Joanne Marie Greer

Introduction

In the early 1990s Fr Ed Hone, an editor of Redemptorist Publications, was wondering what new topic to cover for the weekly Telephone Helpline service, which offered a series of three-minute pre-recorded messages on various pastoral subjects. These Helplines were advertised on the Sunday Bulletin news sheets which are distributed to Roman Catholic Parishes all around the United Kingdom. Having exhausted a range of topics over several years, Ed decided to record a Helpline on the topic of masturbation.[1] The day after it was made available, British Telecom phoned Ed to say that the line had 'crashed'. Ed wondered what had gone wrong, and the British Telecom representative said that nothing had gone wrong. He told Ed that so many people had called the line that the system couldn't cope. This happened again later in the week. Tens of thousands of people accessed the Helpline, and Ed received hundreds of letters, from people of all ages, many of them older women. A common factor in many of the letters was the relief expressed that they were able to hear helpful, non-judgmental advice about a topic that had caused them guilt and distress for years, and about which they had been unable to speak in any meaningful way. He only received one complaint, and that was from a man who said that 'Masturbation' was not a suitable topic title for his sons to see on a Catholic publication when they attended Mass on Sunday.

What this story tells us is that masturbation is still an area of concern for many religious people. Other sources confirm this impression.

1. Fr Ed Hone, CSsR., Personal communication.

John Perito for example, a retired psychiatrist and psychoanalyst who lives near Washington DC, wrote, 'I have listened to so many people struggle with this kind of guilt.'[2] Vincent Genovese SJ, a moral theologian, noted that this seems to be less of an issue for young people today than it was in the past, but issues related to masturbation are still on the minds of the young people whom he teaches.[3] Similarly Martin Saunders, writing in *Christianity*, a monthly magazine that targets the Evangelical wing of the Church of England, writes that masturbation is still 'a key question for many teenagers'.[4]

Adult masturbation is probably the most practised, most joked about, but least talked about, aspect of human sexuality. A survey of sexual behaviour which was carried out in Great Britain in the early 1990s omitted questions on masturbation, because the topic caused such disgust and offence among so many people in the pilot study that it was considered unwise to include it in the final survey, in case its inclusion led to people's declining to participate.[5] Alain Giami, however, suggests that this perhaps rather reflects the discomfort of the researchers who were all women.[6] Either way, the sensitivity of the topic led to it being excluded from the research project, which then failed to produce empirical knowledge of this important aspect of human sexuality. In a similar vein, when Harold Ivan Smith tried to include a chapter on masturbation in a book published in 1979 entitled *A part of me is missing*, a book on sexuality for single adults, he was told by the publisher to remove this chapter as it would be unacceptable to Christian bookshops.[7]

2. Perito, J. E. (2003). *Contemporary Catholic sexuality: What is taught and what is practiced*. New York: Crossroad, p. 91.
3. Genovese, V. J. (1987). *In pursuit of love: Catholic morality and human sexuality*. Dublin: Gill & Macmillan, pp. 300 – 327.
4. Saunders, M. (2009). Gagged and bound, *Christianity*, pp. 22 – 26.
5. Wellings, K., Field, J., Johnson, A. M., & Wadsworth, J. (1994). *Sexual behaviour in Britain*. England: Penguin.
6. Giami, A. (2001). Counter-transference in social research: Beyond George Devereux. M. W. Bauer (Ed.). *Papers in Social Research Methods – Qualitative Series*, *7*. London School of Economics: Methodology Institute. www.ethnypsychiatire.net/giami.htm, retrieved 16/12/2008.
7. Smith, H. A. (2003). Modern Christians and masturbation. In M. Cornog, *The Big Book of Masturbation*, San Francisco: Down There Press, pp. 167 – 173.

Despite these discomforts and reservations, the topic of masturbation has clearly come a long way, as can be seen in the way that it has been presented in a number of recent popular films. In *There's Something about Mary*[8] and *American Pie,*[9] it is a source of humour, in a rather adolescent way. In the Spanish film *Y tu mamá también,*[10] there is a scene where two boys masturbate by a pool, reflecting the behaviour of many adolescent boys. In *American Beauty,*[11] however, there are two scenes where the main character, played by Kevin Spacey, is seen to masturbate; once in the shower, and once while in bed. His wife is aware that their marriage is disintegrating and comments on his masturbation in anger. These contemporary films show a growing societal awareness that masturbation is often part of the sexual life of normal adults.

Developmental aspects of masturbation

In young children, body image is highly correlated with intelligence; engaging with the body is crucial for normal development. Body image is acquired by handling and labelling the parts of the body, and by mirroring one's own body parts against those of another human or a doll. So parents may say, 'my eyes', 'your eyes', etc., touching and pointing. Anyone who has changed the nappy of an older infant will be aware of the child's keen interest in the genital area, from grabbing at it to showing obvious delight when it is sponged, powdered, or creamed. However, the majority of toddlers quickly learn that there is lots of admiration if you touch and name 'my eyes', to a visitor, but general unease if you touch and name 'my penis'. A major reason that Freud was the target of general acrimony was that he, unlike his Victorian colleagues, considered young children sexual beings. He noted that every nursemaid in Vienna knew that

8. Farrelly, B., & Farrelly P. (Directors). (1998). *There's something about Mary* [Motion picture]. USA: 20th Century Fox.
9. Weitz C., and Weitz P. (Directors). (1999). *American pie* [Motion picture]. USA: Universal Pictures.
10. Cuarón, A. (Director). (2002). *Y tu mamá también* [Motion picture]. USA: MGM.
11. Mendes, S. (2000). *American beauty* [Motion picture]. USA: Dreamworks.

young children were interested in their sexual organs, even though adults denied this.

Guarding against 'self-pollution' was both a parental preoccupation and a medical preoccupation until well after World War II. One could buy special corsets to keep children from being able to touch their genitals in bed. Masturbation was considered even more troubling in a girl than in a boy, and sometimes the clitoris was surgically removed to stop childhood masturbation. One of us had an elderly psychotherapy client whose mother's clitoris had been removed at age six, on the order of the client's grandfather, a Methodist minister. This was a life-altering trauma for both mother and daughter. In adulthood the mother had several periods of psychosis during which she would rage about the surgery and smear her own menstrual blood on the walls, terrifying her young daughter.

At the present time, paediatricians and psychologists consider childhood masturbation a problem only if it interferes with general development by taking attention from other developmental trajectories such as peer friendship, cooperation with parents and teachers, attention to studies, etc. But the child who masturbates obsessively will still come to the attention of the therapeutic community. Obsessive masturbation in a child is an indicator of severe anxiety, not of sexual preoccupations. The child who masturbates within public view raises non-sexual concerns, because he/she either does not grasp social-behavioural norms or chooses to defy them.

Some pseudo-sophisticated helpers working with adults believe firmly that childhood masturbation is universal, and regard the client who denies remembering the experience as a liar. It is important to remember that, ordinarily, for the childhood masturbator, self-soothing is the major goal rather than an orgiastic experience. It is not normative for pre-pubertal children to experience anything like an orgasm. Sometimes neither parent nor child recognises an activity as masturbation. For example, consider a five-year-old girl rhythmically rubbing her crotch against mother's leg, as her mother and therapist discussed her treatment schedule. It seems reasonable that she would be anxious about a schedule that would leave her alone with a stranger. Moreover, her mother was proposing to run errands during her session, rather than remaining nearby in the waiting room. As another example of covert masturbation, an adult woman often recalled her delight at sliding down her grandmother's long, curving stair rail. She remembered the sensation of flying, but did not recall the inevitable genital stimulation. Horseback riding is another activity popular with girls that inevitably stimulates the female genital area.

Because of the external nature of the male genitals, males are more likely to recall childhood masturbation experiences. They are also more likely to have been in open conflict with a parent about masturbation. For example, one man recalled his mother tucking in the bedcovers tightly, placing his hands on top, and exhorting him to 'be good'. Another was forced as a young adolescent to sleep with his door open, with his father checking on him periodically throughout the evening. These sorts of parent/child interactions intermix feelings about emerging sexuality with conflicts over autonomy, and may lead to either troublesome passivity, if the child submits, or troublesome defiance, if they do not.

With the onset of adolescence, there is a rise of hormonal secretions and resulting sexual sensations in the young adolescent's body. This is not necessarily a matter of unalloyed joy for the young person. A comfortable body image from childhood is being disrupted. Boys begin to sprout body hair and experience wet dreams. Girls develop breast buds, hips, shapely thighs, waistlines, and may experience clitoral sensitivity. Favourite garments suddenly pull and stretch uncomfortably. Both genders worry about what people think about their changing bodies, and are curious about how their bodies work. Older friends and siblings may make comments, sometimes friendly and sometimes not, about body changes.

Both genders experiment sexually during adolescence, and their experiments may range from fun to frightening. Every so often the newspaper reports the death of a male adolescent who was experimenting with asphyxiation as a way to intensify sexual excitement during masturbation. When one of the authors of this chapter (Joanne Marie Greer) was working in a church orphanage in the 1960s, a thirteen-year-old girl investigated her vagina by inserting a folded fan she had pilfered from her favourite nun. She then became frightened and could not remove the fan. Unfortunately, the Mother Superior in charge saw, not normal curiosity about the vagina, but evil behaviour. She refused help to the child, and called a male doctor to take the fan out, even though one of the resident nuns was a nurse. Not only was the child intensely humiliated before a male stranger, but thereafter she was regarded as 'bad'.

Masturbation to orgasm is a new development during adolescence. Age of puberty and age of beginning masturbation vary,[12] but by mid-teens, the majority of boys and some girls have masturbated, and by 18 years of age 90% of boys and smaller percentages of girls masturbate. It appears to be the case throughout the world that boys masturbate more than girls, although the gap may be narrowing, possibly as a result of growing awareness, understanding and acceptance of female sexuality.[13]

Most parents today accept, at least in theory, that it is better for their children to learn about intercourse from them than from playmates. But most parental communication restricts itself to the bare bones of procreation and communicable diseases. The question of sexual pleasure, and especially of self-pleasuring, is often ignored, even when children approach adulthood. As we will discuss below, the majority of religious adults continue to be perplexed and uncomfortable about self-pleasuring. It is informative to scan the

---

12. Arco Editorial team. (2000). *Sexuality. (La Vida Sexual)*. Cologne: Könemann, pp. 128 – 139.
13. Miracle, T. S., Miracle, A. W., & Baumeister, R. F. (2003). *Human sexuality: meeting your basic needs*. New Jersey: Prentice Hall.

internet for some of the questions that well-educated, upper-middle-class university students have asked about their bodies, e.g., 'Clitoris – where is it? Why doesn't it work?' This particular question was posted on 'Go Ask Alice', the website of Health Services at Columbia University in New York City.[14]

Some history of attitudes toward masturbation

It may be helpful to understand how Western religion and society have reacted over time to masturbation. There are no references to masturbation in the Old or New Testaments. Modern authoritative biblical commentators make clear that the sin of Onan referred to in the Book of Genesis (and which was the source for the word, 'Onanism', an earlier term for masturbation), refers specifically to Onan's ejaculating outside of the vagina, thereby preventing Onan from fathering a child with his bereaved sister-in-law as required by Jewish law. Onan's sin is not masturbation but failing in his legal duty to his sister-in-law. References in Deuteronomy and Leviticus to seminal discharges that make a man unclean were also clearly influential in the future demonisation of masturbation. Also influential was St Paul's teaching on 'not giving way to selfish lust', providing an inferred scriptural support for religious prohibitions against solitary (ergo, selfish) sexual behaviour.[15]

Richards notes that up to the Middle Ages the Church had adopted what one might consider a flexible and sophisticated approach to such everyday realities.[16] In the early Middle Ages masturbation was seen as a rather trivial sin. But Burchard of Worms, who died in 1025, recommended ten days on bread and water for someone who confessed to masturbation using the hand. This was one of the less serious offences in the sexual area. What is interesting is that female masturbation received a more severe

14. http://www.goaskalice.columbia.edu/Cat6.html, retrieved Oct. 29, 2008.
15. Dt. 23:9 – 11, Lev. 15:16, 1 Thess. 4:3 – 4.
16. Richards, J. (1990). *Sex, dissidence, and damnation: Minority groups in the Middle Ages*. New York: Barnes & Noble.

punishment. Over time the penalties, as reflected in the writings of Jean Gerson, a leading fourteenth-century theologian who taught in the University of Paris, became even more serious. He realised that masturbation was common among young people, but was also done by adults, and he recommended that parents and teachers discourage it as it could lead to eternal damnation. St Thomas Aquinas, one of the most influential Christian thinkers in the Western tradition, wrote that since masturbation frustrated the natural purpose of sex, which was procreation, that it was a very serious sin. The inaccurate biology of the Middle Ages saw the man providing a seed for a woman to 'germinate', and masturbation as a waste of precious human seed. To some extent, moral theology cannot escape social context. So it is important to remember that during Aquinas' time one-third of Europe's population died from the Black Death; there was a desperate need for a compensating high birth rate. We can understand that 'wasting seed' would be considered as a very serious – and selfish – act. This social context also led Aquinas to the nonsensical position of considering masturbation a more serious sin than rape, which, from the perspective of Aquinas, was at least in conformity with the divine purpose of sexuality.

The next important voice was Samuel Tissot, who linked masturbation to medical and mental disorders. His book, *Onania, or a treatise upon the disorders produced by masturbation*, originally published in 1716, went through 80 editions and significantly influenced medical thought. Important philosophers such as Kant, Voltaire and Rousseau also condemned masturbation. Kant's comments on masturbation are found in his Lectures on Ethics,[17] in a section revealingly entitled, 'Crimes against the body'.

Tissot's book had a major influence even into the nineteenth century. The book's complete lack of empirical basis for any of its extreme assertions troubled no one; formal empirical research was yet to be

17. Kant, I. (1963). *Lectures on ethics.* (L. Infield, Trans.). New York: Hawthorn Books.

developed. William Kellogg, better known as the originator of Kellogg's cornflakes, dedicated his life to a crusade against the evils of masturbation, and designed his flakes as a healthy alternative to food which he thought might inflame the passions of young people and lead them to the practice of masturbation. Kellogg enumerated 39 signs that parents should look out for, including acne, bashfulness, boldness, nail biting, use of tobacco and bed wetting,[18] many of which are behaviours that can be seen in normal, healthy adolescents. In nineteenth century Western society, masturbation came to be regarded as a source of impotence, immorality, madness, and professional failure.[19] Even well into the twentieth century, similar beliefs were held by many in the health and eugenics movements. For example, as late as 1908 Dr Hoyt F. Pilcher was discharged as director of the Kansas State Institute for the Feeble-minded because his treatment regimen had included castration of chronic masturbators. Pilcher believed that preventing masturbation would reduce mental retardation.[20]

Sigmund Freud originally disapproved of masturbation, but changed his views over time. As the twentieth-century psychological and biological sciences progressed, practitioners and researchers began to question the truth of earlier fears and condemnations of masturbation. In 1948, when Alfred Kinsey brought out his groundbreaking empirical study of human sexuality, it was at last possible to see actual data. Kinsey reported that in his respondent sample of adults over 90% of men masturbated, and 60–80% of women.[21] In the face of these data, it was no longer possible to maintain the opinion that masturbation caused, or was a consequence of, the various diseases and mental illnesses that had been attributed to it in the past.

18. Miracle, T. S., Miracle, A. W., & Baumeister, R. F. (2003). *Human sexuality: meeting your basic needs.* New Jersey: Prentice Hall.
19. Capps, D. (2003). From masturbation to homosexuality: A case of displaced moral disapproval. *Pastoral Psychology,* 51(4), 249 – 272.
20. Barr, Martin W. (1920). Some notes on asexualization. *Journal of Nervous and Mental Disease, Vol. 51*(3), 231–241.
21. Kinsey, A. C., Pomeroy, W. B., & Martin, C. E. (1948). *Sexual behavior in the human male.* Philadelphia: Saunders, p. 513.

However, Kinsey's book shocked many Americans, and even today nineteenth-century thinking still persists among many religious laypeople and clergy.

The perception persists, especially among religious people, that masturbation is 'beginner's sex' and that when young people mature that they are ready for the 'real thing', i.e., sexual intercourse.[22] The perception that masturbation is an adolescent behaviour that will disappear in adulthood, and that it can lead to problems if not relinquished, underlies a lot of current religious writing on this subject. What then do we know about masturbation today, and can this shed any light on the meaning of masturbation in the human sexuality of religious people?

Current empirical research on masturbation

Martha Cornog provides probably the most comprehensive analysis of research on masturbation. Integrating the data from ten surveys of varying quality, she concludes that between 80% and 99% of men report ever having masturbated, and 47–89% of women.[23] The Sex in America Survey (1992) found that despite masturbation's carrying a slight taint of psychosexual failure, 'among Americans aged 18–59, about 60% of men and 40% of women said they masturbated in the past year'.[24] There was a lower rate among young men aged 18–24 (only 6 out of 10 men in this group said they had masturbated in the previous year), and less than half of the men over 54 masturbated. The statistics for women followed a similar pattern with fewer than 4 out of 10 women aged 18–24 reporting they had masturbated in the previous year and fewer than 3 out of 10 aged over 54. People over 55 may be experiencing the beginnings of a general decline in

22. Miracle, T. S., Miracle, A. W., & Baumeister, R. F. (2003). *Human sexuality: meeting your basic needs.* New Jersey: Prentice Hall, p. 353.
23. Cornog, M. (2003). *The big book of masturbation,* San Francisco: Down There Press, p. 67.
24. Michael, R. T., Gagnon, J. H., Laumann, E. O., & Kolata, G. (1994). *Sex in America: A definitive study.* Boston: Little Brown, p. 158.

sexual needs, and younger people may have other sexual outlets, or may want to believe that they have outgrown what has been presented to them as an adolescent behaviour.

In terms of frequency, 25% of men and 8% of women said that they masturbated once a week or more, and 11% of men and 12% of women said they masturbated 1–5 times a year. Notably, most of these people were adults who had regular partners available for sexual intercourse. This finding appears puzzling, as it is often assumed that masturbation is an inferior substitute for intercourse, and is a reflection of loneliness or lack of opportunity for sexual intercourse. One student in a class on human sexuality made the following observation: 'When I was at university I worked with a guy in a call centre who used to go off to the toilets from time to time with his porn mags. And he had a girlfriend.' Once he made the comment there was a pause in the conversation. The student's face then changed to a look somewhere between amusement and surprise when he realised that he had assumed that having a girlfriend would result in there being no need to masturbate. What the American researchers found was that those you would expect to masturbate – single men – masturbated less frequently, while those who had other sexual outlets – people in relationships – masturbated more frequently. The authors of the study concluded that, 'Masturbation is . . . not an outlet as much as a component of a sexually active lifestyle'.[25] They note that the group which is most likely to masturbate is the group which is 'neither young nor old', as nearly 85% of men and 45% of women who were in a partnered relationship had masturbated at some point in the year prior to the study.[26]

It appears that masturbation is not simply an adolescent phenomenon, and that, while there may be a slight decrease in young adulthood,

25. Michael, R. T., Gagnon, J. H., Laumann, E. O., & Kolata, G. (1994). *Sex in America: A definitive study.* Boston: Little Brown, p. 159.
26. Michael, R. T., Gagnon, J. H., Laumann, E. O., & Kolata, G. (1994). *Sex in America: A definitive study.* Boston: Little Brown, p. 165.

masturbation becomes part of the sexual lives of many people, both single and in partnered relationships. The authors of the Sex in America study further weaken the link between masturbation and adolescence when they suggest that many women probably only begin to masturbate after they have experienced sexual intercourse rather than before – as is the case for the vast majority of men.[27]

Does masturbation really retard development and movement towards others? Is this concern actually a disguised way to raise a concern about the frequency of masturbation? It is difficult to believe that an occasional instance of masturbation can affect the normal course of human development. Some authors, when writing about masturbation, contrast 'normal' masturbation and 'compulsive' masturbation. Compulsive masturbation tends to be seen as problematic and requiring therapeutic help; it is viewed as a symptom of other problems in the person's sexual and personal development. However, the question has to be asked: does this refer to compulsion in the same sense that we understand it in 'Obsessive compulsive disorder'? Do we actually mean 'frequent', 'regular' or 'excessive' masturbation rather than compulsive? How can we decide whether or not behaviour is excessive from a mental-health point of view?

One of the authors of this chapter, when working as a therapist with a group of sex offenders, was asked, 'How many times a week is it normal to masturbate?' One of the men in the group reported masturbating once a week and another reported masturbating every day, something that is not uncommon in adolescence, but may be more frequent than is usual for men in their forties. The therapist turned the question over to the group, and this led to a remarkably open and honest discussion of this aspect of their lives. Since that conversation took place, data has been published that may help to answer the group member's question.

27. Michael, R. T., Gagnon, J. H., Laumann, E. O., & Kolata, G. (1994). *Sex in America: A definitive study.* Boston: Little Brown, p. 164.

A survey of 4781 adult men and women in Norway,[28] conducted in the spring of 1996, found that male respondents had sexual intercourse on average 5.5 times per month and female respondents 5.1 times per month. The men masturbated an average of 4.9 times per month and the women 1.6 times per month, which is consistent with differences other researchers have observed in rates of masturbation between men and women. 31% of the men and 61% of the women reported not having masturbated in the previous month. The authors of the study found that in these respondents high frequency of intercourse was positively related to happiness, but high frequency of masturbation was related to unhappiness. They found that respondents who masturbated more than 15 times per month had lower rates of satisfaction with their sexual lives and with life in general. The moderately sexually active, whether via intercourse or masturbation, had similar levels of satisfaction: respondents who had sexual intercourse an average of 4.8–5 times per month had the same level of satisfaction as those who masturbated 0–3 times per month.

Those who did not have sexual intercourse at all had the same low level of satisfaction with life as those who masturbated more than ten times per month. This suggests that masturbation as an occasional sexual outlet is not related to unhappiness, but that when it is a very frequent occurrence that it may be related to poor psychological health, possible loneliness, and reduced happiness. The authors of the study found elevated levels of some other sexual indicators that were also related to unhappiness. They concluded in a response to a critique of their paper that, 'We make the . . . modest claim that it is possible for sexual activities to be excessive, and that excess would likely involve impersonal sexual activities. It would be truly amazing if sexuality was the one area of life where restraint was never of benefit.'[29]

28. Långström, N., & Hanson, R. K. (2006). High rates of sexual behavior in the general population: Correlates and predictors. *Archives of Sexual Behavior, 35:* 37 – 52.
29. Långström, N., & Hanson, R. K. (2006). Population correlates are relevant to understanding hypersexuality: A response to Giles. *Archives of Sexual Behavior, 35:* 643 – 644.

From the perspective of psychological well-being it appears that the issue is not whether or not someone masturbates, but rather how often and why. When asked how they had chosen the cut-off point of 15 times per month, Karl Hanson, one of the authors of the study, noted that this number was closest to the top 10% of the male respondent-masturbators, above which level the individuals were unhappy with their sex life and with life in general.[30]

This study and others like it do not tease out possible differences between suffering from any compulsion, and suffering from a specific compulsion to masturbate. Morton Kelsey, an American Episcopal priest, and his wife, both experienced counsellors, offered the following reflection on the issue of compulsivity:

> It bothers most sensitive people that they are unable to stop something that they want to stop: '. . . We would conclude that, generally, compulsive television watching probably causes more damage than compulsive masturbation – because it robs us of much more time and energy that could be used more creatively.'[31]

Masturbation and the Internet

One area of life where masturbation may be clearly part of unhealthy behaviour is in the relatively recent development of Internet pornography and cyber sex. Many writers raise concerns about the isolating effects of Internet sex. Some people criticise masturbation as it can lead to the objectification of other people, and to viewing them as existing only for sexual gratification. A counsellor who worked in this area asked people what led them to stop viewing pornographic images. Some said that they switched the computer off when they had come to orgasm with masturbation and others said that when

---

30. Karl Hanson, personal communication, (19th January, 2007).
31. Kelsey, M . & Kelsey, B. (1986). *Sacrament of sexuality: The spirituality and psychology of sex.* Warwick, NY: Amity House, p. 219, quoted in Cornog, M. (2003). *The big book of masturbation,* San Francisco: Down There Press, p. 204.

they began to think of the bodies they were watching as real people, that it became more difficult or impossible to continue. These two responses appear to give credence to the criticism of masturbation that it can lead to, or be a behavioural manifestation of, unhealthy sexual attitudes.

In a sample of young adults, one researcher found that 6% viewed explicit material and masturbated online on a daily basis.[32] More male respondents than female respondents were involved in viewing sexual material on the Internet and in masturbating. It was also noted that respondents who were most unhappy with their ordinary (offline) lives, were more likely to seek sexual information on the Internet, or to view stimulating material that might lead to or be accompanied by masturbation. Respondents who did not use the Internet for these purposes were more connected and satisfied in their offline lives. These findings tend to support the view that masturbation can be a consequence rather than a cause of unhappiness and interpersonal disconnection, although it may also be the case that absorption into the online world exacerbates pre-existing problems or personality tendencies.[33]

What does the act of masturbation mean?

Some authors stress that masturbation should not be discussed as an act in isolation, but has to be seen in a moral and psychological context. William Kraft, for example, suggests that 'the act should be seen in the light of a total process'.[34] We have already observed that in the early Middle Ages the Church was flexible and sophisticated in its treatment of this subject, suggesting lesser penalties for masturbation than for other sexual sins. Kraft suggests that along with age, we

32. Boies, S. C. (2002). University students' uses of and reactions to online and offline sexual behavior. *The Canadian Journal of Human Sexuality, 11*(2), 77 – 89.
33. Boies, S. B., Knudson, G., & Young, J. (2004). The internet, sex, and youths: Implications for sexual development. *Sexual Addiction and Compulsivity, 11*, 343 – 363.
34. Kraft, W. F. (1982). A psychospiritual view of masturbation. *Human Development, 3,* 2, 39 – 45.

should consider frequency and intensity, noting that masturbating once a month is not the same as being involved in a compulsive daily habit. The research from Norway sheds light on possible implications of highly elevated rates of masturbation for well-being. It is possible that people who masturbate very frequently are caught in a cycle of using masturbation to release tension, which then builds up and is again released by more masturbation.

Regarding intensity, consider this contrast. Consider a person who masturbates late at night, while in bed, when his reserves of self-regulation have been depleted, and tension prevents sleep. Then consider someone who has daily bouts of viewing pornography, or accessing sex on the Internet, and who uses the masturbation experience to indulge in intense fantasy instead of forming normal, healthy relationships with real people. Roy Baumeister has suggested that people's ability to self-regulate seems to diminish at the end of the day, and he notes that late in the day people are more likely to smoke and drink more heavily, break diets or become involved in sexual acts they might later regret. He offers as corroboration 'most violent and impulsive crimes are committed between 1am and 2am'.[35] If these observations are correct, then a person who chooses to masturbate in bed at night, may not be seeking to increase sexual arousal, as is often supposed by people who criticise masturbation, but may in fact be 'giving in' in order to release the sexual tension and be able to sleep, at a time when the capacity to self-regulate is already lower than earlier in the day. John Perito writes:

> It can be a harmless act, or even an act of self-love, done solely for pleasure, or to confirm one's sense of sexual identity, or to release sexual tension that has become intolerable . . . It may be done to help one sleep and be more rested for the next day.[36]

---

35. Baumeister, R. F., & Heatherton, T. F. (1996). Self-regulation failure: An overview. *Psychological Inquiry, 7 (1)*, 1 – 15, p. 3.
36. Perito, J. E. (2003). *Contemporary Catholic sexuality: What is taught and what is practiced.* New York: Crossroad, p. 91.

These are not descriptions of narcissistic, selfish individuals suffering from arrested interpersonal development, but rather normal people, part of whose sexuality is expressed, or dealt with, by masturbation.

Religious perspectives [37]

In her review of the teachings on masturbation found in the major world religions (Judaism, Christianity, Hinduism, Buddhism and Islam), Martha Cornog notes that there do not appear to be verses in any of their sacred texts which irrefutably condemn masturbation. At the same time all of them have consistent *traditions* of disapproval and condemnation. She reports that in the Jewish tradition the Talmud explicitly condemns masturbation, and that the Tractate Rosh Hashanah (11b–12a) lays the blame for the flood in the story of Noah (Genesis 6:11–12) on those who had sinned by wasting semen. Since 'liquid (semen)' had been wasted, the punishment was also by liquid. [38] Early Christian teachings have already been mentioned, and the contemporary Roman Catholic position will be discussed in a later section on morality and guilt. It appears that the Mormon tradition is very restrictive, as is that of the Jehovah's Witnesses. However the Unitarians and Quakers appear to take a more liberal approach.

Both Islam and Buddhism have traditions of condemnation of masturbation. In the Buddhist tradition it is linked to teachings that suffering is due to desire, and that indulging desires interferes with spiritual progress. Hinduism does not appear to have texts containing prohibitions, but it has a strong tradition of ritual purity, and in that context any sexual behaviour outside of marriage is understood to be prohibited.

Martha Cornog also points out that there are alternative voices in all of these great traditions. She quotes Michael Gold, a Reform

37. This chapter is based on the research provided in Cornog, M. (2003). *The big book of masturbation,* San Francisco: Down There Press, ch. 11, Religion, spirituality and masturbation.

38. The Talmud of Babylonia: An American translation, Atlanta, GA: The Scholar's Press, c. sixth century CE / 1990 – 1995, Niddah 13a – 13b, quoted in Cornog, M. (2003). *The big book of masturbation,* San Francisco: Down There Press, p. 169.

Rabbi, for example, who makes the following comment about the teaching on masturbation from the Orthodox Jewish tradition:

> If their teaching is based on false information regarding male seed, then it is even more important to rethink the ban on masturbation. Particularly to discourage young people from experimentation with others, we ought to declare forthrightly that masturbation as a form of release, of sexual pleasure, and of learning about the body is permissible.[39]

There are also more liberal views being expressed in Hinduism and Islam, which Cornog discusses in her book. She mentions that there are websites where there are ongoing debates about masturbation in these religious traditions. Rabbi Michael Gold bases his comments on changes in medical knowledge. A number of traditions base their condemnation on the belief that seed is wasted in the act of masturbation. If this is not the case, then what is the prohibition of masturbation based on? Perhaps the prohibition is intended to protect and promote marriage. If the marital dyad is seen as the one proper place of sexual acts, then masturbation would appear to be unacceptable. Cornog, however, notes that in Roman Catholicism St Alphonsus Liguori, the great teacher of Moral Theology and a Doctor of the Catholic Church, wrote that 'wives, who are more frigid by nature, can stimulate themselves by touch before copulation so that they may ejaculate at once in the act of marital union'.[40]

Other religions offer other exceptions. Some Islamic authors allow masturbation in order to prevent adultery, for example for soldiers or students separated from wives, or for a man who is not in a financial position to marry. The Buddhist tradition rules out masturbation for celibates. However, according to John Stevens, the Dalai Lama appears

---

39. Gold, M. (1992). *Does God belong in the bedroom?* Philadelphia: The Jewish Publication Society, quoted in Cornog, M. (2003). *The Big Book of Masturbation*, San Francisco: Down There Press, p. 172.
40. Alphonsus Liguori, (1748). *Theologia Moralis*, 6,919, quoted by Peter Gardella. (1985). *Innocent ecstasy*, New York: OUP, pp. 14–15, quoted in Cornog, M. (2003). *The big book of masturbation*, San Francisco: Down There Press, p. 186. Translation provided by Maureen Walker and Margaret Harvey.

to have suggested in a radio interview that it may be permissible to lay Buddhists as a means of 'temporary satisfaction'.[41]

Does religion influence masturbatory behaviour? According to Martha Cornog, the important issue appears to be devoutness rather than affiliation. Men and women who were members of Conservative Protestant denominations, and who were devout in their religious practice, were less likely to have masturbated than other groups. The authors of the Sex in America study found that those with no religious affiliation were most likely to have masturbated, suggesting a link between religious teaching, levels of devoutness and masturbation.[42] An earlier study also noted that women who attended church masturbated significantly less than those who didn't; there was not a statistically significant difference in rates of masturbation among men.[43] Feelings of guilt may deter some churchgoers, or the combination of church attendance and masturbation may intensify feelings of guilt and shame that were already there. For a brief review of the current-day attitudes of various religious groups toward masturbation, the reader may find the Wikipedia discussion on masturbation and religion useful.[44]

Moral issues

Both Perito and Genovese note that the Christian moral teaching on masturbation was heavily influenced by the fact that the male seed was used to impregnate the woman, and that masturbation was a waste of human seed, which also influenced the teachings of other religious traditions, as we have already noted. Perito and Genovese note a major change in society's views of masturbation over the past fifty years. While people may not talk about it, they are hardly

41. Stevens, J. (2003). Buddhist masturbation, in Cornog, M. (2003). *The big book of masturbation*, San Francisco: Down There Press, p. 181.
42. Cornog, M. (2003). *The big book of masturbation*, San Francisco: Down There Press, p. 71.
43. Adams, C. G., & Fishbein, M. (1985). Reported change in sexuality from young adulthood to old age. *Journal of Sex Research, 21*, 126 – 141.
44. http://en.wikipedia.org/wiki/Religious_views_on_masturbation, retrieved on Oct 29, 2008.

inclined to believe that an act of masturbation can lead to eternal damnation. Andrew Greeley compared two surveys of priests undertaken in 1970 and 2002. In both studies the belief that masturbation was always wrong remained constant at only 29%.[45] These data from parish-level priests do not reflect the official bureaucratic position of the Vatican, which describes masturbation as 'an intrinsically and seriously disordered act'. The main reason for this judgement is that it involves, 'the deliberate use of the sexual faculty outside normal conjugal relations', and that this 'essentially contradicts the finality of the faculty'.[46] Other Christian churches vary in response to masturbation, with the Mormons, Jehovah's Witnesses and Evangelicals taking a position similar to the official position of the Catholic Church, and Unitarians, Methodists and Quakers taking a more positive view of its role in sexual development. Judaism is also opposed to masturbation.[47]

In the Catholic tradition, one school of moral theology seeks to benefit from insights of the human sciences, and to see sexual acts in relation to human development and the building of healthy human relationships. Within this context masturbation is seen in a different light. The Vatican also has begun to take account of this position as can be seen in the most recent catechism of the Catholic Church:

> To form an equitable judgement about the subject's moral responsibility and to guide pastoral action, one must take into account the affective maturity, force of acquired habit, conditions of anxiety, or other psychological or social factors that lessen or even extenuate culpability.[48]

This eminently sensible teaching is held in tension with the Church's teaching on the disordered nature of masturbation. Perito writes that sexuality is 'God's way of calling us into communion with each other

45. Greeley, A. M. (2004). *Priests: A calling in crisis.* University of Chicago Press.
46. *Declaration on certain questions concerning sexual ethics* (1975). Sacred Congregation for the Doctrine of the Faith.
47. Cornog, M (2003). *The big book of masturbation,* San Francisco: Down There Press, pp. 167 – 189.
48. *Catechism of the Catholic Church, 2532.* (1994). England: Geoffrey Chapman

through love and procreation'.[49] In this sense, people must guard against sexual selfishness and self-obsession. It is difficult, though, to see individual instances of masturbation as global manifestations of a narcissistic and self-enclosed attitude toward life and relationships. Genovese writes that, 'It is one's pattern of behaviour, more than any particular act in itself, which both determines and manifests a person's moral status before God.'[50] Since we know from research data that many adults masturbate occasionally within a loving relationship and not as a substitute for one, then it is difficult to see occasional acts of masturbation as a deliberate turning away from love, and the embracing of a sinful, self-preoccupied attitude. These are moves in the right direction which avoid creating a twenty-first century theology based on a medieval understanding of biology.

Masturbation guilt

What, then, are we to make of the human experience of guilt? Capps notes that the religious crusade that was waged against masturbation for centuries would be expected to have some influence on people's perceptions of this activity. Even from a secular perspective, the combination of masturbation being viewed as 'beginner's sex', or a substitute for those who are not in a position to have sexual intercourse, and thus the hint of failure and weakness associated with it, make it a difficult subject to talk about. The Sex in America survey found that half of those who were surveyed felt some guilt about their masturbatory behaviour. The authors of the report attribute this to the influence of the history of social condemnation of masturbation. They also noted that feelings of guilt did not appear to prevent men from masturbating, but women who felt guilt masturbated somewhat less.[51]

49. Perito, J. E. (2003). *Contemporary Catholic sexuality: What is taught and what is practiced.* New York: Crossroad, p. 91.
50. Genovese, V. J. (1987). *In pursuit of love: Catholic morality and human sexuality.* Dublin: Gill & Macmillan, p. 322.
51. Michael, R. T., Gagnon, J. H., Laumann, E. O., & Kolata, G. (1994). *Sex in America: A definitive study.* Boston: Little Brown, p. 166.

It has been noted that the experience of guilt can create a vicious circle where the anxiety from the guilt is relieved by masturbation, leading to more guilt and more anxiety. People no longer believe that masturbation is harmful, so it is worth asking what the source of guilt feelings might be. Cornog asks if the guilt experienced today is more because masturbation incites feelings of personal inadequacy rather than moral failure. Perito wonders if such guilt interferes with normal development. In contrast, Kraft suggests that feelings of guilt indicate there is something fundamentally unwholesome about this behaviour. He writes, 'The folly of masturbation is that we silence the Spirit urging us to love'.[52] This comment leads naturally to the issue of masturbation and spiritual development.

Spirituality and masturbation

One of the healthy developments in the teachings of the Christian Churches in the last 50 years has been the rediscovery of positive approaches to human sexuality. Genovese's book is entitled *In pursuit of love*, for example, and Perito introduces his book, *Contemporary Catholic Sexuality*, by noting the shift in Catholic moral thinking. Alan Bartlett, an Anglican writer, has written of the need for a humane Christianity,[53] which is life and body embracing, and not rejecting of the life of flesh, including sexuality. Perito suggests that we should focus on masturbation only if it interferes with other aspects of healthy human functioning. In contrast, Kraft suggests that by embracing a certain personal asceticism, we can develop as more mature spiritual beings. He writes, 'It is not a one-way ticket to hell, nor is it a one-way pass to heaven'.[54] He writes that masturbation is seductive because it is easy and accessible, but that there is need for discipline and restraint in the moral and spiritual life. He suggests that masturbation may be an indicator of a lack of integration in

52. Kraft, W. F. (1982). A psychospiritual view of masturbation. *Human Development, 3*, 2, p. 41.
53. Bartlett, A. (2004). *Humane Christianity*. England: DLT.
54. Kraft, W. F. (1982). A psychospiritual view of masturbation. *Human Development, 3*, 2, p. 40.

parts of the person's life, as its satisfaction is momentary and not growth-oriented. He notes that people who masturbate often have another part of their lives that is over developed, e.g., thinking, work, self-development. He concludes that 'guilt calls us to seek a better life',[55] one where our life is in better balance and we listen to our bodies, our feelings and our thoughts, rather than letting one aspect predominate.

Kraft's views are healthy and helpful. He does not condemn masturbation, but seeks to explore its meaning in a larger psychological and spiritual context. He prefers to see it as an invitation to growth rather than the worst of moral failings.

Celibates

A seminarian recently commented that everywhere he read on the issue of celibacy he also came across the topic of masturbation. It is, without a doubt, a significant issue for those who embrace the celibate life, whether in the Christian, Buddhist or Hindu traditions. Given the moral teaching of the Catholic Church, it is clear that masturbation among Catholic celibate men and women is considered at least *pro forma* unacceptable, since celibacy requires abstaining from all genital sexual activity. There is a tension in those who live the celibate life between being called apart and being different in significant ways (as manifested in the celibate commitment) and yet being the same as other men and women. This tension can be seen in the area of masturbation.

The traditional position is reflected in the attitude of Fr Benedict Groeschel, CFR, an American Capuchin priest who, along with seven other friars who shared his concern that their order was losing its spiritual edge, founded his own order of the Franciscan Friars of the Renewal. Groeschel is quoted as saying, 'And chastity means chastity. You know, it means no voluntary acts of autoeroticism, or anything

55. Kraft, W. F. (1982). A psychospiritual view of masturbation. *Human Development, 3*, 2, p. 45.

like that. And when kids have grown up in this sexually explicit culture that's a bit of a challenge. But they know what's coming. And they embrace it.' Groeschel attributes the growth in vocations to his order to the more authentic, ascetic and challenging lifestyle that aspirants are offered, which includes a clear position against masturbation.[56]

In contrast, Richard Sipe, a psychiatrist and former priest, writes that, 'Masturbation is the most common and frequently used sexual behaviour of celibates'.[57] He estimates that 80% of Catholic clergy masturbate at least occasionally. John Cornwell reports a priest-counsellor saying to a group of priests in Dublin a number of years ago: 'Well, we all get by, Fathers, don't we, on the three excesses: excessive whisky, excessive golf, and excessive masturbation!'[58] This comment may have been delivered tongue-in-cheek and have been a bit excessive in itself, but it implies that masturbation is part of how many priests deal with celibacy. Gerard McGloan, SJ, a Jesuit priest and clinical psychologist, interviewed 80 priests in the United States. He noted that 'most subjects seemed relatively content with their masturbatory fantasies and activities'.[59]

Kraft notes that people who are overly cerebral, like many religious, and who tend to live 'from the neck up', may experience increased yearning to 'live from the neck down'.[60] In that sense, the wish to masturbate is a symptom of a life that is out of balance. These 'thinkaholics' are prime candidates for a practice that more than anything else, focuses attention on their own sexual needs, relieves the intellectual and work pressures they live with, and puts them in touch with sensuality and pleasure. They slow down, relax, and experience rest and relief.

---

56. Boyer, P. (May 16th, 2005). A hard faith: How the new Pope and his predecessor redefined the Vatican. *The New Yorker*, pp. 54 – 65.
57. Sipe, A. W. R. (1990). *A secret world: Sexuality and the search for celibacy*. New York: Brunner / Mazel.
58. Cornwell, J. (2001). *Breaking faith: The Pope, the people, and the fate of Catholicism*. New York: Viking Compass, p. 157.
59. McGloan, G. J. (2001). *Sexually offending and non-offending Roman Catholic priests: Characterization and analysis*. Unpublished doctoral dissertation, California School of Professional Psychology, Alliant University, San Diego.
60. Kraft, W. F. (1982). A psychospiritual view of masturbation. *Human Development, 3*, 2, p. 41.

Sipe notes a number of different mindsets of celibates toward masturbation. One group does not feel particularly guilty. For some priests their own masturbation is seen as the lesser of two evils, a routine way of managing their sexual tensions while carrying out day-to-day ministry. They are hard-working men, whose strength is in administration rather than moral casuistry. Celibacy does not have a great deal of essential meaning for them and masturbation is their way of managing their sexual feelings while conforming to the external discipline of the Church and remaining relationally celibate.

There are those celibates who feel terribly guilty about having a sexual self. Simple reassurance seldom helps them to modify negative judgements of themselves. This group often needs therapeutic help to bring the different parts of their lives together; sexual and celibate, intellectual and spiritual, priestly and human, and to integrate their humanity with their vocational aspirations.

According to Sipe, there are clergy who would be judged hypocrites if their private lives were known, because they indulge their own sexual fantasies through masturbation, but are critical and condemnatory towards others who masturbate. They say that masturbation is sinful, but find ways to excuse or explain their own behaviour. This is the kind of character portrayed in the Australian film, *The Devil's Playground*,[61] which describes the lives of a group of adolescent male students, as well as the vowed Brothers on the staff, at a junior seminary in Australia in the 1950s. One of the consoling outcomes of the plot is that the Brother who is most suspicious of the boys and who is most sexually repressed himself, decides to leave religious life.

Sipe describes yet another group of clergy who do not teach that masturbation is evil or unnatural and who tend to be compassionate toward the sexual lives of other people. This attitude is a result of years of pastoral experience. They can develop mature spiritual lives,

---

61. Schepisi, F. (Director). (1976). *The devil's playground* [Motion Picture]. Australia: Westlake Entertainment Inc.

while accepting that their occasional acts of masturbation are part of being an ordinary, limited human being.

Whether or not we find the various typologies of these authors credible and useful, it is clear that masturbation is one way that many celibate men and women manage their sexuality. It is part of their adult sexuality in the same way that is the case for non-celibates, both single and partnered. It appears that masturbation in the lives of celibates may be a manifestation not of pathology or of weakness, but of the love they have for the people with whom they work, which from time to time, manifests itself in masturbation.

Advice to the pastoral helper

Masturbation is a sexual topic that does not get the respect it deserves. People tend to dismiss it quickly as an inferior sexual practice that substitutes for intercourse among those either too young to have a sexual partner or deprived of a partner for other reasons. Thus masturbation is viewed as a substitute for intercourse rather than a sexual reality in itself.

In pastoral work, there is a need for a balanced approach when dealing with the topic of masturbation. It is important developmentally, and, for many adolescents and adults it is a way of regulating excess sexual tension. Masturbation can be a manifestation of anxiety, frustration or distress, or can be an outlet that enables people to switch off from the pressures of the day and quickly fall asleep. There is a particular spiritual menace to the community from clergy who have split off their humanity and criticise in others what they secretly practise themselves. It is important to be compassionate with ourselves and others, to listen to the call to live a more integrated life, yet to accept with humility that we are not finished creatures, and that our lives are an unfinished symphony. [62]

62. Rolheiser, R. (1999). *The holy longing: The search for a Christian spirituality.* New York: Doubleday, p. 204.

Even in denominations that absolutely maintain a position that masturbation is always sinful, it is important for clerical counsellors to weigh the relative importance of masturbation against other, larger moral issues, rather than hewing to an absolutist position. Here are some examples:

A. Suppose a man is married to a woman who has had a massive heart attack and is forbidden all sexual activity for a period of time. They know each other intimately, and he knows she will be aware of rising sexual tension in him, perhaps aggravated by his anxiety. He fears she will feel ashamed that she cannot satisfy him. If he waits for her to fall asleep and slips off to another room to masturbate, what is the moral value of this act?

B. Suppose a man is married to a woman who is in the last weeks of a difficult pregnancy. He will have to abstain from intercourse with her, not only until the baby's birth but also for six weeks afterward. He masturbates to release bodily tension and this helps him to be unselfishly attentive to mother and baby.

C. A young male secondary school teacher in the USA confides that he feels he has to masturbate every morning just before leaving for school. He says that the young adolescent girls at his school dressed so scantily and provocatively that he is terrified of having an erection when talking with them.

D. A person may masturbate because heterosexual involvement with another human being is not possible, and homosexual involvement is not attractive, or not possible either. In addition to vowed celibates, several possibilities come to mind: the imprisoned and the active-duty military.

E. Heavy disapproval of masturbation in women is probably a contributing factor in reckless liaisons that young single mothers make with men who turn out to be abusive to them or to their children. When the body's sexual demands are at their peak and female masturbation is viewed as sin and/or psychosocial failure, women will be more prone to accept undesirable sex partners. Helping the young woman may involve viewing masturbation as a lesser evil in lieu of promiscuity that exposes her child to a potential physical or sexual abuser.

If you compare these five masturbatory acts with the masturbation of the person who is simply unable to engage emotionally and sexually with another person, you see that the mechanical act of masturbation can take on different psychological and moral meanings. The young woman who uses masturbation to satisfy her sexual needs until she finds a mature and caring man is protecting herself and her children from dangers resulting from indulging her own sexual impulses without reflection. For the two marital partners, there is a virtual engagement with the other. The masturbation is not a solitary gratification, but an act of consideration, even charity, toward a vulnerable partner. The teacher is trying to protect his thoughtless young students from a shocking experience, and himself from possible dismissal. For the imprisoned or the military, the discharge of sexual tensions through masturbation may help protect them from greater moral dangers such as brutality toward others. In such cases, emphasising masturbation and ignoring its context is similar to arranging deckchairs on the *Titanic*.

Even for a person who masturbates simply because of fear of engagement with another human being, the masturbation is a minor symptom of a major psychological problem. Focusing on the masturbation is the wrong helping strategy. Clients may find it much easier to spin their wheels by focusing on being abstinent rather than explore the roots of their emotional alienation.

It seems easy to classify vaginal intercourse according to motive: affection, passion, humiliation, drive to dominate, etc. Mechanically, a rape and a passionate encounter may involve exactly the same actions. The two acts may differ only by motive. We have no difficulty labelling the rape as 'evil' and the passionate embrace as at least morally neutral. The same capacity for nuance seems to fade away in discussions of masturbation. It is perhaps impossible to disentangle all the many reasons that masturbation remains such a delicate issue, even for highly educated and trained pastoral helpers. Nevertheless, when the issue of masturbation is presented in a helping partnership, it is particularly important to maintain a stance of detachment and balance. It is a great act of trust for a client or a parishioner to initiate such a discussion, and this trust should be honoured with care and respect.

FOUR

Cohabitation:
Living in sin or an occasion of grace?

Kevin Kelly

What I am about as both parish priest and moral theologian is 'trying to make faith-sense of experience and experience-sense of faith'.[1] That is why, when couples who have been living together for some time, many with children of their own, come to me to arrange their wedding, I cannot bring myself to tell them that they are 'living in sin'. I do not believe they are! They are coming to me because they want to make a more formal commitment before God to a living and growing relationship which they have already experienced as a grace from God. I was nearly going to insert the phrase 'despite its rough patches' after the word relationship above. However, that would not reflect what these couples are saying to me. Many are encouraged and inspired by the fact that their love for each other has grown through their being able to overcome the difficult problems they have faced together, including problems in relating to each other. They have caught a glimpse of God in the midst of the storms and struggles they have been through. To describe their experience as 'living in sin' would scandalise them and would be a denigration of something they had experienced as sacred and from God. Such language would almost be tantamount to blasphemy. In my experience, most of these couples seem blissfully ignorant that the Church disapproves of the way they have been living. In fact, they are simply grateful that they can come to the Church to celebrate the gift of their love for each other and to give it a new permanence through the solemn commitment of their marriage vows to each other and to God.

1. Mahoney, J. (1984). *Bioethics and belief.* London: Sheed & Ward, p. 112.

To make 'faith-sense' of this new phenomenon of living together before marriage, we need to listen to how such living together affects the lives of those involved. Is it a good thing for them? Does it help them to grow together in love and mutual support? Could it be compared to a kind of novitiate in the religious life, gradually preparing them to make a full and unconditional commitment to each other? If, in fact, it seems to be a 'good' experience in terms of human growth and fulfilment, does the Church need to find a more positive and appropriate way of describing it?

In his book, *Living Together and Christian Ethics* (Cambridge University Press, 2002), the Anglican theologian, Adrian Thatcher lists twenty-five 'probably true' propositions about cohabitation. Some carry a kind of health warning. For instance:

- 'trial marriages' are unlikely to work,
- men are less committed to their female partners and much less committed to children,
- cohabitors with no plans to marry report poorer relationship quality than married people,
- cohabitors with children are very likely to split up,
- their children are more likely to be poorer and victims of abuse,
- cohabitation leads to an increase in the number of single-parent children.

That paints a rather bleak picture, especially if the increase in cohabitation is interpreted as one of the signs of creeping individualism and weakening religious belief.

However, Thatcher also offers some 'good news':

- people who live together with their partner before they marry value fidelity almost as much as married people do,
- the stability of cohabitation and marriage may be measured by the beliefs and attitudes partners bring to each,

- cohabitors with plans to marry report no significant difference in relationship quality to married people.

Another Anglican theologian, Duncan Dormor, has written an equally interesting book on cohabitation, *Just Cohabiting? The Church, Sex and Getting Married,* (London, Darton Longman & Todd, 2004). The way he presents some of the data is more hopeful than Thatcher's. For instance, he is able to report:

> More recent research, conducted when a majority of those marrying have cohabited first, has shown that it is no longer the case that those who cohabit in preparation for marriage are more likely to get divorced after the event. (p.10)

Hence, to maintain that 'the experience of pre-marital cohabitation has a destabilising effect on subsequent marriage' is simply 'incorrect', even though it is 'the simplest and most popular interpretation' (p.10). However, Dormor does accept that 'whilst it is clear that marital stability *per se* is not affected by premarital cohabitation, children born to cohabiting parents are twice as likely to experience parental separation as those born within marriage' (p.88).

A growth process

A post-Vatican II (1962 – 1965) understanding of marriage recognises that it involves a growth process which neither begins nor ends with the marriage promises. At the heart of this process is the couple's growing together into a communion of life and love. The sexual expression of their love in intercourse is such an intimate part of this growth process that the consummation of their marriage lies in the achievement of an integrity between their making love and their living together, rather than in any single post-wedding act of intercourse. Even their consent, which the Church has always put centre stage, is subject to the demands of growth. Time is needed for them to gradually grow in an appreciation of what they are undertaking together and in their mutual capacity for and commitment to this life-long creative task. All of this cannot be contained in a specific moment on their 'wedding day'.

Both Thatcher and Dormor agree that prenuptial cohabitation, that is, cohabiting prior to getting married, is a totally different reality to cohabiting without any intention of getting married. In prenuptial cohabitation the couple accept the values of marriage as their norm and have every hope and intention at some future date to make a solemn commitment to their relationship through the exchange of their nuptial vows in some kind of public wedding ceremony. There are also couples who, for a variety of reasons, do not want to go through a marriage ceremony, but who have every intention of staying together for the rest of their lives. There are, of course, some couples who cohabit without any intention of getting married, and who are, in a sense, simply living together for as long as suits them. It is this form of cohabitation to which Thatcher's health-warnings mentioned above apply.

Dormor reports that less than 1% of couples getting married today actively adhere to the Church's teaching on the undesirability of sexual intercourse before marriage. Certainly, for most couples today, at least in Britain, cohabitation is part of the process of getting married. They do not seem to be rejecting marriage nor seeing cohabitation as a desirable alternative. Rather they seem so aware that the health of a marriage is dependent on the potentiality for growth in their relationship that they are keen to get that growth process established on a solid foundation. Not until that foundation is laid, will they have the confidence to commit themselves for the rest of their lives. They do not see this as denying that marriage is for life. In fact, they would claim that this is their way of trying to ensure that their marriage – or relationship – actually will be for life. In their minds, to commit themselves before experiencing this initial part of the growth process and discovering whether as a couple they are up to it, would be foolhardy and irresponsible. It would be like teaching a person to swim by throwing them into the deep end rather than helping them gradually to feel confident in the water before risking themselves out of their depth. For many years Jack Dominian has argued that trial marriages are a recipe for disaster. Commitment cannot be experimental. Nevertheless, according to Dormor (p.10), many young people today do not see cohabitation as a kind of 'trial marriage'. Rather, many see it as 'a "trailer" for the absolute commitment which marriage entails'. Is this just a clever use of words or is there something more substantial to it?

A warning note

Of course, making faith-sense of experience cannot ignore the negative aspects of cohabitation, however sensitively it is handled in pastoral practice. After all, it contains no built-in expression of commitment or binding framework of rights and responsibilities. Although in theory that can sound liberating and in keeping with the modern emphasis on individual freedom and internalised commitments, in practice when things do not work out, the partner in the weaker economic, social or legal position can be left in a desperate situation. Remember Thatcher's second health warning, 'men are less committed to their female partners and much less committed to children'. While this is patently not true of all men, it would be unwise for pastors to ignore this aspect of male and female sexuality. It is not by accident that many young mothers are left literally 'holding the baby'! Moreover, if, as Christians and most people believe, marriage has a social dimension to it, with or without children, it is hardly doing justice to it to leave it as a purely private arrangement between consenting adults. It should be added that the warning note sounded in this paragraph applies less to prenuptial cohabitation than to cohabitation with no intention of marrying.

Thinking back over the weddings I have been involved with in recent years, I get the impression that the main reasons why many couples live together before their marriage are economic and social. They see the public celebration of their marriage as demanding a 'big do'. It is all part of a key 'rite of passage' for them. If they are Christians, the wedding in church is an essential part of this – but only a part, not the whole. If they had only the church wedding, they would probably feel something lacking – shades of the wedding feast at Cana! But weddings are expensive – though the church celebration is probably the least expensive item! In our contemporary culture of self-sufficiency and independence, many couples feel that they should pay for their own wedding.

Nevertheless, in terms of their embarking on the process of their life-long sharing of life and love together, it is not the wedding which is first on their list of priorities. Before that, they want to set up home together – ideally in their own house, though, tragically, this is becoming more and more an impossibility for many young couples. Some are keen to start a family before they marry – though it is worth bearing in mind that men and women often bring different perspectives to the timing and desirability of having children. I sometimes wonder whether, at least for some cohabiting couples, the baptism of their first child is an important public statement about their growing into marriage together. That would explain the increasing trend to invite family and numerous friends to the baptism and the celebration afterwards. It would also put their cohabitation firmly in the prenuptial category!

Freedom

A very important document, *On the Way to Life*, written principally by James Hanvey of the Heythrop Institute for *Religion, Ethics and Public Life*, has been published by the Catholic Education Service. It was commissioned by the Department for Education and Formation of the Bishops' Conference of England and Wales. Hence, at least implicitly, it has the support of the Bishops' Conference. It tries to analyse the present-day culture which is in the air we breathe and which, inevitably, has an influence on the way we live and the decisions we make. It also offers an interpretation of our own post-Vatican II Catholic culture and tries to discern how we can translate and interpret our Christian vision into language (not just words, but also life and action) which is enriched by the deepest and truest insights of contemporary culture, while refraining from being colonised and taken over by its less desirable elements. *On the Way to Life* sees freedom as one of the dominant values in present-day culture (cf. pp.13–14). It points out that freedom and its associated values 'are not just static concepts but are subtly embedded in our ways of understanding both ourselves and the cultural dynamics in which we are engaged'. In struggling to see if it is possible to make faith-sense of cohabitation, perhaps one important question that needs to be faced is this. Is today's social trend of cohabitation no more than an expression of the kind of freedom which claims that we humans are the sole arbiters of the truth of our actions, and that the only criterion to follow is self-authentication, 'Be true to yourself – do your own thing'? In terms of giving meaning to marriage, Dormor would interpret such an approach as equivalent to Anthony Giddens' notion of 'pure relationship'(cf. Dormor, pp.91–104). In other words, the priority is given to the relationship between consenting adults, which may last only as long as their consent lasts (and presumably that means, as long as they find each other attractive or their relation-ship satisfying their needs), with children having little or no say in it, since it is perceived as an 'adults only' relationship.

I must confess that the cohabiting couples who come to me to be married would be horrified by the Giddens approach. It might be in tune with some of what they see on television but it is certainly not how they would interpret their own relationship. They would see the

Giddens scenario as failing to do justice to how they see themselves as human persons and to the kind of relationship they have struggled to build up as a couple. Love, tenderness and stability are the values they seem to believe in and which they would want to be hallmarks of their own marriage. They would also see these values as offering the right environment for the upbringing of their children, whether already born or hoped for in the future. They believe in freedom, certainly. Perhaps unthinkingly it is their freedom of spirit which has empowered them to leave home and cohabit together. I have even met couples who have seen their cohabitation as a very deliberate way of entering into the marriage process on their own terms and under their own free volition. For them, to start the marriage process with their wedding would be to let their parents and family take over this important stage in their life together.

One of the key insights of *On the Way to Life* is its focus on 'the ordinary' as the realm of God's grace:

> The 'ordinary' is only a problem in a desacralised world in which the secular refuses to be graced. The theology of grace that informs Vatican II recovers 'the ordinary' as the realm of grace, God's 'better beauty'; hence the aesthetic of holiness is not something exceptional but something that is shaped in the realm of the domestic, giving it the weight of glory; the Alchemist's stone is Christ.

In making faith-sense of cohabitation, I am left wondering whether some cohabiting couples might, at least implicitly and maybe even unconsciously, be laying claim to the holiness of 'the ordinary' of their relationship. They are holding back from celebrating that in the solemnity of their marriage until they have sufficient appreciation of the wonder and beauty ('the weight of glory') of this 'ordinary' reality of which they are the co-creators.

In recent years I have also noticed that some couples – admittedly, very few at present – are wanting to mark much earlier wedding anniversaries than their Silver or Golden with a religious blessing or renewal of vows, either in church or as an intimate family celebration. Could this be an indication that they are becoming more conscious of the power of symbols both to consolidate and celebrate key moments in the growth of their marriage and to reveal the sacredness of their 'ordinary' life together?

In this little chapter I have tried to make some kind of 'faith-sense' of the fact that many couples living together before marriage find this a 'good' experience and want to thank God for its goodness when they eventually celebrate their wedding. If there is any truth in what I have written – and I believe there is – maybe it is also a challenge to those of us who are theologians. Does our Christian theology of sexuality need to develop imaginatively and creatively so that what it says about cohabitation actually makes 'experience-sense' for the many Christians who are actually living this reality? If our theology can move in that direction, perhaps such a move could be reflected in some imaginative and innovative moves in the fields of liturgy – and even canon law. After all, the best liturgy emerges out of life – and custom often gives rise to the best laws.

FIVE

Psychosexual development in adolescents and adults: Delays and aberrations

Joanne Marie Greer

Introduction

Delayed psychosexual development is a relatively common problem among religious adolescents and adults, and by no means uncommon in the population in general. By delayed psychosexual development, we mean a failure to progress in psychosexual and biological knowledge and social skills appropriate to the person's developmental level and current role in life. This lack may be purely psychological in basis. For example, it may stem from a puritanical and repressive upbringing, from an internal denial of the differences between men and women, and/or from a refusal to take in sexual information. Or a person may have taken in information but may refuse to use it to meet cultural expectations based on his/her age, gender and social roles. In social interactions, persons with these difficulties may display age-appropriate or even superior general knowledge, but seem sexually naïve. For example, they either do not understand or are unduly embarrassed by mildly sexual jokes.

Conversely, a second type of difficulty in psychosexual development is precocious sexual activity that fails to integrate properly with overall personality development and a growing sense of personal responsibility. A third type of difficulty is the psychiatric diagnosis of Pervasive Developmental Delay, in which psychosexual development is only one of a number of psychological-developmental trajectories that are cut off or inhibited in childhood and adolescence. A fourth source of psychosexual difficulties is some inborn biological defect that impinges on psychosexual development.

Why is delayed psychosexual development a problem?

First of all, it is a source of anxiety. Anxiety is always a problem for successfully living any life choice. Free-floating anxiety is even more of a problem for persons wishing to maintain a peaceful mind to promote a life of prayer. Since all humans are engendered, the source of anxiety will be ever present. Even the person living a silent, cloistered life may be troubled by a hypersensitive response to the slightest touch or glance. Frustratingly, that which one wants to avoid at all cost can become a constant distraction.

Such anxiety may give rise to a wish to avoid all emotionally satisfying relationships, lest they give rise to perplexing sexual feelings. Emotional isolation becomes the price of feeling 'pure'. Further, the irresistible, normal need for human relationships may lead such a person to repetitively initiate friendships which quickly become intense, but then abruptly break them off, leaving puzzled and grieving victims in his/her wake. Such a person is unwittingly a destructive force in any community.

Some sexually naïve persons may engage in behaviours that would be clearly reckless in the view of the more aware. Denial of the reality of sexual attraction leads to unwanted difficulties. Naïve clergy who have lengthy, emotion-laden discussions with parishioners behind closed doors might be unintentionally exposing themselves to seduction by disturbed or exploitative people.[1] When someone directs seductive words or behaviour toward a sexually naïve person, the naïf may fail at appropriate self-protection. A touch or kiss the sexually naïve person chooses to regard as platonic may seem anything but to the other party, and may set off a serious chain of events. Rigid defences

---

1. See the following article regarding Rowan William's account of an experience of trying to help a troubled student at Oxford: http://www.timesonline.co.uk/tol/comment/faith/article5119808.ece, retrieved August 5th, 2009.

against sexuality are apt to collapse just when most needed. A vivid illustration is Somerset Maugham's short story 'Rain'. The story concludes with the minister's rape of a seductive woman he tried to counsel for her 'impurity', then followed by his suicide.

Perhaps most importantly, the integration of one's whole being, body and spirit, is necessary for spiritual maturity. The struggle to integrate sexual feelings and attractions into one's spirituality is not optional. It is a necessary and ongoing aspect of the human journey. Failure to deal consciously with one's sexuality will result in a permanently stunted adult personality burdened with false pride, judgemental attitudes toward 'weaker' colleagues, and coldness toward the emotionally needy.

Sources of delays in psychosocial development

Cultural sources

A frequent source is early moral and religious formation that regards sexuality as dirty or dangerous. For example, an elderly American woman told of, at age 16, being beaten by her aunt for telling her 12-year-old cousin where babies came from, and thus 'spoiling her innocence'. In this old woman's rural Louisiana culture, her generation of brides was supposed to go to the marital bed sexually uninformed; good girls were reliably ignorant. They did not require any sex education, because good girls knew what was right by instinct. Another elderly woman told me of drawing, at age six, a man with a penis. 'What's this?' her mother barked harshly. Cringing, she answered, 'It's a third leg.' 'Well, it had better be,' Mother replied. Another told of being ordered by her mother to kneel and recite an Act of Contrition [a prayer asking forgiveness for sin] after being found 'playing doctor' with two other preschoolers.

Such early experiences send a strong message that it is dangerous or sinful to be interested in bodies. Young persons brought up in this way often do not even know the proper names for their body parts.

They may say instead, 'between my legs', or 'down there', or they may mispronounce sexual terms they have learned from books but never heard spoken aloud. In seminary and formation programmes, reviewing accurate sexual vocabulary as well as discussing common sexual slang may offer a non-threatening start toward undoing engrained shame about the body. Also, practically speaking, it prepares the students to understand what people might say to them in the future.

One should not infer that the sexually naïve are found only in seminaries and novitiates. A touching story about the disastrous effect of deliberate sexual ignorance is found in the novel *On Chesil Beach*.[2] The young bride is very fond of her bridegroom, but regards sex with distaste and trepidation. The young groom is eager but inept. He 'saves himself' for her, avoiding his customary masturbation for a week before the wedding. At her first touch of his penis, he loses control and bathes her naked body in a large ejaculate. She immediately flees him in disgust and the marriage is quickly annulled.

Defensive ignorance or pseudo-ignorance of sexuality

Maintaining 'sexual innocence' in a world full of sexual innuendo and sexually explicit media obviously requires conscious or unconscious effort. This effort is rooted in anxiety, an ill-defined feeling that at least some sexual knowledge and/or behaviours are dangerous to one's spiritual, emotional, or physical safety.

This condition must be distinguished from a mere lack of sexual information. Normal youths who have a benign innocence of sexual matters usually welcome information and find it increases their security and enhances self-image. In contrast, the person with this type of developmental delay may fend off sexual information when it is available, maintaining sexual naïveté by deliberate choice. Freud speaks of the denial of differences between the sexes as a form of

2. McEwan, I. (2007). *On Chesil Beach*. London: Vintage Books.

neurosis, based in fear or anxiety. This formulation bears the test of time. (However, his further speculation that the cause was the male's fear of being castrated as he perceived women to be, and the woman's resentment over already being castrated, has not held up.)

The sexually naïve are not necessarily young. As an example, consider one middle-aged woman's reaction to explicit sexual films as part of a curriculum preparing her to be a pastoral counsellor. 'I have been married 28 years,' she proclaimed indignantly, 'and I never knew and don't want to know these things.' Yet she was an adult and was proposing to practise pastoral counselling as a career; her role in life would require her to understand a diversity of sexual practices. She refused to accept this reality.

Another type of sexually naïve person plays at sexuality rather than avoiding it. Consider the 'hip' clergyman who wears his shirt unbuttoned to the waist, or the female pastoral counsellor who wears a revealing frock to work. At a recent youth event, the presenter did a stunt where he took off one piece of clothing at a time. He presented himself as a living poem, with each piece of clothing having some symbolic meaning that he then explained. Such persons fail to accept prohibitions on the social expression of sexuality that are appropriate to their age and role. This is a form of 'testing the limits' that reminds one of the normal toddler's testing of parental rules to gather information about which rules are 'real'.

A similar problem is denial of proper sexual boundaries between persons. It is as if the person does not actually know when, how, or with whom to speak and act sexually, and so tests the boundaries to see what might develop on the other person's part. Here are two examples.

1. I was participating in a group interview of a prospective entry-level professor in a Pastoral Counselling academic department. The interviewee had had private interviews with each faculty member over two days. We were all impressed. As a final get-

together, the group was dining in a nice, but crowded, restaurant. As dessert arrived, the prospect leaned across the table and whispered to me, 'It wouldn't be a problem if I were bisexual, would it?' Conscious of two young girls dining very close by with their parents, I snapped, 'I don't think it's any of our business!' By sneaking in this important question at the last minute and in a public place, he was also acting more like a child testing the limits than an adult.

2. My husband, also a professor, had taken me to his department's end-of-school-year party. We were chatting with another married couple, casual acquaintances, on neutral topics, when they suddenly inquired whether we had ever tried bondage and whether we would be interested in four-way sexual acts.

These sorts of events are puzzling. At the very least we can say (1) the content is sexual, and (2) there is denial of the shock value of the interaction. So we can say that the person either lacks a grasp of the cultural rules around sexual discourse, or refuses to follow them. This may manifest a sort of political statement, e.g., if the person is a 'flower child' and wishes the whole world to be likewise. Alternatively, the discourse may have an aggressive basis; there is no denying the recipient's sense of being violated. Most importantly, there is a failure to grasp, and honour, the sacredness of sexual relations between human beings. Rather, such persons play at being sexual.

Sexual ignorance can turn up in the most unexpected situations. At one point in my career I was given charge of a portfolio of government research grants on treatment programmes for sex offenders. When visiting one prison, I was astounded to learn that the rehabilitation programme my agency funded was teaching rapists *how to masturbate!* The researchers told of men who treated their own bodies so roughly as to injure themselves rather than cause pleasure. Moreover, it was not unknown for inept rapists to fail at penetrating their victims, torturing them with repeated attempts over a period of hours. The rapists also lacked social-sexual skills. An interesting part of their rehabilitation was formal training in small talk with women, and how to ask for a date. In essence, they were being taught the rules of sexual boundaries.

Sexual over-stimulation in childhood

A common source of delayed psychosexual development is, paradoxically, sexual overstimulation by adults in childhood and adolescence.[3] Where confronting an adult may be impossible, pseudo-stupidity suggests itself as a protective strategy. A client told of being sexually abused on public buses in childhood, as she rode a long distance to school. Trained not to cross or confront adults, she had no recourse. Frotteurs rubbed their penises against her buttocks in crowded buses, and once an exhibitionist sat next to her in an empty bus and exposed himself for 45 minutes. 'I didn't let myself know what was going on. I didn't like it but I didn't know what it meant. I never wanted to know,' she recalled. I know of several women who negotiated growing up in potentially incestuous situations by maintaining a steadfast ignorance of their pursuers' intents but also obsessively locking their bedroom doors. An adolescent who occasionally woke to find her drunken father entering her bed simply moved to the hall carpet to sleep. Father would be removed from her bed by her mother in the morning. None of the three ever spoke of it. Another thirteen-year-old girl had a broken bedroom lock, and her father, a single parent, kept 'forgetting' to repair it. Ultimately, she decided to walk to the hardware store, buy a new lock with her own pocket money, and install it herself. Interestingly, when she was later recuperating from an illness, Father moved her bed into the living room so she could watch TV, instead of moving a television into her

---

3. Weil, John Leopold (1989). *Instinctual stimulation of children: from common practice to child abuse.* Madison, Ct.: International Universities Press.

bedroom. Some parents with unconscious incestuous wishes toward their adolescent children may act out in subtle ways that leave the child confused as to the parent's intent, but nevertheless deeply uneasy. Two examples are the father who never buttons the fly of his pyjama pants as he parades back and forth through the house, or who suddenly insists on a kiss goodbye each morning, even though none of the family ever kissed before.

A defining characteristic of such pathological family situations is *silence*. There is no safety to speak of what is happening. Putting things into words brings them into consciousness. But what is forbidden to speak of remains unintegrated into the personality.

Sexual competitiveness on the part of a parent

Yet another source of pseudo-ignorance of sex, especially in girls, is the mother's jealousy of the developing girl. Mild maternal jealousy is a normal aspect of ageing: the mother is engaged in working through her sadness over the loss of her own youthful beauty just when her daughter is blossoming. A normal middle-aged woman, capable of self-reflection, will recognise what is going on. Her normal love for her child will allow her to overcome her competitive feelings and rejoice in her daughter's new sexual attractiveness. She will support her daughter's developing sexual interests with timely information and advice.[4] In contrast, the narcissistic mother may make it clear that the daughter must not compete with her as a woman. This message can be conveyed in many ways. One mother refused to teach her daughter to cook, using the excuse that she might spoil the meal. One might see an adolescent girl in childish clothing or without a brassiere even though her breasts are developed. Helpers might be alerted to this pathological situation by a myriad of clues: the girl avoids socialising with boys, the mother dresses the girl in a childish

4. Fox, G. L. (1980). The mother-adolescent daughter relationship as a sexual socialization structure. *Fam. Relations* 29:21-28.

fashion, the mother might refer to her daughter as 'my little girl' when she is clearly a young woman, etc. Although chronologically an adolescent, the girl understands, at least unconsciously, that she must stay a little girl to keep mother's love. Such youngsters may develop a defensive over-investment in religion, or a passion for studies or sports.

Projection of parental sexual wishes onto the adolescent child

Other parents may react to a child's adolescence by pushing the child into sexual situations the child fears or is not ready for. For such a child, sexual pseudo-stupidity or pathological shyness may suggest themselves as effective defences. For example, a mother may buy her daughter revealing clothing in which the daughter feels vulnerable, or her father may urge her to 'be nice', by dancing with his drunken friends. Either parent may urge her to accept invitations she feels unready for. Some mothers and fathers who enjoyed sowing wild oats as adolescents, or who had wished for the opportunity to do so, may want to relive adolescence vicariously through their children. For example, the father may pay for a prostitute to initiate his early-adolescent son into intercourse.

While some adolescents might respond to such parental initiatives with zest, others will sense that they are being used as pawns in an unknown parental agenda. I have actually heard adolescent girls wish that their parents would give them a set time to be home, or inquire about where they are going, like the other parents do. Playing dumb, retreating into a shell, and being hopelessly inept at dating are useful strategies in a confusing situation. Conversely, the confused youngster may become indiscriminately promiscuous without understanding the risks involved.

These types of pathological parental behaviour can be one stimulus for a child's interest in a celibate religious vocation. If so, formators need to assist the young person to recognise what he/she is fleeing, and hopefully move beyond a defensive idealisation of celibacy.

It is worth remembering that any psychological defence may be growth-oriented in the short term. This includes defences against sexuality. If a young girl perceives marriage negatively, based on observations of the parental marriage, then she may find it useful to refuse to play the game, and present herself as a so-called 'tomboy' or 'bookworm' when her age peers are 'boy-crazy'. The same strategy may be useful in a family where boys are educated and autonomous and girls are expected to end their educations early and marry young. An acquaintance of mine who grew up in a traditional orthodox Jewish family tells of the despair of her parents, aunts, and uncles when she ignored their presentations of eligible young men and kept her attention firmly on her studies. The relatives finally gave up, assumed she would always have to support herself, and began to encourage her to take an advanced degree. As soon as she had a medical degree, she promptly married.

Medical problems with sexual-developmental aspects

It is important to mention that in some cases delayed psychosocial development in an adolescent may be only one aspect of a serious psychiatric condition such as Pervasive Developmental Delay,[5] or even a gradual onset of schizophrenia. Both adolescents and adults may display a form of high-functioning autism known as Asperger's Syndrome.[6] However, these situations are unlikely to pose a puzzle to the pastoral helper, because the child's pervasive difficulties will usually have been evident long before puberty. Nevertheless, parents will be understandably very concerned as puberty approaches. Assisting them would require other expertise that pastoral workers are unlikely to have, and they should be referred to appropriate medical

5. http://www.webmd.com/brain/autism/development-disorder, retrieved August 4, 2009.
6. http://www.webmd.com/brain/autism/tc/aspergers-syndrome-symptoms, retrieved August 4, 2009.

resources. However, kindly encouragement in a difficult situation is always appropriate and usually welcome. The pastoral worker is more likely to be tasked with the delicate job of running interference for the afflicted youth with the other youth of the parish and their parents. For example, it is possible that some inappropriate touching may occur in social gatherings or even at church services.

Mild cases of Asperger's Syndrome are certainly found in Catholic seminaries and novitiates. (This is unlikely in Protestant seminaries because of their emphasis on preaching; Asperger's sufferers are usually not fluent verbally.) Very traditional religious training settings that emphasise asceticism, silence, strict routine, intellectualism, and avoidance of close friendships may fit well to the deficits of such persons. Further, they tend to be highly intelligent and do well at theological studies.

A rare but very difficult situation one should be aware of is the individual with actual genetic defects related to sexuality. Kleinfelter's Syndrome[7] is the most common example; males with this syndrome have an extra X sex chromosome. While normal males have XY, and normal females XX, Kleinfelter males have an XXY sex chromosome configuration. It occurs in about one out of every thousand males. The syndrome was first reported at Western General Hospital in Edinburgh, Scotland, in 1959.[8] Most but not all are infertile, and adolescents do not develop normal male muscle mass. A minority develops noticeable breasts. According to some experts, XXY males exhibit defensive and inferiority feelings in sexual matters, more than normal comparison subjects.[9] Obviously, adolescent boys with this syndrome are subject to greater psychological suffering than the typical adolescent.

7. http://www.mayoclinic.com/health/klinefelter-syndrome/DS01057, retrieved August 4, 2009.
8. Jacobs, P. A., & Strong, J. A. (January 31, 1959). A case of human intersexuality having a possible XXY sex-determining mechanism. *Nature, 183*, (4657): 302–3.
9. Burnand, G., Hunter, H. & Hoggart, K. (1967). Some psychological test characteristics of Klinefelter's Syndrome. *The British Journal of Psychiatry, 113*: 1091–1096.

Psychosexual developmental delay and 'Call' or 'Vocation'

Formators for the celibate life in religious training houses and seminaries sometimes function as relatively healthier parents, replacing the more pathological parents with whom the trainee grew up. In such a situation, psychosexual development often restarts. What may ensue is a revival of adolescent developmental tasks that were avoided or aborted due to environmental threats. Most prominent are tasks concerned with autonomy and with sexuality. Approval of sexual knowledge and interest in one's body, coming from a respected and loved formator, may result in reconsideration of the choice of vocation, or the perception of being called. Rather than viewing this as a failure of the training programme, formators ought to view such a choice as a win-win situation. The trainee is able, for the first time, to make a healthy free choice, and the religious order or seminary is relieved of the ongoing burden of managing a troubled person.

On the other hand, this re-started development may not displace the trainee's conviction of call or vocation. In such cases, enormous tact is called for. A new emotional freedom may open up the possibility of genuine friendships. These new experiences may have the intensity of early adolescent attachments, may distress or frighten the objects of affection, and may be disruptive to celibate community life. For example, the trainee may impulsively display sexualised expressions of feeling such as hugs, kisses, or touching/holding hands with other trainees or even with formators. The easy solution, but not necessarily the best one, is to send the person quickly on his/her way with advice to marry. A solution which better respects the trainee's possible call and potential spiritual gifts is psychotherapy or psychoanalysis, but with the long-term accompaniment of a sensitive spiritual director who is also psychologically sophisticated. The person's progression through the training will probably have to be slowed by a year or two. Given the increasing rate of poor parenting in current-day society, this scenario will be encountered more and more frequently in seminaries and novitiates. Some women's religious orders in the US even now have a preponderance of poorly parented applicants, and automatically send them all to psychotherapy as part of their training.[10]

Reaching out and helping

What advice can be given to those who must help or guide persons who have various deficits in psychosexual development? Here we are addressing helpers in a wide variety of positions of responsibility: teacher, minister or priest, youth pastor, counsellor, confessor, formator, seminary professor, spiritual director, etc.

1. Deal with your own sexuality. You cannot offer guidance for a journey you have not undertaken yourself. If you yourself are afraid of sexuality, you cannot be a dispassionate, empathic helper to others.

2. Model an open and matter-of-fact attitude toward human sexuality, while avoiding any inappropriate effort to be 'hip'. Create an atmosphere in which it feels safe to seek information and ask serious questions. I recall the story of a Mother Superior who accused a young nun of having a homosexual relationship. The young woman sincerely wanted to know if this were true, but was afraid to ask how her accuser came to this conclusion. So she asked her confessor exactly what it was that female homosexuals actually did. His response was an explosion of temper. Perhaps he didn't know himself, or perhaps he felt she should not know. In either case, he was little help.

3. Do not assume that your own sexual interests and sexual experiences are the full range of acceptable human experience. Come to your work with acceptance and respect for the vast diversity of human sexual practices. A person who has a frightened or constricted view of sexuality cannot help another with sexual struggles of any kind.

10. Personal Communication. Sister Suzanne Mayer, I.H.M.

4. Do not, in a misguided attempt to model frankness, behave or speak in a way that might appear immodest or shocking. Here is an example of an actual interchange reported by a counsellee:

    Counsellee What he did to me wasn't very nice.

    Counsellor You thought it was shitty that a person you trusted felt you up and wanted to screw you.

    The counsellee recalled feeling mocked for her distress. The covert message seemed to be 'You are sexually naïve; I am sexually more knowledgeable and at ease than you, and so is everybody else.'

5. Be aware that often you are dealing with two phenomena simultaneously: the ignorance and the danger against which the ignorance defends. For example, the girl with the jealous mother is defending against the danger of losing her mother's love and support. The person with the repressive upbringing is defending against the danger of sinning or of being viewed as dirty or impure. You should always explore the defensive purpose of the ignorance first. This is a much more difficult task than merely imparting information. For example, ask yourself why it has been dangerous for this person to feel, think, or behave as an average person in his/her situation. Help them realise that about early experiences 'that was then and this is now'.

6. In raising an uncomfortable topic, those seeking help are often vague and evasive. Helpers often make matters worse by asking vague questions themselves. A psychiatrist of my acquaintance makes a great point of asking extremely specific questions. For example, she recommends never asking 'who took care of you as a child?' because people almost always say 'my parents'. It is much more informative to ask 'who woke you, helped you dress, fed you, and got you to school?'[11] This might have been a

---

11. Personal Communication. Shiela H. Gray, M.D., University of Maryland Medical School, Department of Psychiatry.

nanny, a maid, a grandmother, or an older sibling. Similarly, rather than asking if Mother told you about sex, it would be better to ask exactly what Mother told you, and why she told you at that particular time (e.g., your age, something that happened).

7. Cultures (and sub-cultures) vary widely in which authority figures can educate the young about sexual matters, and how open they can be. For example, in the US, parents are so touchy on this issue that they must sign a form permitting sex education in school. Students without signed forms are sent to the library during presentations on sex. Sexual innuendos or touch by a teacher or church youth worker may result in disciplinary action or even firing.

   Missionaries moving into a new culture are particularly likely to be confused about these matters. In a new work setting, it is best to simply keep quiet until the situation is well understood! Here is an example that made a deep impression on me. In Western cultures of the developed world a woman is not supposed to witness her daughter having intercourse. But while living in Mexico in the 1960s I learned of an indigenous tribe in which it had been the custom for the mother to hold her daughter's head in her lap during first intercourse. Westernisation can bring prudishness to traditional sexual practices, disrupting long-established modes of sexual instruction. Consider that in the past Hindus traditionally presented newlyweds with an illustrated 'Bride's Book' explaining a wide variety of sexual pleasuring. In modern times, such books are sometimes used ceremonially, but now contain only blank pages!

8. Be aware that the conversation 'opener' that a person uses may not be what is actually on his/her mind, but it may be related. For example, a conversation with an adolescent that starts out with the topic of embarrassment in communal nude showers may be an opener to move on to the more sensitive topic of sexual

shame. On the other hand, the adolescent may simply be seeking affirmation that such an arrangement is socially unacceptable and should not be forced on him/her. Often people surprise you with where they are going with a 'conversation opener'. Don't assume you know what's coming next.

9. Be sensitive to feelings of humiliation that may surface when a person realises that he/she has kept ignorant of aspects of human experience that most peers know about. In educational settings, using group instruction can ease these feelings for the uninformed, even though many others in the group may already know the information being imparted or reviewed. At the same time, be aware that the more naïve members of the group may be influenced in an undesirable way by discussions of the sexual experiences of the others, e.g., young people who believe that their peers have had sex, are more likely subsequently to engage in sex themselves.

10. A way to protect against adults' feelings of shame or humiliation is to offer something to read in privacy, and then offer to receive questions.

11. Be present non-defensively to the adult's anger and sense of loss, and even of betrayal. When it has become safe to possess knowledge that was dangerous in the past, a person will likely suffer from such feelings. There will be anger at the persons or situations that made ignorance necessary. There may be grief over the normal youthful experiences that were avoided or compromised. For example, a person may have missed out on dating as an adolescent, or a woman may have avoided men until she was past childbearing age. While I myself was in the convent, I was friends with a middle-aged nun who had entered the order primarily because her jealous older sister first taught her to masturbate, and then told her she could not marry, that men would know she had masturbated and would reject her. Knowing

that I taught biology, she asked me if this was true, and I told her that it was not. She left the convent at age 37, married and had a child. A wonderful Christian, she not only forgave her sister but also prayed for her.

Some necessary cautions

It is important to be aware of proper role boundaries within your religious group or community. You may identify the need for education or intervention but not be the appropriate person to conduct it. There may be social or role prohibitions in your group that militate against your taking an active role in helping a person who is sexually naïve. For example, a confessor may realise that a penitent lacks an age-appropriate knowledge of sexuality or is pathologically fearful of it, but the confessor is obviously not the appropriate person to remedy the situation.

Secondly, although we all appreciate enthusiasm, it is important to avoid a shift from sex being unmentionable to sex being the latest 'in' subject of discourse in teaching and preaching. This accomplishes nothing except the complete embarrassment of the listeners. Such behaviour is socially inappropriate, and the embarrassment of the listeners is not due so much to the sexual content as to witnessing the preacher make a fool of himself!

Thirdly, there is a tendency for people highly trained in one field to feel competent in another field with little justification! Sex counselling/education is actually a highly developed specialty with its own professional journals, professional organisations, and training and certification processes.[12] It is unlikely that a person primarily trained in theology, religious education, or pastoral counselling will do the work appropriately based on casually obtained information. The role of the pastor or religious counsellor is rather to support the client during interactions with other helpers.

12. A good source for further information is: http://www.siecus.org/, retrieved August 4, 2009.

Ignorance: an inescapable human condition

Here is an old anecdote that circulates periodically among American Catholic women:

> A priest is preaching about the glorious calling of motherhood and the wonder of the woman's labour that brings a new life into the world. One old woman whispers to another, 'Glory be to God, I wish I knew as little about it as he does!'

There are always aspects of other people's sexual experiences about which we know little, or only know academically rather than experientially. It is an inescapable result of being engendered; man cannot know woman's experience and woman cannot know man's experience. It is also the usual outcome of making limiting choices in one's adult life: the celibate cannot fully experience marriage, the married understand little of the celibate's emotional life, the heterosexual cannot fully experience a homosexual relationship, the homosexual cannot fully experience a heterosexual relationship, etc. We elect a choice and we grow as adults within that choice. The alternative is a Peter Pan type choice of never growing up, never fully choosing anything.

Why make such an obvious point? Because sooner or later someone may seek your counsel who has life experiences absolutely unimagined by you. This has two implications: never assume you know what people mean, and ask as much as you need to know, to fully understand what they are trying to tell you. I once saw a man in psychoanalysis for four years, who continually complained of how frustrating his marital relationship was. I never thought to ask him *exactly* what happened in bed. He, and I, erroneously blamed his ample bundle of other neurotic complaints for his sexual frustration. Finally I did ask, and assured him that, at least in my opinion, any normal man would find his wife's behaviour utterly frustrating. (While this departure from proper technique made me feel better, it was of little help to him, since he promptly discounted my opinion.)

It is especially important to be aware of the difference between academic knowledge and experiential knowledge. As an example, consider the differences between reading about rape, versus witnessing a rape, versus being a rapist, versus being a rape victim. This caution applies to anyone, but is particularly relevant for celibates, whose chosen role requires purposeful restriction of experiential knowledge of many sexual matters.

It rings false, and may set us up for failure, when we pretend to have knowledge or experience we don't actually have. Some religious helpers, having been disenchanted with a repressive religious stance toward sexuality, swing too far to the other extreme and strive a bit too much to be sexually sophisticated. I was once very friendly with a nun-counsellor working at a Catholic student centre on a USA secular university campus. She once made a comment to me that betrayed she did not understand the mechanics of sexual intercourse, but thought that she did. She was assigned by her order to present religious workshops for hundreds of Catholic students aged between 18 and 22, and felt fully qualified to do so. (I am deliberately avoiding discussion of how her superiors could have thought this an appropriate situation.) She took satisfaction in presenting herself as deeply involved in the students' decision-making about being sexually active. I think that students would have respected her straightforward admission of limited knowledge of physical mechanics, if the matter became relevant, and still accepted her as an important source of value exploration. It was more likely to have hurt her credibility if they realised that she was presenting herself as having knowledge she didn't actually have.

In conclusion

Sex and gender are core aspects of our human identity. As such, aberrations in how we think and act sexually are basically a form of identity disturbance. Persons in such a situation are especially emotionally vulnerable. If they offer their trust and are open to being helped, they present us with both an honour and a responsibility. We must strive to be worthy of that trust.

SIX

Sexual concerns in marriage

Alison Moore

Introduction

A couple in their early thirties are sitting, nervously, in their first session with a relationship counsellor. They've explained that they are there because they are facing difficulties in their sexual relationship.

'When did the difficulties start?' asks the counsellor.

'Oh we were fine until we got married.'

This is a much more common experience than might be expected. People fall in love, are strongly attracted to each other, perhaps live together for a while and then marry. They don't discuss the sexual side of the relationship – it just happens. Later, after children or moving house or getting into routines or changing roles or being ill, a couple can find that sex has changed too. What was a source of pleasure, fun, excitement or relaxation is now a chore, a pressure, a lever in a power game, a way of avoiding dealing with conflict, a source of arguments or guilt.

Another woman in her fifties says with exasperation, 'What's the big deal about sex? Why do people go on about it? It's just a part of marriage – I've never enjoyed it much, but I just put up with it. We have a good marriage anyway. I'm more interested in other things in life.'

This person's underlying question is important: does sex contribute something essential to a happy marriage? And if so – how? What difference does a couple's sexual relationship make to the success of their marriage in general, or their children's and family's well-being?

Perhaps there is an impact on the wider church community if the married couples are experiencing a fulfilling sexual life.

> A man of forty says, 'I used to enjoy making love to my wife, but I feel constantly guilty because I just don't find her attractive any more now we have children. I'm sure none of the other dads in church are like this. I have prayed about it but it hasn't changed and I have no peace.'

This man's dilemma arises from the assumptions he is making: about what is normal, about other people's experiences, about failure of desire being a sin. It touches on the complexity of sexual response, on what is going on at subconscious levels in committed intimate relationships, and on the connections between faith and sexual activity.

This chapter is about the sort of issues these people are raising: concerns about sex that can arise in marriage, in a long-term committed relationship, in the context of a Christian church. No one embarks on adult sexual relationships as a 'blank slate'. Each brings thoughts and feelings, experiences and learning, assumptions and expectations. Some conscious and others not, these are shaped by all that has happened in life. Christians, of course, also bring experience and learning from their belief and the Church's teachings, which can sometimes enlighten and liberate and sometimes trap and confuse in the area of sex in marriage.

The first section will attempt to define what is meant by 'sexual difficulties in marriage'. In the second, which forms the main part of the chapter, we will explore some sources of difficulty, and why difficulties can become entrenched. This section will include something about normal marriage issues and dynamics. The final section has suggestions about what can help to resolve difficulties. Before embarking on these, however, it is worth making some comments about the context in which these relationships take place, in both church and society.

Society and the Church

All sexual relationships within marriage exist in a social context, and for Christians that context includes the church they belong to. History and culture, beliefs and values will impact in one way or another on attitudes and behaviours in marriage.

Our Western society's current habit of discussing sex as if it were something that stands alone, unhooked from any relationship between real people, does not help couples understand what is happening sexually in their particular marriage. Our society also obsesses (some would say tediously) about anything in the sexual arena. It seems to be taken for granted that everyone needs and has a right to a fulfilling and satisfying sexual relationship – and that to question this demonstrates a repressive denial of what is healthy, normal, and 'good'. It considers the individual's freedom of choice as paramount, and therefore makes assumptions about the rights of the individual to make his or her choices in sexual matters as in others. Of course everyone does have the right ultimately to 'say no' and withhold consent to sex, but there are many contexts where this decision is not as straightforward as this would imply. Sadly, public discussion about this can end up being unhelpfully simplistic. On a positive note, however, our society has normalised talk about sex, so that sexual concerns can be spoken about more freely. This is preferable to the secrets and myths that caused misery and mystery in the past. Also, women's experience of sex is now taken much more seriously than in earlier generations.

The Churches for their part have to admit that Christian history is a sorry catalogue of denial of the joy of the sensual and sexual. Early attitudes to women, sex and lust have affected the mentality of western Christians of all traditions to this day – as has the prevalent but unbiblical theology that separated body from soul, seeing the physical as the source of sin and the spiritual of holiness. This has contributed to a Church culture whose response to sexuality of any

kind has been characterised by silence, secrecy, furtiveness, embarrassment, idealism, condemnation and guilt. People who grow up in a
Christian culture which deals with sexual urges and desires in a dis-
approving or authoritative way, often find their marriages affected by
the after-effects of the mixed emotions of guilt and pleasure about sex
exploration in their teenage and young adult years. It is not surprising
that from time to time prominent and respected church leaders turn
out to have been living split lives, engaging in illicit sexual activity
which belies their marriage vows. In the Church we have yet to learn
from society how to normalise discussion of ordinary sexual concerns,
instead of avoiding the issue by proclaiming fervently about others'
behaviour and beliefs.[1]

However, at the heart of the Christian faith is a strong affirmation
of the physical. Christianity is incarnational, because Jesus was a
real, embodied, person. People are created in God's image, as both
body and spirit. The Old Testament contains the erotic love poem,
the Song of Songs. The New Testament shows a high view of sexual
union, describing it both as an image of our relationship with God,
indicating its potential for great satisfaction and significance and in a
very down-to-earth way as a central part of a marriage, that shouldn't
be lightly denied. Sexuality, of which actual sexual activity is just a
part, is an integral part of being human.

Although Christians may find themselves welcoming much that is
positive in society's attitude to sex, they will also differ. For example,
they know that a joyous and fulfilled life is not *absolutely dependent*
on having a satisfying sexual relationship. A Christian might be content
to live with a less than satisfying sexual relationship because other
people's needs may be more pressing than their own; or a Christian
might by chance or choice live a celibate life. Christian language is
more about 'responsibilities to others' than 'rights for oneself'.
Christians still believe in the value of sometimes being able to put

1. see chapter 13, Sexuality in ministerial relationships, re. projection.

the needs of the partner first, even while acknowledging that this truth has often been twisted, for example to ensure that women meet the sexual and other needs of their husbands with no regard to their own.

Christians are affected by the mixed messages from society and the Church, and undoubtedly have swallowed some of these messages without realising it. These internalised messages about sexual behaviour can lead to guilt and shame that affect the sexual relationship in marriage. Even no-longer practising Catholics can joke about themselves that they are 'hard-wired' for guilt; and evangelical Christians who are offered very clear lines about what is and is not acceptable pre-marriage sexual behaviour can suffer lifelong guilt about boundaries transgressed in their youth. Sadly, this means that many Christian couples struggle with unhappy sexual relationships without being able to share what is going on.

On a positive note, however, sex plays a central and enjoyable place in relationships, so it is worth reflecting on what the sexual relationship can mean to a marriage. The marriage service has it beautifully and accurately when it talks about joy and tenderness. Sexual connection can cement a relationship. Sex serves a very serious function in maintaining both the quality and the stability of the relationship, replenishing emotional reserves and strengthening the marital bond.[2] Some would see this as the sense in which sexual intercourse is 'procreative', not because each act should produce a child, but because the sexual connection bonds the couple and sustains a long-term partnership which provides the safe and healthy environment for the raising of the children. The marriage promise of 'forsaking all other' marks sexual boundaries, which create a safe environment from which to resist outside sexual pressures and enjoy healthy relationships and friendships with others. Sex within the sacramental bond

---

2. see Wallerstein, J., & Blakeslee, J. S. (1996). *The Good Marriage*. London: Bantam Press, p. 192 from ch. 15 'Exploring sexual love and intimacy'. The book describes a long-term study of committed and happy couples, drawing some conclusions about the common ingredients of these relationships.

enables play and relaxation, fantasy and fun; it gives pleasure, relieves tension; it expresses living as a whole person, physically as well as spiritually; it affirms value and identity; it embodies intimacy, with the exchange of giving and receiving intense pleasure; it demands risk-taking and vulnerability, because it requires letting go; it even has a close connection with the central sacramental act of the Eucharist ('this is my body, given for you').[3]

Marriage has been described as a wheel, with the spokes representing different aspects of shared life and the hub as 'the most intimate and reparative part' where the sexual relationship is the major component. With the hub in good order, the wheel turns smoothly.[4]

What are sexual difficulties?

Any description of sexual concerns is prone to inexact definitions. Serious writers and researchers on sexual issues confirm ordinary people's experience that sexual response in a committed couple's relationship is a subtle, nuanced and delicate business – as complex to describe as any other aspect of a couple's relationship. So there are a few things to bear in mind when attempting to define marital sexual difficulties:

- It is *normal* to have periodic 'sexual concerns' in a marriage! It would be a strange relationship where both partners were entirely happy with every aspect of their sexual life together over a lifetime.

- If one partner has a 'sexual difficulty' the couple has a *shared problem*. Too often, this person is blamed or told to get sorted out. Of course, for a woman particularly, an atmosphere of anger and blame is likely to kill any sexual desire, so the accusations from the apparently blameless partner in fact perpetuate the problem. If the

---

3. see Radcliffe, T. (2005). *What is the point of being a Christian?* London: Burns & Oates. Ch. 5, 'The Body Electric,' is a powerful affirmation of our sexual nature.
4. Laverack J., & Laverack S. (1994). *The essential red guide to couple relationship counselling theory.* Published privately, Tynewydd, Blaenwaun, Whitland, Carmarthenshire, SA34 0DB: Perceptions, p. 26.

partners try to work together there is greater chance of success in working things out.

- It is said that the most important sexual organ in the body is the brain – and without doubt the first sexual difficulty people face is often the difficulty of knowing how to *think and talk* about what they are experiencing sexually.

- It is known that *anxiety* is a prime inhibitor of sexual arousal. It doesn't matter what has caused the anxiety; the end result will be the same.

- *Lack of communication* is another inhibitor. In sexual connecting, as in many other areas of marriage, people tend to assume that the partner is a mind reader. So when the partner inevitably gets it wrong, he or she can be blamed.

  'If you really loved me, you would know what I like. If I have to tell you what makes me happy sexually, that kills the romance. If the romance has gone, I can blame you because you obviously don't love me any more.'

- It is a truism in marriage as in other areas of life, that 'it's only a problem if it's a problem'. In other words, what might be a serious concern in one marriage may not be difficult in another. The objective facts about the issue are not necessarily the determining factor.[5]

- What is happening sexually is likely to mirror in some way what is happening in the rest of the relationship.

To locate where difficulties arise, the approach of the 'five levels of erotic life' can be helpful.[6] We all experience our sexual nature in five different areas: sexual identity (man or woman); sexual orientation (attracted to men or women); sexual interest (what arouses sexually); sexual role (gender expectations); sexual performance (what actually

---

5. I have heard many people say after discovering an affair, 'I always said that if he/she did this to me, that would be the end of the marriage. But actually we love each other and we're going to work through this.'
6. see chapter 12, Contemporary issues in gender and sexual identity.

happens – desire, arousal, orgasm). Each level is connected to the previous one, so for example, a difficulty in sexual performance may in fact have its roots in inherited gender expectations.

As the focus here is on marriage, this chapter assumes heterosexual relationships,[7] and concentrates on difficulties associated with the three levels of sexual interest, role and performance. Within these areas the range of sexual difficulties is likely to include:

- aspects of desire, aspects of performance, aspects of what arouses sexual interest, aspects of sexual satisfaction
- the relationship between emotional, relational and sexual satisfaction
- a range in severity from, for example, lack of interest by one person for a short period of time to complete withdrawal from any kind of sexual connection for years
- a range from lack of knowledge about how normal sexual response works in men and women to entrenched religious ideas about what should happen
- difficulties that look the same but are in fact different (for example if a man finds it difficult to maintain an erection, this is normal for a man in his sixties, but not for a man in his twenties).

A few specific difficulties in sexual performance have been identified as 'dysfunctions', for which there are well-proven approaches that can really help.[8] However, as the above list demonstrates, it is not always easy to define what is normal and what is not. Just to add to the confusion, there is a danger of unconsciously using a medical model which necessarily needs to define what is or isn't healthy or normal, thereby implying that everything else is abnormal or 'dysfunctional'. Descriptions of women's sexual experience have fallen

7. It is important to acknowledge that just like other people, some married Christians will find people of their own or both sexes attractive; also some are transsexual. Any of these situations are likely to present challenges to a marriage.

8. Dysfunctions include: impotence; loss of desire; premature ejaculation; retarded ejaculation; erectile problems; vaginismus (involuntary contraction of the muscles around the vagina); orgasmic difficulties; pain on intercourse. The section on 'Problems' in Relate's *Sex in Loving Relationships* by Sarah Litvinoff includes useful advice on how to recognise and deal with these. England: Vermilion 2001.

foul of this in the past, with unsubstantiated assumptions being made about what is normal for them.

Where do sexual difficulties come from?

Useful metaphors for initiating discussion of sexual difficulties

Marriages are made up of many factors, some predictable, others not. People talk about the 'recipe' for a successful marriage, as if the ingredients can be hand-picked and mixed together. Some cooks follow recipes to the letter, measuring exactly and timing to the minute. Others have a mixed approach, knowing broadly what they are planning to produce, but adapting ingredients and timing depending on what's to hand. Successful marriage 'recipes' are more likely to follow this model than the first, which will probably lead to disappointment. Certainly a successful sexual relationship will develop out of a couple's ability to adapt, respond, change and experiment.

Another way of describing what might be in a marriage is to think of two people coming to stay in a house, each arriving with a suitcase. The house is the marriage relationship, the suitcases represent all that each person brings to that relationship. Beforehand they have talked about the sort of things they will be bringing in their cases, and once inside, they each unpack what they've brought, which will probably include one or two surprises the other hasn't seen before. Neither will be aware, however, that their suitcase also has a hidden compartment. Out of this from time to time will jump other things – responses, thoughts, memories, fears – that they had no idea were there. Of course, amongst the plethora of experiences, histories, families, assumptions, expectations, hopes, fears, to be found in both the open and the hidden compartments, will be those to do with the sexual. Over time, the couple find homes for their individual items in the shared 'house' of the relationship. But of course the house too will turn out to have hidden cupboards and crannies from which secrets or surprises will sometimes emerge.

Among this sexual 'luggage' will be much more than actual sexual relationships and encounters; there will also be the unexamined expectations and assumptions from their first families, schools, friends, relatives; and the messages about sex that they grew up with, consciously and unconsciously. These will include the overt messages they were given about the body, the genitals, being a 'proper' girl or boy, facts of life, the way puberty was approached. Some families speak openly about sexual matters, with parents discussing clearly with their children what the issues are. Others don't do this. In the suitcase too will be the subliminal messages given by parents: how at ease they were with their own bodies, how much they were able to relax and have fun with each other as well as with their children; how they resolved and approached differences of opinion; how much they touched and held and were physical with each other and the children; how much they were able to show vulnerability and take risks.

In this picture, the couple who achieve a happy sexual relationship will be able to remain interested in and have an understanding of whatever turns up next from the other's suitcase or the shared cupboard under the stairs.

The following sections will look at the contents of the suitcases, some of the many factors that influence a sexual relationship: common myths and gender issues, normal couple experiences, life stages and transitions.

Myths – I just know these must be true

In spite of the availability of much more knowledge and information about sex, many of the old myths remain.[9] Here are a few examples that can cause difficulties for couples.

---

9. Again, see Litvinoff, S. (2001). *Sex in loving relationships*. England: Vermilion, ch. 2 for a fuller list of common myths.

- *Good sex 'just comes naturally' – it should be spontaneous and feel right.*
  This of course is no more true than in any other area of a marriage relationship. Most areas of marriage demand attention from a couple, in much the same way as playing a sport or a musical instrument demands time, attention, familiarity, practice, mistakes before reaching the point where it seems to 'just come naturally'.

- *Sex means 'sexual intercourse' – anything else doesn't count.*
  This ignores the full cycle of sexual arousal and response, which is what adds up to a satisfying experience for both partners. It also disregards the pleasure to be had from each bringing the other to orgasm without actual intercourse.

- *Good sex means both partners coming to orgasm during intercourse, preferably simultaneously – anything else is a failure.*
  Women used to be labelled as 'dysfunctional' if unable to experience orgasm during intercourse. In fact, most women don't have this experience, so the norm for a woman will be to come to orgasm through stimulation – from herself or from her partner.

- *Sex is a failure if it's not exciting, 'the earth doesn't move', 'if you don't respond to me as quickly as you did' or 'if you don't reach orgasm'.*
  A tutor on a training course for couple counsellors observed drily that she didn't eat a great banquet every night of the week, and she wouldn't expect that in her sex life either. Sometimes the sexual encounter is like 'egg on toast', other times it's more of a three-course dinner. Taste and variety make the difference.

Why can't a woman . . . be more like a man? Or vice versa?

Gender expectations

In the 'house' that is a marriage will be gender expectations. The couple has chosen some of these, but others (in the hidden compartments and cupboards) have been unconsciously accrued over a lifetime, from parents and other sources. Doing the following exercise can be revealing. The idea is to complete the sentences very quickly without thinking too deeply about them, preferably twice, once for oneself and the second time guessing what the partner would say:

Being a married woman means . . .
Being a mother means . . .
Being a married man means . . .
Being a father means . . .

For example:

Being a married woman means . . . being respectable, always (or never?) being on a diet, making my way in the world of work, dressing well, making sure I am sexually attractive . . .

Being a mother means . . . being asexual, cooking, laughing, worrying, always looking a mess . . .

Being a married man means . . . being responsible, taking the initiative sexually, sorting the bills, mowing the grass, looking after house repairs, playing with the children, working long hours, helping to wash up dirty dishes. . .

Being a father means . . . setting a good example, being a disciplinarian, watching from the sidelines, cooking . . .

These sorts of gender expectations will affect the sexual relationship one way or another. A man or woman who instinctively feels that 'mothers are not sexual' may well find it more difficult to pick up a sexual relationship after childbirth. If a woman believes that 'married men should take the initiative sexually' then she may well be increasingly frustrated when her husband appears not to be interested in sex, but she can't make the first move.

Men and women really are different

Enormous distress, frustration and misunderstandings happen simply because people don't make allowances for the different ways men and women experience sexual encounters. Here are a clutch of generalisations that could helpfully be stuck on the wall of every marital bedroom:[10]

- for men passion leads to intimacy – having sex makes them feel close;

- for women, intimacy leads to passion – feeling close makes them want to have sex;

- men tend to be sexually aroused by what they see; women tend to be sexually aroused by how they are touched;

- a man's sexual arousal is hormone-driven, a woman's is thought-driven;[11]

- men don't have to work at being aroused, women often need to put in more effort;

- if a woman says no to sex with her husband, this does *not* mean that she has stopped loving him or that she finds him unattractive.

Normal couple experiences

Couples in long-term relationships fall into habits and patterns of relating that develop gradually without either person actually choosing them. Inevitably this happens with the sexual relationship too. Each partner goes along with whatever the other person has seemed to prefer, and patterns develop. These habits are not necessarily right or wrong in themselves, but partners can gradually become dissatisfied. If something opens their eyes to re-evaluate the habit or pattern, this 'crunch point' gives an opportunity either for growth and change or for the opposite, resentment and blame.

---

10. Of course these don't apply to everyone, but many couples will recognise their wisdom.
11. Basson, 2000, quoted in Edna Astbury-Ward. (2003). Menopause, sexuality and culture. *Sexual and Relationship Therapy Journal, 18(4)*, who writes: 'Female sexuality differs from mens' in three distinct areas: women are not driven, as men are, by their hormones; women's motivation (or willingness) to be sexual stems from a series of rewards or gains that are not strictly sexual; and "women's sexual arousal is a subjective mental excitement that may or may not be accompanied by awareness of vasocongestive changes in her genitalia."'

The questions and comments that follow describe the sort of habits a couple may have developed in their sexual relationship. Each question describes something with the potential to be difficult:

- How do we know we're going to make love? Who decides?
  'I'm going to have a shower', 'Let's have an early night', 'A hug when we get into bed'. These are examples of codes that couples use to show that they would like to make love.

- What, if anything, do we call sex? Do we use a euphemism? How did we decide? Do we both like what we call it?
  One partner might comfortably use a word like 'shag' and wrongly assume that the other is happy to do the same. Some couples invent their own 'coded' phrase and enjoy the shared privacy of this.

- What do we mean by 'sex'? Can we be physically affectionate without this leading to sexual intercourse?
  Some women say they avoid any kind of touch because they know this will be taken as a sign that they want to make love. So they – and the relationship – are starved of other kinds of touching, for affection, reassurance or comfort.

- When we make love, I don't really like what you're doing to me, and I don't know whether you like what I'm doing to you, but I can't say anything in case I hurt your feelings.
  If this habit of pretence has crept up over years, a couple might not be aware of it. The individual may not even know what he or she actually likes physically. Many people live so much 'in their heads' that they will have to concentrate hard on recognising physical sensations to begin to identify what they prefer.

- How do we know what's normal frequency for making love? Are we normal?
  It seems that there's no such thing as 'normal' when it comes to how often people make love. If it suits a couple to make love six times a week or once every two months, then for them that is 'normal'. Difficulties

arise when couples have different views on how often they want to make love – a mature relationship will manage some give and take on this point.

A young man shared his anxiety that there was something seriously wrong with him because he had lost his appetite for sex, although he and his wife were very much in love. When questioned about what was actually happening he said that they were now making love only 5 times a week instead of once or twice every day. His wife was so distressed that she was doubting her attractiveness and his love. Once he reassured her that it was exhaustion not lack of love that was affecting him, they were able to adapt their love-making habits to suit their current life demands.

- How long do we typically spend making love?
  If the answer to this question is 5–10 minutes, the wife is probably not getting much enjoyment! Women usually need longer to get in touch with their sexual sensations and feelings. They are not usually aroused by their partner rushing to touch the obviously erotic areas of breasts or genitals. There are plenty of good books that give helpful advice about this, describing normal patterns of sexual response.[12]

- Are we typically male and female – the man thinking about sex often and being instantly aroused; the woman rarely thinking about sex and needing time to become interested? If so, do we make allowances for this?
  Although these are stereotypes, many couples will recognise themselves. When partners remember that these are typical responses they are more likely to adapt rather than blame each other for them.

- I don't always have an orgasm, but I enjoy what we do.
  There are no rules about this – if you are not left frustrated and tense then this is working for you.

---

12. For example the Relate guides, published by Vermilion. Also *One flesh – A practical guide to honeymoon sex and beyond,* by Amelia and Greg Clarke published by Matthias Media (2001), distributed in the UK by The Good Book company. This short book from Australia takes a clear evangelical perspective with a down-to-earth approach.

- We always do the same thing when we make love. Are we boring? *Magazines suggest techniques and positions as if variety and lots of good techniques are essential for improving love life. However, the sexual relationship is a good arena for adults to retain their ability just to relax and to play. Allowing more time and using imagination and humour could prove just as successful as reading up on techniques. If a couple is happy with the same routine, for them it is not a difficulty.*

Changing life stages

A sexual relationship is affected by age and life stage. By definition, the early months or years of a relationship are likely to be made up of shared hopes and experiences. But as the relationship continues, there is much scope for incompatibility. Each partner will be moving through the life stages separately. The five-year age gap that meant nothing when they fell in love in their twenties will take on a new significance when one hits 40 and faces midlife challenges while the other is still firmly feeling a youthful 30-something. Sexually, women reach their peak later than men. Facing the reality of menopause and no more fertility takes a woman into experiences that her husband may not understand. Losing desire and erectile function with advancing years can impact deeply on a man's sense of identity and value, in ways his wife finds hard to take seriously.

Marriages themselves go through transitions – in our society, people who marry are more likely to have lived together for a while and be sexually used to each other by the time the wedding takes place. Many people have considerable experience of sex without love before committing to a marriage relationship, and can be taken aback by the different emotions involved when love is present – the vulnerability of total self giving to the other. Sometimes however the very act of marriage can kill sexual desire (making love with a wife feels very different from making love to a girlfriend).[13] Childbirth

13. As may have been the case for the man quoted on p. 129.

and the invasion of marital space by family have an impact on the opportunities for sexual encounter, physically, emotionally and mentally. Living with teenagers who are entering their own sexual experience and discovering their own sexual identity can disturb the parents' views of themselves. Rediscovering the marriage relationship when family have left home, or feeling impatient because adult family have not left home, impacts on sexual relating. The ageing process too can surprise and unbalance, causing sexual difficulties.

The rest of this section explores the kind of sexual difficulties that these normal life stages can bring.

Early years

Jan and Dave came to see a counsellor because they were so unhappy with their sexual relationship. Jan said that she was obviously a failure and she didn't believe Dave when he said he found her attractive. The evidence for this was that he was slow in getting an erection when they made love, however provocative she was. It emerged that her previous relationship had been tempestuous, with extremes of behaviour that in the end had made her decide to leave. She enjoyed the calmer atmosphere of her marriage to Dave. However, sex in her previous relationship had always been exciting and highly charged, with both partners easily aroused. So she and Dave, in a much calmer relationship, had to learn new ways of making love, which for Jan involved unlearning previous habits.

Previous long-term relationships do not get left behind with the start of a new one – former partners are often around, more or less visibly, whether they're alive or dead. Their presence can be felt even in the bedroom, setting expectations and comparisons. This can continue for years if neither partner realises and challenges what's happening. Also, high expectations can be pressurising, as Dave found. And a secure marriage can be a less exciting environment for sex, as Jan found.

Children – or not

If a decision to have children is not followed soon by conception then the impact on the sexual relationship is likely to be strong, as the anxiety about conceiving outweighs the pleasure of lovemaking. And for couples who remain childless but not by choice, the inevitable link between sex and disappointment can cast a shadow into the long term. Of course also the opposite anxiety about conceiving can spoil sexual relationships that have previously been satisfying.

Pregnancy

Pregnancy brings many challenges, differing between couples, women and the individual pregnancies. Many women are as sexually interested during pregnancy as at other times; many men find women as attractive during pregnancy as at other times, although this can dip at the beginning and towards the end of pregnancy. And although many people feel anxious about the possibility of harming the foetus through sexual intercourse, there is no evidence to suggest that this is the case. Psychosexual therapists find that a lot of women who describe having lost desire for sex say that this started during or after a pregnancy, but researchers have struggled to identify precisely how pregnancy affects sexual desire and performance. Again, this probably reflects the individual complexities of every sexual relationship. If everything is compared to a mythical 'normal' way of functioning, most couples would be defined as 'abnormal'. In a first pregnancy particularly, this is the last idea a couple needs when they are likely already to be feeling some anxiety.

Difficulties are likely to be the result of physical changes – sickness, discomfort, exhaustion, hormonal effects, size; or emotional responses – fear, anxiety, short-temperedness; or skewed thinking – dislike of the changing body shape, resistance to stereotyping; or context – social pressures or expectations, financial changes, lifestyle changes.

Psychologically, with the first pregnancy, this is the start of introducing a third person to the family, so both partners have to be able to adjust to this. Without the benefit of hormonal change, the man has to make a big adjustment to no longer having the first claim on his wife, both physically and emotionally. He will have to put to one side or postpone his own desires and needs for the good of the child.

When the baby is born, the father has to put his own sexual needs on hold for a while. This will allow the mother to bond and be absorbed with the baby as well as recovering from the physical impact of the birth. If he cannot do this, the marriage will suffer in one way or another: a man can make unreasonable demands, becoming angry and unsupportive, which will build resentment or guilt in the relationship; he can seek sex elsewhere, betraying trust that can take a long time to rebuild. The mother's physical recovery can take some time; hormonally she will feel different for some months if she is breastfeeding and renewed sexual desire can take longer again. Sooner or later, though, it is important that they both make time to re-establish the sexual connection, to nurture their own bond that is separate from the bond with the new child.

Laura, now in her forties, was looking back to those early months after childbirth. 'I really couldn't even think about sex after our second baby was born, I was so exhausted and I'd put on so much weight anyway that I couldn't bear to look at myself in the mirror. My husband was very understanding. Then one day when by some miracle both the children were asleep in the afternoon he just insisted that we took the chance and made love. I was very reluctant and didn't feel at all sexy, but I went along with it. I just remember us both getting the giggles because my breast milk suddenly spurted out in the middle of it. It wasn't the greatest lovemaking ever, but it certainly got us back in touch with each other. It sort of ring-fenced our marriage again.'

Family life

Exhaustion and preoccupation with small children and their needs can impact the sexual relationship. Also the subconscious arena (the hidden compartment again) can be powerful: Am I a mother or a lover? How can I move from one to the other? Can I make love to a mother? I have to share my lover with the baby, who has first claim on the breasts that were mine!

Older children take up time and space that might have been private for the couple. 'The children don't go to bed early any more – we've lost our evenings.' Making love at the end of an already long day means exhaustion, anxiety about interruptions, and need for speed, which can lead to mounting exasperation and dissatisfaction. Equally if both partners enjoy the demands of family life, they can develop a mutual understanding to abandon their own sexual relationship for a while and then find it difficult to pick up later.

Fear of conceiving more children can become a strong subconscious inhibitor to sexual response, so discussion and research about contraception is important.

Work

Work can inspire or inhibit the sexual relationship. Bringing together the two worlds of home and work can be mutually enriching, whether one or both partners are working outside the home. Or each can pick up the unspoken cultures of the work world[14] and reinterpret their own sexual desires and needs in that way. Sexual desire can come to be associated with the spark of the working environment, with stimulating colleagues or meals out, with the intimacy of team-working or shared jokes. Then the reality of home can disappoint: here both partners show their worst as well as their best; talk, tensions and stresses become focused in little events and

---

14. see section on systems and culture in chapter 13 on Sexuality in ministerial relationships.

details (the dentist appointment or leaving the toilet seat up). Sexual desire and arousal can simply close down.

> Barry, a police officer and treasurer for his church, described how he became involved with a work colleague: 'We work in a team, and we're very close – we have to be because we rely on each other in dangerous situations. And we work long shifts and strange hours, so I could go for days hardly seeing the family and not getting to church very often. My wife was always complaining about it, but what can you do – it's a good job and I love it. I'd always got on well with Sue, who's in my team, but I didn't realise how close we were until we all went for a drink after a long shift. She gave me a kiss as we left – not particularly passionate, but I kissed her back, and that's how it all started.'

Midlife

In spite of much talk about the 'SKI' generation (the 55-plus-year-olds who are enjoying life 'Spending the Kids' Inheritance'), negative images of midlife and old age abound in our culture, particularly of women. Interestingly, although the physical and psychological signs of the menopause make it a significant and often difficult life stage for women in the Western world, it is barely marked in other cultures, where ageing is respected and older women valued.

In the Churches too, there is a mixed reaction to midlife. Highly anxious about ageing and declining congregations, the Churches are at the same time highly dependent on them. For increasing numbers of people, midlife is a time of much responsibility and many roles – servicing the needs of three generations of the family, elderly parents, young adult children and grandchildren, at the same time as being at the peak of responsibility at work. Also important are the physical and psychological changes associated with ageing, which many people start to notice 'for real' around the age 55 mark.

So it is not difficult to see that these factors are likely to affect sexual relationships in marriage. Physically, patterns of sexual desire and response are likely to change in men and women, often becoming slower and less frequent, and the menopause for women can affect sexual activity. Certainly the fall in the oestrogen level during the menopause has an effect, as it leads to decreased lubrication so that intercourse can be more difficult. Psychologically, this is the time when unresolved earlier issues can come home to roost as couples are left facing each other with no 'buffer' of children around. Jung[15] described the need in the second half of life to make a 'journey inward' – in other words, to get to know oneself again, and face up to the inner world. This applies to couples too. Jokes about men in midlife crisis who buy the sports car they've dreamed of and have an affair with someone the same age as their daughter are not funny when they happen for real. Christian couples are not immune from this.

One writer concludes that if women are unhappy with their sexual relationships in midlife, it is likely to be 'a multicausal and multidimensional problem combining biological, psychological and interpersonal determinants'.[16] It would be reasonable to assume that the same will be true for men.

It is a challenge to hold on to identity and value, one's own and each other's, while meeting obligations and making time for tending the sexual relationship. On the other hand, with the possibility of more undisturbed time together, there is great potential for renewed sexual interest and deeper and more fulfilling sexual relating. Many couples rediscover their sexual relationship, and happily move on to the next stage of their marriage.

Older age [17]

Amongst the many myths about sex in old age is the well-established one that sexuality is one of the first faculties to diminish. In fact it

---

15. Carl Gustav Jung (1875 – 1961) Psychiatrist and psychologist. See http://en.wikipedia.org/wiki/Carl_Jung
16. see '*Menopause, sexuality and culture*' article.
17. see chapter 9 on Sexuality and ageing.

seems that it is one of the last. The joke about the 80-year-old man's birthday suggestion to his wife that they 'go upstairs and make mad passionate love' that is met with the rejoinder that she could 'manage one or the other but not both', nicely sets the record straight on sexual desire in older people. Research has shown that continuing with regular sexual relations is a determining factor in being able to maintain sexual activity in later life.[18]

With increasing numbers of us living longer, most couples will share many years of marriage post 65 years old. Marriage is the context for retirement for most people, and a potential source of immense satisfaction, physically and psychologically. However, as in midlife, marriage issues that have been ignored for years are likely to re-appear now, if they haven't already with the children's departure – and the sexual relationship can be among them.

The ageing process affects the intensity, frequency and quality of sexual experience, which is likely to be less intense but no less satisfying. Of course, age-related physical conditions, illnesses or medication will have an impact on how either partner feels and some of these will affect sexual functioning. For women, physiological changes associated with the menopause can have an effect on sexual functioning. Similar to men, women's orgasms can take longer to reach, but can still be satisfying and multiple. It is natural for desire to slow down, along with other faculties, but there is no reason for it to disappear.

Difficulties of sexual relationships in older couples are therefore likely to be caused by lack of knowledge about how normal sexual response changes in older age, and about how to adapt lovemaking activity to take account of this. Unrealistic expectations will play a part too, either that sex should remain the same as earlier in life, or that it should not happen at all. The persistent negative attitudes of

18. see Trudel, G., Turgeon, L., Piché, L. (2000). Marital and sexual aspects of old age. *Sexual and relationship therapy, 15(4),* 381 – 406.

our society can be internalised so that everyone comes to think that sex and old age shouldn't go together. This may change as younger people are more realistically educated about sexual responses, so that future generations of elderly marrieds will be more able to enjoy sexual activity. Not surprisingly, couples who are reasonably happy with themselves and their life together are more likely to enjoy some sort of sexual activity whatever their age or state of health.

Concerns about particular sexual dysfunctions and behaviours

Sexual dysfunctions

There are some defined and recognised dysfunctions that can seriously spoil long-term relationships if they are not recognised and dealt with. Couple counsellors regularly come across these – difficulties with erection and ejaculation, lack of desire, inability to come to orgasm, difficulties in becoming aroused. Referral to specialised sexual therapists is appropriate for these couples. Such specialists make a thorough question-and-answer assessment with each person separately and together and then design a structured sexual programme for the couple to follow privately. These impairments can originate in a variety of causes, physical or psychological, and sometimes discovering the cause can help to shift the problem. It is important to investigate the cause. It is senseless to worry that a man's lack of erection stems from a psychological anxiety about failure, when a visit to the GP would confirm that it is a normal side effect of the medication he is taking. Being supportive of one's partner and following the sex therapy programme together is often enough to be able to move on. Because men and women have such different sexual responses, it can be the case that simply learning to slow down and appreciate sensual touch enables sexual responses to follow once some relearning has taken place.

Other sexually related behaviours

Obsessions, addictions, pornography, affairs, erotic fantasy, fetishism, cross-dressing, jealousy: married Christians can experience any of these. They are deliberately grouped in the same list, because any one of them *can* seriously destabilise a marriage relationship, though not all of them *will* do so. Accessing pornography via the Internet is an ever-growing business, skilfully designed to draw casual site visitors further in.[19] Christian men (this is mostly aimed at men) who become drawn in, perhaps to addictive extent, are likely to respond with denial or guilt or both. The impact on the wife can be devastating as she cannot compete with the other women with whom a sexual 'encounter' can be perfect every time in the fantasy world. Jealousy and obsessions can become dangerous, and it is wise to seek help. On the other hand, marriages can absorb cross-dressing, fetishism and erotic fantasy. An affair is nearly always a shock to a marriage once it is revealed. For those couples who do not split up, the affair can precipitate a creative re-evaluation of the marriage, which can lead to a deeper and more fulfilling relationship.

What can help?

Useful advice for the couple themselves

- Become more self-centred. Ironically, this will improve a sexual relationship. This is not to suggest ignoring what the other needs. But if each person can learn to observe and take notice of their *own* physical sensations, they will become more attuned to what gives them pleasure. They are then more likely to sense what gives their partner pleasure. The combination leads to a better sexual relationship for the couple.

- Get informed. With plenty of books and websites available, finding information about normal sexual responses and common difficulties

---

19. see chapter 11, Sex and the Internet.

is straightforward. It is better to check out anxieties with a doctor or couple counsellor than worry alone.

• Make some changes. Experimenting by adapting sexual thoughts, expectations or behaviours can make a big difference. It doesn't even need both partners in a couple to do this: if one does something different, the other will be affected.

• Think about what sex means in the relationship. This may be different for each partner. Does it express intimacy and tenderness, a way of expressing love or relaxation and fun? Is it a useful way to de-stress or an obligation? Has it come to mean a reward for good behaviour or a way of making up after a fight? Is it demanded as a right? Perhaps it's simply a Friday-night habit. Most couples recognise a variety of meanings. If sex has only a single function, or partners have very different views, an honest discussion is called for.

When things change because of illness, ageing, disability or absence

• Use the imagination or fantasy. The imagination has a wonderful power to transport and transform. As we know when our heart thumps from watching a scary film, we respond physically to a fantasy scenario. Imagining romance without arthritis on a sunny holiday can be arousing and transform the experience of making love at home in a chilly bedroom.

• Be realistic. Some people are able to 'shut down' sexually until their partner is available again; others masturbate. Change positions, place or timing; buy lubricating jelly; allow more time and slow down; concentrate on caressing; give pleasure to each other or masturbate[20] rather than have intercourse. [21]

• Beware of always acting like the parent in the couple. This can happen when one partner is disabled or ill and the other takes on

---

20. see chapter 3, Masturbation: A sensitive pastoral issue.
21. see Thoburn, M., & Powling, S. (2000). *The Relate guide to loving in later life.* London: Vermilion, in particular ch. 13.

a full-time caring role. Quite apart from the practical challenges, making love can be difficult because the marriage feels more like a parent-child relationship than a mutual one.

- Remember it can be difficult to distinguish between a 'dysfunction' and a normal response to ageing or illness. If in doubt, check with a doctor.

Advice for ministers or friends

- Don't be afraid of the subject of sexual difficulties. Ministers do not have to be experts, nor have a wonderful sexual relationship themselves, in order to be helpful. It is sensible to be informed about basic facts and myths about sex. The five levels[22] can be useful background to help you sense where to locate the problem. Briefly stated, the five levels are:

  1. Sexual identity. This is almost always consistent with our genitals, but there are men who feel they are a woman trapped in a man's body and vice versa.
  2. Sexual orientation. Who do we fall in love with, and who is the focus of our erotic attraction; men, women or both?
  3. Sexual interest. This relates to the type of persons, parts of the body and situations that are the focus of sexual fantasy and arousal.
  4. Sex role. This relates to the public expression of sexuality, i.e., how we indicate that we are a man or a woman. This can vary from culture to culture.
  5. Sexual performance. Problems in this area are known as 'dysfunctions' and relate to desire, arousal and orgasm. People with difficulties in this area can be helped by psychiatrists, psychologists and those who specialise in sexual problems.

- Just listen. Like all powerful pastoral encounters, the most important experience is usually that of being listened to very attentively.

22. see Seligman, M. E. P., & Rosenhan, D. L. (1998). *Abnormality.* New York: Norton & Company, pp. 416 – 449, also chapter 12: Contemporary issues in gender and sexual identity.

- Don't minimise: if this couple think it's a problem – it is a problem.

- Do mention the subject. Sex is a private area of a couple's life, and other people must not be voyeuristic about it in the name of 'being helpful'. However, introducing a question about 'the physical aspects' of the relationship in a calm and low-key way can give a couple welcome permission to speak.

- 'It takes two to tango.' As with any marriage difficulty, remember that one partner might describe the situation very differently from the other. And both are right.

- Sex always has a context. Sexual 'problems' often reflect other patterns or issues in a relationship.

- Be open to reflecting on your own experience in light of previous sections, but also remember that your own or other people's experience won't necessarily be relevant to this couple.

- Always encourage people to seek information and advice from doctors and/or couple counsellors. There is plenty of help available.

Conclusion

Couple counsellors see many people who are distressed and damaged by their experience of sexual relationships in marriage. Sadly, the Churches have often contributed to problems by loading Christian couples with unrealistic expectations and skewed views of sexual responses and behaviours, and then discouraging open discussion of difficulties. This chapter has illustrated the complexity of sexual relationships in marriage, affected as they are by society and the Church, life experience and practicalities, conscious and subconscious factors. So it's good to conclude by remembering that countless couples testify to the joy of their sexual life as part of the love they share. Over many decades of marriage, they ride the difficulties and challenges to enjoy sex as part of a lively, committed, deep and increasingly satisfying relationship.

SEVEN

Homosexuality

Ashley Wilson

Scope of chapter and definitions

Over the last few years, the issue of homosexuality has, for the Churches, become highly controversial. The issues have been frequently debated and the interpretation of relevant passages of scripture has been endlessly argued. Some official statements have been vitriolic and condemnatory; others have been positive and conciliatory. Different groups have reached several different conclusions and advocates for and against have taken up entrenched positions. For some, a particular understanding of homosexuality has become a test of Christian orthodoxy. At present, the Anglican Communion is facing the prospect of schism (or, at least, some form of secession). For some Christians (e.g., members of the Lesbian & Gay Christian Movement) and some Churches (e.g., the Episcopal Church of the USA or the Canadian Episcopal Church) there is no problem in accepting gay men and lesbians as full members of the worshipping community. For others (e.g., the Archbishop of Nigeria, Peter Akinola) the issue is so serious that it is worth splitting the Anglican Communion.

The furore has, I think, been prompted by the increasing acceptance of gay and lesbian relationships in secular society that has resulted in demands for similar acceptance within the Church. Gay and lesbian Christians want the Churches to face up to the issues and to take their experiences seriously. However, the debate has unfortunately become rather abstract and theoretical. Sometimes it seems as though the 'real people' whose experiences the Church is seeking to understand have been forgotten and their voices suppressed by abstract arguments. On many occasions theology and ethics have simply displaced pastoral care and compassion. Many gay and lesbian Christians have felt unwelcome and have left the mainstream Churches in favour of Churches such as the Metropolitan Community Church or, in many cases, have simply been put off church altogether. This cannot be right. Of course, the Church shouldn't blindly follow the prevailing culture; but neither should it be countercultural simply for the sake of it.

My own experience of preaching and teaching on homosexuality is that many people are personally affected – they may have sons, daughters, brothers, sisters, or even parents who are gay or lesbian – and are relieved to hear it discussed in church. In the Western Churches at least (and I suspect in other parts of the world) there are already many gay and lesbian Christians in churches as members of congregations and in positions of leadership – some of them are 'out' (i.e., their sexual orientation is a matter of public knowledge), while others feel under immense pressure to keep their sexuality hidden. The Church needs to be willing to listen to all those gay and lesbian members who are prepared to speak about their experiences.

Considerations of sexuality require careful listening and honest thinking; above all, they require recognition that all human beings are children of God and loved by God, that all are sinners, and that we are all in this mess together. Churches do not like talking about sex (hence the need for this book). But there cannot be any excuse for failing to care for our fellow Christians and fellow human beings. Whatever our views may be on the theology or the ethics of homosexuality we simply must obey the command to love our neighbours.

This chapter is based, in part, on interviews with lesbian and gay Christians and their partners. It examines ways in which the Churches can respond pastorally to the needs of homosexual Christians, and engage with those outside the Church. It is, of course, an impossible task to write this in a way that will satisfy every reader. The varied denominational policies; the range of personal convictions; the differing interpretations of scripture; and the huge range of contexts in which churches are facing up to these issues mean that almost everyone will be able to take offence at something I have written . . . ![1]

Priests, ministers, pastors and congregations need to be well-informed; churches should get into the habit of talking about sex and listening to people's experiences. It is important that we as individuals take time to reflect on our own sexuality and our own prejudices in this area. I apologise in advance for my own prejudices and bias – but so that you might more easily recognise them: I am a white, Anglo-Saxon Protestant; I am ordained as a priest in the Church of England; I am a liberal (at least on this issue) Catholic; and I am a married heterosexual man. I have tried to be even-handed but will more than likely have failed. Hopefully, though, this chapter will nonetheless contain useful information, insights, suggestions and resources. Readers will need to reflect on these in the light of their own personal convictions and their own denomination's pronouncements. They will need to reflect further in relation to specific congregational situations. Above all they will need to remember that we are not debating an abstract issue, rather we are engaging in dialogue with our brothers and sisters.

Perhaps the most important question we need to address is one raised by Archbishop Rowan Williams.[2] He suggests that Christian ethics should always be good news and asks how that can be so for a gay Christian who wishes to live in obedience to Christ, who does not see him/herself as rejecting something in his/her being, who lives a moral struggle like the rest of us, and who believes it is hard to hear good news from a church that insists that her/his essential identity is spiritually compromised. It seems to me that we have a responsibility before God to do our best to answer this question.

---

1. It must be acknowledged that our theology and ethics will influence our understanding of the goals of our pastoral care – whether we are seeking to support people in loving relationships, or to encourage celibacy, or to 'convert' homosexuals will clearly alter our listening.
2. Williams, R. (2003). Knowing Myself in Christ. In T. Bradshaw (Ed.), *The way forward?: Christian voices on homosexuality and the Church* (2nd ed., pp. 12-19). London: SCM.

We must now turn to some matters of definition. Sexuality and sexual orientation are considered in chapter 12. 'Homosexuality' is not a singular concept and the term does not always refer to the same thing. As Oliver O'Donovan observes:

> If there is anything more disconcerting than the hesitation and uncertainty with which theologians propose their answers on this subject, it is the dogmatic certainty with which they frame their questions.[3]

One simply cannot take one's own assumptions about sexuality and homosexuality into cultural or sub-cultural settings other than one's own and assume they apply in the same way. Philip Groves offers a list of 20 different 'homosexualities', among which are the following examples:[4]

- A homosexuality that has no or little relationship to sexual desire. For whatever reason, a cultural group has decided that certain formalised homosexual experiences are needed for personal growth and maturity or for full inclusion in the cultural group. The homosexual practices promote what is perceived as the common good. People may derive incidental sexual pleasure from the experience, but that is secondary and unimportant.

- A homosexuality in a culture in which the number of sexes and/or genders is expanded beyond two (male and female) to a third gender and/or sex. Members of the third group may be thought to have special spiritual powers or perform special services for the culture as a whole.

- A homosexuality that is transient, apparently a normal part of adolescent human development, and eventually relinquished in favour of heterosexuality.[5]

---

3. O'Donovan, O. (2002). Homosexuality in the Church: Can there be a fruitful theological debate? In E. F. Rogers Jr. (Ed.), *Theology and sexuality: cassic and contemporary readings* (pp. 373-386). Oxford: Blackwell, at 377.
4. Groves, P. (Ed.). (2008). *The Anglican communion and homosexuality: A resource to enable listening and dialogue.* London: SPCK, 210.
5. Editor's note: This is the classical Freudian position. JMG.

- A situational homosexuality rooted in a large number of people of the same sex living together and sequestered from contact with the opposite sex (prisons, boarding schools, theological colleges, religious communities, plantations, mines). Contact with those of the opposite gender is impossible, so homosexual relationships are all that are available.

- A homosexuality arising from both deep mutual friendship and deep-seated same-sex sexual desire, that seeks to combine permanent friendship and exclusive sexual intimacy, perhaps aspiring to the model similar to heterosexual marriage – a permanent, faithful and stable partnership.

- A sublimated homosexuality that recognises the same-sex attraction but channels it into one or more non-sexual friendships and maintains sexual abstinence within those relationships.[6]

- A homosexuality of transient episodes of same-sex intercourse with close male friends, engaged in by persons who do not regard themselves as 'homosexual', either because their sexual fantasies are heterosexual or because they also have a heterosexual marriage. There are several American slang expressions for this: 'MSM' = 'Men who have sex with men', and 'getting down'.

Of course, no Christian, however liberal, thinks that all homosexualities can be incorporated into the Christian way – there is no support in the Church for behaviours which are seen as unworthy of human beings and the kind of lives they are called to live, nor for behaviours which are demeaning, exploitative or damaging to others, such as rape, prostitution or paedophilia. Such activities would be rightly condemned, whether heterosexual or homosexual.

What are the problems for Christians concerning homosexuality?

The Churches need to remember that many of the pastoral problems faced by their gay and lesbian members are the direct result of the

6. Editor's note: This is another classic Freudian formulation. JMG.

161

Churches' attitudes and pronouncements on the issue. It's hard enough for heterosexual Christians to ask for pastoral support in relation to sexual concerns; the added fear of rejection or condemnation can make it almost impossible for lesbian and gay Christians. So, any problems may remain hidden, and unaddressed, for long periods. There can also be a good deal of resentment if gay men and lesbians are seen as being in need of pastoral care simply because of their sexuality – they may see it as a rejection of their full humanity when they become, by definition and not by need, the objects of 'sensitive pastoral care'. Homosexual Christians and homosexual non-Christians (just like heterosexual people) are deserving of pastoral care not because they are homosexual *per se* but because they are fellow children of God struggling to live a good life in a difficult world with the same pastoral needs as anybody else.

Homophobia

Homophobia is a fear of, or aversion to, homosexuality often resulting in serious discrimination or hostility. In my opinion overt acts of homophobia simply should not be tolerated within any congregation. Even if one sees homosexuality as a 'sin' one should still 'love the sinner'. Hatred and hostility have no place in the Kingdom of God.

Rejection

One gay Christian friend observed that because the Church did not make him feel welcome, and was unable to bless his civil partnership, he did not imagine that the Church would be able to support him if, for example, his partner should die. In Anglican parish life even non-churchgoers expect the Church 'to be there for them' and to provide pastoral support at significant moments such as baptisms, weddings, and funerals. Lesbian and gay Christians often feel they are denied even that.

Bullying

Whilst society generally is increasingly accepting of gay and lesbian relationships many individuals still face bullying at school or work – especially young gay men. Such stressful situations can produce the usual consequences of anxiety, fatigue, poor performance, poor self-image, depression and even suicide. There is an obvious need for pastoral care and support in these situations.

Coming out

The whole process of telling other people about one's sexuality – choosing whom to tell and when – is much more difficult if one is expecting a negative reaction from family, friends, community or the Church. Many gays and lesbians speak of periods of self-loathing and guilt before finally 'coming out to themselves' and accepting their sexuality.

Celibacy

Some Christians who are aware of their homosexuality will choose to live celibate lives. Also, some who have chosen celibate lives at a relatively young age, such as Roman Catholic priests and members of religious orders, may subsequently recognise that their sexuality is homosexually oriented. Such a realisation can produce a good deal of stress and tension. Because some Churches insist that all homosexual Christians *must* be celibate, there can be a correct perception of being coerced rather than helped to make choices informed by personal integrity.

Lack of recognition of relationships

Even long-term, stable, faithful committed homosexual relationships are generally not recognised liturgically by the Churches (there are exceptions where individual churches or dioceses have developed rites for the blessing of same-sex couples (perhaps after civil partnerships)).

For many lesbian and gay couples this can leave them feeling excluded or 'second-class'.

Denial and pseudo-heterosexuality

Many lesbian and gay Christians will marry people of the opposite sex and often even raise families. Sometimes this is about conforming to expectations of respectability but it can also be on the direct advice of priests or pastors. For example, 'Robert' was reasonably confident by age 16 or 17 that he was gay. His Roman Catholic priest urged him to marry in order to 'straighten himself out'. After twenty-five years of marriage, and raising two children, he finally came out as gay with predictably traumatic consequences for his wife and children. One is driven to ask which is the greater sin: Robert's overt homosexuality, or the priest's covert exploitation of the unsuspecting young woman who became Robert's wife.

Homosexual affairs

It is not uncommon for married men (and to a lesser extent married women) to indulge in transient affairs with same-sex partners. Sometimes this may reflect a degree of bisexuality or a desire to 'experiment', but it may also reflect the gradual acceptance of an emerging orientation. Such affairs were certainly part of Robert's experience before finally coming out to his wife. The psychological consequences are the same as with any form of unfaithfulness – anger, pain, confusion, lack of integrity, breach of trust, loss of confidence, and so on – but the extra dimension of homosexuality can dramatically increase the intensity of feelings for a straight spouse (or partner) of a gay or lesbian adulterer. The spouse may also endure psychological trauma, puzzling over serious questions about sexual identity and the nature of the marriage (was it all a sham?).

'Fiona' spoke of the intense guilt, shame, fear and pain that she felt when her husband came out as gay after nearly ten years of marriage. She felt completely unable to discuss the situation or her feelings

book *Sexual Issues - understanding and advising in a Christian context*, which I would be grateful if you could consider for review. It is priced at £34.99 and is available from most Christian bookshops and online at www.kevinmayhew.com

If you have any questions, please don't hesitate to contact me. Many thanks in advance for your consideration.

Yours sincerely,

Abbie Goldberg

Marketing Manager

www.kevinmayhew.com

www.kevinmayhew.com

kevin mayhew publishers

Buxhall • Stowmarket • Suffolk • IP14 3BW

Tel: 01449 737978 • Fax: 01449 737834 • E-mail: info@kevinmayhewltd.com

Kevin Gillespie SJ PhD
Pastoral Counseling Department
Loyola University in Maryland
Suite 380
8890 McGaw Road
Columbia
MD 21045 USA

3rd February 2010

Dear Mr. Gillespie,

with any members of her church (even her vicar) because it was 'too much of a hot potato'. Fiona became very angry that her husband received plenty of emotional and practical support from the gay community but that she had to face the situation completely on her own.[7] Amity Buxton observes, 'The coming out thrusts the spouse into the closet as well.'[8]

Conversion ministries

Some Churches offer 'treatment' to gays and lesbians to make them 'straight'. Despite a few claimed successes there is little empirical research evidence to suggest that such treatment is effective. The effectiveness may depend upon the type of homosexuality and strength of same-sex attraction in individual cases but treatments generally seem only to produce temporary changes in behaviour, leaving orientation unchanged. For some the whole process is highly traumatic and can itself create serious psychological problems.

Children in homosexual households

Many homosexual couples wish to raise families. They may have custody of children from former relationships; they may wish to foster or adopt; or they may (in the case of lesbian couples) wish to have children using donor sperm. Whatever the Churches' views on such reproductive strategies, we need to recognise the stresses and tensions associated with the desire for children and the pressures that such couples can experience.

Homosexuals in Christian ministry

Some homosexual Christians have a strong sense of vocation to ordination or other forms of licensed ministry. They can experience

7. see also the stories in: Buxton, A. P. (1994). *The other side of the closet: The coming-out crisis for straight spouses and families.* New York: John Wiley & Sons.
8. Buxton, *The other side of the closet*, xiv.

a good deal of confusion, anger, frustration and resentment when such vocations are denied or blocked not on the basis of their faith or their abilities but simply on the basis of their sexuality. Alternatively such people may be allowed to follow their vocation but are then encouraged to deny their sexuality and to keep secret any same-sex relationship.

'John' is a trained Reader in the Church of England. On moving to a new diocese he requested to be licensed but was refused because of his homosexual relationship despite the fact that the parish was without a priest and desperately in need of pastoral care and teaching. Another man, 'James', left parochial ministry because the challenge to his integrity of keeping hidden his relationship with his partner (as he was required to do by his bishop) became too great. James described his experience as a gay priest in the Church of England as invisible, hidden and unacknowledged. Several Christian traditions ordain gay men and even lesbians while officially denying that they do so.

Causes of the problems

We must be careful here: are we talking of the problems experienced by lesbian and gay Christians, or of the 'problem' of homosexuality itself? In fact, it will be worth making some pertinent comments on the causes of homosexuality but whether or not one sees homosexuality as a problem in itself will depend on the conclusions one has reached in the theological and ethical debates. Among the questions the Church needs to address are:

- What is homosexuality?
- What does it mean (and how does it feel) to be gay or lesbian?
- What does it mean to be gay or lesbian *and* Christian?

Biological bases of homosexuality

After reviewing the scientific evidence for a biological cause of homosexuality it seems likely that sexual *orientation* has a biological (probably genetic) basis, but that the superimposition of personality variables results in a range of sexual *behaviour* which is also affected by cultural, environmental and sociological factors. In other words, human sexuality is a lot like human handedness (known as a stable *bimodalism*) – most people are right-handed, some are left-handed, and a minority exhibit varying degrees of ambidexterity. Left-handed people can be trained to use their right hand but most often revert. Ambidextrous people can be influenced to use either hand. The Church for centuries condemned people for being left-handed. Handedness is a genetic trait that can be substantially modified by environment and upbringing.[9]

Homosexuality is sometimes condemned as being 'unnatural'. The term 'natural' has to be used with care – much that is natural is considered immoral and much that is thought unnatural is considered moral (nakedness may be natural but is in many cases immoral; monogamy may be unnatural but is usually considered moral). The American Psychological Association released a Statement on Homosexuality in 1994. It is worth quoting the first two paragraphs in full:

> The research on homosexuality is very clear. Homosexuality is neither mental illness nor moral depravity. It is simply the way a minority of our population expresses human love and sexuality. Study after study documents the mental health of gay men and lesbians. Studies of judgement, stability, reliability, and social and vocational adaptiveness all show that gay men and lesbians function every bit as well as heterosexuals.[10]

Nor is homosexuality a matter of individual choice. Research suggests that the homosexual orientation is in place very early in the life cycle, possibly even before birth. It is found in about ten per cent of the population, a figure which is surprisingly constant across cultures, irrespective of the different moral values

9. see: http://www.religioustolerance.org/hom_caus.htm
10. http://www.apa.org/pi/sexual.html

and standards of a particular culture. Contrary to what some imply, the incidence of homosexuality in a population does not appear to change with new moral codes or social mores. Research findings suggest that efforts to repair homosexuals are nothing more than social prejudice garbed in psychological accoutrements.

Sources of difficulties for homosexual Christians

Ignorance of fellow believers

Many of the problems for homosexual Christians are caused by ignorance, or lack of clarity in the debate. As we have already seen, the topic of 'homosexuality' is complex and varied; we must beware of simplistic assumptions and stereotypes. There is an enormous variety of gay men – from 'Screaming queens' to 'Village People' to pillars of the community (and the Church). Lesbians are not all 'butch and hairy'. This should really come as no surprise given the huge variety of heterosexual personalities that we accept without question.

The danger, of course, in all this is that we tend to assume that our stereotypes actually represent the totality of possibilities. In fact, not all gay men are promiscuous – some are, but then so are a great many heterosexual people. Not all gay men are active on the 'Gay Scene' – and there are heterosexual equivalents in the culture of clubbing and one-night stands. Not all gay men are transvestites – in fact, relatively few are, as are similar numbers of heterosexual men. Not all gay and lesbian relationships are sexually active – just as with heterosexual relationships. Not all gay relationships involve anal intercourse though some do; this is also true of heterosexual relationships. Not all homosexual men are paedophiles – in fact very few are; paedophiles are in fact more likely to be heterosexual in their adult attraction.

The debate about homosexuality cannot be framed in terms of sexual *acts* (there are no straightforward criteria by which all homosexual relationships can reliably be distinguished from all heterosexual relationships). The debate must then turn to the quality of the relationships and whilst the Church may have views on certain sexual behaviours, the debate about homosexuality logically reduces to the simple matter of the gender of the partners. The Church here, it seems to me, has missed an opportunity. Instead of extolling the virtues of stable, faithful, life-long, committed partnerships entered into in the sight of God, it has got caught up in an interminable discussion about the rights and wrongs of 'who puts what where' in sexual encounters. While promoting marriage as the appropriate context for sex for heterosexual couples, partly as a defence against promiscuity, it has failed to offer anything remotely similar to homosexual couples, despite condemning them for their perceived lack of faithfulness and commitment. The Church must define the limits of the debate more carefully. There is still plenty of room for disagreement but we need to be clear on exactly what we disagree about.

Reticence

Many of the problems faced by gay men and lesbians (including some of the ignorance just mentioned) are caused or exacerbated by a general reluctance in society (at least in the West) to discuss matters of sex and sexuality – it's just not done in polite society. Consequently, many people grow up with inadequate or inaccurate sex education and issues of sex and sexuality may be poorly understood. For Christians the problem is even greater. The Church is even more reluctant to discuss the issues, even those relating to heterosexual couples and marriage. Thankfully, the truth that sex and sexuality are gifts from God that can be properly celebrated is being more widely preached, but there is a long way to go before congregations generally can be said to understand the issues. Arguably, the Church has failed to develop an integrated and comprehensive theology of human sexuality (though it is urgently needed) and is only beginning to face the issues.

Male sexual stereotypes

Society's prevailing understanding of male sexuality is that it tends to be macho, aggressive, domineering and resolutely heterosexual. Some men seem to feel threatened by any male sexuality that does not fit this model. This may be accompanied by a fear of subservience or disgust at the thought of a man as a passive partner in penetrative sex. Interestingly, in prisons (where homosexual activity is relatively common) it is only the passive (penetrated) partner who is labelled as 'homosexual' or 'gay'; the active partner's macho heterosexuality is not brought into question by such encounters ('needs must . . .').

Patriarchy

Gene Robinson, the openly gay Bishop of New Hampshire in the Episcopal Church of the USA (ECUSA) says:

> I believe with my whole heart that what we are up against in this struggle is the beginning of the end of patriarchy. For a very long time now, most of the decisions affecting the world have been made by white, heterosexual, educated, Western men. Ever so gradually, people of colour have been invited to the conversation, then women and now gay and lesbian people. And things are never the same when the oppressed get their voice.[11]

The Church's understanding of marriage

We are not here concerned with questions of same-sex marriage. Rather, with the observation that the Church's emphasis means that the Church views 'sexuality' as a subdivision of 'marriage', whereas it

---

11. In a lecture at Emory University's Center for the Study of Law and Religion reported in *All God's children: The magazine of the lesbian and gay Christian movement* (April, 2009).

might be more helpful and more accurate to see 'marriage' as a sub-division of 'sexuality'. The strong identification of sexuality solely with marriage may be at the root of the Church's difficulties in addressing issues of sex and sexuality as they relate to singleness, celibacy, adolescence, masturbation, and cohabitation as well as same-sex relationships.

Being helpful – roles, strategies, etc.

This section discusses the general ways in which we can and should support and help all our fellow Christians – by accepting them for who they are, by showing respect and being courteous, by making them welcome, and offering pastoral care and advice when needed. For the Body of Christ, worship, discipleship and mission are the true priorities and we should support one another in living the Christian life. Some specifics, though, may be helpful.

Listening

The very least we can do to support gay and lesbian Christians (and indeed non-Christians) is to listen carefully and patiently to their accounts of their experience of sexuality and of spirituality. Before we disagree with someone we must first demonstrate that we under-stand what they say. Simply treating people with respect can be tremendously positive. Gay men may say things such as:

> Don't you see, I've lived all my life afraid of people. When you treated me with the same respect you'd give any other human being, it had a profound impact on me.[12]

The Anglican Communion characterises its 'Listening Process' in this way:

> A listening process is an open commitment to engage actively in the world and thought of the person or people to whom you are listening and a corresponding commitment on the part of

12. see Jim's story 'The Joy of Openness' in Buxton, *The other side of the closet*, pp. 259–267.

the other person or people to enter into yours. It does not presume agreement or disagreement; it presumes a striving for empathy.[13]

Where possible our listening should be non-judgemental. Of course for those Christians or those denominations who take a negative view of homosexual activity there may be some implied 'judgement' on a person's behaviour but hopefully there need be no condemnation of a person's orientation.

Creating welcoming communities

Interestingly, many gay and lesbian Christians struggle with the official pronouncements of the Churches and with the attitude of denominational institutions and yet report very positive experiences in individual congregations. John (the Reader mentioned previously) speaks very highly of the congregation in his local parish church who have been welcoming and tolerant. John's partner now attends church and is considering confirmation, largely because of the warmth of the welcome. John and his partner are both committed to village life and are prominent local residents. To some extent they are probably accepted in their rural Anglican church community because they are committed members of the village community.

Listening to the experience of gay and lesbian Christians, together with meeting real people and making them welcome can transform a church's culture. The Episcopal Church of the USA, for example, sees itself at the end of a forty year 'listening process' with its own momentum in which they have already heard the voices of lesbian and gay Christians. Pastoral sensitivity now demands their full inclusion. They have no wish to impose such an answer on the whole of the Communion; they simply want the autonomy to proceed as they feel called by the Holy Spirit.[14]

---

13. The Anglican Communion, 'The Listening Process Website: What Is the Listening Process?' 2007: http://www.aco.org/listening/whatis.cfm
14. see The Episcopal Church of the USA (2005), *To set our hope on Christ: A response to the invitation of Windsor report.* New York: ECUSA, paragraph 135, 40 – 43 (also foreword and appendix).

Education

Churches need to overcome the ignorance and reticence that surround issues of sex and sexuality – we have to start talking more openly about such things. We need to find ways to stimulate discussion and reflection and to educate ministers, priests and pastoral assistants about sexuality during initial training and continuing education programmes. Possibilities for this include:

- Set up discussion groups in parishes or congregations specifically to look at issues of sex and sexuality in a Christian context,

- Discuss the issues in house groups or cell-groups,

- Provide access to the wealth of resources available – many denominations and organisations produce study guides. ECUSA has produced a DVD entitled *Voices of Witness* and in the UK, the Anglican Diocese of York has produced a DVD *Listening to Gay Men and Women's Experiences within the Church*. Either could be used in a study-group setting. A number of helpful websites are listed at the end of the chapter,

- Preach on the issues,

- Include relevant articles in church magazines and newsletters.

Prayer

As in all things, Christians should be praying. We should pray for gay and lesbian Christians and their needs. We should pray for ourselves; for an awareness of our prejudices and fears. We should pray for clarity in the interpretation of scripture. We should pray for the Churches and for ourselves in the process of discerning God's will for the future and we should be open to the guidance of the Holy Spirit.

Support at times of crisis

We should be prepared to offer pastoral support to gay and lesbian members of our congregations and local communities at times of crisis or at significant moments in their lives (though they may not feel they can ask unless they already feel welcome). Examples might include:

- Rites of passage such as baptisms, weddings and funerals,

- Times of ill-health. There may be specific issues in relation to sexual health and HIV,

- A confidential 'listening ear',

- Support for individuals 'coming out'. Gay and lesbian Christians face huge pressures when coming out and there can often be nobody to speak to. It can seem that there is no place to turn where they can be sure they won't be condemned. Support could include, encouraging people to keep a journal and to reflect on their emotions throughout the process; help in managing the process and timing of disclosure; support as individuals mourn the loss of lost or broken relationships; or celebration of the individual's new status ('coming-out parties'),

- Support for spouses and families of people who come out as gay. You will recall that Fiona (mentioned earlier) felt there was nobody in the Church that she could turn to for advice or support. Yet the whole episode she says hit her 'like a ton of bricks' and raised issues of sexual rejection, challenge to her understanding of the marriage, concern for the children, a crisis of sexual identity and integrity. Robert (mentioned earlier) experienced a 'stomach-churning' freefall of emotions when he came out to his wife. At the same time he felt enormous relief and enormous guilt, together with compassion for his wife whom he genuinely loved,

- Support at times of relationship infidelity. The issues are the same as in supporting heterosexual people through the trauma of adulterous relationships. Physical faithfulness can be difficult for men (gay or straight) after about five years of a relationship and many will have affairs.

Counselling

Provision of (or signposting to) counselling services. The need for counselling may not be directly related to issues of sexuality but lesbians and gay men often live with considerable stress and tension. They may need help to deal with attendant problems such as risky behaviour, addiction (sexual or substance) or mental-health issues.

Spiritual direction

We should not be blinded by a person's sexuality to their need for spiritual support and discipleship training.

Inclusion

As far as possible, allowing lesbian and gay Christians to take an active role in congregational life. There may be particular constraints in certain denominations – like the issue of John and reader ministry.

Liturgy, paraliturgy and ritual

Most lesbian and gay Christians say that they would appreciate the opportunity to mark significant moments and events in their lives with appropriate liturgy or ritual. How far this can be accommodated will depend on the official stance of the denomination and the inclusiveness of individual churches. Such liturgies could, for example, include same-sex marriage, the blessing of same-sex partnerships, or the renewal of commitment together with rites to mark the ending of relationships. Fiona certainly would have valued some way of marking the end of her marriage with prayers in church.

Reaching out to all kinds of families

The Church is sometimes guilty of unthinkingly using the word 'family' to mean a heterosexual couple with children. Increasingly (at least in the West) this picture excludes a great many domestic arrangements that people nonetheless think of as 'families'. This obviously includes same-sex couples (with or without children). Whatever the Church's view on these 'alternative' families it should at least acknowledge their existence and recognise that careless use of language can leave many children and adults feeling ignored, alienated or offended.

Developing a clear policy on ordination and ministry

The current policy (in the Church of England, at least) of bishops 'turning a blind eye' to the ordination of gay men and lesbians in sexually active relationships (in contradiction of its official position) causes a great deal of tension in the lives of gay clergy and the bishops who are responsible for their pastoral care. Sometimes gay clergy are even encouraged to deny the truth of their relationships and refer to their partner as 'the lodger'. There may be laudable motives behind such policies (perhaps a desire to find a way of accommodating gay clergy within the Church while waiting for the official position to change) but a way needs to be found for all concerned to act with integrity.

Inescapable limits on our usefulness

Our ability to provide pastoral care is always limited by our knowledge, skills and experience. Good pastors will know their strengths, weaknesses and limitations. There are particular things that can limit our usefulness in the pastoral care of gay men and lesbians (and our response to sexual concerns more generally):

- Lack of specialist knowledge or expertise in e.g.,
  - Sexual counselling
  - Relationship counselling
  - Personal counselling
  - Mental-health problems
- Being 'straight' (if we are)
- Being unaware of our prejudices

- Failure to reflect on our own sexuality
- Being part of a Church that is condemnatory and discriminatory.

Cautions – avoiding making things worse

Perhaps the greatest danger in the pastoral care of gay and lesbian Christians (as in much other pastoral care) is that of unquestioned assumptions. It is all too easy to think one understands the issues when in fact one doesn't. As with all pastoral care the focus should be on the person one is seeking to help. However much theory we know 'in general', we must not assume that we know what other people think or how they feel. Attentive listening is the only option.

Churches can certainly make things worse by allowing people with inadequate training to provide pastoral care. People should not 'dabble' in these issues. If they do not have the expertise to deal with the issues or are not confident of their own ability they should pass on the responsibility for pastoral care to someone more appropriate.

People providing pastoral care in relation to sexual concerns need to be pretty much unshockable which will usually require extensive prior consideration of the issues they are likely to encounter and reflection on their own responses. Panic, fear, disgust and abhorrence are rarely helpful in pastoral encounters. Love and compassion are indispensable.

Any attempt to compel people to adopt a particular course of action is likely to be unhelpful. Advice is one thing, but 'gratuitous ministry' in the form of forced exorcism or healing should be avoided. If one's denomination insists on celibacy for homosexual Christians it is an issue that should be introduced with the greatest sensitivity. Any suggestion of homophobia must be avoided.

Conclusion

In one sense the pastoral care of sexual concerns among homosexual people is little different from that of heterosexual people. However, our approach has to be very different – not because homosexual people have different essential needs but because of other people's attitudes to them, and in particular the response of the Church. We would do well to remember that people and situations are complicated and that in areas of sexual concern there may be no quick fixes and no easy answers.

As Christians, whatever our views on the issues of homosexuality, we are called to be obedient to the two great commandments – to love God with our whole beings and to love our neighbours as our selves. The parable of the Good Samaritan is surely sufficient warrant for accepting gay men and lesbians as our neighbours. Amity Buxton dedicated her book:

> . . . with encouragement to those who view gay and lesbian issues from extreme positions to consider the middle ground, where the human condition common to us all plays out its uneven course in individual lives.[15]

The Churches, and we as members of worshipping Christian communities, have to answer Rowan Williams' question: how is Christian ethics good news for a gay Christian who wishes to live in obedience to Christ, who does not see him/herself as rejecting something in his/her being, who lives a moral struggle like the rest of us, and who believes it's hard to hear good news from a church that insists that her/his condition is spiritually compromised?

Your conclusion may be very different from mine but, as disciples of Christ and servants of God's Kingdom, none of us can escape the pastoral and gospel imperatives to find an answer.

Suggested reading

Vasey, M. (1995). *Strangers and friends: a new exploration of homosexuality and the Bible.* London: Hodder & Stoughton.

15. Buxton, A. P. (1994). *The other side of the closet: The coming-out crisis for straight spouses and their families.* New York: John Wiley & Sons.

Bonnington, M., & Fyall, B. (1996). *Homosexuality and the Bible.* Cambridge: Grove Books.

Fowl, S. E., & Jones, L. G. (1991). *Reading in Communion: Scripture and ethics in Christian life.* Grand Rapids, MI: Eerdmans.

Burridge, R. A. (2007). *Imitating Jesus: An inclusive approach to New Testament ethics.* Grand Rapids, MI: Eerdmans.

Hays, R. B. (1997). *The moral vision of the New Testament: a contemporary introduction to New Testament ethics.* London: T & T Clark.

The House of Bishops. (1991). *Issues in human sexuality.* London: Church House Publishing.

The House of Bishops. (2003). *Some issues in human sexuality: A guide to the debate.* London: Church House Publishing.

Gaede, B. A. (Ed.). (1998). *Congregations talking about homosexuality.* Herndon VA: The Alban Institute.

Hallett, M. (1997). *Grove Pastoral Series 69: Sexual identity and freedom in discipleship.* Cambridge: Grove Books.

Brown, T. (Ed.). (2006). *Other voices, other worlds: the global Church speaks out on homosexuality.* London: Darton, Longman & Todd.

Buxton, A. P. (1994). *The other side of the closet: The coming-out crisis for straight spouses and families.* New York: John Wiley & Sons.

Useful websites

Extensive website on homosexuality with articles from all viewpoints (recommended)
http://www.religioustolerance.org/homosexu1.htm

The Lambeth Conference, 'Resolutions from 1998'
http://www.lambethconference.org/resolutions/1998/
(See Resolution 1.10)

The Anglican Communion's Listening Process
www.anglicancommunion.org/listening

Methodist resource paper on homosexuality
http://www.methodist.org.uk/index.cfm?fuseaction=opentogod.con
tent&cmid=1547

Christian denominational positions
http://en.wikipedia.org/wiki/List_of_Christian_denominational_po
sitions_on_homosexuality

Fulcrum – renewing the evangelical centre
http://www.fulcrum-anglican.org.uk/

Anglican Mainstream http://www.anglican-mainstream.net/
Conservative evangelical group committed to 'promote, teach and
maintain the scriptural truths on which the Anglican Church was
founded'

British Association for Counselling and Psychotherapy,
'Guidance for Good Practice in Christian Pastoral Care'
http://www.bacp.co.uk/expert_areas/apscc/practice.php

Lesbian and Gay Christian Movement www.lgcm.org.uk
A UK-based international Charity who are praying for an
inclusive Church

Changing Attitude
http://www.changingattitude.org.uk/home/home.asp
Working for gay, lesbian, bisexual and transgender affirmation
within the Anglican Communion

Metropolitan Community Church http://mccchurch.org

New Ways Ministry http://www.newwaysministry.org/
A gay-positive ministry of advocacy and justice for lesbian and gay
Catholics and reconciliation within the larger Christian and civil
communities

Gay magazines
http://www.attitude.co.uk/
http://www.gaytimes.co.uk/

EIGHT

Sexual perversions: Some background and useful pastoral responses[1]

Joanne Marie Greer

Introduction

This chapter discusses sexual behaviours regarded as deviant either by the general public, mental-health professionals, or both. Obviously, the more rigid and traditional the social context, the fewer sexual behaviours will be considered normal, and the more behaviours will be labelled deviant. For example, for many Victorians, 'normal' sexual behaviour was limited to heterosexual intercourse in the so-called missionary position (man on top), while such behaviours as intercourse with the woman on top or oral sex were regarded as deviant. Masturbation was considered deviant because it appeared to be forbidden in the Old Testament, didn't allow for conception, and was thought to cause bodily wasting or mental illness. Today, none of these sexual behaviours are considered unusual.

In the West today, there are more liberal views of sexuality, and social disapproval of a sexual behaviour is sometimes based on justice issues or social issues rather than reproductive concerns. Here are some examples. Paedophilia (sex with children) is disapproved of because the power differential between adult and child results in the exploitation of the child. Exhibitionism (public display of one's genitals) is disapproved of because it imposes a shock on the unwilling viewer. Frotteurism (rubbing one's genitals against others in public) is disapproved of because it violates another person's private space. However, some sexual behaviours with no offensive content continue

---

1. The editors would like to thank Professor Fred Berlin, MD, Ph.D., Director of the National Institute for the Study, Prevention, and Treatment of Sexual Trauma, Baltimore, USA, who reviewed this chapter before publication.

to be regarded as deviant simply because they are so perplexing. An example would be a 'foot fetish' in which the person becomes sexually excited only by feet and footwear. Rape is a special issue. The earliest modern sexual researchers such as Krafft-Ebbing would not have regarded it as a perversion when it resulted in coitus only, but many contemporary social psychologists probably would, because the victim is unjustly deprived of sexual self-determination.

The term 'perversion' is historically well established in mental-health literature, going back to the time of Sigmund Freud 's *Three Essays on Sexuality*.[2] Although Freud insisted the term was morally neutral, the general public regarded it as derogatory. Perhaps for this reason, a later Freudian, Otto Fenichel,[3] proposed the alternative term, *paraphilia*, a neologism based on the Greek root for 'love' for this group of sexual problems. Both terms remain in common use, although contemporary sexologists consider the term 'perversion' offensive and judgemental, and prefer the term 'paraphilia'. However, I prefer to use the term perversion because of its historical roots. Moreover, for the ordinary person the term 'perversion' does connote the usual societal response to the sexual behaviours in question. While it may or may not be desirable that society accepts all forms of sexual behaviour with equanimity, the fact is that society does not do so. Indeed, some 'paraphilias' are expressly forbidden by law.

Why the pastoral worker needs to know about perversions

Perversions ordinarily come to the attention of the pastoral worker because the dominant culture has already spoken. The law, the sexual object, the sexual actor, or neutral witnesses have had a negative response to a sexual behaviour. For this reason, this chapter will focus instead on the developmental and intrapsychic aspects of sex-

2. Freud, Sigmund (1905/1962). *Three essays on the theory of sexuality*, trans. James Strachey. New York: Basic Books.
3. Fenichel, Otto (1945). *The psychoanalytic theory of neurosis*. New York: W. W. Norton and Co.

ual perversion, rather than social and legal definitions and responses. Near the end of the chapter we will give general advice on legal reporting demands on the pastoral worker, but it will be necessary for each reader to obtain precise guidance from local secular and church authorities about reporting responsibilities.

Our main interest in this chapter will be to understand why these behaviours occur and what purpose they might serve in stabilising the personality for some adults. Viewing the matter from this perspective will make it easier for a pastoral worker to offer non-judgemental support and guidance to the sexually aberrant.

What makes a sexual act perverse?

The classification of a sexual act as a perversion can be approached from several perspectives. From the perspective of ordinary people, a perversion is any sexually exciting behaviour they consider abnormal and repugnant, i.e., any sexual act they cannot imagine themselves participating in. Different cultures might have different standards. Among some Arabs who take child brides, it is reported to be socially acceptable to enjoy a sexual practice known as 'thighing', i.e., reaching male orgasm while holding the little girl's thighs firmly around the penis. Many other cultures would regard such a behaviour as perverse.[4]

From a philosophical point of view, Thomas Nagel[5] points out that desire plays a crucial role in classifying a sexual act as a perversion. Perversions must contain fantasy and satisfy desire; thus, e.g., contraception cannot logically be considered a perversion even by persons who consider contraception an unnatural act.

A contemporary psychological reference work, *The Gale Encyclopedia of Mental Disorders*,[6] offers the following definition: 'sexual feelings

---

4. see 'Baby Tilth' at http://www.islamreview.com/articles/madinasuras.shtml, retrieved on March 8, 2009. Many other discussions of thighing can be found via Google.

5. Nagel, Thomas (1969). Sexual perversion. *J. of Philosophy, 66*, (1):5-17.

6. http://www.encyclopedia.com/searchresults.aspx?q=Gale+Encyclopedia+of+Mental+Disorders, retrieved March 8, 2009; also available in hard copy and e-book form.

or behaviours that may involve sexual partners that are not human, not consenting, or which involve suffering by one or both partners'.

From the psychodynamic developmental perspective, a perversion is a substitution for and avoidance of ordinary adult-with-adult consensual sexual intercourse. The substitution of the perversion for intercourse allows the person to attain sexual release without arousing the psychological anxiety he or she associates with adult intercourse. Many 'perverse' sexual acts are variations on acts that are normal in a young child but outgrown by the normal adult. Here are some examples. It is normal for children to find it exciting to play Peeping Tom. It is normal for an uninhibited small child to try to touch others' sexual parts; the child must be taught not to. Two-year-old boys will often enjoy exhibiting their penises to others, and must be taught not to. But an adult who looks, touches, or exhibits in exactly the same way is considered a pervert.

Some specific perversions

The current *Diagnostic and Statistical Manual of Mental Disorders* (DSM-IV-TR), the reference work used by Western mental-health professionals to diagnose mental disorders,[7] offers the following list: exhibitionism, fetishism, frotteurism, paedophilia, sexual masochism, sexual sadism, transvestic fetishism, and voyeurism. The manual also includes a category for 'paraphilia not otherwise specified', which is the category for extremely unusual perversions such as zoophilia (discussed below), or even perversions unique to an individual.

As noted above, culture comes into play in defining perversion. Therefore, it would be impossible to compile an exhaustive list of perversions of cross-cultural relevance. The *Diagnostic and Statistical Manual of Mental Disorders*[8] instead offers a list of perversions that are well-documented in Western mental-health literature and are met

---

7. http://www.behavenet.com/capsules/disorders/dsm4TRclassification.htm, retrieved on March 8, 2009.
8. American Psychiatric Association, 2000. The following article gives a good discussion of this text:
    http://en.wikipedia.org/wiki/Diagnostic_and_Statistical_Manual_of_Mental_Disorders

in serving Western clients. It is useful to begin with one that is quite unusual because it will aid in further exploring the nature of perversion.

Fetishism

This is a perversion that causes the person to be erotically excited to orgasm by a physical object. Perhaps the most well-known example is the foot fetish, whereby a man is excited to orgasm by viewing women's feet and caressing women's shoes. Freudians thought the fascination was due to the very rough resemblance of the slender foot to the penis. Many years ago, on first reading of this perversion in a nineteenth-century tome[9] I thought surely the writer is making this stuff up! But not long after, my local newspaper reported a robbery of a home with the headline 'Thief steals 38 Pairs of Shoes; Leaves Valuables'. So I inferred that shoe fetishism still happened in contemporary Washington, DC.

How to interpret this behaviour is perplexing. Without necessarily accepting it, it is interesting to read the comments of Kraft-Ebbing, an early sex researcher, on the foot fetish:

> It is highly probable, and shown by a correct classification of the observed cases, that the majority and perhaps all of the cases of shoe fetishism, rest upon a basis of more or less conscious masochistic desire for self-humiliation. In Hammond's case (case 59) the satisfaction of a masochist was found in being trod upon. In cases 55 and 58 they also had themselves trod upon. In case 59, equus eroticus, the person loved a woman's foot, etc. In the majority of cases of masochism the act of being trod upon with feet plays a part as an easily accessible means of expressing the relation of subjection.

---

9. Project Gutenberg: Full text of *Psychopathia Sexualis,* with especial reference to the antipathic sexual instinct, a medico-forensic study; R. v. KRAFT_EBBING, http://www.gutenberg.org/etext/24766, retrieved January 2009.

Recall the religious custom of kissing the feet of Jesus portrayed on the crucifix, as well as the medieval religious custom of kissing the feet of another as an act of humility and penance. These customs would have been familiar to Kraft-Ebbing's Victorian-era cases, and perhaps influenced his interpretation of their foot fetishism, which differs from Freud's interpretation.

Brendan Geary[10] reports this fetishism case from an inpatient hospital-therapy group he led during the 1990s: the patient was erotically aroused by women's feet. He said that, 'For me, walking down the street on a summer's day when women are wearing sandals, is just like it would be for other men if they (the women) were all walking down the road topless.' He would sometimes find in high-school annuals the photographs of young women whom he found attractive. He would then find their phone numbers, and phone them up pretending to be a shoe salesman so that they would describe their feet. While this was happening he would masturbate. He said, 'I got masturbation down to less than a minute as I was terrified of being caught.' He also picked up a nurse's shoes at the hospital when she was out and started to masturbate with them until she came in and caught him. He had been through psychodynamic counselling, which identified possible childhood events that could have influenced his desires and behaviour, but it didn't cure anything. The supervising psychiatrist put him on antiandrogen medication and it brought him tremendous relief. He was still able to have a sexual life with his wife, though it was not as easy as before.

Pastoral counsellor and Baptist minister Tom Rodgerson reports a rather bizarre example of a variation on a foot fetish, in which the man needed to tickle the foot of a woman (who had been bad to him) to the point of pain. The woman would be restrained in some way and this would continue until she begged for mercy.[11]

---

10. Personal Communication, March 2009.
11. Rodgerson, T. E. (2001). Pastors and paraphilias, *American Journal of Pastoral Counseling, 4,* (1) 19 – 36.

A combination of sadism and foot fetish involving animals is before the US Supreme Court's 2009 session. A state law passed to prevent animal cruelty was used to stop the creation and distribution of 'crush videos', i.e., videos depicting women's feet inflicting torture on animals. The feet were either bare or wearing high heels. The videos were reported to appeal to persons with a very specific sexual fetish because the videos show only the woman's foot or shoe inflicting pain. The question before the court is whether the law in question is an unconstitutional restriction of free speech.[12]

Why is foot fetishism theoretically interesting? Because it illustrates the developmental 'falling off the tracks' which we speculate is involved in perversion. It would be normal for a lover to enjoy his love's pretty feet but then move on to admire the rest of her body and ultimately join with her in intercourse. What makes it abnormal is the derailment of this trajectory, leading to the experience of orgasm without the denouement of physical and emotional union with the love object. Instead, orgasm is reached via a symbolic substitute that in this case is gender-ambiguous: is the fantasy of a pretty woman's foot, or of a man's penis, or both? Is the emotional experience one of pleasure or of pain?

Fetishes may involve other objects than feet. Geary reports,[13] 'I worked with a client who loved the touch of women's underwear. He didn't desire to wear it; just to touch it. He was caught touching the lingerie in the homes of women he did work for. He also stole underwear from the clothes-drying lines of neighbours.'

Transvestism

Strictly speaking, transvestism could involve either a woman's use of male clothing or man's use of female clothing. But in contemporary

---

12. http://www.washingtonpost.com/wp-dyn/content/article/2009/04/20/AR2009042003196.html?sub=AR, retrieved April 21, 2009.
13. Personal communication, March 2009.

Western society, it usually refers only to male behaviour. Public cross-dressing is a very extreme version of male transvestism. More often, transvestism involves the private use of female clothing, especially extremely feminine objects like silk lingerie, to attain orgasm. It would be normal for a young child to experience both excitement and comfort in snuggling with silken clothing saturated with the mother's scent. It would also seem normal for an adult to use a lover's garments the same way. What makes the act 'perverse' is that the preferred mode of attaining sexual orgasm is through caressing the garment rather than a human, bodily encounter.

One cannot help but be impressed by the similarity of such self-comforting to the young child's use of a special soft blanket or stuffed animal that he has held in his mother's arms. The mother is often mystified at the child's unhappiness if she washes the blanket, not realising that the skin-smell of the cloth is a necessary aspect of its comfort. British paediatrician and psychoanalyst Donald Winnicott called such a blanket or toy a 'transitional object', and also called it 'the first not-me object'. He regarded this special cloth object as both a transitional tie to original mother/baby symbiosis and a way of exploring the me/not me contrast.[14]

Early in my training as a psychoanalyst, I treated a very handsome, virile-looking young man, a professional athlete, who was able to have sexual enjoyment only when clad in women's satin underwear. Otherwise, his sexual tastes were heterosexual and conventional. He planned to marry soon, and one of his treatment issues was whether he should tell his bride-to-be about his sexual habits. He decided to do so, and she broke the engagement. He then broke off treatment, blaming me for the failure of the engagement.

Brendan Geary reports the following occurrences of transvestism within a religious order, involving ordinary members not in mental-health treatment:

14. http://en.wikipedia.org/wiki/Transitional_object, retrieved April 21, 2009.

A member of a religious order, who was in his seventies and needed a lot of attention and 'stroking', approached me as he wanted to talk about something. He had not had an easy life, and perhaps the religious order provided a refuge from a world that was too difficult for him. He said halfway through a fairly inconsequential conversation that, 'Of course I am one of those men who likes to wear women's clothes . . .' As a child he would snuggle up to his mother's clothes in a wardrobe. He may have masturbated with them in adolescence. He felt ashamed and embarrassed about this; but didn't know how to stop. The position of the order was that what he did in his room was his business, but that he was not permitted to wear female clothes in the community spaces as this affected other people negatively.

Here is a final example: an Anglican clergyman who taught in a secondary school. At the end of the day, when the students had left, he would lock his door and take a box of women's clothes out of a cupboard. He would put them on and do his corrections. He found it soothing and comforting. He would then return them to the box and go home.

Many people lump transvestites with homosexuals, and of course there are transvestite homosexuals, but this is not a necessary conjunction. Transvestites can and do marry successfully, and can enjoy sexual intercourse, provided the lover is tolerant of the necessary fantasies and supporting props. He may be sincerely attached to a sweetheart, and want marriage and children. Ethical men often confess their unusual sexual needs to the prospective partner beforehand. This is a point at which the woman may well seek the advice of her pastor, who has a delicate task to perform in helping the couple determine what is best for both.

Frotteurism

The frotteur (from the French *'frotter'*, which means to rub or to scrape) is a person who achieves erection or orgasm by rubbing against a nonconsenting person, usually a stranger. This behaviour usually occurs in public places, such as on busy streets or crowded buses or subways (tubes). It can also occur on the dance floor. The offender pushes against a young or vulnerable victim and rubs the penis against the victim's buttocks or thighs. Typically the offender times his motion to the motion of the vehicle. This perversion is under-reported because the victims are often children and young adolescents who are not sure what is going on or whether they should take offence. Sex researcher Gene Abel[15] conducted a study in cooperation with the subway police in New York City, helping them spot frotteurs. The suspect men were removed from the subway and taken for a strip search. The systematic frotteurs were found to wear a rubber garment to contain their ejaculates, and those were arrested. In addition to blatant crowding against a victim, another identified sign of a frotteur was a man who got off the subway and immediately got back on in the opposite direction, cruising for a likely victim.

A common sign of frotteurism is a man with his legs spread wide, taking up more than his 'share' of the seating area. He rubs his thighs against his seat-mate's, and often conceals his penis with loosely folded hands. Frotteurism usually begins in adolescence, and peaks between ages 18–25.

Exhibitionism

Exhibitionism is the exposure of genitals to a non-consenting person, most often but not always a stranger. The victim may also be some known vulnerable person, such as a child in the family or neighbour-hood, or a young household worker. In some cases, the individual may also engage in masturbation while exposing himself. Some-times, no additional contact with the observer is sought; the individual is stimulated sexually simply by gaining the attention of and startling the observer. This ploy for attention is completely normal in a very

15. Personal communication, 1980.

young boy. Psychodynamically, exhibitionism is a developmental fixation, i.e., being stuck at an early developmental stage in one's sexual development.

The following case, reported by Brendan Geary[16] illustrates very clearly the developmental issues involved:

> G. was a man in his late forties. He was a pleasant man, and a pleasure to have in the therapy group. He had been caught exposing himself many, many times throughout his life and had spent time in prison. He would find himself thinking of exposing himself and find the idea arousing. If he left immediately he was OK. If he remained, he would lose his ability to control himself, and end up exposing his penis. He used antiandrogen medication, which led to problems with erection.
>
> In the group I asked him about what may have led to this and he told the following story:
>
> 'When I was eight years of age I was at home jumping up and down on the bed wearing only my underpants. I was with my brothers and sisters and having fun. At one point I looked down and saw my 4-year-old niece looking up at me with a look of wonder and surprise on her face. However, her gaze was not on my face but between my legs. When I looked down, I could see my penis hanging out of my underpants. I loved the admiring gaze on her face.'
>
> The exhibitionism only emerged as a behaviour in late high school, where he began to get into trouble for this, leading to expulsion from school. He did not want to shock women, but wanted to see an admiring gaze on their faces.

In younger men, this perversion sometimes occurs in combination with frotteurism (see above). The usual location for this combination

16. Personal communication, March 20, 2009.

is nearly empty public transportation. Typically, the victim is sitting by an isolated window, the aggressor takes the aisle seat, exposes the penis, presses his thigh firmly against the victim's thigh and rubs the victim's thigh. He may or may not masturbate as well.

Exhibitionism in an elderly person who has not previously been sexually inappropriate may signal an early onset of senile dementia. One of the early markers of Alzheimer's disease is socially inappropriate speech and actions.

Sexual masochism

Masochism is a term with a rich history in mental-health literature. Broadly speaking, it is used for the personality characteristic of taking pleasure in suffering pain. Thus, the literature speaks of 'moral masochism' in the person who sacrifices pleasure for a moral purpose. In the context of sexual disorders, the masochist is a person who must suffer pain in order to achieve orgasm. In general, the pain may be inflicted by others or by self, but for a particular individual it always follows a stereotypic script. The source can usually be traced to childhood experiences combining love and pain, e.g., of whippings by a loved person. The term 'masochism' was coined by Kraft-Ebbing from the name of a nineteenth-century Austrian novelist, Leopold von Sacher-Masoch.[17] He created fictional characters fixated on the combination of sex and pain.

In the broader sense, masochism refers to any experience of receiving pleasure or satisfaction from suffering pain. One psychodynamic theory is that masochism is aggression turned inward, onto the self, when a person feels too guilty or is too afraid to express aggression outwardly.

Freud was puzzled by women's acceptance of painful genital experiences, such as first intercourse or childbirth. He concluded that they were somehow 'hard-wired' to seek pain in order to accomplish their

---

17. http://everything2.com/title/Leopold%2520von%2520Sacher-Masoch, retrieved on April 21, 2009.

biological destiny. Therefore, he considered masochism normal in women but not in men.[18]

Sexual sadism

The term 'sadism' is so named from the notorious and insane Marquis de Sade.[19] The plots of his obscene novels involved the combination of lust and cruelty.

A sexual sadist must inflict pain on another person in order to achieve orgasm. Logically, the sexual sadist usually partners with a sexual masochist, and this relationship paradigm is called 'sado-masochism'. The relationship may be very satisfactory to the two individuals, and yet not be in the interest of society. This is the case when the life and health of the masochistic partner are in danger. Such cases are often identified by physicians or even in hospital emergency rooms. While some sadists stick to a stereotypic script, there is the danger that the violence will escalate over time.

In line with the increasing social tolerance for other people's sexual preferences, the DSM manual (referred to previously) requires that there also be significant distress or impairment of the ability to function as a result of the perverse sexual behaviours or fantasies. In other words, no mental disorder exists if both parties are happy with the situation. In most jurisdictions, public law would not be so liberal, if the masochist is actually harmed. However, legal prosecution would not be for sadism, which is a mental-health term, but for bodily assault. In some sad cases, the prosecution may even be for manslaughter, when both partners fail to anticipate the effect of catastrophic excitement on a weak constitution.

Some psychoanalytic theorists explain sexual sadism as a psychological defence against a neurotic fear of castration or bodily harm during sex. The defence is known as 'turning passive into active'. Instead of the sadist's suffering harm as a passive victim, she/he becomes

---

18. http://www.enotes.com/psychoanalysis-encyclopedia/feminine-masochism, retrieved on April 21, 2009.
19. http://supervert.com/elibrary/marquis_de_sade, retrieved on April 21, 2009.

the aggressor and inflicts pain on someone else. Instead of the masochist's suffering harm as a passive victim, he/she actively seeks to be harmed. This is thought to create a sense of safety and well-being, leading to the possibility of orgastic release.

Either sadism or masochism may be limited to fantasy scripts needed to achieve orgasm in outwardly nondeviant sexual relations. Sadomasochism occurs in both males and females, and in both hetero-sexual and homosexual relationships. Sometimes psychoanalytic treatment can link the fantasy script convincingly to childhood psycho-logical trauma. An example is a woman I treated many years ago, with a traumatic memory of her father forcing whisky down her mother's throat, in order to get her to submit to sex. The grown daughter was able to achieve orgasm only while imagining an elaborate fantasy of a man force-feeding women.[20]

Sadism (and masochism) occurs in an attenuated form in a normal sexual relationship, with gentle biting and all sorts of horseplay. Kraft-Ebbing comments: 'Woman no doubt derives pleasure from her innate coyness and the final victory of man affords her intense and refined gratification. Hence the frequent recurrence of these little love comedies.' He also comments that he considered it a mild form of sadism when Victorian men demanded the sexual act in unusual places, to provoke confusion and embarrassment in a modest woman.

Sexual sadism in its extreme form is the lust-murder. There have been sufficient case reports in the media to document this reality.[21] Often the corpse is genitally mutilated and dismembered. Very rarely, the flesh may be eaten. Lust-murderers almost always have been treated with extreme brutality as children. However, not all children treated sadistically will become lust-murderers. The reality, and unpredictability, of the interaction of nature and nurture underlies this conundrum.

20. Greer, J. M. (1994). 'Return of the Repressed' in the analysis of an adult incest survivor. *Psychoanalytic Psychology*, *11*:545-561.
21. http://en.wikipedia.org/wiki/Lust_murder, retrieved April 21, 2009.

Paedophilia

Paedophilia will not be discussed in detail here because it is taken up in a separate chapter. Briefly, paedophilia is sexual activity of an adult with a child. For the crime of paedophilia, the upper age limit for the child is legally defined and may vary from country to country. There is a logical problem if two persons are close in age, but one is classified as a child and the other as an adult, and the sexual activity is consensual. The DSM-IV-TR addresses this difficulty by diagnosing paedophilia if the aggressor is at least 16 years of age and at least five years older than the child. However, the local law may not offer this latitude. Paedophiles may be attracted to either males or females or both.

Individuals with this disorder develop procedures and strategies for gaining access to and trust of children. Schoolteacher, scout master, tutor, babysitter, and youth pastor are some of the work positions that paedophiles seek out. Church ministries are attractive careers for paedophiles because they provide easy access to a child's trust.

Paedophilia also occurs in the context of incest, a separate crime. There is some dispute among experts in child sexual abuse, as to whether paedophiles are a distinct category from incest perpetrators. A number of experts view the incest perpetrator as simply a 'lazy paedophile',[22] using the sexual object nearest at hand, i.e., a child of the family.

Covert paedophilic sadism may be in play when children are treated with physical brutality, e.g., being harshly beaten.[23] This is especially likely if the child is partially or totally nude during the abuse.

Voyeurism

Voyeurism is a perversion in which a person finds sexual excitement in watching unsuspecting people who are nude, undressing, or having

---

22. E.g., see: Coleman, H. and D. Collins. (1990). Treatment trilogy of father-daughter incest. *Child and adolescent social work* 7:339-345.
23. E.g., see: Weil, John Leopold. (1989). *Instinctual stimulation of children: from common practice to child abuse.* Madison, Ct.: International Universities Press.

sex. Again, normal young children and even adolescents engage in such viewing if they can arrange the opportunity. However, a normal youngster eventually relinquishes such behaviour voluntarily, because of social disapproval.

In areas of the world with an Anglo heritage, voyeurs are popularly known as 'Peeping Toms', based on the eleventh-century British legend of Lady Godiva. Tom was a tailor who 'peeped' at Lady Godiva's nakedness, while the rest of the townspeople respectfully looked away.

Adult voyeurs are almost always male. A voyeur may have fantasies about having sex with the person he is viewing but the voyeur almost never approaches the person. The voyeur is highly inhibited with regard to adult sexual performance, and may never actually have had sexual relations with anyone. Such persons are said to be fixated at the early childhood level of curiosity about sex rather than active participation in sex. 'Fixated' in this context suggests that normal development has been stopped or 'fixed' at a certain stage or age of development, and that normal adult development has not taken place.

As with other perversions, there can be childhood events that instigate a perverse tendency in one child, while another is un-affected. One cannot really predict the vulnerability of any particular child. For this reason, it seems highly inadvisable for parents to stimulate voyeurism in their children by, e.g., roaming the house nude or semi-naked, or allowing the children to hear or see sexualised contacts between the parents, or allowing the young child to examine and handle the parents' breasts or genitals. This point is particularly difficult to make to educated parents who consider themselves liberal and enlightened with regard to sex.

Modern technology offers variations to the voyeur. Binoculars are used to view through distant windows. There have been a number of cases of proprietors of businesses creating viewing holes in restrooms, or even filming customers at the toilet. Recently a high-school girls' sports coach in the USA was fired and prosecuted for filming his adolescent charges in the dressing room. And of course the Internet offers relative safety to the voyeur who does not require a flesh-and-blood view of the sexual object.

Necrophilia

Necrophilia (literally, 'love of the dead') is a sexual perversion that involves fantasies or actual attempts to use a corpse for sexual stimulation. While many other perversions seem to fall within the realm of the understandable, particularly if one is psychodynamically inclined, this one does not.

In the nineteenth century, Kraft-Ebbing reported that a number of cases appeared in Austrian legal proceedings of his day, but unfortunately none of them were examined for psychosis. In these cases the corpse was that of a stranger murdered by the pervert. Kraft-Ebbing proposed that overcoming the natural repugnance which man has for a corpse and having sexual relations with a cadaver, implies the actor must be psychotic. In one of Kraft-Ebbing's case reports from the Austrian government files, he reports that on autopsy the offender's brain showed several abnormalities. He reports another case in which there was a family pattern of manic attacks with homicidal impulses.

When the corpse violated is that of a lover rather than a stranger, the break with reality may involve a psychotic grief response of failing to accept that the lover is indeed dead. One is reminded of Heathcliffe's desperate embraces of the dead Cathy in the classic novel, *Wuthering Heights*.

Sexual asphyxia

This perversion is an effort to intensify the sexual orgasm by reducing or stopping breathing in the moments leading up to orgasm. The orgasm may be via masturbation or intercourse, and breathing may be cut off by the self or by the sexual partner. Various strategies are used to cut off breath. The active partner may suppress the breathing of the passive partner during intercourse. An individual may masturbate while using a rope around the neck to partially cut off breathing. There have been a number of cases in the USA of adolescent males accidentally hanging themselves while practising sexual asphyxia.[24]

Telephone scatologia

In this perversion, the offender attains sexual excitement by 'talking dirty' to an unwilling listener. Most often, the offender dials at random until finding a girl or a naïve woman who is polite enough, or curious enough, not to hang up immediately. This offence occurs sufficiently often in the US that telephone companies provide a special short phone number (e.g., '*69' for one telephone company) to alert the company's computer system to make a record of the caller's phone number.

Telephone scatologia seems to have particular appeal to adolescent males, and to males who fail to mature past adolescence. If the listener is known to the adolescent male, the purpose may be overtly hostile, e.g., an attempt to shock or frighten a girl who has rebuffed him.

Telephone scatologia should be distinguished from 'phone sex'. Phone sex is a more recent phenomenon in which two consenting adults engage in sexually arousing conversation over the telephone. They may also masturbate during the conversation. Partners who are separated by temporary circumstances, especially stressful circumstances such as war, may practise phone sex. Phone sex can also be carried out through a business intermediary, by paying for the partner's time on a per-minute basis.

Zoophilia (aka Bestiality)

Zoophilia involves sexual feelings or behaviours focused on animals, usually domesticated animals such as dogs, sheep, cows, or goats.

---

24. Rosenblum, S. and Faber, M. M. (1979). The adolescent sexual asphyxia syndrome. *J. Am. Acad. Child Psychiatry,* *18* (3):546-58.

This is an uncommon behaviour in developed countries in the present day. In less-developed nations, the practice seems to have persisted into the present day. A 2002 news report from South Africa claimed that contemporary adolescents were practising sex with goats to avoid HIV infection.[25]

If the behaviour is that of a child or adolescent, it may simply manifest the child's sexual curiosity and exploration of those animals available to it near the home. But if this behaviour is driven and repetitive, it begs the question of whether the child is being penetrated by someone, and is defending against helplessness by 'turning passive into active'. For example, in a case of mine, a child subjected to repeated enemas by both parents, would attempt to anally penetrate a pet dog with a stick.

On farmsteads it is not unknown for a young male to use his penis to anally penetrate a docile animal. This may be a passing stage in exploring his sexuality, or it may lead to a fixation on this approach to orgasm. The final outcome will depend on the structure of the personality and the vicissitudes of the environment.

The phenomenon was much more common in the nineteenth century, when animals were more available. Kraft-Ebbing was loath to categorise it with more serious perversions, commenting that 'Low morality and great sexual desire, with lack of opportunity for natural indulgence, are the principal motives of this unnatural means of sexual satisfaction, which is resorted to by women as well as by men.' He also reports another contributing factor during his historical era, a belief originating in Persia, that intercourse with animals could cure gonorrhoea. 'Experience teaches that bestiality with cows and horses is none too infrequent. Occasionally the acts may be undertaken with goats, bitches, and . . . hens.'

---

25. http://www.news24.com/News24/South_Africa/Aids_Focus/0,,2-7-659_1161152,00.html, retrieved April 15, 2009.

According to Kraft-Ebbing, older writers classified both bestiality and pederasty under the general term of sodomy. (See Genesis 19 for the origin of the word 'sodomy'.) Later, sodomy was often used synonymously with bestiality. However, he notes that moral theologians distinguished correctly, in the sense of Genesis, between *sodomia, concubitus cum persona ejusdem sexus,* and *bestialitas, concubitus cum bestia.* He offers as a source a work of his contemporary, Olfert, on 'Pastoralmedicin', (pastoral medicine).

Urolagnia

Urolagnia can be one expression of the sadistic impulse, to force contempt and humiliation upon partners by defiling them. An example is the 'Golden Showers' perversion, in which one partner attains sexual excitement by urinating on the other.[26] I knew of such a case because I was the psychotherapist of the woman involved. She was struggling with a wish for a divorce, versus accepting the advice of her confessor to continue in the marriage. Her husband sensed her wish to flee and began several perverse sexual practices. The goal seemed to be to intimidate her, as well as to express his rage.

There are persons who claim to enjoy being urinated upon and defecated upon. There are websites that cater to such inclinations.

Multiple perversions

It is not unusual for one person to have more than one sexual perversion. As mentioned above, frotteurism and exhibitionism often occur together in public places. Here is a different example of two combined perversions: Brendan Geary reports, 'I had a client who sought to have pain inflicted upon him; it seemed to be part of self-loathing. He had been a victim of multiple abuse as a child and this seemed to be a constant re-enacting of his abusive childhood. He

---

26. For example, see: http://edstrong.blog-city.com/whats_sex_without_a_fetish_ill_take_a_golden_shower.htm, retrieved April 15, 2009.

had also had sex with animals.' Such combinations fit well with Freud's formulation of childhood sexuality as 'polymorphous perverse', i.e., involving many forms of divergence from normal adult sexuality. Sex researcher Gene Abel and his co-author report data that indicate that many paraphiliacs carry out a variety of perverse behaviours and cross a number of boundaries within individual perversions.[27]

Theories about how perversions develop

As most readers already know, the intrapsychic approach to understanding human thoughts and actions was the dominant approach until the advent of behaviourism. Behaviourists and social psychologists discounted the importance of the intrapsychic world of feelings and fantasies, and emphasised the importance of environmental influences on adult behaviours. However, the social-behavioural approach fails in the face of perverse behaviour. Ordinarily, no childhood authority figure even knows of the individual's perverse behaviour, much less teaching it to or modelling it for them. Even films and books can hardly be blamed for engendering such well-defined, narrow sexual needs. Perverse pornographic material does exist, but it is usually out of reach of the developing child. So the perversion has to develop from intrapsychic sources. Several clues are available to help us understand the process.

Already mentioned is the 'pre-oedipal', i.e., 'early childhood' quality of many perverse behaviours. Gender-ambiguous thinking is characteristic of normal young children as they try to sort out the social and physical roles of the two sexes. I still chuckle when I recall a comment of my three-year-old son's playmate from a conservative Jewish household. The two children were watching me re-paper the hallway. The visiting child speculated, 'Your Mommy must be a man because she hangs wallpaper.'

27. Abel, G. G. and Osborn, C. (1992). The paraphilias: the extent and nature of sexually deviant and criminal behaviour. *Psychiatr. Clin. North Am. 15*(3):675–87.

Because 'man' and 'woman' are not yet fully sorted out, to a young child the penis and the breast may seem interchangeable. Many a father who shaves in the nude has been startled and worried by a boy toddler's attempting to suck his penis. Part of the process of attaining maleness (or femaleness) involves the gradual dwindling of fantasies and behaviours inappropriate to the ultimate gender identity. In contrast, the pervert is 'stuck' at the polymorphous perverse stage of development, still using the multiple forms of non-standard sexual behaviour and fantasies characteristic of young children. And like young children, they are usually incapable of empathic identification with those who may be startled or repelled by their behaviour.

If appropriate adult sexual partners are available, as is usually the case, why does the person not move on toward adult sexual behaviours? The usual psychodynamic reason for avoiding any activity otherwise to one's advantage is fear/anxiety. Somehow the attainment of adult sexuality is threatening, so the person clings to childlike sexual behaviours. Thus, the adult physical need for orgasmic release is satisfied without the psychic risk of ordinary sexual intimacy.

Why should it be dangerous to move on toward adult sexuality? Why should a developing adolescent feel a need to somehow meld old ways of comfort with the new experience of orgasm? To undertake any new risk in life, one requires a certain sense of self-worth and self-sufficiency: one thinks, 'I can handle this; the risk is not too great; the risk is worth the reward'. Moving on from the parental orbit to create a new world of one's own has many trajectories. It may feel safe to move forward academically, for example, but not emotionally. Many 'perverts' are educated, highly accomplished people.

Certain configurations of the family of origin are more likely to result in sexual developmental failures for males, who make up the vast majority of adult perverts. The mother's affirmation of the son's masculinity is key to normal development. If he sees mother rejoicing as he moves out of her orbit to enter the male world of games, interests, and peer socialisation, he is also free to find a peer love object. Mother's heart will not be broken, she will not be abandoned, and she will not abandon him in anger. But this disengagement process does not start in adolescence, or even in middle childhood. Such a mother probably also encouraged autonomy from early on, as the child began to walk, talk, and say 'no'. A mother who does not continually let go at each appropriate moment will elicit responses of rebellion, sulkiness, or overt rage from a male child. Rage and a sense of human alienation persist as undercurrents in adult perverse behaviour.[28] This is a partial explanation of the pervert's usual lack of empathy for his victims.

Another contributing factor is pathological self-centredness (narcissism) that has developed defensively due to a feeling of being at disadvantage in dealing with a dominating, controlling mother and with later power figures. A defining characteristic of narcissism is an inability to empathise with the perspective of another person, or here specifically with the victim.

For the mother to appropriately let go of her son, she needs an engaged male partner. The father's role is to come between the mother and young son, disengaging them from their outgrown mother/baby symbiosis, and engaging each of them with himself. In those households without fathers, of course, other males such as uncles or grandfathers can play this role for the child. But a distant, absent, frightening, or hostile male authority figure will fail at engaging the son in the masculine world and reassuring him of his masculinity.

Difficulty also ensues for the child if the father engages him appropriately, but fails to re-engage the mother. This appears to leave the mother in the position of being abandoned, and makes it difficult for the child to leave her orbit without guilt. This may happen because the father has little sexual interest in his wife. He may also

---

28. Khan, M. (1979). *Alienation in perversions.* International Universities Press, New York.

fail to re-engage her because she is disappointed in him as a man. Women who hold their menfolk in contempt, e.g., for lack of education or achievement, or failure to earn an appropriate income, can fix their ambitions on a son instead, so that his life becomes his mother's project rather than his project. Although the son may appreciate his mother's ambition on his behalf, his sense that he is unfree engenders resentment and even unconscious rage toward her. Such conflictual feelings toward his first female love object may make it impossible to disengage from childish sexual satisfactions and undertake an adult male sexual role with another woman.

It appears that I am saying the psychodynamic cause of perversion is over-involvement between mother and child. Not necessarily. Under-involvement can be just as devastating. Male transvestites, for example, may have learned early that Mother's embrace was not available, that she was cold and withdrawn, and comforted themselves with her garments and her scent instead.

Is there no way for things to turn out well if parental nurturing is flawed? This is far from the case. Most children are naturally resilient, and when faced with parental peculiarities will learn eventually to shrug them off and move on. A child who will not is the vulnerable child who either (1) is genetically disposed to intense emotional reactions, or (2) is bombarded with too many disruptive events at once, even though he/she could have handled each one individually with ease. The child genetically disposed to intensity is well-described in the early pages of Marcel Proust's *Swann's Way*,[29] the opening section of *Remembrance of Things Past*. An example of too many disruptive events might be the mother's extramarital affair coinciding with the father's temporary absence and also the first year of school attendance.

In my clinical work I have noted that both heterosexual men and women who have difficulty enjoying heterosexual sex frequently

29. Available from Project Gutenberg: http://www.gutenberg.org/etext/7178, retrieved April 15, 2009.

report a childhood of unfulfilled longings for Mother's attention. They may engage in heterosexual sex for other reasons, but they 'take care of themselves' as far as orgasm is concerned, via either fantasy or direct self-stimulation. They often report that their mother took little interest in their childhood activities and conversation, although perhaps providing for material wants. A sad example was a woman who recalled eavesdropping on her parents as they had a pre-dinner drink each evening, just to hear her mother's voice. Her mother was a local government administrator who wanted to spend her evenings with her husband, leaving her children to servants.

Pastoral workers are well acquainted with the phenomenon of complicated grief, in which the bereaved person is unable to work through the loss, come to closure, and begin again. Perversion has some of the characteristics of complicated grief, in that the loss of the mother's appropriate attention and care is not grieved, accepted, and let go of. Instead, the repetitive, stereotypic scenario of the perversion makes one aborted attempt after another to resolve the pain.

One might well ask how unresolved grief over maternal loss can explain aggressive perversions, in which the sexual object is humiliated or caused pain. Aggression is based in rage, and rage functions as a defence against grief. Grief cannot get underway until loss is accepted at least to some small extent. Rageful behaviour tries to compel the human object to conform to expectations and thus make grief unnecessary. Thus, rage-based perversions are more out of touch with reality than the more gentle perversions, and such persons tend to be more dangerous to others. The unconscious target of the rage would ordinarily be a neglectful, cruel, or seductive mother, but not always. In the 1970s in California, a long-distance trucker picked up a teen girl hitch-hiker, raped her, and cut off the arm with which she thumbed the ride. He was deeply upset with his teen daughter, who had been hitch-hiking against his orders. His own previous history was not reported.

Noted sex researcher Gene Abel, in the article co-authored with Osborn and previously cited,[30] speculates that Fenichel's idea of matching specific paraphilias to specific developmental deficits is not the most parsimonious explanation of a paraphiliac career. Abel and his co-author Osborn speculate instead that the explanation is rather a general deficit of control.

Perversion in women

Since female homosexuality has become widely accepted, a woman being labelled a sexual pervert is relatively rare. In my opinion, this is because women are allowed wider latitude of behaviour before they are considered peculiar or deviant. Transvestism is a good example. Women can adopt extremely masculine dress without arousing much comment. They may even be at the height of current fashion. Undoubtedly, they have different motivations than the male transvestite. Some women find it exciting or sexually titillating to appear gender-ambiguous, while others adopt a sloppy style of masculine dress to avoid sexual attention. If they do dress in clothing or lingerie reminiscent of the mother, no one takes it amiss. Further, although the observed behaviour may be the same, it may not be in the service of desire or orgasm.

Masochism is the only paraphilia in which a number of women participate – about 5% of masochists are female. As previously noted, Freud was of the opinion that normal women were naturally masochistic, because nature required them to submit to the male sexually, and to permit the developing foetus the use of their bodies, including all the pains incidental to pregnancy, labour, and nursing. His view of feminine masochism, however, was quite different from the deliberate seeking of bodily abuse, which is clearly a mental disorder.

---

30. Abel, G. G. and Osborn, C. (1992). The paraphilias: the extent and nature of sexually deviant and criminal behaviour. *Psychiatr. Clin. North Am.* *15*(3):675-87.

Women who seek and submit to sexual abuse from a partner typically suffer from low self-esteem and a sense of ill-defined guilt. The abuse restores their psychic equilibrium, like taking well a deserved punishment, and permits the enjoyment of sex. This is an important obstacle to persuading the woman to leave the abuser.

Sexual sadism does occur in women, usually toward children, and most often toward boys. In this case, the sexual excitement is provoked and enhanced by hostility toward males. Hostile control of a male body is the exciting objective. The means might be carried out by beatings, enemas, forced feeding, or insertion of objects into the penis or anus. The single case of which I personally knew was a woman who was a pillar of the community. Her young son had no recourse; he would not have been believed. I met him as an adult and he told me his story. He was being treated for genital scar tissue at the time. The scarring was caused by his mother's forcing beads from a broken necklace up his penis. He had enraged her by breaking her necklace, and the forcing of the beads into his body became a repetitive ritual with her.

The dominatrix of adult masochistic men is seldom a sexual sadist, although to outward observation she may appear so. Since she is, in effect, marketing a service to men who require domination to achieve orgasm, an empathic identification with the man's goals is necessary for her continuing success. Hostility would not be helpful. Instead, the successful dominatrix obeys the man's fantasies in the service of his orgasm.

A complex form of disguised sexual sadism observed among celibate nuns is emotionally abusive behaviour toward the attractive love object, with the dual goals of both safely distancing the love object and continually churning up emotional tension centred on the love object. Thus, a Mother Superior might experience a diffuse excitement in assigning harsh punishments to her favourite subordinate while treating the other nuns with calm equanimity. The classroom-based nun might harass and criticise her favourite pupil, regularly bringing her to tears and then reconciling with her. This may occur among celibate men also, but I have no knowledge on this point.

The sexual offender in a pastoral setting

The support and comfort available from churches and church institutions often attract people with all sorts of difficulties. Religion can be used as a tool in a struggle against perceived sin. A malformed conscience may reason that prayer and service can substitute for relinquishment of harmful behaviours. Misinterpretation of particular theologies, e.g., predestination, may offer reassurance that it is unnecessary to change. Further, many perversions require a sexual object, a vulnerable target. Pastoral settings are full of children and relatively innocent, unwary adults, making easy prey for predators.

Since the recent onslaught of clerical sexual abuse cases, administrative responses to sexual acting out have been formally programmed in many denominations. Often there is a requirement for all paid and volunteer staff to attend periodic training to learn reporting requirements, as well as setting prudent standards for staff-parishioner interactions.

Realistically, the sexual pervert who acts out on church property is not likely to receive pastoral care at that particular facility. Nevertheless, he/she is due pastoral care, and provision must be made. How provision is made will be up to higher-level administrators in hierarchical denominations. In independent churches, arrangements are more difficult, but there is a responsibility to care for the pervert who is a church member. Those who actually break the law may receive pastoral care from a prison chaplain.

Pastoral approaches to the person who suffers from a perversion

Sexual perversion is a type of human brokenness. Pastoral workers are usually well-prepared to deal with this subject in general. The difficulty comes from feeling at ease specifically with sexual human failings. In my opinion, it is imperative that pastors, pastoral counsellors, spiritual directors, etc., all receive a thorough sex education during the preparation for their ministries. This will help to prevent a reaction of disgust rather than compassion toward the person seeking help. It is highly undesirable that any pastoral helper hear about a sexual practice for the first time from a person seeking help. In addition to knowing the sexual practice exists, the pastoral worker should also have some knowledge of the usual psychological configurations and needs of a person who uses that practice.

The person will seek help either because of being repelled by the self, or being proclaimed repulsive by someone else. A normal response to these experiences is despondency, often followed by a wish to change, to be different. Again, the pastoral worker is familiar with helping people change. But in this specific instance, it is important that both parties realise that it may not be possible for the pervert to achieve the most satisfying sexual release without the perversion. If the perversion depletes self-esteem, is illegal, or interferes with desired relationships, the pervert may need to sacrifice full sexual satisfaction for overall well-being. Sex researcher Vernon Quincy has told of a heterosexual paedophilic client whom he advised to pursue petite, girlish young women with small vaginas. He reported that the client established a fulfilling marriage this way. But such a 'way out' is not likely in most cases. It is easy to imagine how stressful the renunciation of full sexual satisfaction will be. Such a person, if religious, is in need of pastoral accompaniment in a long, difficult journey.

Pastoral workers who are prone to self-doubt may wonder if they are equipped to help in such complex situations. The advice of D.W. Winnicott,[31] a renowned British psychoanalyst, is relevant. In speaking to a group of pastors, he advised that you can help if the person

---

31. Masud Kahn's Introduction to Winnicott, D. W. (1986). *Holding and interpretation.* New York: Grove Press.

interests you. If you find the person boring, then the situation is beyond your skills and you should refer them to someone else. The psychological basis of this handy rule-of-thumb is that boredom in a counselling situation is ordinarily a defence against strong emotions, such as, in this case, revulsion. Of course, if the sense of revulsion is conscious, it is clear that a referral is necessary.

Perversion and the Church's role in sex education

For the devoutly religious parent, the pastor, an assisting 'youth pastor', or a nun-educator is the authoritative source of guidance about sex education of their children. This is a heavy responsibility. Too much information may shock, while too little information may fail to protect. At present, it is hardly controversial to give pre-adolescents the standard 'birds and bees' information about where babies come from. But in many religious traditions, there is still controversy about giving contraceptive information to unmarried youth. And it is safe to say that almost no religious tradition sufficiently educates children against assaults from perverts. This is particularly difficult in religious traditions that emphasise respectful submission to adult authority. Many children have submitted to incest or to sexual overtures from teachers or pastors because they felt they must obey adult authority figures without question.

In my opinion, there is no possibility of resolving this dilemma without encouraging the child in the formation of an autonomous conscience. That is, one must acknowledge the possibility of the child's judging the parent's (or other adult's) action as sinful and refusing to participate in it. The child should be taught that he/she is responsible before God for his/her own decisions, and obedience to an adult is not an acceptable excuse before God. At the same time we need to ensure that no child who does submit under this kind of pressure is left feeling that they will be judged by God for behaviour in which their freedom to choose was limited. One way of introducing such ideas might be to discuss appropriate responses to a more common adult failing, such as destructive gossip. The discussion might go as follows: How should a child respond? To point out the adult failing might offend the adult. The child can walk away, refuse to listen, and pray for the adult to see the error of his/her ways.

Another necessary religious teaching is the child's right and responsibility to protect his or her own body from intrusion by others. As an example, some denominations speak of the body as 'the temple of the Holy Spirit'. In this area, advocacy groups and government agencies have developed teaching materials suitable even for nursery schools. One such resource is a colouring book entitled 'Good Touch/Bad Touch', developed under contract to the [US] National Institute of Mental Health in the 1980s. This concept has been incorporated into many other teaching resources for children.[32]

Concrete advice about 'bad touch' is difficult to craft. However, a few examples may be sufficient for the child or adolescent to generalise from. Children can be taught to avoid people who try to touch them in 'sneaky' ways, e.g., they might be told to avoid sitting by men who sprawl their legs far apart, or to get up and move immediately if the man rubs them with his thighs. They should move away immediately from men who press the genital area against them in a crowded place. They should move away immediately from adults who take off clothing and expose their private parts. Children can be taught to dress quickly and leave quickly if they observe an adult focusing on them, e.g., at the swimming pool dressing room. A good piece of advice is to stand or sit as near as possible to the person in charge, e.g., the driver on a bus, the lifeguard at the swimming pool. These sorts of examples might be followed by the general advice to escape any situation that is uncomfortable or scary, and that it is OK to make a public scene. Then, we may hope that the child will be able to deal resourcefully with threatening situations for which he/she has no prior preparation.

---

32. For example, see: http://www.cfchildren.org/issues/abuse/touchsaferules/, retrieved April 15, 2009.

The pastor or confessor may also have to function as sex educator for adults at times. The vast majority of adults have had neither the opportunity nor the interest to study the huge variety of human sexual expression. Consequently, it can be upsetting when they, or someone close to them, display a 'deviant' sexual interest or impulse. Here are some real examples: the father who experiences a sudden erection when an adolescent daughter's breasts are accidentally exposed; the mother who suddenly experiences sexual excitement when spanking a child, the mother who observes herself wanting to touch her daughter's husband.

The development of human sexuality begins at birth, and beneath the normative sexual activities favoured by psychologically healthy adults are lurking all sorts of abandoned childhood excitements. We are all of us still voyeurs underneath our civilised veneer. Although we might consciously disclaim any interest in cruelty as a pathway to sexual satisfaction, such a connection still exists beneath the surface, particularly for those who were brutalised or exposed to views of brutality in childhood. And the incest prohibition is a matter of moral knowledge, not bodily impulse. A useful piece of advice for those startled by their own impulses is 'feelings don't count'. You can't always control what you feel, but you can control what you *do*.

What use civilised people make of their latent perverse tendencies is an interesting question. Most of us simply suppress them quickly. But some professions the average person would find repelling are highly satisfactory as civilised diversions of perverse tendencies. A particularly clear example is the diversion of sadism into the careers of butcher or surgeon.

Legal requirements

Pastoral workers must juggle advocacy for their clients with the needs of victims and the requirements of society in general. The situation is further complicated by possible conflicts between secular law and Church law. An example is the 'seal of confession' in the Roman Catholic Church, which forbids the confessor, under pain of excommunication, from reporting the penitent's confessions to a third party. If the penitent has broken the civil law, a potential conflict may exist between Church and state. If the pastoral worker also is licensed in a secular profession, such as counselling, more conflict is possible, between the ethical standards of that profession versus Church law and also civil law.

Each pastoral worker must be informed as to his/her duties and responsibilities under civil law and professional standards, as well as his/her Church's guidance about dealing with secular authorities. It is impossible to give more than this general advice, because civil law varies from place to place, and Church law varies from denomination to denomination. The important thing is to recognise one's duty to be informed, and to seek training as needed. It may be necessary to seek expert advice in a specific complicated situation.

Special burdens fall upon those church ministers who are responsible for the selection of candidates for a ministry. As noted above, church settings are attractive to perverts, and especially to paedophiles. The conscious motive for seeking a church career may be self-redemptive, but the unconscious motive may be easy access to victims.

Because of the impact of sex-abuse lawsuits against a number of churches in recent years, legal guidance has been developed on showing due diligence in trainee selection. Such guidance usually advises a psychological evaluation of an applicant that includes an in-depth exploration of the individual's sexual history.

Hierarchically organised religions are more likely to have formal systems for evaluating applicants. More informally organised churches, such as independent non-denominational churches, need to examine their procedures in light of current reality. At particular risk are those evangelical churches that recognise only one necessary qualification for ministry, i.e., a 'call' perceived interiorly by the applicant. Many of these groups are considering a more formal approach to selection of candidates, if for no other reason than to avoid future harmful publicity and even possible lawsuits.

NINE

Sexuality and ageing

Jocelyn Bryan

Introduction

In the developed world, Christian congregations often have a preponderance of retired members. This suggests that sexual issues in the later years should be an aspect of pastoral care. Sadly, the topic is rarely mentioned or acknowledged. There is an underlying assumption in the Church and society that sexuality is not an issue for the elderly. Contemporary attitudes towards old age and sex have had a negative impact on both sexual experiences in the later years and the attention this has received from those who offer pastoral care. This chapter will challenge these attitudes by exploring the current research and it will also seek to offer insights as to how we might help and support those who encounter sexual difficulties in old age.

It is important to be clear that for purposes of this chapter the definition of sexuality is a broad one. It encompasses much more than vaginal intercourse to orgasm. It includes myriad forms of bodily and mental eroticism, such as stroking a loved one or fantasising about intimate contact with the loved one. For example, a couple that are no longer physically able to achieve penetration or orgasm may nevertheless delight together in memories of their lovemaking in younger years. They may enjoy their usual foreplay while realising that they lack the strength to complete intercourse.

A simple anecdote illustrates the importance of bodily contact in the life of the elderly. For over 20 years I have exercised a preaching ministry in my local Methodist Circuit in County Durham in the north of England. I preach to predominantly elderly congregations. One Sunday I reflected on the text Mark 5:21–43, and explored the significance of touch in our lives, relating it to Jesus' healing touch. After the service an elderly woman shared with me how, since the death of her husband, one of the major losses in her life was the experience of being touched. She related that during the week her only experience of human touch was limited to the accidental, when someone brushed against her in a queue or a cashier touched her hand. Her family were living a long distance from her. She grieved for the hugs and kisses and the intimate language of physical affection that she had shared with her husband.

The language of physical affection changes throughout our lives. Passion and tenderness, and the physical acts that we use to express this, from sexual intercourse to a gentle touch on an arm, are shaped by the dynamics of our relationships but also by our psychological and physical state. In our later years when our bodies are likely to be less supple and illness is more frequent, the expression of physical affection must adapt to these changes.

Change and loss have been identified as important characteristics of this life stage. The changes that follow upon retirement include loss of work, change in routine, a reduction in income, adjustment of self-image and a possible loss in self-esteem. One can expect to experience the death of more friends and relatives in older life and many also experience a loss of social status and role. In contrast, for some elderly the later years can be a time of freedom, choice and fulfilment. The impact of negative and positive psychological states on sexual activity is well recognised in younger people. However, there is very little research exploring how these factors work out in the lives of the elderly. Sex and old age are disassociated from one another, not only in the majority of the psychological literature, but also in the way that society views this later phase of life. The stereotype of the 'asexual older person' pervades the research and has been a major factor contributing to the hiddenness of sexuality in our later years.

It is unsurprising that the Church's attitude has been in line with this stereotype, especially since the Church struggles to deal straightforwardly with sexual issues at any point in the lifespan. The literature on pastoral care for the elderly offers very little, if any, explicit acknowledgement that sexuality is an active issue in old age. Hence, it is rarely, if ever, referred to in pastoral conversations or the exercise of pastoral care in a Church setting.

This chapter seeks to dispel some of the myths surrounding older people and their sexuality and to increase our awareness of sexual issues that occur in this stage of life. There are many factors that contribute to the complexity of this task, not least the dearth of empirical data. At the outset it is important to recognise that like any other group of people in *society* the elderly are not homogenous. Older people have had a variety of experiences and hold a diversity of views about sexuality. Hence, we must be cautious about our assumptions and generalisations.

Our attitudes, and indeed our behaviours, in this fundamental area of our lives are shaped by social norms and the prevailing sexual culture. Sexuality is associated with youthfulness, beautiful bodies, health and vitality. In contrast, old age is linked with physical illness and decline, failing senses, greyness and loss. Gott[1] notes that even though representations of sexuality in later life might not necessarily reflect the experiences of older people, they have an influence on their self-perceptions and expectations. For elderly who take pleasure in their sexual experiences this has consequences for the way they view themselves, just as it does for those who experience sexual difficulties. It is not surprising that some elderly people will not confess to having sexual difficulties because they are 'not supposed to be doing it' and feel a sense of shame regarding both their desire and their performance difficulties. Those who enjoy sexual experiences may find this contributes to a sense of positive self-esteem or, on the

---

1. Gott, M. (2005). *Sexuality, sexual health and ageing.* Maidenhead: Open University Press, pp. 7–8.

other hand, fear that they are being seen as lecherous or depraved. The stereotype of the 'dirty old man' and other images that elicit disgust may well have a negative effect on the self-image and esteem of older people.

The perceived incompatibility of old age and sexual activity is not only a popular stereotype but also a common assumption of academic researchers. In the United Kingdom, the 1990–1991 National Survey of Sexual Attitudes and Lifestyles adopted an age cut-off of 59 years. In a 1998 follow-up study the oldest respondents were 44.[2] This is also the case with many studies in the United States. On the one hand, the perceived embarrassment and intrusion involved in asking older people about their sexual experiences has deterred researchers from investigating this aspect of their lives. On the other hand, many working in this area would concur with the view that research into the sexuality of older people is simply of low priority. Furthermore, as Gott[3] points out, the little work done conforms to the traditional approach of sexologists in counting specific sexual acts. The affectional and fantasy dimensions of sexual experience associated with intimacy have received little or no attention. However, it is precisely in these that older people are more likely to express their sexuality and find sexual satisfaction.

Many have concluded that this largely hidden part of the lives of older people remains so because it is not a major issue for them. It is thought that sex is not something which troubles the over-60s. However, from listening to the stories of older people it is evident that, just as with any other groups of people, the importance of sex varies amongst them. For some, sex is a valued aspect of their relationship, which expresses love for a partner, enriches and maintains their relationship, gives them pleasure and enhances their self-esteem.[4] For

---

2. Johnson, A. M., Mercer, C. H., Erens, B., Copas, A. J., McManus, S. and Wellings, K. et al. (2001). Sexual Behaviour in Britian: Partnerships, practices, and HIV risk behaviours, *The Lancet, 358(9296):* 1835-42.
3. Gott, M. (2005). *Sexuality, sexual health and ageing.* Maidenhead: Open University Press, p. 2.
4. Gott, M. (2005). *Sexuality, sexual health and ageing.* Maidenhead: Open University Press, p. 73.

others their sexual life has had to adapt dramatically because of loss of a partner, illness, loss of interest or some form of sexual dysfunction.

Sexuality

Sexuality is an elusive term. What is and is not part of our sexuality challenges any attempt at definition, especially in the light of writings of Foucault who suggests that it is the 'truth of our being'. Tiefer[5] makes this point more explicitly by posing the following questions regarding sexuality: how much of the body to include, which behaviours, thoughts and feelings can be categorised as sexual?

Sexuality is not a singular measurable phenomenon. There is a wide range of feelings, behaviours, attitudes and thought processes encompassed by the term. It is far more than the obvious physical responses involved. There are physical, social, emotional, spiritual and cognitive aspects to it.[6] However, a lot of research has reduced sexuality to be operational, and sexuality is measured in terms of sexual acts, usually acts of intercourse. Clearly this has implications for the relationship between sexuality and ageing. Whilst not engaging in full sexual intercourse, many elderly people would describe their sexuality as continuing to be positive and life-enriching. For this population it is important to be attentive to all five aspects of sexual expression: the physical, social, emotional, spiritual and cognitive.

Ageing

Until recently the study of ageing tended to focus on the social problems and failing health associated with old age. Of course it is important that we understand the effect of ageing on health and functioning but this has reinforced the perception that ageing is only about decline and dependency. Ageing and growing old are perceived as

5. Tiefer, L. (1995). *Sex is not a natural act.* Boulder, Co: Westview Press p. 20
6. Miracle, T., Miracle, A. & Baumeister, R. F. (2003). *Human sexuality: Meeting your basic needs,* New Jersey: Prentice Hall, p. xxiii.

unattractive prospects we will all have to face. Ageing is associated with chronic illness, dependency, physical unattractiveness, failing sensory perception (hearing, sight, smell, touch, taste) and declining psychological functioning (memory and thinking). The wealth of consumer products which promise to stop the wrinkles, thicken the hair, and maintain a youthful complexion, indicate that the physical effects of ageing are seen by many as things to be staved off for as long as possible. It seems too that people do not want to be classified by their age according to what they wear, the colour of their hair, even the music they listen to or the leisure activities they engage in. Rather there is a concerted attempt by many to break the stereotypical image of old age and the lifestyle associated with it. Slowing down or resisting the inevitable characterises Western society's attitude to ageing. For many, growing old is something which is feared.

On the other hand, while the majority view old age as a fixed stage in life, which most of us have to endure before death, it is evident that people are increasingly choosing the ways in which they will manage this stage of their lives, rather than being passive and allowing the process of ageing to happen to them. Added to this is the more general recognition that it is not age *per se* which determines our state of well-being, but a number of different factors including lifestyle, diet, living circumstances, socio-economic class, as well as age cohort.

Sexual experience and ageing

What do we know about the sex lives of older people? First it is important to state that many older people engage in sexual activities until their eighties or even nineties. A study in America[7] found that, in healthy residents in retirement homes in California, two thirds of men and almost a third of women over 80 had had recent sexual

---

7. Bretchneider, J., & McCoy, N. (1988). Sexual interest and behaviour in healthy 80 – 102-year-olds. *Archive of Sexual Behavior 17*: 109–29.

intercourse and a significant majority of men and women reported having had physical intimacy of some sort. A similar study[8] found that almost one third of those who responded had engaged in some sort of sexual activity during the past month and two thirds were satisfied with their current level of sexual activity. The limited studies available suggest quite clearly that many elderly people enjoy sexual activity and have a satisfying sex life. There is also evidence to suggest that those who had a keen sexual interest and activity in their younger years are likely to retain this in their later years.[9]

As already noted, the majority of studies have considered sexual intercourse as the main measure of sexual activity, but one study investigated a full range of sexual behaviours from touching to sexual intercourse and also examined levels of sexual satisfaction.[10] Questions about specific behaviours and preferences for those behaviours were asked in a questionnaire. The sample size was 166 and the average age 76 years. There were several significant findings from this study. First, it is clear that older adults want to remain sexually active. Touching and kissing are important features of this and the majority in the study had some experience of this in their present lives. They also found, unsurprisingly, that the age of the person and state of health affects both the type of sexual activity engaged in and the level of desire. As would be expected, younger, more healthy elders are more likely to want and engage in sexual intercourse. What is also interesting is that most of the elderly people reported that they wanted more sexual activity than they were currently experiencing, and that for many the main issue was not having a sexual partner.

These studies all suggest that the incompatibility of old age and sexual activity is nonsense. Older people both desire sexual activity and engage in it. Those who seek to help and support the elderly

8. Matthias, R. E., Lubben, J. E., Atchison, K. A., Schweitzer, S. O. (1997). Sexual activity and satisfaction among very old adults: Results from a community dwelling Medicare population survey. *Gerontologist 37:* 6-14.
9. Kaluger, G., Kaluger, M. F. (1979). *Human development: the span of life*, 2nd ed. St Louis, MO, USA: Mosby, pp. 441–442.
10. Ginsberg, T. B., Pomerantz, S. C., Kramer-Feeley, V. (2005). *Age and Ageing 34:* 475 – 480.

need to be sensitive to the importance of sexuality at this stage in life, and how the elderly cope when loss of a partner, chronic illness or a change in living circumstances, such as loss of privacy, make sexual activity increasingly difficult.

Both the elderly and their pastoral caregivers experience a natural diffidence when it comes to talking about sex. Married couples who have known each other for many years and engage in a mutually fulfilling sex life might still find it difficult to discuss sexual matters even with each other, much less an interviewer. For many well-intentioned helpers, talking to older people about sex is taboo, due to fear of causing offence. These inhibitions interfere with gaining a fuller understanding of the importance of sexual activity in the lives of older people, and its effect on them. However, Gott and Hinchliff[11] used both a questionnaire and semi-structured interviews to explore this. It is helpful to look at their findings in detail because they indicate some of the characteristics of the sexual experiences of older people as well as suggesting some important areas to engage with pastorally, especially when we consider them in combination with the other studies referred to earlier.[12]

The responses of those who attached little or no importance to sex indicate a number of important points. It seems that those who are without a partner, or are not having sex with their partner, often come to believe that they will not be sexually active again, and this was a major factor in dismissing sex. They reached this conclusion for a number of different reasons. Let's look at the following example:

Vera had been married to Bill for 47 years. They had two children and were happily married and enjoyed their sexual relationship. Bill died suddenly, and two years later, Vera attaches no importance to sex in her life. She misses the intimacy of the physical

11. Gott, M. & Hinchliff, S. (2003). How important is sex in later life? The views of older people. *Social Science and Medicine 56(8)*: 1617–28.
12. Gott, M. (2005). *Sexuality, sexual health and ageing.* Maidenhead: Open University Press, pp. 63–76.

relationship and is still coming to terms with 'the empty bed' she faces each night, but does not want anyone else.[13]

Sex can become unimportant for other reasons:

David was 80 when his wife died. Sex had been important to them both throughout their married life. But now as a widower experiencing various health problems, he recognises that he would be unable to engage in full intercourse and hence David no longer experiences any desire to engage in any sexual activity.

Couples whose sexual desire for each other has reduced over the years can also reach a point where sex ceases to be important to them. This may be a reflection of other chronic problems in their relationship, health issues, or loss of sexual confidence by one partner. It is clear that the nature of the previous relationship has an influence on the importance attached to sexual activity after a partner dies or leaves. When a marriage or relationship has been satisfying both sexually and emotionally it seems that there might be a fear of comparing all future relationships with it. It is also the case that during illness preceding the death of a partner and after the death, sexual interest is likely to decline, and a lower level of desire may be seen as helpful in adapting to the loss of sexual activity following bereavement.

Just as in other stages of the lifespan, when a sexual relationship is no longer satisfying to one or both partners, then a coping strategy of resignation and a reduced importance attached to the sexual aspect of the relationship can take place. Health issues can reduce interest and importance. Sometimes illness can lead to an acceptance of the physical constraints the body now imposes, and moderating expectations and desire in the light of this. Psychological conflict can have the same effect.

One researcher found that those who rated sex as only moderately important referred to health issues and a decline in interest. Yet a

13. Examples given are anecdotal and not from Gott's research.

number of those respondents mentioned the importance of being cuddled and experiencing some form of physical intimacy.[14] This is reflected in advice I got from an elderly friend before I married: 'Always share a bed with your husband, then no matter what, you can always cuddle each other.' For many elderly people who are unable to engage in sexual intercourse, being held, cuddled, stroked and kissed becomes for them the means by which they share and express the precious intimacy of their relationship.

Where sex was rated as very important, the closeness of the relationship and the sexual attraction for their partner was strong. For some of the 'young-old', sex in the later years can be experienced as better than in earlier years. This can be attributed to no longer having fears about pregnancy, knowing each other's bodies well, the benefits of the sexual skills acquired over the years, being more relaxed about sex generally, and having more leisure time to attend to one another sexually. Below are the important points to note from this research:

- Sex has some importance in old age
- Health issues and no longer having a partner are significant factors in less importance attached to sex
- The older we are, the less importance we are likely to attach to sex, but this is associated with health and the loss of partner, and not necessarily age *per se*
- The closeness and satisfaction of the relationship has an effect on the importance of sex in old age just as in other life stages.

Sexual problems

Passion and intimacy are highly valued in the lives of elderly people. Intimacy, understood as the warmth and affection that exists between two people, continues to be expressed physically in sexual activity, which may include passionate arousal and intercourse throughout

14. Gott, M. (2005). *Sexuality, sexual health and ageing*. Maidenhead: Open University Press, pp. 63–76.

old age. But the frequency and the importance attached to this are influenced by a number of factors that are more frequently salient at this particular phase of the lifespan. This presents us with the fresh challenge of seeking ways of helping elderly people both to enjoy and cope with this aspect of their lives when it is largely unspoken of and, as we have seen, shrouded in misconceptions.

Sexual problems can arise at any stage in life, but for the elderly some sexual problems are more likely to occur than others. Although some of these have been referred to previously, they will now be explored in more detail.

It is widely acknowledged that sexual interest and activity decline with increasing age. Masters and Johnson[15] describe how in later life more time is needed to engage in sexual activities. Arousal is delayed and more attention to genital stimulation is required. Men may be less rigid, and take longer to achieve an erection. Women often experience vaginal dryness. Inevitably some men may have a loss of sensation of ejaculation, and achieving orgasm in both men and women can take longer and may be achieved less frequently or not at all.

Erectile dysfunction has consistently been found to be most strongly associated with age. This is defined as a persistent inability to attain and/or maintain a penile erection sufficient to complete 'satisfactory' sexual intercourse (National Institute of Health, 1992). This leads to an increase in sexual dissatisfaction with age and a subsequent lowering of sexual desire.

There are a number of medical factors that may decrease sexual activity:[16]

- Medications can cause impotence or reduction of sexual desire
- Chronic illnesses associated with impotence e.g., diabetes mellitus
- Loss of erection or sexual sensation as a result of surgery, e.g., removal of prostate or uterus

15. Masters, W. & Johnson, V. (1966). *Human sexual response*. Boston: Little Brown.
16. Kessel, B. (2001). Sexuality in the older person. *Age and Ageing 30* :121-124.

- Depression
- Physical barriers to genital contact, e.g., catheters or pessories
- Change of body image e.g., after mastectomy, or limb amputation
- Poor mobility due to arthritis or stroke.

The treatment of sexual problems in most cases does not differ according to age. Kessel[17] offers the following advice:

- Women with vaginal dryness: lubricants, oestrogen creams and pessaries and hormone replacement therapy can help
- Urinary incontinence can sometimes be managed by intermittent catheterisation or pelvic floor exercises
- Men with impotence can take drug treatments such as Viagra. If men have an indwelling catheter they can still have intercourse using a condom or suprapubic catheter.

Social factors are also important. For many older people the loss of or lack of a partner is the main reason they no longer engage in sexual activity. Those who live in residential or nursing homes find the lack of privacy inhibits their sex lives. We must also acknowledge the effect of current social attitudes make some ashamed to engage in sexual activity, even though they experience desire.

Gender differences

Men and women differ in their attitudes towards sexuality and sexual activities in later life. There is still the popular notion that men and women are fundamentally different in their sexual natures. Male sexuality is active and powerful and has to be released or expressed, whereas female sexuality is commonly understood as receptive and nurturing. For many older women their sexual activity is still controlled by their male partner. Men instigate sexual activity and also are the main influence in determining whether a woman sees herself as attractive or not.

17. Kessel, B. (2001). Sexuality in the older person. *Age and Ageing 30* :121-124.

The ageing process is considered to make the body less attractive. Especially for women, who generally invest more time and money than men in attending to their appearance, growing old can undermine their sexual confidence and self-esteem. For many women, how often their partner is able to perform intercourse, or the availability of a partner at all, rather than their own lack of desire, is the major deterrent to active sexuality. These women would welcome more sex if it were possible.

For other older women sex is more seen as something they have a lifelong duty to provide for their husbands. Ageing is seen as reducing the need to satisfy their husbands, partly because of the anticipated reduction in male sex drive.

When older people consider the option of re-marriage there is a clear gender difference. Widows often do not want to re-marry because they don't want sex any longer, but widowers wish to re-marry because of their desire to resume a sexual relationship.

One further significant difference to note is that the nature of sexual problems differs between men and women. Men more often report physical problems and women's sexual problems tend to be psychological or social. Problems with arousal, inability to reach orgasm, and lack of enjoyment or sexual satisfaction in women are often associated with problems in the relationship. It is always difficult to discern whether it is the relationship difficulties that lead to the sexual problems or vice versa, but women seeking help usually identify the relationship as their main concern.[18]

Remarriage and new intimate relationships

The 2001 UK Census shows that divorce and re-marriage are increasing amongst the over-50s. For older people, being in an intimate relationship increases the likelihood of being sexually active. Generally older individuals are less likely to engage in casual sex, and view sex

18. Gott, M. (2005). *Sexuality, sexual health and ageing*. Maidenhead: Open University Press, pp.78–82.

within marriage as important in enriching married life. However, alongside this there is evidence that *some* older people are now engaging in intimate but non-cohabiting relationships.[19] Dating agencies for the elderly are growing in numbers and organisations such as Older but Bolder, www.lovingunlimited.com and Senior Dating *SeniorFriendFinder.com* help to encourage new intimate relationships following divorce or bereavement. This suggests that in this later stage of life, many people are embarking on new sexual relationships. The increase in lifespan through better health care and improved lifestyle means that in some cases couples who marry in their 60s or 70s, after a previous marriage has ended, can look forward to perhaps 20 years in this new relationship.

For many a new sexual relationship is exciting and fulfilling. However, previous sexual relationships undoubtedly cast a shadow on expectations, and comparisons may lead to difficulties as well as new positive experiences. This is the case for both older and younger individuals.

> Jane had been married for 29 years. She and her husband Tom had not considered sex to be important, especially during the last 5 years of their marriage. Tom was always gentle sexually. In the last years of their marriage they rarely had intercourse, and although Jane was anxious that Tom might be having an affair, she was frightened to talk about their sex life with him. After their divorce, Jane met Phil and sex took on a new importance to her. Compared with Tom, Phil made her feel special because he openly expressed the physical attraction he felt for her. Their lovemaking was passionate in a way she had never experienced with Tom. Phil gave her a new confidence in her looks and her body at the age of 64.[20]

19. Borrell, K., Ghazazfarreon Karlsson, S. (2003). Reconceptualising intimacy and ageing: Living apart together. In S. Arber, K. Davidson, K. J. Ginn. (Eds.). *Gender and ageing: Changing roles and relationships.* Buckingham: Open University Press, pp. 47–62.
20. Anecdotal evidence.

Gay and lesbian relationships

The growing social acceptance and legal recognition of gay relation-ships has given lesbian and gay elderly couples the confidence to be more open about their sexuality, and encouraged those who had repressed their sexuality to 'come out' and form gay partner-ships. This is recognised by organisations such as Age Concern (www.AgeConcern.org.uk) which now offers advice for gay couples on its website. The rising rates of HIV/AIDs amongst people over 50 years of age also points to the need to acknowledge the sexual activity of this age group.[21]

For many years gay and lesbian older people have remained largely ignored or invisible. They have endured a lifetime of discrimination and social rejection. For the majority during their younger years their expressions of love, intimacy and sexual desire were labelled as deviant, illegal and even a sickness. To 'come out' at that stage in their lives might well have resulted in loss of a job and in many cases family, as well as social, ostracism and a life of poverty. However, in more recent times this group of men and women have witnessed or been part of the transformation that has taken place in attitudes and gay rights.

The limited research in this area paints a mixed picture. For many gay older people the lifetime of stress and stigma has left them vulnerable to depression, suicide, addictions and substance abuse.[22] When social and health-care professionals are insensitive to needs of older gays and lesbians this often causes them to avoid seeking the help and support they need. In contrast others have commented on the strength of the social support networks amongst older gays and

21. Health Protection Agency (HIV/STI Department, Communicable Disease Surveillance Centre) & the Scottish Centre for Infection and Environmental Health, Table 6.1: UK AIDS cases and HIV infection for individuals aged 50 and over at diagnosis by sex: to end of December 2003, 2004.
22. Brotman, S., Ryan, B., & Cormier, R. (2003). The health and social service needs of gay and lesbian elders and their families in Canada. *Gerontologist, 43*:192–202.

lesbians, suggesting that they have lively social lives with plenty of mutual support.[23]

The apparently youthful world of the contemporary gay scene means that for many older people to be 'gay and grey', or to be an old lesbian leaves them feeling marginalised and misunderstood. Their stories are ones of both vulnerability and resilience. They have lived most of their lives with little support or recognition within church or society, and their stories of pain and prejudice have never been heard.

Sex and health

Another growing influence in the way society responds generally to sexuality is the notion that intercourse and orgasms have a significant part to play in being healthy and being contented. Sex is regarded as good for you with many health benefits. Satisfying sex is understood to contribute positively to well-being. This has resulted in an increase in the medicalisation of sexual problems. Doctors now prescribe drugs such as female sex hormones and Viagra to improve sexual performance and increase pleasure. For many men over 50, erectile dysfunction drugs have enabled them to maintain erections and perform intercourse. However, a study in New Zealand suggests that Viagra has created a culture where not engaging in sexual intercourse is now considered to be abnormal.[24] Yet, recent research suggests that older people continue to be anxious about the appropriateness of being seen as sexual at their age. This presents a major barrier to seeking help and advice.[25] Some elderly may not wish to seek medical treatment for sexual performance, and the prevailing culture may make them uncomfortable with their choice.

23. Pugh, S. (2002). The forgotten: A community without a generation – older lesbians and gay men. In D. Richardson, & S. Seidman,. (Ed.). *Handbook of lesbian and gay studies.* London: Sage, pp. 161– 81.
24. Potts, A., Gavey, N., Grace, V., & Vares, T. (2003). The downside of Viagra: Women's experiences and concerns about Viagra use by men. *Social Health Illn. 25*: 697-717, quoted in Gott, M. (2006). Sexual Health and the new ageing. *Age and Ageing 35* : 106-107.
25. Gott, M. Hinchliff, S., & Galena, E. (2003). Barriers to seeking treatment for sexual problems in primary care: a qualitative study with older people. *Fam. Pract. 20* : 690-695.

The elderly tend to use many more medicines on a regular basis, some of which have sexual side effects. Although many more people are aware of sexual side effects from medicines, there are barriers to successful consultation. Much of the literature and training for health-care professionals tends to focus on younger people. Gott[26] notes that the myth of the asexual older person still underpins the attitudes and approaches of most health-care professionals. Hence, in situations where sexual-health issues should have been raised, they are not mentioned: e.g., when a particular medication has erectile dysfunction as a possible side effect.

> Bob had been suffering with high blood pressure for several months. His GP prescribed him a drug with a possible side effect of reduced penile rigidity, but made no reference to this in their consultation. Up to this point Bob and his wife Joan had enjoyed regular intercourse. After three weeks Bob returned to his GP to have his blood pressure checked. It had improved and the GP prescribed the drug for a course of three months. Bob was too embarrassed to mention the effect that the drug had on his sex life. In fact at the age of 75 years he could not be sure it was the drug which was causing his reduced penile rigidity because he had been half expecting this would occur at some point in his later years. When the GP asked if he felt better in himself, he responded 'yes'. Both Joan and Bob found this very difficult to cope with. It took until the following three-month consultation for Bob to find the courage to discuss this with his GP.[27]

For those who have health issues making intercourse impossible, the physician's encouragement of appropriate sexual touching and love play can support them in continuing to experience sexual satisfaction and intimacy. For those who are adjusting to a loss of a partner, dating

26. Gott, M. (2005). *Sexuality, sexual health and ageing*. Maidenhead: Open University Press, pp. 128–147.
27. Anecdotal example.

agencies and even use of prostitutes are sometimes proposed. Recent literature[28] advises that health professionals should suggest masturbation to relieve anxiety and promote well-being. Those of us who minister in a church context may have ethical concerns about some of these developments, however it would be naïve to pretend that these issues do not exist, or to pretend that older people will not seek outlets for their sexual needs which may not be in accordance with the teachings and views of their particular Church. It is important for pastoral helpers to be prepared to respond empathically and appropriately if their advice is sought in these matters.

HIV and STDs

There is a tendency to assume that older people will not contract a Sexually Transmitted Disease (STD), but the evidence available suggests this is not the case, and it is something which may well increase in the future. The stigma associated with contracting a STD coupled with the embarrassment of sexual activity with old age conflates the difficulties in dealing with this issue for elderly patients. A study in America showed that the stigma attached to contracting HIV was experienced as very difficult and isolating in older persons.[29] Another American study[30] highlights that HIV infection is likely to be under-reported amongst older individuals, suggesting again that the stigma and taboo of sexuality and ageing might be preventing older people from seeking necessary treatment.

Sexual abuse of the elderly

Abuse of older people, like many other forms of abuse, has been hidden from society. Elder abuse is defined as:

---

28. Griffiths, E. (1988). No Sex Please, we're over 60. *Nursing Times 84:* 34–35.
29. Nichols, J. E., Speer, D. C. & Watson, B. J. et al. (2002). *Aging with HIV, Psychological, social and health issues.* San Diego: Academic Press.
30. Zingmond, D. S., Wenger, N. S., et al. (2002). Circumstances at HIV diagnosis and progression of disease in older HIV–infected Americans. *American Journal of Public Health, 91(7):* 1117–20.

A single or repeated act or lack of appropriate action occurring within any relationship where there is an expectation of trust, which causes harm or distress to an older person.[31]

A BBC report in 1999[32] highlighted the issue and claimed that 5% of some 5 million older people have been abused. It described the sexual abuse of elderly people as one of society's latest taboos. The impact of such abuse can be devastating, and may include considerable emotional distress, loss of self-esteem and self-confidence, depression and attempts at suicide or self-harm, as well as a negative effect on physical health. There are many barriers which prevent older people from reporting sexual abuse or seeking help. These include not only the taboo which is associated with sexuality and ageing, but also fear concerning the consequences of reporting the abuse. The fear associated with the abuse and the trauma experienced as part of the abuse may fuel other fears which might include embarrassment, shame, fear of being blamed in some way, and being alienated from friends and family. The growing awareness of this issue particularly, in health care and social services, will hopefully mean that professionals are more alert to this abuse and will seek to address it and care for the victims in sensitive ways. Hopefully this will result in limiting the impact of such appalling trauma in the lives of some older people.

Sexuality and institutional care

For those older people who live in institutional care the lack of privacy and attitudes of the staff can prevent any sexual activity or sexual expression. For many their only physical experience of touch by another human being is when they are washed and dressed by an attendant. For those whose partners visit or share the institutional accommodation the opportunities for sexual activity are few – if any – and again it seems that there is little recognition that sexuality is of

31. http://www.elderabuse.org.uk/What%20is%20abuse/what_is_abuse%20define.htm accessed 16 June 2009.
32. BBC News Report, 21 October 1999.

any significance to this group. It has been suggested[33] that sexuality in institutional care is a taboo. Although some double beds are provided for married couples, in residential care the majority of beds are single ones. Furthermore, there is little provision for privacy or the availability of a double bed when one partner is in residential care and the other partner visits. There is always a need to balance the concern for personal safety and the need for privacy in these institutions. However, it is encouraging to see that those who advocate the provision of appropriate opportunities for sexual expression in nursing and residential care have already achieved the introduction of training packages to address this issue.

> Anne suffered from a stroke 6 months ago and is paralysed down her left side. Raymond, her husband, is 5 years older than Anne and suffers from arthritis and angina. They had hoped that Anne could return home, but her care needs were such that Raymond could not cope. Anne is in residential care and Ray visits her daily. Within the past 6 months they have had to adjust to their sexual activity being reduced from occasional sexual intercourse and daily closeness to a kiss and a hug in the care home.[34]

Often staffs in homes do not acknowledge this issue and are embarrassed, confused, prejudiced and negative about older people's sexuality.[35] It seems that the process of education and changing attitudes along with recognition of the importance of touch is beginning to open up this issue, but there is a considerable way to go. Cases of abuse by staff reported in the press have undoubtedly increased the amount of caution surrounding provision of privacy to residents.

33. Kessel, B. (2001). Sexuality in the older person. *Age and Ageing 30*:121-124. Borell, K. and Karlsson, S. (2002) 'Reconceptualising intimacy and ageing: living apart together,' paper presented at the *Reconceptualising Gender and Ageing* conference at the University of Surrey, Guildford, 25-27 June.
34. Anecdotal evidence.
35. Ehrenfeld, M., Tabak, N., Bronner, G. & Bergman, R. (1997). Ethical dilemmas concerning sexuality of elderly patients suffering from dementia. *Int J. Nurs. Pract. 3*:255–9.

Some concluding reflections

Touch, tenderness, passion and intimacy

A lot of both secular and pastoral writing about sexuality has focused on sexual intercourse in adolescence and adulthood. However, as stated earlier, sexuality involves more than sexual intercourse. It includes touching, caressing, physical closeness and warmth, feelings of love and affection expressed verbally or otherwise, fantasy and masturbation. For many their sexuality is more focused on unique expressions of intimacy they share with the partner, rather than the mechanics of intercourse. For example, Greer[36] reports the interesting case of a rape victim who submitted to vaginal penetration without a struggle, but began to resist angrily when the rapist tried to suck her breasts, protesting, 'Only my husband can do that!'

The word 'intimacy' is derived from the Latin word '*intimus*', meaning 'inmost'. We can think of what this means both psychologically and physically in the area of sexual intimacy. Intimate couples have a sense of each other's presence, whether they are with each other or not. This is characterised by a number of things. The first is the knowledge each has of the other. Intimacy involves sharing experiences, emotions, thoughts and dreams. When couples are intimate, the one responds sympathetically to the other, with acceptance, and together they build up mutual understanding. Secondly, intimate couples care for one another and protect each other, as well as sharing emotionally with each other, so that when one is sad or disappointed, the other feels upset on the partner's behalf. Finally, intimacy is expressed in affectionate words and actions, from love letters and gifts to kissing and having sex. Gentle teasing and play are one aspect of intimacy. Although frequency of penetration and intercourse may decline with the ageing process, there is no reason to suspect that intimacy and the expression of affection, passion or sexual satisfaction, declines.

36. Greer, J. M. Personal communication. July 20th, 2009.

The two following examples illustrate how the expression of love and passion can adapt to the limitations sometimes imposed by the ageing process.[37]

> Richard is 75 years old and sexual intercourse has become more difficult due to penile erectile difficulties. He reflects how the desire to show your love to your partner is still there, and cuddling can be as special as sex. As he gets older Richard considers that physical intimacy is just as important, but he has found other ways of achieving it.

> Julia reflects that even at the age of 78 years her desire and need for sexual activity is strong. The physical closeness, warmth and holding which she shares with her husband are very important to her, especially as they do not make love as frequently as they used to. It shows that they still love and care for each other in a special way.

For many older people who love each other, the tender and passionate affection they feel for each other continues to find its expression in physical closeness and sexual activity even if this does not culminate in sexual intercourse. Couples who feel connected, close and bonded to each other continue to share their intimacy in a number of different ways, adapting to the changes which they face in the later years. For many, touch is the primary means by which this happens.

Touch is important because it allows us to communicate feelings and emotions beyond the limits of our words. When two people hold hands they become aware not only of the bond this makes between them but also of how the other is feeling, whatever it might be, whether they are contented, anxious, angry or embarrassed. When couples are in a state of conflict or are unhappy with each other then they usually avoid touching one another. Touch is revelatory

---

37. Anecdotal, but supported by Gott, M. (2005). *Sexuality, sexual health and ageing.* Maidenhead: Open University Press, pp. 70–1.

and can be deeply healing. It forms the language of intimacy and desire.[38] For older people the language of touch assumes a greater significance in their intimate relationship, which means that the death of a partner is a significant loss which many feel unable to share, even with their children or others close to them.

The term 'personal sexual communion' has been used to describe a presence between a couple which is primarily psychological but most complete, intense and satisfying when it is both physical and psychological.[39] It is a passionate preoccupation with the other which involves thinking and caring about the other in such a way that they have a sense of each other's presence even when they are physically apart. It is not uncommon for elderly couples to experience this.

Rousseau and Gallagher[40] emphasise the importance of touch in deepening intimacy. Sexual touching is often neglected by couples and is a very powerful way of communicating intimacy. This is sexual but is not necessarily genital (although it can be). It has been developed in a process Rousseau and Gallagher call 'Skin-to-Skin Prime Time' (SSPT). They stress how important nakedness is, especially holding each other in complete nakedness. Further, they suggest that 'prolonged non-genital touching may be more powerful, more effective in making spouses present to each other than intercourse'. Often in acts of cuddling and caressing, couples are aware of each other and communicate with each other in ways which are subtle, warm and tender, thus enhancing their sense of sexual communion. As health problems prevent couples from sexual intercourse in later life, the significance of sexual touching as an expression of affection, passion and tenderness, takes on greater significance. This can be especially

---

38. See Richards, A. (2007). *Sense making faith: Body, spirit, journey.* London: Churches Together in Britain and Ireland.
39. Rousseau, M. & Gallagher, C. (1991). *Sex is holy.* Shaftesbury: Element Books Ltd, p. 86.
40. Ibid pp. 84 – 98, for full description of process.

important in situations when one partner has to offer a great deal of physical care for the other partner. For example:

> George's wife was severely disabled with arthritis from her early 60s. For over 15 years George washed her every day and brushed her hair. He lifted her into the bath and into their bed. Their intimacy and tenderness were expressed in the daily physical tasks of gentle washing and making her hair look tidy. These tasks were the means by which they shared their sexuality and maintained a sense of intimacy.

For older people, the language of touch often becomes more subtle and nuanced as couples learn to express tenderness and passion in new and often surprising ways. In many couples, their continuing intimacy is a source of deep contentment and support as they face the changes and challenges the later years present. It leads to a profound sense of contentment and sexual communion, as mentioned above.

Reclaiming and celebrating intimacy

The creation story suggests from the very beginning that God's relationship with human beings is one characterised by intimacy. Genesis 2:7 describes how the Lord God formed man from the dust of the earth and breathed into his nostrils the breath of life. In Eve's creation, Genesis 2:21–2, God took one of Adam's ribs and closed up its place with flesh. The rib that the Lord God had taken from the man he made into woman. Both of these acts of creation suggest a powerful sense of intimacy, in which God kisses Adam into life, Eve and Adam are created from one flesh, and later become one flesh. The relationship between touch, intimacy and creation is also expressed in the imagery found in Psalm 139:

> You created my inmost self,
> Knit me together in my mother's womb. *Psalm 139:11*[41]

41. *The New Jerusalem Bible.* (1985). Darton, Longman and Todd.

Another example is when Isaiah (Isaiah 64:8) refers to God as the potter and human beings as the clay. God is the one who shapes us, breathes life into us, embraces us, and holds us in his arms.

Jesus' life was infused with intimacy from the moment his mother Mary held him in her arms to the time when Mary anointed him with precious ointment and wiped his feet with her hair. Throughout his ministry Jesus physically touched people, either in greeting, healing, or, on Maundy Thursday, through washing and drying the apostles' feet. He gave and received love and prayed for intimacy between his followers and God:

> That they may all be one. As you are in me and I am in you, may they also be in us, so that the world may believe it was you who sent me. *John 17:21*[42]

Jesus then prays that we will live in loving intimacy with each other and that this will enable the rest of the world to understand who he is and his relationship with God.

As human beings we are often fearful of intimacy because it requires us to be vulnerable to another by sharing our thoughts, feelings, and, in the case of sexual intimacy, our bodies. This avoidance of becoming too close to others can often be rooted in a sense of unworthiness, shame, or a feeling of being unlovable. Older people who have long-lasting loving relationships model for a fresh understanding of what relationship means and the blessings that stem from it. Intimacy can only develop with the realisation that we are lovable and are loved. Love enables us to trust and open ourselves up to others and to God. It draws us together so that we have a sense of communion with each other. We carry each other in our hearts and minds. It requires an openness and generosity to both oneself and to another. For many people, sexual activity – touching or intercourse – is a way of expressing love and intimacy which helps maintain

---

42. *Holy Bible NRSV Anglicized Edition* (1995). OUP.

their loving relationship as well as sharing in mutual pleasure with their partners. Relational intimacy is not just about intercourse or our bodies; it nourishes our souls and our spirits. It is expressed in warmth and touch, in acts of loving care. Elaine Storkey notes that:

> If in our lives there is no sexual union with another, perhaps because we have accepted celibacy or gone through bereavement, illness or divorce, we are no less fully human or fully sexual. Deeply satisfying human intimacy, whether in marriage or outside, is in the end not dependent on copulation but on faithful sharing of our hearts and lives with those whom we love and a longing for their well-being and peace.[43]

Older people who have sustained their loving relationships over many years, whether this involves sexual intercourse or not, have something deeply significant to celebrate. They also offer us an important insight into an enriched understanding of intimacy.

43. Storkey, E. (1995). *The search for intimacy.* Hodder & Stoughton, p. 207.

PART III

Contemporary issues in human sexuality

TEN

Victims and perpetrators in the parish: The struggle to accept terrible truths

Tony Robinson, Andrew Peden,
Gerard Fieldhouse-Byrne and
Gerardine Taylor-Robinson

Introduction

Churches are perhaps the only institutions in our society that attempt to 'hold' both victim and perpetrator within a community context. Child sexual abuse is such an abhorrent crime that it tends to fracture communities, moving people into opposing camps. A faith community believes, however, that, by being present to both victim and perpetrator, grace may somehow enter in. Churches in the past have been guilty of denying the reality of abuse, by not listening to victims and simply moving priests or pastors to another location. It is our belief that a Church wishing to be faithful to its call to be a source of healing to all, needs to respond to victims, perpetrators and parish communities. In this chapter we explore the implications of abuse in a parish for all concerned, and discuss ways that a church can respond with justice and compassion to all three groups.

Sexual abuse is never a positive event in a child's life. However, because of a range of factors that can generally be captured around the notion of 'resilience', it is estimated that about 11% of victims report that they are relatively unharmed by the abuse and are able to get on with their lives and put the event behind them. On the other hand, Professor Bill Marshall[1] likens child sexual abuse to Russian roulette. He explains that you could have two identical twins abused

1. William L. Marshall, Ph.D., Professor Emeritus, Departments of Psychology and Psychiatry, Queen's University Kingston, Ontario, Canada.

in the same way by the same person and one may emerge relatively unharmed whereas for the other, his or her life may be for ever changed and there may be no significant recovery.

The reality we are confronted with is that children suffer abuse and cruelty mostly at the hands of their various caregivers. In the United Kingdom one child dies each week, murdered or neglected by their primary caregiver. We would all hope that our homes, our schools and our parishes are the safest places for our children. When they are, the best happens for a child.

There is a saying 'be careful what you wish for', and there is a psycho-dynamic notion that a wish holds, in equal part, a fear. Our wish for the pristine beauty of good love and care for our children, is balanced by the truth that most harm comes to children by loved-ones and caregivers and that, looking on as bystanders, we often can't tell the difference between the two types of care.

Professor Gill Straker was a young woman in South Africa during the apartheid struggle. Her experience led her to develop the victim/perpetrator/bystander triad:

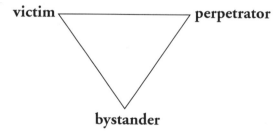

Straker suggests that within each of us, there is an internal (intrapsychic) triad where, as we war within ourselves, we are at different times in a position of victim, destructive perpetrator or bystander in this battle. When there is pathology (ill health) within a social system and where power and/or cruelty are present (e.g., in the apartheid regime or dysfunctional families or organisations), then the victim/perpetrator/bystander triad existing inside each of us is more likely to be acted out rather than remain an intrapsychic dynamic.

Statistically, children will be victims of abuse in every parish, in every school, and in most neighbourhoods. Within our parishes, many adults will carry the burden of a history of an unwanted sexual advance. As bystanders, we usually cope with this dichotomy (that children are most loved and most at risk in their homes, schools, parishes) by demonising the bad caregiver. However, it is only when we are able to hold our profound ambivalence that we can be deliberate in moving from the position of bystanders (denying, minimising or panicking) to becoming change agents in effectively safeguarding children in our parishes.

In this chapter we will begin by exploring the issue of the definition of sexual abuse. We will then provide a description of different kinds of abusers, and move on to a description of victims. There is a section on what signs to look for if sexual abuse is suspected, and guidelines about how to respond if a child decides to reveal their abuse. The central section of the chapter will focus on the parish as victim, with a discussion of the impact on a parish community, and advice regarding how to respond to this situation in a way that helps a parish community to deal with the issue honestly and openly, grieve losses, and move on to a healthier future. The chapter ends with a discussion of the importance of responding to the victims and the issue of the treatment of offenders.

Sexual abuse: The problem of definition

The very definition of what constitutes sexual abuse is often unclear and complex, reflecting diverse cultural, social and legal differences. The National Society for the Prevention of Cruelty to Children (NSPCC) offers the following definition: 'Sexual abuse occurs when an adult exploits their power, authority or position and uses a child sexually to gratify their own needs'.[2] The NSPCC has developed a Child Protection Awareness Programme which seeks to teach educators,

---

2. NSPCC. (2007). *Keeping children safe: Module one, Understanding the basics.* p. 2. Warwickshire: Educare.

priests, seminarians and other care workers about important effects of child abuse (sexual, physical, emotional) and neglect. It is important to bear in mind that sexual abuse involves both touching and non-touching behaviours. Showing pornography to a victim, exposing genitals, watching a victim undress or use the bathroom, or initiating an unwelcome conversation about sexual development or adult sexual topics, also constitute abuse, as they invade the private world of the victim.

Historically, there has been considerable evolution in thinking about sexual abuse and there are marked cross-cultural differences even today. For example, in the United Kingdom it was only in 1991 that rape within marriage was made a criminal offence. Male homosexuality was not decriminalised in the United Kingdom until 1967, at which time the age of consent was set at 21 years (now reduced to 16 years). Lesbianism has never been illegal in the United Kingdom; until relatively recently it was not recognised in law to exist. Indeed, the failure to recognise lesbianism for many years meant that child sexual abuse allegations against women were simply dismissed by many as impossible, and even today are still viewed with incredulity by some professionals.

In both research and practice, the term sexual abuse is broad in scope, and tends to include abusive acts ranging from any form of unwanted non-contact sexual suggestion or advance, to indecent exposure, to forcible rape. Research is also clouded by the fact that different societies have different ages for the ability to give sexual consent. Although the average age across the world for consensual sexual intercourse is around 16 years, there are wide variations between countries, ranging from the age of 12 in the Philippines to the age of 20 in Tunisia. In the United Kingdom the age of consent was raised in 1885 from 13 to 16 in order to protect children from prostitution.

Even within a single country there may be federal and regional variations. For example, in the US the federal age of consent is 16, but in Texas young people may marry at 14 with parental and judicial consent. In many Middle-Eastern countries, any form of sexual contact outside of marriage is deemed illegal, regardless of age. These variations create moral and legal ambiguities, and are often cited by child sex abusers as a justification for their behaviour: i.e. the rationalisation and minimisation of their abuse on the basis that sex with children and young people is more traditionally accepted in other countries around the world. Moral ambiguity is particularly marked in 'borderline' cases, where the age of the abuse victim falls close to the age of consent, the victim declares that the relationship was consensual, and the purported abuser is only a few years older than the purported victim.

Prevalence

Including such examples in the abuse statistics alongside more extreme examples makes it very difficult to establish true prevalence rates and to share a common language of what constitutes abuse. Indeed, because of these difficulties, it is simply impossible to calculate the true prevalence of sexual abuse. This is, in part, because of the problem of definition, but also because of the probable under-reporting of abuse by victims, and because criminal conviction is extremely difficult to secure. Despite these difficulties, it is widely accepted that the prevalence of childhood sexual abuse is high, with general population studies suggesting anywhere up to 20–30% of women and 10% of men worldwide were victims of sexual abuse in their childhood, with much higher reported prevalence rates in certain subgroups, particularly for female drug addicts, psychiatric patients and those in prison.

Sex offenders

A sex offender is someone who engages in sexual behaviours that are considered illegal. This simple definition is important to clarify, as laws regarding age of consent vary in different countries and may be different for boys and girls. Researchers, as a rule of thumb, will use age 16 as a cut-off point, with the perpetrator being at least five years older than the victim. Many legal jurisdictions also recognise that adults of limited intelligence or life experience, or subjected to force or trickery, cannot give consent.

The most surprising thing about sex offenders is how ordinary they are. Men and women from all social classes and walks of life are found among sex offenders. While offenders are mostly men, there is a growing awareness of women who also abuse. Most child molesters tend to be family members or people in positions of responsibility or trust (priests, teachers, probation officers, clergy). Abusers of adults, unless they use force, are also ordinarily in positions of authority or trust. Force or aggression are seldom used by either group. They often use what are known as 'cognitive distortions' to justify their behaviour. Cognitive distortions are distorted ways of thinking that help to excuse, minimise, rationalise or deny abusive behaviour. The following examples will help to illustrate this kind of distorted thinking:

1. I was showing affection and was misunderstood.
2. The victim came on to me. I didn't initiate this.
3. He/she never told me to stop.
4. I was not given any sex education myself and I did not want this child to grow up ignorant like me.
5. She knows I did this because I love her.

These 'cognitions' (ways of thinking) enable the offenders to commit the offence without experiencing the anxiety, shame or guilt that would normally accompany these actions or help the adult resist an inappropriate erotic impulse.

Child molesters

There are a number of issues to bear in mind when trying to understand child molesters:

1. Is the person attracted to boys, girls or both?
2. What age range is the molester attracted to/involved with?
3. Has violence or aggression been a part of the abusive behaviour?
4. Does the abuser also have an interest in adult sexual relations or is s/he only interested in children?
5. Is the abuse restricted to family members or is the focus on children who are not related to the abuser?

It is possible to consider three broad types of child molesters: paedophiles, familial offenders, and ephebophiles. It is important to note, however, that no system of categorisation adequately captures the extraordinary range of deviant sexual interests and behaviours. This categorisation is broadly useful but also limited.

Paedophilia[3]

Mental-health professionals make use of the *Diagnostic and Statistical Manual of Mental Disorders*, currently in its fourth edition, which is commonly known as DSM-IV. This provides criteria for a range of psychiatric disorders, and is often a useful starting point for discussion of a mental-health problem. The criteria for paedophilia are as follows:

A. Over at least six months, recurrent, intense sexually arousing fantasies, sexual urges, or behaviours involving sexual activity with a prepubescent child or children (generally 13 years or younger).
B. The fantasies, sexual urges, or behaviours cause clinically significant distress or impairment in social, occupational, or other areas of functioning.

While these criteria are useful they are not without difficulties when it comes to providing a clinical diagnosis. It is also evident that the word paedophile is often used incorrectly in the media, as it is frequently used to describe any sexual behaviour involving an under-age child

---

3. The following sections are based on the chapter on Child sexual abuse by one of our editors, Brendan Geary, see, Geary, B. (2008). Child sexual abuse. In B. Geary & J. Bryan (Eds.), *The Christian handbook of abuse, addiction and difficult behaviour* (pp. 22 – 29). Suffolk: Kevin Mayhew.

or adolescent. The word paedophilia comes from the Greek words for 'child' and 'love'. In some ways it is a misnomer, as the behaviour we are describing is not about love, but about abuse, power, and control. Professor Bill Marshall prefers to use the term 'child molester', which focuses on the behaviour and does not depend on strict adherence to the criteria described above. The term 'paedophile' will continue to be used for the moment in order to distinguish this group (who are sexually interested in prepubescent children to whom they are not related) from other groups.

Some paedophiles are attracted only to children. These are called 'exclusive type'. Others are attracted to adult men or women as well as children. These are known as 'non-exclusive type'. The key feature for a diagnosis of paedophilia is an attraction to children who do not have the visible characteristics related to puberty (breast buds, pubic hair, etc.). This most often involves children who are twelve years of age and younger. A second important distinction is whether or not the abuser is fixated or regressed. The fixated child abuser is attracted to only children in a specific age range. The regressed child abuser has regressed (retreated) from a normal interest in adult partners. The word 'regressed' in this context suggests that the person is capable of functioning emotionally and sexually at his or her biological age, e.g., a thirty-year-old, but is *at this time* relating emotionally as a child or adolescent. Those who are fixated can have very high numbers of victims, often more than one hundred. Those who are regressed tend to have fewer victims, as their sexual acting out often originates in more or less transient experiences of stress, and responds to coincidental situations, whereas the fixated offender will often seek out and create opportunities, purposefully grooming their victims over a period of time.

Familial sexual abuse

A useful (but not absolutely clear) distinction can be made between those who abuse children outside their own families and those who abuse family members. Within this category it is important to distinguish between blood relatives (parents, siblings, grandparents, uncles and aunts) and relatives by marriage (stepfamily, uncles and aunts by marriage). While the word incest is commonly used, 'familial offenders' is a more accurate descriptor. In situations where fathers abuse their own daughters, it has been suggested that this may be as a result of the mother/wife losing interest in sexual relations with her husband, who then turns to his adolescent daughter to have his sexual needs met. The daughter may remind the father of his wife when she was younger. In other situations, the perpetrator may be experiencing stress, and the combination of loneliness, attractiveness of the victim, power imbalance in the relationship and poor self-esteem may combine and lead to sexual abuse. It is not uncommon for alcohol to be a contributory factor as it leads to losing the inhibitions that normally put constraints on behaviour that they know to be wrong or could lead to personal embarrassment. It should be absolutely clear that offering an explanation for familial abuse does not mean it is being condoned. Men who experience difficulties in their sexual relationships with their partners have no right to abuse or impose on their daughters or stepdaughters in order to attempt to have their own needs met.

Ephebophiles

The word 'ephebophile' comes from the two Greek words, 'Ephebos', meaning adolescent, and 'philia' meaning love. This is not a diagnostic term, but is used to describe adults who become sexually involved with adolescents in the 14–18 age range. As with paedophiles, they fall into two categories, those who are fixated and those who are regressed. It is not uncommon to hear stories of high-school teachers (male and female) who become sexually involved with adolescents whom they are teaching. This was recently made the subject of a film, *Notes on a Scandal,* starring Judi Dench and Cate Blanchett, who plays the role of an art teacher who becomes involved in a sexual relationship with one of her (male) pupils.[4] Whether or not the victim is under the age of consent, the behaviour constitutes a breach of trust and abuse because there is an imbalance of power in the relationship.

Problems can also occur due to relationships formed over the Internet. Without excusing them, some men who have found themselves involved in relationships with adolescents might never have done so before the availability of Internet chat rooms. Young people expose themselves to exploitation and deception in these Internet relationships.

Our society makes a judgement about the ability of young people to make an emotionally mature decision regarding their readiness for sexual relations. Many adolescents start having sex at a relatively young age. However there is a difference between sexual experimentation with an adolescent of the same age, and becoming involved with a person who is more than five years older. Sexual involvement of an adult with an adolescent is considered sexual abuse, as our society concludes that young people under 16 (or whatever the local age of consent is) still need the protection of the law.

Recognising abuse and its effects

The signs of abuse are often subtle or indirect. The problem is even greater because the gross or overt signs are seldom unique: behavioural and emotional problems are the outward manifestation of a multitude of possible causes.

The impact of abuse upon children or young persons, and how they might manifest that abuse through disturbances in behaviour, will in large part be determined developmentally: that is, it will differ depending upon the age of the child concerned.

---

4. Morris, R., Fox, R., & Rubin, S., (Producers), & Eyre, R. (Director). (2007). *Notes on a scandal* [Motion picture]. United States: 20th Century Fox Home Entertainment.

Sexual abuse seldom occurs in isolation; it is more likely to occur in situations where emotional and physical abuse also take place, where there are general disturbances of parent-child relationships, or where there is parental psychopathology (mental-health problems). Therefore, disentangling the effects of the sexual abuse from the impact of neglect and other forms of abuse is often very difficult.

With those caveats in mind, it is important to briefly consider some aspects of child development. Very young children will not have the language skills in which to express their experiences: they will not be able to tell in words that they have been abused. Even slightly older children may not have the vocabulary or the emotional sophistication to enable them to clearly state what has happened, perhaps even to know and understand that they have been abused. Older children may be more aware and better able to say what has happened to them, but threat, secrecy, shame and fear may prevent then from openly reporting it. Children are more likely to signal their abuse through actions rather than words. Fear of or avoidance of the abuser is one signal. Aberrant sexual behaviour is another common signal of sexual abuse. For example, explicit erotic gestures, either oral or genital, are extremely rare in children who have not been abused, but fairly common in sexually abused children. Children between the ages of 1 and 4 are typically comfortable with their own bodies and nudity. However, they seldom act out sexual acts. Although they may be comfortable touching the breasts of women, they seldom touch the genitals of others; they are very unlikely to attempt to engage in sexual intercourse. Although they may kiss adults, so-called French kissing is rare; and in their play they are unlikely to use dolls or stuffed toys to engage in simulated sexual acts. They normally do not include genitals in their drawings of human figures.

Children aged 4–6 are typically less comfortable with nudity. Although they may engage in sexual exploration, they seldom touch others' genitals, seldom draw genitalia, and tend not to act out sexual behaviours in their play.

Children aged 7 years and older will be more likely to have the language to say what has happened to them, but because of issues of fear, shame and secrecy, it is important to be attuned to clues in their behaviour which might indicate internal distress or a disturbance of relationships. However, it is important to remember to look at the child's social context and not any one isolated behaviour – a cluster of worrying behaviours is more indicative of possible abuse. (See chapter 2 for a useful checklist.)

Older children and teenagers may show a preoccupation with sexual matters, early pregnancy, venereal disease, sexual identity issues, promiscuity, identification with the abuser (i.e., they form an attachment with the person who is abusing them – see chapter 2), perplexingly distorted relationships, anxiety, depression, post-traumatic stress disorder, self-harming behaviour, suicidal attempts, loss of concentration, character change, withdrawal, poor school work, peer relationship problems, aggression, delinquency – a gamut of problems. If the situation is impossible to disentangle, removal of the adolescent to a safer environment such as a boarding school or specialised nursing home may result in marked improvement.

In adulthood, the effects of childhood sexual abuse may be far reaching and include difficulties of sexual adjustment in marriage, promiscuity, parenting deficits (the so-called cycle of abuse), and varied personality and mental-health problems. Worse adult outcomes are thought to occur when the exploitation is within the family, when the abuse is genital, and when force is used, with father–daughter consummated incest often considered to be the most traumatic. There are special difficulties when the victim lacks a developmental grasp of the sex act, and instead perceives penetration as an attack intended to rip his/her body apart.

What parish workers and parishioners should do when they think abuse has occurred

First and foremost, procure your local area child-protection guidelines, your society or agency child-protection guidelines, and the names and contact numbers of any appointed representatives and resources. If you work or volunteer in a parish or parish school, update yourself with these on a regular basis. Make sure that you attend regular training events on child abuse and protection and keep yourself up-to-date with current thinking and practice.

If you have any reason to suspect that abuse may have occurred, in the first instance seek advice, support and guidance: don't keep it to yourself, don't ignore it, and don't hope that someone else will act upon it instead of you. Equally, don't go it alone and try to investigate and deal with the situation on your own. That is not your responsibility; in many cases well-intended but clumsy intervention has contaminated the legal process of investigation and made prosecution of the offender impossible.

In situations where a victim discloses abuse to you – even if you are uncertain that they are actually naming abuse – the most important thing is simply to listen. Don't ask them questions. Children over 5 years of age say what they think adults want to hear, they may be quite concrete in their thinking, they will have difficulty in understanding the motives of others, and often they cannot hold simultaneously opposing views of others as good and bad. It is often impossible to undo the effects of leading questions at the early stages of disclosure, and many a criminal prosecution has failed because of this. Remember, dedicated police and social services child-protection workers receive highly specialised training in interviewing victims and gathering evidence.

Disclosure is thought to be less likely if the abuser is a close family member. Some will only be able to tell someone outside of the family

— a neighbour, teacher, or a priest. Even then, their telling may be subtle or indirect. It is not typical in such circumstances for a victim to blurt out a full disclosure; they are more likely to test the water with a little piece of information in order to see if they are believed and to test the reaction of the person to whom they disclose. Consequently, your reaction to any attempt at disclosure is vitally important; a negative reaction may shut down further disclosure or produce a retraction. Express genuine concern but try not to show disbelief, or emotions of anger or disgust. Try not to be embarrassed yourself, and avoid transmitting any sense of shame or moral outrage you may be feeling; the abused are often expert readers of non-verbal communications: their very lives may depend upon it.

Particularly with children, don't try to 'save' the child; you cannot do that. If a child has made a disclosure, discuss the boundaries of confidentiality and follow your child-protection guidelines. Do not promise to keep the information a secret; this can put you in an impossible position as it is your duty to inform appropriate statutory bodies about what you have heard. You should not make a promise you will break, as this would further undermine the child's ability to trust adults. If you are uncertain that a disclosure has been made but you have some worries, seek advice and support from appropriate sources.

Under no circumstances should you confront the alleged or suspected abuser of either a child or an adult. As soon as possible after disclosure, make detailed, accurate notes, if possible quoting the victim's words accurately. Date and sign these notes and keep them in a safe place so that they can be provided to legal authorities if required.

Look after yourself: speak with your line manager or supervisor in order to debrief and process your feelings, which are likely to be complex and powerful. Do not keep your thoughts and feelings entirely to yourself; sexual abuse thrives in darkness and secrecy, and its reach extends beyond its immediate victims.

Faith issues

If the perpetrator is connected to the victim's church, there are added dynamics such as a potential loss of faith. The victim might ask, for example, 'How could my God let something like this happen to me at the hands of God's representative?' There may have been moral distortions by the perpetrator to seduce the victim or to keep secret the abuse (for example, telling a victim that the abuse is a way of sharing God's love), or to shift blame and sin away from self and onto the victim (by blaming the victim for precipitating the situation). The victim may not feel safe attending church.

Recovery is both a spiritual and a psychological task, engaging a triad of pastor, victim, and therapist. A pastor is not trained to provide psychological treatment or healing to the victim. The therapist may be inept at the spiritual. Of the three, the therapist, the pastor and the victim, clearly the most important person in the recovery triad is the victim. The other two need to be careful to not over-step their boundaries (as sexual abuse is a fundamental disregard for boundaries of the other). The therapist will assist the victim's recovery task by helping the victim minimise the disruption of this past (or present) trauma in their lives and maximise their pre-abuse competencies. The pastor, along with the social supports of the parish community, needs to allow the victim to speak from intuition. Intuition is a deep internal sense of what needs to be done next. Abuse often decimates intuition, as 'what came next' was shocking and incomprehensible. The Spirit broods in our intuitions and grace will be given at the right time in the right amount and if others can quietly and unintrusively 'hold' the recovering victim.

Forgiveness

An effective and sensitive pastor will realise that some of the usual spiritual tools-of-the-trade will not necessarily apply. Bishop Robinson, a victim of sexual abuse who later had to deal with cases of sexual abuse in the diocese of Sydney, Australia, in his capacity as Auxiliary Bishop, wrote the following thoughts on what victims had taught him about forgiveness:

> Forgiveness after a truly serious offence takes its own time and cannot be hurried. Even when a person begins to gain some control of the process, forgiveness has little to do with how one 'feels' about the offender and more to do with two conscious decisions. The first is a conscious decision not to let the offence rule one's life but to do one's best to leave it behind and get on with life. The second is the conscious decision to want not just punishment for the offender, but also change and growth.

A victim must never be given the message that they *should* be able to forgive. Pastor, victim and perpetrator need to wait on God's timing. Often a perpetrator will wish for forgiveness to feel better, whereas a more true grace is for a perpetrator to understand that they never have the right to ask or expect forgiveness and that they would want the victim to be as angry for as long as need be. Sometimes, pastor or parish will also want forgiveness to come quickly so the community can settle back into a comfortable space and put this situation behind them. Sadly, this movement, while seeming to promote peace, is actually a retreat into denial where abuse could occur again. The healing process of the victim within a parish community, even when unknown to the parish, is nevertheless a beautiful grace for the parish.

Parishes as secondary victims

When a clergyperson's sexual abuse comes to light in a parish, using Gill Straker's triad model, the parishioners, in the first instance, become victims. For many parishioners, the revealed secret means that what was, what they thought and had hoped in, can never be the same again. They may also wonder how it came to be that they did not see what was happening in close proximity to them and thus were also bystanders of the abuse.

The parish may need to experience a mourning process. A trusted pastor sexually abusing those in his care can be like a terminal illness for the faith life of the parish. When the pastor abuses, they lose a total sense about whom they need to be for the victim and who their victim is and what he or she needs. For the bystander parishioners, the terrible news of a pastor's sexual abuse evokes potent feelings of betrayal and violation. In this process of grieving, of helping the parish to speak out at each stage of collective grief, something new can emerge in the parish.

Diocesan or Church leadership needs to offer ongoing support to the replacement pastor and to the parish. The other clergy and staff who have lived and worked with the abuser also suffer feelings of betrayal, and sometimes also irrational feelings of shame.

There have been some devastating mistakes made in the service of protecting the good name of the perpetrator. Some replacement pastors have not been fully or fairly briefed, and left on their own to navigate a minefield of mistrust and anger. Often, Church leaders are themselves anxious and do not know how best to respond. They might enter the parish in an attempt to 'control the scandal'. Most parishes are made up of intelligent adults with a mature spirituality and faith life. When Church leaders enter into the parish process in an anxious, controlling, non-transparent fashion, they inadvertently create a parallel to the abuse, where they 'forget who the other is' (mature adult parishioners with rich experiences of life) and (unintentionally) take on a dominating and patronising role, to 'get what they want'.

Church leaders such as bishops are often themselves secondary victims, experiencing similar grief processes as the parish community. Caught in a bystander position, they need support and advice so that when they attempt to be present to the victim, the perpetrator and the parish, they are not carrying unprocessed bystander material that could see them act in a way that perpetuates some of the abuse dynamics of the first offence. For example, a common dynamic in bystanders is that they feel guilty. This drives them to deny or minimise the consequences of the events that they have failed to intervene to prevent.

Parish response to sexual abuse

Responding to the needs of a parish after the pastor's sexual abuse comes to light demands a joint response from various stakeholders in this wounded community. There is no quick-fix solution and the road ahead will be difficult, but healing is possible. It may seem a cliché but it is 'Truth' that will ultimately enable this broken community to journey on towards healing and new life. Facing the horror and destruction of the pastor's sexual abuse is the only life-giving way to respond in justice to the victim and the parish community, which is trying to come to terms with this devastating news.

The first principle of response in the parish has to be caring for the victim of sexual abuse. Knowing that the victim's needs are being responded to appropriately enables the parish community to also receive support and encouragement for the onward journey. Justice and healing demand this first principle, and without it the parish community will remain stuck in the destruction that sexual abuse brings.

In many ways, responding to the parish community is intimately linked to the victim, but there are also significant departures and needs that a corporate body inevitably demands. There are also fundamental Christian building blocks that should be part of the journey and ongoing response. Experience suggests that there are key areas of response that enable the parish to journey from death to life.

Appropriate communication

In the context of sexual abuse appropriate communication within the parish can be complex, but it is essential. The authorities responsible for the parish, with their various advisory bodies and legal advisors, need to give the parish community information about the abuse that is factual and accurate. The parish community should not be left to find out information which has a direct effect on them from the newspapers or other media. Concern for the victim, any police or court proceedings, legal implications and an awareness of the community will affect what information can be shared, and the timing of that sharing. That being said, the parish community needs to have ongoing updates, particularly in the early stages of the response to the abuse. As time moves on and the specific information in regard to the case reduces, this need changes. If the parish is given information in an appropriate manner along the journey, then there will be a natural progression from the acute phase of response, through to various stages of moving on with parish life. We can see that accurate and sensitive communication, when used appropriately, is a tool for healing and parish re-building.

The healing journey takes time

Given the complexity of issues affecting the parish community, diocesan authorities and the new pastor should be aware that the journey to healing is a process needing time and a clear commitment to proactively address this negative experience. The diocese, their advisors and the new pastor should all be clear that the parish community will best move on in the process if they take the lead. There will always be members of the community who journey at a slower pace, and there will be others who, for various reasons, will stay stuck in the trauma of abuse. Experience shows, however, that there is a desire in the majority of parishioners to move on with parish life. This does not mean that they want to ignore the abuse, but that they do not want to be defined by this trauma. The professionals involved in advising the diocese and the new pastor will offer ideas around the cycle of recovery from trauma, and what has been learned from this collective human experience. This information is helpful when we consider the next point, which is the development of a clear pastoral plan for the parish community.

The journey of healing for the parish is, in reality, a process which will be ongoing for many years. However the initial two-year period seems to be a key time for proactive and sensitive parochial planning. In every case planned responses and professional input need to be fleshed out in the particular context of the parish. Each parish will have specific issues which have been affected or caused by the abuse and these areas of concern need to be taken into account. In broad terms the first six months after the court hearing and final decision on the abuse is a crucial time as this period will set the tone for the process of healing. The parish members will need to have the truth of the abuse presented and handled in a way that also enables them to see that, as a family of faith, both justice and mercy have been done. There will be significant difficulties and personal and public searching, but new life is possible.

The leadership of the new pastor is crucial here, as is the visible support of the bishop and other diocesan authorities. The parish is not just healing from within but also as part of the diocese and wider community. It is important to maintain the liturgical cycle of the parish, with a balanced approach to seeking healing and grace at this time for the victim, the perpetrator and the parishioners. For the new pastor this early period is the most difficult personally and relationally as the parish begins to trust a priest again. The need to support the new pastor cannot be underestimated and there should be a balance of autonomy and the existing support structures that every minister needs.

After this first period the community moves into a sense of 'what now?' and the gentle but clear guidance of the new pastor and parish council or pastoral team is important. Parishioners will be looking for truths, about who they are as a family of faith and members of the wider community, to be reinforced and supported, and this can be accomplished by doing the things that 'normal parish life' demand. Confidence will gradually build and the parishioners will take ownership of their renewed identity and their ongoing process of healing.

Clear pastoral vision

As already discussed, it is important for the parish community to have some normality and rhythm of prayer life that is not hijacked by the abuse. The parish community will need the diocese and new pastor to take the lead in re-igniting parish life, as otherwise the community will stagnate. This re-igniting of parish life means fostering a balance between maintaining the familiar whilst being open to change and the new. In the early weeks and months the focus of this pastoral plan will be to allow people to reflect and take on board what has happened, to pray about it, and discuss it openly within the parish context. Time for the new pastor to meet and listen to the community is critical, as mutual respect and knowledge grow. Being able to talk about the abuse with other parishioners after church services, or over coffee during parish hospitality time, is an important way for parishioners to process what has happened. This also enables them to support each other through the various emotional responses that each person may have at different stages of the journey. Re-invigorating the ordinary things of parish life, whilst hard at this juncture in time, allows the healing process to have life. As stated above, appropriate ongoing communication in the parish newsletter is also helpful and this should always be balanced with information on other parish news and events.

The reality of this abuse in the parish context will bring to the surface previous difficult issues around trauma or abuse for some parishioners. It is also a real possibility that there will be others in the parish community who are experiencing emotional, physical or sexual abuse and the parish situation will compound this. The diocese has a duty of care for these people and appropriate professional support should be made available confidentially for them. Putting information on how to access this support in the parish newsletter and on notice-boards offers a clear but gentle way for parishioners to see that their needs have been thought about. It will also be helpful for the new pastor to remind people about this service in various ways. Although few people may use it, many will appreciate that the diocese has provided this support, which is a visible sign of care. As stated earlier, it is important that the parish knows what the diocese is doing to support the victim and the immediate family; this needs to be done with sensitivity for victim privacy, but it is necessary that the wider parish community have this information.

Whilst it is important to maintain the familiar rhythm of parish life and liturgy, it is also important that this proactive pastoral plan should include visible signs of change so that the journey of moving on and healing can be seen in a concrete practical way. It may seem contrived to make this suggestion, but it is our experience that fostering healthy emotional growth and change for the community is greatly helped by visible signs. It is hard to stay stuck in the past when events around you speak of change and new developments. On a pastoral level this could include new parish initiatives around hospitality and spending time together. For example, in one parish, having tea and coffee after each church service and every parish event enabled people to spend time together without making an issue of asking for it. The parish went on to establish a hospitality team to plan a social calendar for the parish. Changing the garden surrounding the church enabled a group of parishioners to gather together after the service each Saturday morning. Over time they planned and then gradually changed the appearance of the church grounds. In the 1960s, a New Orleans parish that lost a 12-year-old girl to rape-murder by another parishioner decided to consecrate a small garden in her memory, featuring a statue of St Maria Goretti, another teen victim of rape-murder. These symbolic acts mirror other more fundamental changes in the community. In cases of sexual abuse by a liturgical presider, changing the decoration of the church and liturgical vestments will also help people to disassociate from the abuser; the subliminal connections like this cannot be underestimated when exploring emotional attachments and bringing about change and healing. If the new presider wears the same parish vestments as the abuser then the connections made at various levels will be very destructive for the healing process. One pastor learned this the hard way. On his first weekday service, the reader who came in to the sacristy to speak to him froze when she saw him; he was wearing the familiar vestment, and that meant she did not see the new pastor but the man who used to wear it.

Sexual abuse often brings the good name of the parish into the mud in the newspapers and other media. It will also be important for the parish community to have a wider community project so that they can actively be involved in restoring their good name in the wider community. Working collaboratively with other faith communities on projects of interest can also help foster life and a renewed sense of the community changing.

As the parish community journeys toward healing it will be important, on the diocesan level, for the authorities to make a real psychological and financial investment in bringing new life to the parish community. These visible signs of change bring home the truth that the parish community is not held captive by the abusive situation; it is part of the parish history but is not their only identity. In real terms these suggestions enable the parishioners to become proactive in writing a new parish history that is life-giving.

The priest (pastor) that follows

In many respects the diocese has no control over the personal and communal journey to healing that the parish community needs to make. One area of control that the diocese has, which is crucial for parish healing, is the appointment of the priest who follows. The new pastor will have oversight and control of the healing process and ongoing healthy life of the parish. It is a priority for the diocese that they appoint a person who is a good pastor, secure in his/her sense of self as a person and as a priest or minister, and someone who is a woman/man of the Church who is able, through the ups and downs of the healing journey, to love the parish. They do not need to be a therapist or have all the answers but rather be open to working collaboratively with the parish, diocese and other support structures, yet have the confidence to be the pastor of this flock entrusted to them.

It is a daunting task to be asked to be the 'priest that follows'. There are many reasons why priests or ministers may say no to such an appointment, usually resulting from their own stories, limitations or personal needs. The person who accepts the appointment will experience powerful realities of who they are called to be as a priest. On many levels and in various ways their life as pastor of this community will challenge them in every aspect of their being, but it will equally affirm and reveal to them most powerfully Christ working in and through human weakness and sinfulness to bring new life. The reality of holding the pain and trauma of sexual abuse with the real sense of the goodness and blessedness of the body of Christ in the parish community is profound. In order to live this ministry in a healthy way the new pastor will need to be attentive to their own support structures for there will be times when they are shaken to the core.

The documents on ministerial and priestly life of our various Churches provide a blueprint for the important structures that will enable the new pastor to fulfil their pastoral responsibilities, whilst maintaining a healthy awareness of self, gifts and limitations, and overall balance.

Having a personal prayer life is the building block on which everything else rests; without this foundation the new pastor will never be able to make sense of their ministry, nor re-dress the distortions that the abuse brings to priesthood, church and life. This may sound pious, but many years of research conducted with priests faltering in and leaving ministry highlights a fundamental lack of prayer as the primary cause. The priest that follows must be a person of prayer – not 'perfect', but sure of their relationship with God and their personal faith journey in priesthood or ministry.

With this foundation the other support structures make perfect sense; regular spiritual direction, friendships that are challenging and life-giving, diocesan supportive mentoring/supervision, days off and time away, relationships with other clergy and diocesan involvement, spiritual retreats and, if necessary, an openness to seek supportive counselling. There is much here that the Church asks of every pastor but it is absolutely essential for the 'priest that follows', in a context of sexual abuse, in order to have a healthy life and ministry. The priest is responsible for availing of these supports, but it remains the obligation of the diocese to facilitate and monitor the well-being of the pastor that follows until the community is in a good state of recovery, and the particular challenges brought by the sexual abuse give way to a restored vibrant parish life.

Responding to victims

The problem of the sexual abuse of children in church and society is not new. There is a long history of denial of the existence of abuse and minimisation of its consequences. Thankfully, at the present time – certainly in the English-speaking world – there has been a heightened awareness of this issue. In the past victims were often revictimised through being bullied or shamed into silence, blamed for the abuse or punished for their behaviour – if they dared to report it. Within the Churches this was often the result of an in-appropriate respect and trust in clergy, and adults and systems that were overly deferential, and refused to investigate properly or to intervene effectively.

In recent years governments, statutory authorities and Churches have articulated the 'Paramountcy principle', which, as the word suggests, makes it clear that the needs of the victim are paramount in any discussion of this topic. Where abuse has occurred the priority has to be care of the victim. Most dioceses and churches now have protocols that give clear directions for reporting, investigating and, if necessary, the removal of the accused if there is any danger to a victim or possible future victims. Clearly parishes and dioceses should make use of counselling support for the child and his or her family. Steps should also be taken to avoid revictimising the victim.

There is often a tension between care for the victim, the appropriate protection of the legal rights of the accused (innocent before proven guilty) and the rights of a diocese, religious order or church. This has led to churches in the past behaving in ways that were – or perceived as – cold, uncaring or defensive. A balance has to be struck between pastoral care for victims, protecting the rights of the accused (as well as providing support for them) and due care for the reputation of a diocese, church or religious order, and those members who are innocent of any abusive behaviour.

Responding to the perpetrators

Recent reflection on the Catholic Church's response to the crisis of sexual abuse indicates that the first intervention was often to provide treatment for the perpetrator. Treatment can be effective, and is the best strategy in reducing the likelihood of future abuse. However, a critique of a 'treatment first' approach is that in providing treatment for priests and religious, there may not have been appropriate attention paid to the crime committed, and a disinclination to allow the perpetrator to face the judicial consequences of their actions against their victims.

We propose an approach to treatment that never excludes the judicial consequences of the crime. However, treatment will be based more on a dignified commitment of the perpetrators to living the rest of their lives with 'no more victims', and with daily direct or indirect amends to the victims, whatever those amends may be. If a perpetrator can see the victim as another person who has been harmed by their actions (whereas in the moment of abuse, they lost the other's sense of personhood and treated the child as an object for sexual gratification) and now places the victim's daily needs as superior to their own, then they have made a fundamental shift, and from this new position, it is hoped that it would be almost impossible for them to offend again.

The 'Good Lives Model' of Professor Tony Ward and his colleagues provides a strong argument for this approach to treatment since previous, more-confrontational models exacerbated perpetrators' shame. The 'Good Lives Model' emerged out of critical reflection on the standard approaches to sex-offender therapy, and some of the assumptions and punitive attitudes that underlay it.[5] There is a saying that shamed people do shameful things. Previously, in our efforts to break through an offender's denial system, we tended to echo the dehumanising chants of society about sex offenders being 'monsters and rock-spiders'. If sex offenders were monsters, then they could and would do monstrous things. If, however, sex offenders were able to commit to a value system where they lived a 'good life' for the rest of their lives, then that good life would hopefully be guided by values that kept children safe, and the offenders free from future criminal acts. An approach to treatment that attempts to enhance the quality of life of offenders, and that supports alternative goals and values that offer satisfying rewards, is more likely to be effective if offenders feel good about themselves and feel that their life is getting better. This suggests that therapists, without losing

5. http://www.howardleague.co.nz/newsletters/40.pdf

sight of the primary goal of keeping children safe, should intentionally aim to enhance offenders' feelings of safety, esteem and well-being. Those who have studied the efficacy of treatment programmes for sex offenders have concluded that programmes based on cognitive-behavioural principles, using group therapy as the primary means of therapy, have made a difference to rates of re-offending. For this reason – if for no other – treatment makes sense. Our societies have not chosen to imprison sex offenders for life. It is therefore in the best interests of society to provide treatment that minimises the possibility of re-offending.

There is a danger in some fundamental faiths where some perpetrators use the notion of conversion (the old self slain in the Lord) as a reason not to undergo treatment (since my old self and the perpetrator are dead now) nor put in place the usual safeguards that are needed for the rest of their lives. However, if the conversion is authentic then the new person will co-operate with treatment.

Recovering the place of perpetrators within faith communities

Philip Zimbardo, who recently reviewed the cruel actions of individuals in Abu Graib prison in Iraq,[6] writes of abuse within a system with the provocative saying, 'there aren't any bad apples – just bad barrels'. We need to look respectfully but with clear eyes at structures within our churches to identify any possible 'bad barrel' dynamics that may facilitate an unhealthy system. Karl Rahner, a Catholic theologian, describes a faith community as existing between 'the mystery of the already and the not-yet'; how it already is living true to its charism and, at the same time, 'not-yet' practising what it preaches. He sees this as a true reflection of what it means to be human. As we are imperfect and incomplete, grace can enter into the 'not-yet'. Using this

6. Zimbardo, P. (2007). *The Lucifer effect.* New York: Random House.

understanding of what it means to be a discerning faith community, dioceses or parishes can then identify what elements of their current living shut out the grace of sexual continence. Some may be attitudes to women, issues of inclusion and exclusion, use of power and authority etc. These are some examples of potentially 'pro-offending attitudes'.

This challenge is just as vital for society in general. While society, for example, allows advertising that sexualises minors, this 'bad barrel' can be used by a perpetrator as a justification of his aberrant behaviour. Some faith communities that preach rigid standards of perfection in sexuality, without the balance of grace and reconciliation, run the risk of what our co-editor, Professor Joanne Marie Greer, has pointed out 'When people try to live like angels, they often act like demons', or the wisdom of the 12-step movement that 'the Perfect is the enemy of the Good'. Each member of a faith community and each member of society is called to live a good life and while we hope for a perfect life in heaven, we will do less harm on earth by simply striving to be good people open to transforming grace in our lives.

In the moment of offending, the perpetrator often has no sense of the victim as a person. The perpetrator probably has faulty intimate relationships. Many perpetrators will have faulty sexual moral development. Often the sense of sexual sin has been in terms of misuse of one's own body or sexuality rather than the gravity of the sin being determined by the harm to the other. For some celibate pastors, an immature celibacy may make them vulnerable to a sexual transgression, though we do not see a mature and spiritually based celibacy in any way connected to the crisis of sexual abuse in the Catholic Church. The past custom of entry into ministry training at age 14, before sexual identity has been consolidated, has been a deterrent to the development of a mature celibacy in some priests. Perpetrators typically exhibit faulty morality, immature sexuality, an egocentric sexual ethic, inadequate spiritual and social supports, and pre-existing faulty attachment styles. In contrast, a graced and mature celibacy is fundamentally disposed to the safeguarding of children and vulnerable adults.

There is life after prison, and churches face the challenge of how to allow perpetrators to attend church services but, at the same time, safeguard the children in the parish. The Circles of Support and Accountability movement was established by a Mennonite church in Canada. Mennonite churches practise the notion of restorative justice. This movement involves surrounding a perpetrator with a group of ordinary members of a congregation who provide both support, in terms of companionship and social inclusion, and accountability, regarding temptation to re-offend or behaviours that contain different levels of risk. This is currently the most promising model of care for offenders once they are released from prison, with re-offence rates that are significantly lower that other approaches to treatment.

Conclusion

We began this chapter with a reference to Professor Gill Straker's model of victims, perpetrators (oppressors) and bystanders, and suggested that all of us can play various roles at different times in our lives. The mature person can recognise these various parts of the self, and live in such a way that the person does not get lost in any one role (or denial of a part of the self). In the same way a mature church is able to recognise that within the broken body of the community there are parts that are victims, parts that are oppressors, and parts that can stand by and watch without getting involved. In this chapter we have explored the various people who are affected by the unspeakable violations of sexual abuse. It is our belief that when sensitively handled, we have the resources to reach out to all concerned, and can offer healing in ways that are consistent with best practice and the values of our Churches.

Do's and don'ts

1. Do take a child seriously if he or she tells you that something inappropriate has been done to him/her.
2. Don't rush to interfere. Do contact Social Services, Childline, NSPCC helpline, or Stop it Now! for advice and information.
3. Do follow child-protection proceedings of your own organisation.
4. Do provide supportive counselling or help for relatives, work colleagues or others who are affected.
5. As an employer or priest/minister, contact a lawyer before making any decisions regarding employees who have been accused or found guilty of sexual abuse.
6. Do advise families to report any crime that has been committed.
7. Do not ask unnecessary questions of victims or abusers, but offer support as long as it is necessary.
8. Do not promise to keep information a secret if it involves a child who is being sexually abused.
9. Do not ostracise the perpetrator if you previously had a relationship with him or her. People who are guilty of abuse need as much support and contact as possible as they go through the stages of discovery, trial, treatment, probation and rebuilding their lives. Personal support does not mean you condone their actions.

Recommended reading

Geary, B. (2008). Child sexual abuse. In B. Geary & J. Bryan (Eds.), *The Christian handbook of abuse, addiction and difficult behaviour*. Suffolk: Kevin Mayhew.

McGlone, G. J., Shrader, M., & Delgatto, L. (2003). *Creating safe and sacred places: Identifying, preventing, and healing sexual abuse*. Minnesota: St. Mary's Press.

Marshall, W. L. (2007). A proposal for the prevention and treatment of child molestation by Catholic clergy. *Seminary Journal, 13*, (3) pp. 20 – 36.

Robinson, G. (2008). *Confronting power and sex in the Catholic Church: Reclaiming the Spirit of Jesus*. Minnesota: Liturgical Press, pp. 217–224.

Ward, T., & Brown, M. (2004). The good lives model and conceptual issues in offender rehabilitation. *Psychology Crime & Law*, 10, (3), pp. 243–257.

Wilson, R. J., & Prinzo, M. (2001). Circles of Support: A restorative Justice Initiative. *Journal of Psychology and Human Sexuality*. Gloucestershire: Hawthorn Press Inc.

Yantzi, M. (1998). *Sexual offending and restoration*. Ontario: Herald Press.

ELEVEN

Sex and the Internet

Brendan Geary and Ed Hone

Introduction

The Internet is unquestionably a resource which has had a significant positive impact on the lives of many people, as a source of information, for the sharing of knowledge, flexible working arrangements and research, for swift and convenient shopping, making travel bookings, ways of paying for services, merchandise or settling bills, mobilising people to support a cause or complain about an issue to politicians or other people who hold power in various areas of life. The Internet has contributed to circumventing censorship in countries like Iran[1] and China,[2] where governments prefer to keep the people in ignorance, and has created international communities of scholars and friends who can communicate instantly across countries and continents.

The Internet, however, also has its dark side. Hackers have found ways of penetrating protected sites (especially credit-card agencies, banks, and government databases). Racist, inflammatory and extremist sites have been created, including sites that incite people to hatred. Violent, exploitative and sexually demeaning sites exist which provide spaces for criminal or simply offensive material. There are also people who create viruses and 'worms' which can damage, corrupt or render people's computers and databases unusable. At the very least this anti-social behaviour can cause considerable inconvenience and expense to ordinary people.

---

1. Iranian government blocks Facebook access. (25th May, 2009). *The Guardian*. Retrieved on 25th May, 2009, from http://www.guardian.co.uk/world/2009/may/24/facebook-banned-iran
2. Macartney, J. (3rd June, 2009). Twitters silenced as Web services blocked. *The Times*. Retrieved on 4th June, 2009, at http://www.timesonline.co.uk/tol/news/world/asia/article6414510.ece

This chapter will focus on the way that the Internet has made pornography easily available, and will explore the impact this has had on individuals, children and families, and on relationships. While the main focus of this chapter is on sites that are not deemed to be illegal, special attention will be given to the issue of Internet child pornography, which is illegal. There will also be a section on clergy, some of whom appear to be vulnerable to inappropriate use of the Internet. The related issue of sexual addiction will also be considered, as a number of people who engage in Internet sexual searches become trapped in compulsive and ultimately damaging online activity. The chapter will present ways in which people seeking out or addicted to Internet pornography can be helped. We will also consider ways that Internet pornography can create an opportunity for pastoral conversations not possible before the development of this medium. The issue of treatment will be discussed and information will be provided regarding organisations which can be of help, and websites which can be accessed for further information.

Clarifying terms

The World Wide Web (WWW), which was created by Tim Berners-Lee as a means of instant communication between scientists,[3] is the international network which enables contact to be made, emails to be sent, sites to exist and be accessed etc. While one of the benefits of the Web is the extraordinary freedom that exists, a related difficulty is how to monitor, police or track criminal or offensive material. The word 'cybersex' is often used in discussions about Internet sex. This word is used as a collective term to describe the various ways that people can access sexual material on their computers. It also refers to making use of the Internet in an attempt to have relational, sexual and erotic needs met. When this type of relationship generates contact and dialogue, using some of the means indicated below, then the

3. http://en.wikipedia.org/wiki/Tim_Berners-Lee

person is involved in 'cybersex'.[4] There is a range of ways that cybersex can be made available:

- *Newsgroups:* These are 'communities of interest', where people who share a similar interest can communicate and share materials (e.g., erotic pictures). For example, people with particular fetishes (unusual sexual interests – see chapter 8 on Sexual perversions) can find other people online who share their tastes.

- *Email:* Emails can be used to make contact or share materials, e.g., photographs or video clips, or other weblinks, with persons who hold similar interests. Email can also be used to move from the virtual world of the Internet to the real world of personal contact. It is also fairly common for ordinary users of the Web to receive unwanted emails of a sexual nature.

- *Messenger systems:* These can be used to have online conversations – Internet fantasy sex – with one or more persons.

- *Chat rooms:* Similar to newsgroups and messenger systems, chat rooms become a sort of 'café' or 'marketplace', where people can make contact with others.

- *Videoconferencing/video chatting/webcam:* Many computers are equipped with cameras able to transmit pictures of the user. This takes the virtual reality a stage further by enabling people to see each other, or to view activities of the other person. While this can enhance a normal conversation, it can also take cybersex to another level of titillation or exploitation.

- *Peer-to-peer file sharing.* This enables people to share resources, photographs, materials, video links etc. with people who share their interests.

- *Online fantasy games:* People can take on roles in games. Internet-based games of all sorts are a popular recreational activity with

---

4. Young, K. S., Griffin-Shelley, E., Cooper, A., O'Mara, J., & Buchanan, J. (2000). Online infidelity: A new dimension in couple relationships with implications for evaluation and treatment. *Sexual Addiction & Compulsivity,* 7(1 – 2), pp. 59 – 74.

many children and young people. But in the world of cybersex the dimension of sexual stimulation and/or activity is added. People can adopt different *personae*, creating 'avatars' who have parallel 'second lives', thereby living out sexual fantasies which may otherwise have been suppressed.[5]

- *Cyberaffair:* This is a way of describing a relationship which develops online and continues using the various means described above. It may or may not lead to a real personal or sexual encounter.[6]

- *Pay-per-view webcams:* Individuals can make contact with Internet sites where they can pay to watch live sexual activity, and, in some cases, direct the activity they wish to see.

Some research findings

Despite being a relatively recent phenomenon, the world of Internet pornography has already been the focus of research. One of the earliest, and still valuable, pieces of research analysed data from 9265 respondents who submitted completed questionnaires via the MSNBC[7] website in March–April 1998. The survey was promoted through various media, including television, radio and newspaper interviews, and data was collected electronically over a seven-week period. Cooper, Delmonico and Burg, the authors of the study, divided Internet sex users into four groups, by using scores on the Kalichman Sexual Compulsivity Scale:

- *The nonsexually compulsive:* 83.5% of the people who participated in the study fell into this group.

- *The moderately sexually compulsive:* 10.9% of those who responded fell into this category.

- *Sexually compulsive:* 4.6% of the respondents fell into this category.

5. Daniel, D. (2008). The self-set free: Stepping into virtual worlds. *Therapy Today, 19*(9) 4 – 9.
6. Morris, S. (November 14, 2008). Second Life affair leads to couple's real-life divorce. *The Guardian*, p. 5.
7. Microsoft National Broadcasting Company: A cable channel based in the USA.

- *Cybersex compulsive:* Only 1% of respondents fell into this category, but they reported spending more than 11 hours per week in online sexual activities. These people, as well as being sexually compulsive, made use of the Internet as a significant part of their compulsive sexual behaviour.[8]

This research found that the vast majority of users are able to limit use of the Internet to a 'recreational' basis. This is confirmed by research undertaken by Mark Griffiths of the International Gambling Research Unit at Nottingham Trent University, who has concluded after years of research that, 'There are very few people who are addicted to the Internet'.[9] However, for a small percentage (but not a small number) of people in the population, the Internet is a focus of compulsive behaviour, and for some this involves sexual behaviour. It has been suggested that 40% of couples who approach counselling agencies with difficulties report that use of pornography has been one of the sources of their problems.[10]

The 'Triple A' engine of online sex

Al Cooper, one of the first people to research Internet sex, coined the phrase, 'The Triple A' engine, to describe what makes sex on the Internet unique and alluring. He suggested that, in the first place, it is easily *Available*, 24 hours a day, seven days a week. There is no need to find a shop selling pornography, or use a TV for a video or DVD. Once you have switched on your computer (and some addicts will talk of not being able to contemplate switching *off* their computers), the material can be accessed in seconds.

As well as being readily available, the Internet is also *Anonymous*. Before the days of the Internet, people who wanted to look at pornography often had to go to a shop specialising in this kind of

---

8. Cooper, A., Delmonico, D. L., & Burg, R. (2000). Cybersex users, abusers, and compulsives: New findings and implications. *Sexual Addiction & Compulsivity, 7*(1 – 2), pp. 5 – 29.
9. Daniel, D. (2008). The self-set free: Stepping into virtual worlds. *Therapy Today, 19*(9), p. 9.
10. Barnes, A., & Goodchild, S. (28th May, 2006). Porn UK, *The Independent on Sunday*, pp. 1 – 2.

material, often in the seedier parts of major towns, and make the physical act of crossing the threshold into a shop to look at and buy pornography. In recent years, 'soft porn', and 'lads' mags' have been made available in many newsagents and at petrol stations, but they are still kept on top shelves, and are often sold in protective wrapping. In America, this may be required by local ordinance in some towns and cities. Buyers need to overcome feelings of shame and the reality of being seen to browse and/or purchase materials, even if it is only the shopkeeper or salesperson seeing them. Internet anonymity, of course, is an illusion, as every stroke on a computer is recorded and saved at some level. The Internet access provider firms, if presented with a legal demand such as a subpoena, can usually trace a person's Internet traffic. Lawyers, probation officers and therapists who work with people charged with Internet offences, will be familiar with large files of emails or chat-room conversations which have been printed, put in a folder and presented in court.

Al Cooper also highlighted the fact that the Internet is *Affordable*. Many sites are free and, where payment is required (with a credit/debit card) the costs are often minimal. There are countless sites available, creating competition for users which keeps charges low. That being said, it is not unknown for people to spend a considerable amount of their earnings on Internet pornography sites.[11]

Cyberhex

Pornography (like prostitution) has been available since recorded history. People speak of men (usually) who have 'stashes' of porn. We also know that there have always been people whose sexual behaviour was out of control, and people with unusual, bizarre, dangerous or criminal sexual interests.[12] The question needs to be asked,

---

11. Cooper, A. (1998). Sexuality and the Internet: Surfing into the new millennium. *Cyberpsychology and behavior, 1*(2), pp. 181 – 187.
12. Money, J. (1999). *The lovemap guidebook*. New York: Continuum.

though, what it is about the Internet that has led to the increasing levels of problematic behaviour that we are currently witnessing.

David Delmonico, Elizabeth Griffin and Joe Moriarty, who have researched and written extensively in this area, have developed what they call the 'Cyberhex' as a way of understanding the powerful draw of Internet sex (see Figure 1).[13] Their model has six dimensions, hence the hexagon graphic, but the title also contains the word, 'hex' which suggests a spell or trance. This captures well the psychological state addicts experience while interacting sexually on the Internet. These authors suggest that the Internet is integral to our lives, but also imposing, isolating, interactive, inexpensive, and intoxicating. One man, for example, wrote:

I had finished reading some papers for work at 9.30pm and intended to go online for 30 minutes before watching the news and going to bed. My wife goes to bed early, and she is used to me staying up to finish work. However, once I connected to the Internet I thought I would look at some images of naked women. I know the addresses of some free sites and tend to use them. I clicked on to the first site and was stimulated by what I saw. I noticed the banner for another site and decided to check it out. I then followed this to another site which seemed more exciting and was full of video clips that held me glued to the computer screen. It was mesmerising. Needless to say, I lost track of time. Before I knew it, it was well past the time for the news, but I decided (with little resistance) to adjust my 'threshold,' and stay online until midnight. Not for the first time, it was nearer one o'clock in the morning when I finally drew myself from the computer and went to bed. Thankfully my wife was asleep. Up until now no one knows about my attraction to Internet pornography.[14]

13. Carnes, P., Delmonico, D. L., Griffin, E., & Moriarty, J. M. (2007). *In the shadows of the net: Breaking free of compulsive online sexual behavior.* Minnesota: Hazelden, pp. 13 – 18.
14. Private communication.

This man's story is not unusual; many people find themselves devoting far more hours to online activities than they had planned or wanted. The Cyberhex model provides a neat and useful explanatory model for this behaviour.

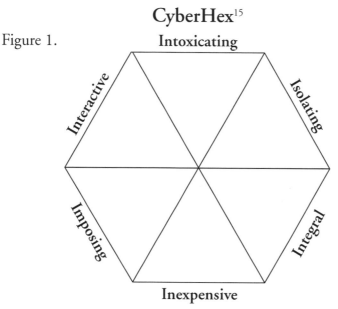

CyberHex[15]

Figure 1.

Integral

As already stated in the introduction, the Internet has become an integral part of our lives. In March 2007 it was estimated that 51% of the population of the European Union used the Internet.[16] That figure rises to 71% in North America.[17] February 2009 data indicate that 75% of US citizens have access to the Internet, with 45.2% having broadband connections.[18] The data are similar for other developed countries. In the developing world the Internet has brought access to places that, in the past, were geographically remote. Poor road systems, mail systems, and telephone systems are no longer a barrier to connecting with others.

15. Carnes, P., Delmonico, D. L., Griffin, E., & Moriarty, J. M. (2007). *In the shadows of the net: Breaking free of compulsive online sexual behavior.* Minnesota: Hazelden, p. 14.
16. http://www.Internetworldstats.com/eu/eu.htm
17. http://www.Internetworldstats.com/stats2.htm
18. http://www.websiteoptimization.com/bw/0403/

In many families there are computers in children's and adults' bedrooms, personal offices or 'dens'. As well as providing rapid access, this arrangement also increases the dangers of inappropriate use, or the exploitation of children by adults. The Internet is also available in libraries, schools, at airports, in cafés, etc. The 2008 American Presidential election demonstrated the way that the Internet has become the dominant means of communication for younger generations across the globe.[19] The Internet has become part of the way we now live.

Imposing

If something is imposed on us, it means we have no choice. We can, for example, choose to watch, or even whether or not to have, a television or drive a car. This is becoming more difficult with the Internet as more and more transactions require the Internet, or, as stated above, favour Internet use. Non-Internet users are often penalised or disadvantaged as goods can be cheaper when bought over the Internet, and bills are cheaper (or there is an extra levy when paid in person or by cash/cheque). The Internet is imposing in other ways. If you click on an email it often sends a 'cookie' to the originating person or site, thereby adding your address to their list of contacts. Some sites will not allow you to process a transaction unless you allow a cookie to be returned. Many people invite friends or contacts to social networking sites. This can lead to your own details being made available to people whom you do not know. An abbot once described poverty as 'having no choice'. If that is true, then the Internet is the polar opposite, as the amount of choice available to users is overwhelming, to the point of being imposing. Search engines like Google often offer access to thousands of sites or images related to a topic of interest. On the one hand the Internet is a wonderland of opportunity; on the other hand it is a labyrinth drawing people in, constantly luring them with more alternatives.

19. Williams, S. (29th November, 2008). Obama's winning option for the poor. *The Tablet*, pp. 6 – 7.

Isolating

The following personal account by Tim Guest is taken from an article on the 'Second Life' phenomenon:

> I found myself longing for my second life. Halfway through one dinner party, I abandoned the table to sneak moments at my PC. I lounged in my virtual office, chatting with my virtual friends, when I should have been in my apartment, entertaining my real friends.[20]

Rather than spend time with his real guests, he chose to disappear into the privacy of his office to spend time in his 'second life' world. Computers are not communal spaces. While they connect us to people all over the world, and to 'virtual communities', both physically and psychologically they require the time and presence of only one individual. They demand that individual's concentration and focused attention. When this is coupled with sexual arousal, we have a formidable combination. In the early years of personal computing people talked of 'Apple Mac widows'; there are now partners who feel rejected and psychologically separated from their Internet-addicted significant others. The isolating effect of the Internet is one of its main problems. On the one hand it promises illicit sex without the risk of infection or disease, or relationship complications. On the other hand it exacts a price in terms of social communication, personal freedom, and managing feelings of guilt, shame and personal disappointment. People speak of seeing their lives fading away.[21]

Inexpensive

As Carnes, Delmonico, Griffiths and Moriarty suggest, the Internet provides 'a low-cost alternative to a sexual high'. Magazines are expensive. Real-life affairs or use of prostitutes are expensive, fraught

---

20. Daniel, D. (2008). The self-set free: Stepping into virtual worlds. *Therapy Today, 19*(9), p. 8.
21. Cavaglion, G. (2008). Narratives of self-help of cyberporn dependents. *Sexual Addiction and Compulsivity, 15,* 195 – 216.

with complications, and risky on several levels. A person afraid of someone's noticing a drop in available income, can use the Internet without bank withdrawals raising a spouse's suspicions.

Intoxicating

The Internet has been called the crack cocaine of sex. Crack cocaine takes seconds to pass the blood–brain barrier and stimulate the part of the brain that produces dopamine, the neurotransmitter related to pleasurable sensations.[22] The Internet has a similar effect. There is no need to expend the effort to go to a bookstore, a lap-dancing bar, pick up a prostitute, or shop for magazines or books. Within seconds the images, conversations, stories etc. are available and accessible. Addicted users often talk about the 'rush' that they get, and how difficult it is to give this up. One recovered addict wrote:

> Often when I was at work I would be doing a fairly routine task at my computer and the thought would pop up, 'Just take a quick look. This is boring and you will feel better if you amuse yourself for a few minutes.' One click and I was excited, stimulated – but also afraid of getting caught, which added to the excitement. The combination caused my heart to beat faster. Paradoxically time went slowly, as I was reacting faster, but time also disappeared, as I could find myself 'distracted' for significant periods of time. Getting home was just another chance to feed the high which became more important in my life.[23]

These six factors all work together to create the context and culture that facilitate online sexual activity. Even where, as in most cases, it does not lead to full-blown addiction, it can still contribute to unhealthy outcomes and damaged or impoverished relationships.

22. Carlson, N. R. (2005). *Foundations of physiological psychology* (5th ed.). New York: Pearson, p. 518.
23. Personal communication.

Gender differences

In her chapter on Gender Issues, Jocelyn Bryan discusses the ways in which men and women are similar and different. Roy Baumeister and Dianne Tice[24] suggest that one of the areas where there are clearest differences between men and women is in the area of sexuality. They propose that male sexuality is predominantly visual, and female sexuality is predominantly relational. They also provide data suggesting that male sexuality is more prone to aggression and even violence, and that this is much rarer in women. These observations have been related to the presence of significantly higher levels of testosterone in some men. Testosterone levels can be extremely high in sex offenders, and one form of treatment uses anti-androgen medications to lower their testosterone levels.[25] At the same time, generalisations and averages do not apply to every single individual. Many men are also attracted to sex in a relational context. Women can and do respond to visual stimulation. It should be noted, for example, that 30% of visitors to pornographic sites are women.[26]

For women who do use the Internet for sexual purposes, they are more inclined than men to make use of chat rooms, while men prefer to download pornography significantly more than women,[27] with chat rooms as only a second choice.[28] A higher proportion of women than men progress from online chatting to real-life sexual encounters. For women the Internet can provide the illusion of romance, courtship, fantasy, an atmosphere of manipulation, seduction, intrigue and the promise of a perfect relationship – the stuff of romantic fiction.

For homosexual and bisexual men the Web becomes a virtual marketplace to meet partners for sexual encounters. They can also

---

24. Baumeister, R., & Tice, D. (2001). *The social dimension of sex.* Boston: Allyn & Bacon.
25. Geary, B. (2008). Child sexual abuse, in B. Geary & J. Bryan (Eds.). *The Christian handbook of abuse, addiction and difficult behaviour.* Suffolk: Kevin Mayhew.
26. Carnes, P., Delmonico, D. L., Griffin, E., & Moriarty, J. M. (2007). *In the shadows of the net: Breaking free of compulsive online sexual behavior.* Minnesota: Hazelden, p. 7.
27. Schneider, J. P. (2000). A qualitative study of cybersex participants: Gender differences, recovery issues, and implications for therapists. *Sexual Addiction and Compulsivity, 7,* 249 – 278.
28. Cooper, A., Delmonico, D. L., & Burg, R. (2000). Cybersex users, abusers, and compulsives: New findings and implications. *Sexual Addiction and Compulsivity, 7*(1 – 2), pp. 5 – 29.

arrange to meet partners for sex without having to cruise the streets, with all the inherent dangers involved. Paedophiles can also use it to identify victims, groom them for seduction and arrange meetings.

Another significant difference from women is that men appear to be able to put their lives into separate compartments. This enables them to separate their lives with their families and partners from their online activities. Compartmentalisation appears to be particularly common among men who have authoritarian tendencies.[29] This psychological profile is fairly common in highly conservative Christian groups. In the USA in summer 2009 the media exposed several prominent conservative 'Born-Again' Christian politicians as having secret sexual lives. Interestingly, these men had been highly vocal in condemning former President Clinton's sexual escapade and demanding his impeachment.[30]

It appears that men and women view Internet sex differently in terms of what it might mean for the relationship with a real-life partner. When women discover that their partners are using the Internet for sex, it can feel like betrayal, and women may speak of adultery. Research studies have found that women tend to regard online sex as a form of infidelity.[31] One woman, for example, wrote:

> I am no longer a sexual person or partner to him, but a sexual object. He is not really with me, not really making love to me . . . He seems to be thinking of something or someone else – likely those porn women . . . He is just using me as a warm body.[32]

Men do not always perceive things in the same way.[33] When working with couples, it is important to help the man to see and understand

---

29. Levert, N. P. (2007). A comparison of Christian and Non-Christian males, authoritarianism, and their relationship to Internet pornography addiction/compulsion. *Sexual Addiction and Compulsivity, 14,* pp. 145 – 166.

30. http://www.nytimes.com/2009/06/28/opinion/28dowd.html?scp=1&sq=Maureen%20Dowd%20Sanford&st=cse

31. Whitty, M. T. (2003). Pushing the wrong buttons: Men's and women's attitudes toward online and offline infidelity. *Cyberpsychology & Behaviour, 6*(6), 569 – 579.

32. Manning, J. (2006). The impact of Internet pornography on marriage and the family: A review of the research. *Sexual Addiction and Compulsivity, 13,* pp. 131 – 165.

33. Dew, B., Brubaker, M., & Hays, D. (2006). From the altar to the Internet: Married men and their online sexual behaviour. *Sexual Addiction and Compulsivity, 13,* pp. 195 – 207.

how this is affecting his wife, and to help the wife to understand that her husband's behaviour may mean something different to him.

Effects on users

In this section we will explore the impact of Internet sexual activity on users and then on other people. The material available on Internet sites can vary from 'soft porn' sites where, for example, women can be viewed wearing lingerie, to sites with increasingly explicit nudity and sexual activity to the more 'hard core' sites where there can be scenes of sexual violence or degradation of people – including children – or sexual abuse or torture of animals.

Researchers have found reliable and strong associations between viewing pornography and aggressive behaviour, especially when the pornography also depicts some kind of violence.[34] Drake, building on the work of two researchers who reviewed the available research, concluded that male exposure over time to standard, non-violent pornography had the following possible effects on users:

- Increased callousness towards women
- Trivialisation of rape as a criminal offence
- Distorted perceptions about sexuality
- Increased appetite for more deviant and bizarre types of pornography
- Devaluation of the importance of monogamy
- Decreased satisfaction with partners' sexual performance, affection and physical appearance
- Doubts about the value of marriage
- Decreased desire to have children
- Viewing non-monogamous relationships as normal and natural behaviour.[35]

34. Manning, J. (2006). The impact of Internet pornography on marriage and the family: A review of the research. *Sexual Addiction and Compulsivity, 13*, pp. 131 – 165.
35. Drake, R. E. (1994). Potential health hazards of pornographic consumption as viewed by psychiatric nurses. *Archives of Psychiatric Nursing, 8*(2), 101 – 106, quoted in Manning, J. (2006). The impact of Internet pornography on marriage and the family: A review of the research. *Sexual Addiction and Compulsivity, 13*, p. 135.

All of these outcomes undermine the values of religious groups. They also have a sometimes subtle, but insidious and corrosive effect on existing intimate relationships.

Use of the Internet for sex has other consequences for users, interfering with developing real relationships, which require time, effort and a range of communication and social skills that some people find to be a strain or lack altogether. Writers in this area have noted that people who become involved in Internet sex often have problems with self-esteem or in the area of establishing and sustaining relationships. The Internet promises the high without the hassle, and, as such, is very seductive. There are consequences, though. The Internet, while promising to overcome these handicaps, actually exacerbates them. It has been suggested that while the Internet promises to overcome loneliness, it can actually create it.[36]

Those who are involved in Internet sexual activity speak of feelings of shame, boredom and depression, of feeling socially isolated, and, especially for those for whom it becomes a true addiction, of feeling powerless. There are also feelings of anxiety, and, of course, the guilt and fear associated with being discovered by significant others or employers.[37]

Sex is a very private area of our lives. Women may be able to talk about intimate matters, but this is unusual for men. When sex enters men's conversation it is usually dealt with through humour, or possibly bragging about experiences and conquests. This makes it difficult for men to talk about the Internet in any way other than swapping details of sites or sending pictures, clips or jokes to each other.

Shame is a very unpleasant emotion, and men often use defences such as rationalisation or denial to avoid being honest about this feeling. It also involves a global sense of being a bad, unworthy or

36. Yoder, V. C., Virden, T. B., Amin, K. (2005). Internet pornography and loneliness: An association? *Sexual Addiction and Compulsivity, 12*, pp. 19 – 44.
37. Cavaglion, G. (2008). Narratives of self-help of cyberporn dependents. *Sexual Addiction and Compulsivity, 15*, p. 196.

defective human being.[38] The Internet has a particularly severe impact on self-esteem for people who belong to Churches or faith communities, as this is clearly an activity that is not approved. Paradoxically, the Internet provides an escape from such unpleasant emotional experiences, while creating the conditions that maintain them. The privacy and individual focus associated with the Internet becomes a corrosive secrecy, creating difficulty in admitting a problem or seeking help.

It is not unusual to have moments of boredom, or to find some aspects of work to be drudgery. The Internet provides endless opportunities for 'displacement' activities. All of us do this to some extent, but only a minority of us have the neurological propensity for true addiction. For the potential addict, once the brain discovers a pathway that 'works', it will find ways to have it repeated. In the way that a person who becomes an addict begins by responding to a thought stimulus, the Internet user will find that the thought of going on to the Internet becomes increasingly common. It is also powerfully reinforcing as it quickly provides the emotional shift that is being sought.

It has been noted that people make use of the Internet as a way of dealing with stress. Sex is a powerful stimulant, which is inherently rewarding. The various stages of courtship; attraction, flirtation, romance, intimacy, sexual contact and commitment, all bring feelings of risk, excitement, stimulation, heightened arousal and awareness, and pleasure.[39] The Internet seeks to circumvent this process and offer instant gratification of sexual and emotional needs. People who use the Internet in this way, however, often experience emptiness rather than intimacy, and depression rather than delight. When an Italian man using the name 'Marco' set up his site to create a support network for Internet sex users, he wrote that he was trying to make contact with people:

38. Tangney, J. P., & Dearing, R. L. (2002). *Shame and guilt*. New York: Guildford.
39. Carnes, P., Delmonico, D. L., Griffin, E., & Moriarty, J. M. (2007). *In the shadows of the net: Breaking free of compulsive online sexual behavior*. Minnesota: Hazelden, pp. 77 – 87.

Who are living my experience, to confront each other, to talk about our anxiety, our big and small victories, depression when we slide back, our attempts to understand why we are in such a state of social isolation and crisis in our relationships with women, our problems with output on the job, our loss of relationships with friends, the terrible temptation to frivol hours in front of the screen . . . lack of self-esteem and anger at ourselves . . . our lack of dependability to be in charge of our lives . . . feelings of shame about our dependence.[40]

While not all Internet sex users may feel these things as intensely as someone who is trapped in addiction, it is not uncommon for people to experience discomfort regarding their use, and to sense that this is not a productive use of time, that it goes against their values, that it is not actually helping them to feel better, as they keep having to return for more stimulation, and that it is a part of their lives of which they feel ashamed.

Feelings of guilt and discomfort are often the spur for someone to approach a priest or minister for help in this area. The development of the Internet has led to a number of men, in particular, approaching priests and ministers to talk about feelings of guilt that they experience as a result of Internet use. Like shame, guilt is an unpleasant feeling. The difference, though, is that in order to get rid of feelings of guilt we either have to desist from a particular behaviour, or apologise to someone whom we have hurt. Fundamentally, guilt tells us that we have 'done a bad thing', but that we are not necessarily a bad person.[41] A recent article summarising the research in this area offered the following observation:

The capacity for guilt is more apt to foster a pattern of lifelong moral behaviour, motivating individuals to accept responsibility and take reparative action in the wake of the occasional failure

40. Cavaglion, G. (2008). Narratives of self-help of cyberporn dependents. *Sexual Addiction and Compulsivity, 15*, p. 200.
41. Tangney, J. P., & Dearing, R. L. (2002). *Shame and guilt*. New York: Guildford.

or transgression. In contrast, research has linked shame with a range of illegal, risky, or otherwise problematic behaviours (Tangney et al., 2007, p. 355).[42]

Involvement in Internet pornography is sometimes illegal, often risky, and, as we have seen, can be problematic. It is hardly surprising that it leads to feelings of shame in those who access it.

Pastoral issues

The whole issue of Internet pornography has significant implications for priests, ministers and pastoral workers, as they find themselves responding to the ways in which this is affecting individuals, couples and families. Many men who use the Internet have a gnawing sense that something is not right, particularly when they think of their wives or girlfriends, as they know that in some way they are being unfaithful or, at the least, that this behaviour is not consistent with involvement in an exclusive, intimate, affectionate relationship.

The following are examples of the kinds of situations that have presented themselves to priests and ministers in the pastoral context:

- Simon is in his mid-twenties and sometimes, when bored at work, he looks at Internet pornography. He feels guilty because he is stealing work time, and also putting his company at risk. Whilst part of him knows he should stop, he finds himself unable to do so, and is concerned about the lack of freedom in this area of his life.

- Pete is a man in his forties who occasionally, late at night whilst his family are in bed, views pornography on the Internet and masturbates. Afterwards, he joins his wife in their bed, and is troubled that in some real way he is being unfaithful, even adulterous, in using other women as sex objects.

---

42. Tangney, J. P., Stuewig, J., & Masek, D. J. (2007). Moral emotions and moral behaviour. *Annu. Rev. Psychol.* 58: 345–72.

- Matt occasionally looks at pornography online, and is usually careful about erasing his browsing history on the home computer. One evening, his partner, however, inadvertently discovered he had been in an Internet chat room having sexually explicit conversations with another (female) forum member. When confronted, Matt at first denied that there was a problem, then confessed to his wife that this was something he did on occasion, and had been doing for some time, in spite of his feelings of shame after each time.

- Michael has been married for almost thirty years and has grown-up children. After accidentally accessing a gay pornography website, and finding the images arousing, he was forced to confront his latent homosexuality. Until that point in his life, he had managed to avoid dealing with this aspect of his sexuality.

Internet pornography has resulted in the breaking down of long-standing taboos with regard to speaking about, and confessing, sexual thoughts and activities. People with Christian religious affiliation would, in the past, often find ways to talk indirectly about their sexual feelings and behaviours. Increasingly, the conversations are becoming more frank and direct, with less beating around the bush. Where once a person would speak about 'committing an impure act by myself', for example, now they are more likely to speak about 'masturbating' and 'using pornographic images to masturbate'. 'Sinning against the sixth Commandment' literally covered a multitude of sins, and was usually a thinly veiled reference to sex, often adultery. The liberalisation of social mores around sex, encouraged by the accessibility, even prevalence of pornography on the Internet, means that even older people will speak of 'having sex with someone' who was not their spouse or long-term partner. This can have the effect of freeing up the conversation, and enabling a more mature, adult discussion about the issues involved.

In talking about fantasies or actions that have subsequently troubled their conscience, both women and men are increasingly able to be more reflective about *why* they have done what they have done. It is not unusual, for example, for someone to speak about having viewed pornography on the Internet, and then go on to explain that it is not simply the viewing of sexual images that troubled them, but the fact that it left them feeling somehow degraded, or that their subsequent masturbation was 'not dignified'. Similarly, there are older people who have conducted themselves 'modestly' (i.e., without looking at or seeking out sexually stimulating material) all their adult lives, who are now unable to resist the easily available content on the Web: 'I feel as though I'm becoming a dirty old man, and would die of shame if I thought my grandchildren would ever know what I'd been looking at.'

On the other hand, there are those men (and women) who speak of their guilt and shame with regard to their sexual thoughts, desires and actions, but cannot do so with any level of candour. Talking about sexual matters may never have been easy for them, and their involvement in Internet pornography may lead to increased feelings of shame which makes talking about their behaviour even more difficult. Their pornographic viewing habits may not be very different from those of others, but the ability to view 'pornography on demand' adds to their moral anguish when they 'give in to temptation', leaving them feeling trapped, oppressed, and vulnerable.

Whilst accessing pornographic content on the Internet is often seen as the preserve of men, especially younger and middle-aged men, experience indicates that no age group or sex is immune: women and men of all ages speak of the effect on their lives of Internet sexual content. One minister described how it was usually men who spoke of viewing Internet pornography, but he had two recent examples of women having sexual affairs as a result of contacting previous partners via social networking sites. (This is consistent with what was noted above about gender differences in Internet sex use.) This phenomenon is perhaps the latest phase of the Internet sex revolution.

Traditional Christian moral responses to sexual activities outside marriage often use the language of sin, emphasise the shamefulness of 'illicit sex' (which can mean anything from masturbation to sexual promiscuity) and stress the need for complete abstinence from any sexual behaviour apart from within the married relationship. Clearly, the challenges posed by the various forms of Internet sexual content demand a new, more dynamic moral response, where the issues involved are examined reflectively, not only in terms of law, theology and spirituality, but also in terms of anthropology, psychology and sociology.

It is easy to approach the issue of Internet pornography from a moralistic and judgemental perspective, however a number of ministers are discovering that, paradoxically, the issue can actually facilitate more mature, open conversations, creating an opportunity for emotional and spiritual growth. Christian reflection holds that sexuality finds its full expression in the context of a loving relationship. The easy accessibility of Internet pornography, with its tendency to dehumanise sex and isolate the individual, whilst inevitably being in tension with the Christian view, can also present an opening for serious reflection on the place of sexuality in human relating.

Partners

It has already been suggested that men who are involved in cybersex will not necessarily be aware of or understand the impact that their behaviour can have on their wives. According to Jennifer Schneider, partners of men who were involved in cybersex felt hurt, betrayal, rejection, abandonment, devastation, loneliness, shame, humiliation, anger, loss of self-esteem.[43] The women said that being lied to repeatedly was a major cause of hurt and distress. Almost a quarter of the women

43. Schneider, J. P. (2000). A qualitative study of cybersex participants: Gender differences, recovery issues, and implications for therapists. *Sexual Addiction and Compulsivity, 7,* 249 – 278.

who responded to her survey were separated or divorced and many others were giving serious thought to leaving their husbands.

It is difficult for many women to understand how men can operate sexually outside of a relational context. Married women view Internet pornography usage as a threat to the relationship more than women in a dating relationship. The distress increases with frequency of usage. This perception is supported by a survey of America's top matrimonial lawyers that was conducted at their annual meeting in 2002. The lawyers were surveyed and, of the 350 present, 68% said that the Internet had been a contributory factor to divorces they had dealt with in the previous year.[44]

Many partners come to doubt themselves and often blame themselves for their partner's behaviour, believing that there is something they can do to stop it. This usually leads to initiating sex or trying to provide more frequent or more varied sex, before succumbing to feelings of worthlessness, sadness, loss of self-esteem, and despair of ever being able to do anything to regain their partner's interest or reignite the passion in their relationship. In reality, there is little the partner can do, as the use of the Internet is seldom a substitute for an unsatisfactory or unaffectionate spouse.[45] At a recent workshop a woman was relieved to hear that her husband's Internet use was not her fault, and, in a sense, that there was nothing she could do. This led her to encourage her husband to seek help, which he did.

There is a 'magnitude' gap between the perceptions of partners in this area. As stated above, men can often separate their Internet or pornography interest and dismiss it as a bit of fun, or a distraction. For many casual users, it does not appear to interfere with their affectionate or sexual relationships with their spouse.[46] This changes

44. Manning, J. (2006). The impact of Internet pornography on marriage and the family: A review of the research. *Sexual Addiction and Compulsivity, 13*, pp. 131 – 165.
45. Schneider, J. P. (2000). A qualitative study of cybersex participants: Gender differences, recovery issues, and implications for therapists. *Sexual Addiction and Compulsivity, 7*, 249 – 278.
46. Dew, B., Brubaker, M., & Hays, D. (2006). From the altar to the Internet: Married men and their online sexual behaviour. *Sexual Addiction and Compulsivity, 13*, p. 204.

when the usage becomes more frequent or there is a dependency. At this point partners can notice changes in personality, psychological and emotional withdrawal, and time spent away from real people. For the wives there is an experience of rejection and distance, which is painful and distressing.

Children

The arrival of the Internet and the rapid expansion of home computers have led to a range of concerns for children and adolescents. Households with children are more likely to use computers and access the Internet than homes without children.[47] There are issues around the amount of time that children spend online, the kind of material they may be accessing, sites or images to which they are inadvertently exposed, accidentally viewing websites that one of their parents has accessed, as well as the dangers of predatory and exploitative behaviour from other adults.

Children have adapted to use of new technology much faster than many adults. For them the Internet has become a natural medium for social networking, a source of information, and entertainment. It is not without its perils, though, as it has led to the phenomenon of cyberbullying,[48] and other forms of exploitation and harassment. There was, for example, a recent report in the media of 'friendship addiction'. This refers to the pressure among young people to acquire hundreds of friends. It appears that young women are particularly at risk since number and quality of relationships is more important for their self-esteem than is the case for young men.[49]

Children and adolescents are particularly vulnerable as this is a time of personality and character formation. Societies have laws and

47. Manning, J. (2006). The impact of Internet pornography on marriage and the family: A review of the research. *Sexual Addiction and Compulsivity, 13,* p. 149.
48. For the United States: http://www.cyberbullyalert.com/blog/2008/08/cyber-bullying-statistics-that-may-shock-you/, retrieved August 6, 2009. For the United Kingdom: http://yp.direct.gov.uk/cyberbullying/, retrieved August 6, 2009.
49. *Therapy Today.* (2008). Facebook to blame for 'friendship addiction.' 19(10), p. 10.

taboos as ways of protecting young people from inappropriate and damaging experiences. The Internet has rendered much of this ineffective, as it is very difficult to police this medium. There is evidence, for example, of children from 2 years of age upwards being exposed to pornographic material online.[50] There is also research to suggest that 93% of boys and 62% of girls had intentionally viewed pornographic material online by 18 years of age.[51] Young people are vulnerable because they can be coerced into viewing or participating in online activities. A BBC TV programme interviewed an adolescent who said that a man contacted him over the Internet and offered to send him £50 if he would masturbate in front of his webcam so that the man could watch. The adolescent agreed, perhaps not realising that he was, in effect, prostituting himself.[52]

A report from 2002 found that 70% of young people had encountered unsolicited sexual material online and almost a quarter said this happened very often. Misspelled words can lead to porn sites, and some sites make it difficult to exit, or will then lead you to another site. This is known as 'mouse trapping'.[53] Young people may not be able to process, cognitively or emotionally, the material they encounter, and there is a danger of believing that what they see represents normal or acceptable behaviour, leading to the development of skewed beliefs about people and human relationships.[54]

Some researchers are concerned about the effects of Internet sexual activity on young people's development. Patricia Greenfield, for example, analysed communications in chat rooms and concluded that the following effects could follow from participation in this medium:

50. Manning, J. (2006). The impact of Internet pornography on marriage and the family: A review of the research. *Sexual Addiction and Compulsivity*, *13*, p. 150.
51. James, O. (15 October 2009). Internet porn affects children more and more. *The Guardian*, Family Section, p.2, http://www.guardian.co.uk/lifeandstyle/2009/aug/15/internet-pornography-sex-addiction, retrieved 20 November 2009.
52. *One click from danger*. (2008, 7th January). Panorama, London: BBC.
53. Manning, J. (2006). The impact of Internet pornography on marriage and the family: A review of the research. *Sexual Addiction and Compulsivity*, *13*, p. 150.
54. Freeman-Longo, R. E. (2000). Children, teens, and sex on the Internet. *Sexual Addiction and Compulsivity*, *7*(1-2), pp. 75 – 90.

- Disinhibition in sexuality, aggression and racism
- Precocious sexual development
- Modelling of negative attitudes towards women, homophobia and racism
- Encouragement of irresponsible behaviour due to the protection of anonymity.[55]

Greenfield raises the issue of the kind of values that we wish to promote among young people, as the Internet is an almost value-neutral zone. This should also be a concern for families who share a religious value system.

Young people can also be victims of another person's use of pornography. Emma Cook explored this issue in an article in *The Guardian*, asking what, if any, level of pornography use by a partner was acceptable, and discussing the disturbing experience of children encountering pop-up ads, or of putting a word in a search engine to find that address auto-completion quickly offers a topic of sexual interest, leading to pornographic sites. One adolescent boy, for example, whose parents were separated, was using his father's computer to do research for homework. He began to enter words relating to his topic and inadvertently came across pornographic sites that his father had been accessing. The Internet History feature on computers keeps a record of the sites a person has been visiting. One woman wrote of the impact on her family life:

> Suddenly I felt I couldn't be honest with my son, Will. I've always been very open with him. I told Peter (husband) I'd die if Will found out what he had been looking at, and that's a horrible feeling because I try not to have those awful secrets. So I felt angry with Peter for creating that distance. My first feeling was

---

55. Greenfield, P. M. (2004). Developmental considerations for determining appropriate Internet use guidelines for children and adolescents. *Applied Developmental Psychology, 25,* 751 – 762. Quoted in Manning, J. (2006). The impact of Internet pornography on marriage and the family: A review of the research. *Sexual Addiction and Compulsivity, 13,* p. 151.

that he had brought something into my house that implicated me and my son and it affected us all with something that is violent and degrading.[56]

Research suggests that 60% of children already knew of their parent's use of Internet pornography, and while they experienced a range of feelings including anger, embarrassment, fear for the family (financial implications of discovery), guilt and confusion, there was also relief that the topic was now open and could be discussed, and their fears and anxieties validated. There was also some concern about the need to find appropriate language to help children to understand what was happening, and advice that helping children to process this information required more than a single conversation.[57]

Contrary to some people's beliefs, young people are often embarrassed and upset by exposure to Internet pornography. Many have found it disgusting and offensive. It appears that those who use it as a stimulus for masturbation are less likely to have negative reactions. Males tend to have more positive feelings, but both young men and young women can react with shock, surprise, anger, fear or sadness. Very few report unsolicited incidents of exposure to online pornography to adults.[58]

For a Christian community there will be concern about the impact of adult online pornography use on children. Jennifer Schneider, based on her research with 91 women and 3 men, concluded that there should be concern about the following effects on children:[59]

- Loss of parental time and attention
- Exposure to arguments between parents, and increased experience of stress in the home

---

56. Cook, E. (September 27th, 2008). Daddy's Internet secret. *The Guardian.* Retrieved from http://www.guardian.co.uk/lifeandstyle/2008/sep/27/family.Internet/print

57. Manning, J. (2006). The impact of Internet pornography on marriage and the family: A review of the research. *Sexual Addiction and Compulsivity, 13,* p. 148.

58. Manning, J. (2006). The impact of Internet pornography on marriage and the family: A review of the research. *Sexual Addiction and Compulsivity, 13,* pp. 150 – 151.

59. Schneider, J. P. (2000). Effects of cybersex addiction on the family: Results of a survey. *Sexual Addiction and Compulsivity, 7 (1-2),* p. 47.

- Children viewing pornography or encountering masturbation in the home
- Adverse effect on children's development (imitating parental behaviour, acting out sexually).

Many young people use the Internet responsibly and use it to network with friends, meet other people, find information about sexual topics or be entertained. However, it appears that young people who do not use the Internet for these purposes are more satisfied with their real lives and more connected to family and friends. Using the Internet as a tool for increased sexual knowledge appears to have value for youngsters who have no other sources. But when it is used as a replacement for real relationships, or as a way to find an identity or avoid forming relationships with real people, then there is a danger of decreased social integration with potentially unhealthy long-term effects, in particular a move towards compulsivity and addiction.[60]

Internet sexual addiction and compulsivity

Before leaving the topic of Internet pornography it is important to give some consideration to the issue of Internet sexual addiction and compulsivity. Some people question whether or not it is correct to talk about someone being addicted to sex, however, in the way that people can become addicted to substances like alcohol, cocaine or heroin, or activities like gambling or shopping, some people can become addicted, or compulsively engaged with, sex. Jennifer Schneider writes that, 'Any addictive disorder comprises loss of control (i.e. compulsive behaviour), continuation despite adverse circumstances, and obsession or preoccupation with the activity'.[61] Clearly there are people for whom this has become a major concern. The research by Cooper, Delmonico and Burg suggested that 4.6% of the respondents

---

60. Boies, S. C., Knudson, G., & Young, J. (2004). The Internet, sex, and youths: Implications for sexual development. *Sexual Addiction and Compulsivity, 11,* 343 – 363.
61. Schneider, J. P. (2000). A qualitative study of cybersex participants: Gender differences, recovery issues, and implications for therapists. *Sexual Addiction and Compulsivity, 7*(4), pp. 249 – 278.

to their survey could be described as sexually compulsive and that 1% were cybersex compulsives. This group reported spending more than 11 hours a week in online sexual pursuits. The Internet is their 'drug of choice'.[62]

In recent years the phrase, 'addictive personality' has achieved a certain prominence. The difficulty with this phrase is that it suggests that there are people who are fated to fall into addiction. In a similar vein, people who find themselves involved in addictive behaviour may use this phrase to justify or explain away their behaviour, as if there is nothing they can do to overcome their problems. It is true that some personalities may be more prone to becoming involved in addictive behaviours. We know, for example, that there is a genetic component to addictions; children whose parents are addicts have an increased chance of becoming addicts themselves. Also, people who experience more negative emotions than the majority of the population, or who experience a good deal of anxiety, may make use of substances or experiences to help to change their mood. If this is coupled with poor impulse control, a high need for variety, an attraction to high-risk behaviours and poor management of time and life goals, then the chances of succumbing to addiction are stronger.

Most sexual compulsives are men. While an early study suggested that married men were less likely to become addicted to Internet sex,[63] a more recent study has come to an opposite conclusion. Now the majority of men with problems with Internet sexual addiction appear to be married, in a committed relationship or dating. From the point of view of a priest, minister or leader in a church congregation, the key issue is that any member of a congregation can potentially fall into this group. In one study, those spending more than 15 hours online were more likely to be involved in risky interactive or

62. Cooper, A., Delmonico, D. L., & Burg, R. (2000). Cybersex users, abusers, and compulsives: New findings and implications. *Sexual Addiction and Compulsivity, 7*(1 – 2), p. 11.
63. Cooper, A., Delmonico, D. L., & Burg, R. (2000). Cybersex users, abusers, and compulsives: New findings and implications. *Sexual Addiction and Compulsivity, 7*(1 – 2), pp. 5 – 29.

partner-seeking activities (including responding to sex ads or contacting prostitutes). This raises dangers of involvement in affairs or promiscuous sex, with the consequent dangers of sexually transmitted diseases.[64] It appears that homosexual and bisexual men are over-represented among the cybersex compulsives. Possibly the Internet is a place where they can experiment with greater anonymity and find outlets to express their sexuality. This is a particularly difficult area for women who are married to homosexual or bisexual men, as aspects of their husband or partner's sexuality may only come to light through Internet behaviours, with the resulting shock, hurt, confusion and anger that may ensue from this discovery.[65]

Those who have studied people who become addicted to Internet sex have found that many appear to come from emotionally disengaged,[66] overly authoritarian or dysfunctional families. One author identified the following characteristics of people who are sexually compulsive:

- They are victims of abuse
- They come from rigidly disengaged families
- They see themselves as shameful, bad, unworthy persons
- They are co-dependent, and believe that no one will love them as they are
- They see sexual activity as the most important way of taking care of their emotional needs
- They engage in a variety of sexual behaviours.[67]

They have difficulty trusting others, have a need to be in control of their lives, and have difficulty forming and sustaining intimate relationships. Their Internet behaviours have a negative impact on their

64. Daneback, K., Ross, M. W., Mansson, S. (2006). Characteristics and behaviors of sexual compulsives who use the Internet for sexual purposes. *Sexual Addiction and Compulsivity, 13*, 53 – 67.
65. Cooper, A., Delmonico, D. L., & Burg, R. (2000). Cybersex users, abusers, and compulsives: New findings and implications. *Sexual Addiction and Compulsivity, 7*(1 – 2), pp. 5 – 29.
66. Carnes, P. (1991). *Don't call it love*. New York: Bantam.
67. Davies, M. (2003). Clergy sexual addiction: A systemic preventative model. *Sexual Addiction and Compulsivity, 10* (2-3), 99 – 109.

relationships, families, work, and social lives. It often interferes with sleep and leads to depression, anxiety and isolation. Those who are addicted often continue the behaviour despite adverse consequences, and, like other addicts, develop levels of tolerance that require more and more time online, and lead to seeking more and more stimulating, bizarre, unhealthy or demeaning materials or experiences.[68]

Recovery

Recovery from sexual addiction is not easy. A psychologist who has worked in the area of addictions for many years said that in his experience it was the most difficult addiction to deal with in therapy.[69] Recovery requires an admission that the person has a problem, and a willingness to seek help. For married couples or partners in a relationship it may require couple as well as individual counselling. If children have been exposed to the pornography or the ongoing arguments or tension, then sessions of family therapy may also be helpful. These sessions, with trained therapists, may make some aspects of communication easier, as sex is a difficult topic to talk about for most families. Families may need help to talk through the feelings involved, as well as assistance to identify necessary changes in behaviour to support the recovering addict and prevent younger members from acting out in unhealthy ways themselves.

Those who work in the area of addictions readily recognise the effectiveness and value of self-help groups such as Alcoholics Anonymous. There are also similar groups for those addicted to sex, such as Sex Addicts Anonymous, Sex and Love Addicts Anonymous, Sexual Compulsives Anonymous and S-Anon. We have already referred to the Internet support group in Italy for those who have lost control of the sexual aspects of their lives. A list of relevant web addresses will be given at the end of this chapter. Further discussion of the issue of

68. Cavaglion, G. (2008). Narratives of self-help of cyberporn dependents. *Sexual Addiction and Compulsivity, 15*, p. 196.
69. Mark Schwarz, PhD. *Annual Clinical Conference on Compulsivity, Masters and Johnson Institute*, River Oaks Psychiatric Hospital, New Orleans, May 10th – 11th 2002.

sexual addiction and the recovery process can be found in the booklet entitled *Sexual Addiction and Internet Pornography* by Mark Brouwer and Mark Laaser, which is also published in *The Christian handbook of abuse, addiction and difficult behaviour.*[70]

Clergy

Clergy are not exempt from the problems related to use of the Internet to view pornography, or the dangers of falling into addictive or compulsive behaviour. The magazine *Christianity Today* conducted a survey of its readership in 2000. They found that for the majority of the clergy Internet sex was not a problem. However, 33% of the clergy subscribers and 36% of the lay subscribers said that they had visited a pornographic site at some time. The following statistics were reported for those who had visited sexually explicit sites:

	Clergy	Lay Readers
Have visited sites a few times in the past year	53%	44%
Spouse knows about it	28%	30%
Prayed about this area of their lives	69%	60%
Sought professional help	4%	7%

It is interesting to note how many members of the clergy or laity had prayed about this, but how few had sought professional help. It is also important to note that while 18% of the clergy said they visited sexually explicit sites between a couple of times a month and more than once a week, 69% of those who visited such sites said they did so at first out of curiosity, or justified their viewing by saying that they needed to know what people in their congregations were watching. Clergy with problems tended to be younger and, like lay addicts, could spend over 11 hours a week online. [71]

70. Brouwer, M., & Laaser, M. (2008). Sexual addiction and Internet pornography, in B. Geary & J. Bryan (Eds.). *The Christian handbook of abuse, addiction and difficult behaviour.* Suffolk: Kevin Mayhew.
71. Gardner, C. J. (2001). Tangled in the worst of the Web: What Internet porn did to one pastor, his wife, his ministry, their life. Posted at http://www.ctlibrary.com/ct/2001/march5/1.42.html

People who work in the area of spiritual formation and human development are aware that this is becoming a growing problem. One priest said that a friend who was an ambulance driver reported that he often passed his parish church in the early hours of the morning. Over time he noticed that there was often a light on in an upstairs room of the presbytery. At first he presumed the priest was working late, but he gradually wondered if the priest whom he respected and liked was having a problem with compulsive use of the Internet. His problem was trying to decide what, if anything, he could do about it. There have been reports from all parts of the world, involving married and celibate clergy, from a number of denominations and faiths, of clergy who become involved in inappropriate online activities, including downloading child pornography.

Some people become clergy as a way of coping with addictive behaviours. There is a hope that God will take care of things after ordination, or after a good retreat or effort to renew personal prayer. For many, this leads to further feelings of failure, which can make it more difficult to continue a personal relationship with God because of the feelings of failure or shame that they experience. Clergy are in a difficult position as they are often put on a pedestal by their parishioners, and the results of exposure can lead to loss of their ministry and possibly their home. This may be particularly frightening for married clergy.

Mark Laaser found the following characteristics in his experience of working with clergy who were sex addicts:

- Hope that ordination would reduce the shame they feel in their lives
- Have their needs met by seeking the approval of others
- Are in denial about their sexual needs and behaviours
- Often display lack of flexibility in their thinking, which is mirrored in their rigid theology
- Often have a great deal of unexpressed anger.[72]

72. Davies, M. (2003). Clergy sexual addiction: A systemic preventative model. *Sexual Addiction and Compulsivity, 10*,(2-3), 99 – 109.

It has been suggested that an unconscious motive for choosing ministry is sometimes a refuge from childhood traumas.[73] Ministerial service can be seen as a way to avoid or redeem a painful past. The clergy role is very public and involves a certain degree of scrutiny by the congregation. Their own sense of sinfulness and perfectionism may drive them to high standards of moral behaviour. However, the wound at the centre of their lives may manifest itself in unhealthy ways if the original trauma is not addressed.

Spirituality and recovery

The process of recovery for clergy, and indeed for all people who are caught in the tangle of Internet sexual addiction, appears to involve a renewed spirituality. It is interesting to read the messages left on the Italian self-help website, many of which refer to spiritual concepts. They talk of being 'lost navigators', who are on a journey of soul searching. The word 'confession' is used, and members pray together when in need of help, and refer to their brothers and sisters as a 'gift of God'. Faith in a supreme power is seen as a part of the road to recovery. The leader has stressed that their 'eyes ravaged their souls'.[74]

Spirituality is now seen to have a place for people recovering from a range of addictions, and the same appears to be true of those addicted to Internet pornography. This should hardly surprise us since sex and spirituality are so closely linked. Scott Peck has called them, 'kissing cousins'.[75] Both sex and spirituality spur us on to connect the broken and disconnected parts of the self and our relationships. A healthy sexuality invites us to glimpse the divine in the pleasure, awe, mystery, humour, clumsiness, complexity and reverence involved in sex. The Internet offers shortcuts that turn out to be blind alleys.[76]

73. Laaser, M., & Adams, K. (2002). Pastors and sexual addiction. *Clinical management of sexual addiction* (pp. 285 – 297). New York: Brunner-Routledge.
74. Cavaglion, G. (2008). Narratives of self-help of cyberporn dependents. *Sexual Addiction and Compulsivity, 15*, 195 – 216.
75. Scott Peck, M. (1978). *The road less travelled.* London: Ryder.
76. Carnes, P., Delmonico, D. L., Griffin, E., & Moriarty, J. M. (2007). *In the shadows of the net: Breaking free of compulsive online sexual behavior.* Minnesota: Hazelden, pp. 220 – 221.

Internet child pornography

While this chapter is not primarily concerned with illegal Internet activity, it is important to devote some attention to this disturbing topic. The Internet Watch Foundation (IWF) reported that 71% of adults surveyed said that their top concern about the Internet was the availability of child pornography. Most adults who had come across images of children being sexually abused were not sure how to report them. There has been a considerable decrease in the number of sites containing child pornography hosted in the UK (down from 18% of such sites in 1997 to 1% of sites in 2007), however 2755 such child-pornography sites were identified in 2007, all of which were hosted abroad, and half of which depicted brutal and severe forms of abuse.[77]

40% of sites accessed in the United Kingdom are hosted in the United States of America, and 28% come from Russia. If a site is identified in the UK it is usually shut down within 48 hours, whereas in the United States the police wait to gather evidence in order to conduct a sting operation to arrest those involved. It appears that there is currently no liaison with Russia. These differences mean that this global problem is not currently being tackled in a uniform way, and more children are being exploited.[78]

Elena Curti courageously wrote about her own experience of discovering that her husband had been downloading images of child pornography:

> A few weeks ago my husband was sentenced for viewing child pornography on the net and is now serving a three-month prison sentence . . . My overwhelming desire was to discover how the man I loved and thought I knew so well could have done such a thing . . . It felt like a manifestation of pure evil . . . Stress at work, depression, insomnia and alcohol had all played

---

77. IWF Newsletter (28th October, 2008). newsletter@iwf.org.uk
78. Doward, J. (26th February, 2006). Massive rise in child porn sites. *The Observer*, p. 5.

their part in his addiction. Christianity offers an explanation which I have never understood as well as I do now: all human beings are to a greater or lesser extent drawn towards evil, and once we succumb it is hard to break free.[79]

Elena Curti found support and help from her elderly parish priest. She also arranged to have her house blessed again when her husband returned from prison. They then renewed their marriage vows on their twentieth anniversary. As well as offering a perceptive and honest discussion of this problem, Elena Curti's experience shows how significant clergy, the Church, and spirituality can be in the process of recovery for all members of a family affected by this behaviour.

Conclusion

The purpose of this chapter was to examine the issue of Internet pornography and to explore its impact on users, families, partners, and children. We have shown how the Internet draws people because it is affordable, accessible, and anonymous, and how it is isolating, compelling, intoxicating, imposing, interactive, and has become integral to our lives. The special issues related to child pornography, and addiction and compulsivity have been examined. Specific issues related to members of the clergy have also been explored. The devastating impact of the use of Internet pornography on families has been discussed briefly, as well as the process of recovery. The place of spirituality has been discussed and ways in which members of the clergy can be in a privileged position to offer help to all members of a family, but in particular to those who are involved in this kind of behaviour. It appears, then, that opportunities are now presenting themselves for pastoral conversations around sexuality, relationships, self-esteem, having needs met in healthy ways, respect for self and respect for women, and the corrosive effects of Internet pornography.

79. Curti, E. (28th February, 2004). Evil in the virtual Eden. *The Tablet*, pp. 8 – 9.

It is important that priests, ministers, counsellors, people in positions of leadership – such as employers or head teachers – and others respond in a non-judgemental way, but also that they be careful not to underestimate the extent of the problem or its impact on the person who is coming for help.[80] While it is not necessary for everyone to be an expert on all aspects of cybersex, it is important that all understand the effect that this can have on individuals, families, communities like parishes or schools, and relationships.

Do's and Don'ts

- Ensure that the computer is kept in a place where everyone can see what is being viewed

- If children have their own computers, ensure that blocking software is installed. It is not foolproof, but is highly effective

- Monitor your children's use of the Internet. This may be difficult, but avoiding the issue may lead to unhealthy behaviours

- If you notice secretive behaviour, or evasive answers to simple questions, it may be necessary to have a frank conversation with your partner or member of your family

- Do not underestimate the impact of use of pornography on members of your family, or on the values you are trying to instil in your children

- Break the silence. Talk to someone who can help you.

Reading

Brouwer, M., & Laaser, M. (2008). Sexual addiction and Internet pornography, in B. Geary & J. Bryan (Eds.). *The Christian handbook of abuse, addiction and difficult behaviour.* Suffolk: Kevin Mayhew. (This chapter is also available as a booklet.)

---

80. Schneider, J. P. (2000). Effects of cybersex addiction on the family: Results of a survey. *Sexual Addiction and Compulsivity, 7(1-2)*, pp. 31 – 58.

Carnes, P., Delmonico, D. L., Griffin, E., & Moriarty, J. M. (2007). *In the shadows of the net: Breaking free of compulsive online sexual behavior.* Minnesota: Hazelden.

Hudson Allez, G. (2009). *Infant losses; Adult searches. A neural and developmental perspective on psychopathology and sexual offending.* London: Karnac.

Useful websites

Sexual Sanity

http://sexual-sanity.com/

A web site run by Mark Brouwer which offers help, tele-seminars and resources for people who are affected by Internet sexual addiction.

Sex Addicts Anonymous

http://saa-recovery.org/ (USA)

http://saa-recovery.org/Meetings/OtherCountries/meeting.php?country=United%20Kingdom (United Kingdom)

Sex and Love Addicts Anonymous

http://www.slaauk.com/

Sexual Compulsives Anonymous

http://www.sca-recovery.org/

S-Anon

http://www.sanon.org/

A programme of recovery for those who have been affected by someone else's sexual behaviour. There are meetings in the United States, and in London and Manchester in the UK. Phone numbers are provided on the web page (see Meetings).

Dr. Thaddeus Birchard and Associates

http://www.sexual-addiction.co.uk/?gclid=CJHAqunTkZwCFY4U4wodm1noeQ

This group specialises in providing help for those who are affected by sexual addiction or compulsivity.

BBC website

http://www.bbc.co.uk/relationships/sex_and_sexual_health/
probs_sexaddiction.shtml

TWELVE

Contemporary issues in gender and sexual identity

Jocelyn Bryan

Introduction

When I am faced with an application form asking for personal details I happily tick the relevant boxes which identify me as a female, in her mid-forties, who is married with three children. These facts reveal both my gender and my sexuality. I am female and I am heterosexual.

For most of us, most of the time, we apply the categories of sex and gender without question. Male, female, masculine, feminine, man, woman, boy, girl are familiar terms which we use to identify and classify our fellow human beings. But it is not always this straightforward. A few examples might illustrate the point. Is every man just masculine or would we categorise some men as more masculine than others? How about the women who choose to wear stereotypically male clothes, does that imply something about their sexuality, or do they just happen to like that style of dress? What about the masculinity of a man who entertains an audience dressed in drag, compared with a transvestite who secretly dresses in lingerie in the privacy of his bedroom?

The media, from TV chat shows to documentaries and in-depth articles, has a fascination – some would say obsession – with gender and sexual issues. Comedians such as Julian Carey and Eddie Izzard are explicit in their experimentation with gender boundaries and how we perceive masculinity. The 'gender benders' such as Boy George and David Bowie, along with the influence of such stars as Madonna, confront us with how we make sense of what it means to be male or female, and how we express our sexuality.

How we understand gender and sexuality shapes our personal relationships and the lived experience of being physical sexual beings. For many women their gender identity has led them to experience oppression, inequality, exploitation and abuse. Likewise many homosexual men and women have endured social ostracism, loss of family ties, abuse, poverty and pain because of their sexual identity. It is fair to say that the definition, understanding and categorisation of sexuality and gender in any culture influences not only how individuals see themselves but also how they view others and the nature of the relationships they form with each other.

This chapter will explore how current thinking in gender and sexual identity informs our understanding of both relationships and sexuality. It will consider the current research and different psychological perspectives on gender differences, before examining different sexual identities and the factors which influence their development. Although this chapter is necessarily theoretical, where possible it will highlight areas where help and support can be offered. To conclude it will offer a Christian reflection on gender identity and transsexuality.

Definitions

Sex

For many years social scientists have defined sex in terms of the biological difference between males and females. It is therefore a biological category and is assumed to be fixed. It refers to the physiological and biochemical differences between males and females.

Gender

Gender is a social category. It is the way culture defines and responds to the sex differences between males and females. For this reason, it includes roles, practices, attitudes, values and characteristics which the culture associates with one sex or the other. It works as a social label by which people categorise one another into one or the other of the sexes. Although we can all understand and respond to our gender in different ways, we are created to belong to one or other of these categories and this has a profound influence on how others respond to us, what expectations we have of ourselves and others, and also the course of our lives.

Sexual identity

Sexual identity refers to the way in which one identifies oneself in terms of whom one is sexually attracted to, whether one is attracted to members of the same gender as one's own or the opposite gender. This develops over time and determines the social and sexual expectations we hold of ourselves and others.

Gender identity

Gender identity is the way in which a person identifies themselves as male, female or some combination of these. Hence, it is a sense of the maleness or femaleness by which a person's social behaviour is organised. It is the psychological sense we have of being male or female. Gender identity disorders occur when there is discomfort with one's own gender or a desire to identify oneself as the opposite sex.

Therefore sexual identity and gender identity refer to different aspects of oneself, but because personal identity is formed from a combination of these different aspects, there is often confusion and overlap in the way these terms are used. We can say that gender and sexual identity are distinct but that they are related to each other. This relationship varies from person to person. A homosexual male's gender identity and sexual identity are integrated in his personal identity in a very different way from that of a heterosexual woman.

Gender roles and stereotypes

Gender roles and stereotypes vary from culture to culture. These are the ways males and females are expected to behave within their society.

In some cultures women are expected to care for the children, in other cultures they are excluded from roles which carry with them overt power and authority. There are certain occupations which are more or less exclusively assigned to men. In most cultures there are numerous transgender roles which are socially approved and are neither male nor female, and there are also cross-gender roles, for example when a woman takes on a role which is normally assigned to a man.

Stereotypes are beliefs concerning the 'typical' man or woman. They are fixed ideas about how women and men are expected to behave and include some personality characteristics. They function as shorthand ways of thinking, but can often lead to prejudices and closed minds regarding some of the complexities of human existence, particularly in the areas of sexuality, ethnicity and religion.

Sexual orientation

Sexual orientation concerns a person's erotic, emotional and romantic attachment to other individuals of the same, opposite or both sexes. It not only concerns sexual behaviour but involves love, identity, and desire. Some psychologists believe it is best understood as a range or a continuum.[1]

Gender

There are numerous similarities and differences between men and women, and these have an impact on all of our lives in many ways. Yet from the book of Genesis to the twentieth century the emphasis has been on the difference between men and women, and this has shaped the course of social and political history. The latest national statistics present us with a glimpse of some of the sociological differences which exist in the United Kingdom today.[2]

1. Miracle, T., Miracle, A. & Baumeister, R. F. (2003). Human sexuality: Meeting your basic needs. New Jersey: Prentice Hall, pp. 325 – 326.
2. see www.statistics.gov.uk/focuson/gender/, accessed on 3 February 2009.

- In 2006 75% of men owned a house compared with 60% of women
- Employment rates were higher for men (79%) than women (70%) in 2008
- Although the gender pay gap is narrowing, men still earn over 12% more than women, when measured on median hourly pay for 2006–2007
- 80% of offenders are men.

Although statistics such as these can be used to emphasise differences, they paint a picture of similarities too. There are still gaps in pay levels, but more than half of all men and women are in employment and are home owners. However, the differences between men and women have come to dominate gender studies and the psychology of gender for many years. The common rhetoric of the 'battle of the sexes' suggests difference and competition rather than similarity and harmony. It is encouraging to read that more recent research is moving away from the emphasis on difference and the male/female dichotomy, to explore the overlap between the sexes and a consideration of gender in terms of a continuum on which similarities and differences exist. Furthermore, psychology is asking questions of context; when and under what conditions do similarities and differences occur?[3] In this way we are beginning to gain insights into the causes of both sex differences and sex similarities and this may enable us to navigate through the political minefield of gender with more success, as well as encourage more people to take note of what science is revealing.

Gender and sex differences

Sex differences exist and we experience them every day of our lives. Just listen to the content of what children recount about their school day. Girls are more likely to talk about their friends and how they

3. Eagly, A. H., Beall, A. E., Sternberg, R. J. (Eds.). (2004). *The Psychology of Gender* (2nd Edition) London: The Guildford Press, pp. 4–6.

feel about them than what they did; in contrast boys are more likely to communicate factual information; what lessons they had and which team won the lunchtime game of football in the yard.

Many of the popular books written on sex differences say that men and women are so different from each other that they fail to understand one another and struggle to communicate. *Men are from Mars, Women are from Venus* clearly plays on this, suggesting that men and women do not even originate from the same planet. There are, of course, occasions when communication and understanding are challenging. Evidence suggests that men and women think and communicate differently,[4] but most of the time we communicate with each other effectively, and most of us can show empathy towards those of the opposite sex.

It is important to note that acknowledging differences between the sexes should not result in oppression or justify sexism in any way. Difference does not imply inferiority or superiority. Nor does it justify gender stereotyping which can be equally destructive. The danger in interpreting any research is leaping to assumptions and making generalisations which overlook the individuality of each person.

Here I offer a description of what we know at present and some explanations for this. The possible causes of these differences and their effect on gender and sexual identity are the main focus of this chapter. Much of this will, I hope, confirm what you know and experience already. However I also hope to offer new insights which may inform how we engage with our personal gender and sexual identities, as well as those of others.

Sex differences

Numerous studies from the psychological literature have identified psychological sex differences. Below is a summary of some of the ones that are best known and which have been supported by research.

4. Tannen, D. (2001). *You just don't understand.* New York: HarperCollins.

1. Physical aggression tends to be greater in males than females.

2. Females tend to perform better than males on tasks involving verbal skills.

3. Males tend to perform better on visual spatial tasks.

4. Males tend to perform better on mathematical problems, but this is not as firmly established as the other differences.[5]

We can see how these differences are borne out in our experience. A boy showing physical aggression would be viewed as normal whereas a girl who shows a similar amount of aggression is identified as a child with a behavioural problem. A very talkative girl is not remarked upon, whereas a very talkative boy would be.

We also categorise personality characteristics according to sex. These form the basis of our gender stereotypes. Males are portrayed as active, dominant, aggressive and confident, and females as passive, submissive, fearful and compliant. The assertive female managing director is still viewed by many as an anomaly, or in a cross-gender role. The shy, hesitant father who does not shout on the goal line of the school football pitch is often not considered as manly as those who encourage their sons (or daughters) with aggressive language and a lot of gesticulation. The only personality characteristic which has been linked to sex differences is aggressive behaviour. There is no basis for any of the other characteristics being associated with one sex more than the other. However, these stereotypes continue to persist in our culture, despite the cultural changes which have taken place over many decades, including the effects of feminism.

Interestingly, there is some evidence of changes in our understanding and acceptance of gender roles and gender stereotypes associated with a number of occupations as some cross-gender roles become more common. We no longer comment on a female medical consultant's gender in the same way as we might have done 40 years

---

5. Shibley Hyde, J. (2005). The gender similarities hypothesis. *American Psychologist, 6 (6)*, pp. 581–592.

ago. Women ministers are now accepted and fully integrated into ordained ministry in the Methodist Church and other non conformist traditions, so they are no longer seen as an anomaly. This is also beginning to be the case in the Church of England. However, some jobs, e.g., male midwifes and female firefighters, continue to challenge conventional understanding of gender roles.

The effects of feminism on gender identity and gender roles in this post-feminist age are still being worked through. For some men, feminism precipitated a redefinition of masculinity and the male identity. This has brought about some changes in the roles men now engage in, and there has been a realignment of some gender stereotypes in our culture. Men are more likely to do housework, spend more time involved in child care, and there has been a notable shift in men expressing their feelings. It is noticeable, for example, that we now frequently witness men being more expressive about their emotions in the media. But for other men, the present age has led to an identity crisis. Many have resisted what they interpret as the feminisation of the male sex and feel that the essence of the male nature needs reclaiming. There is also evidence that women value equality, but want to maintain their sense of femininity.

The essential maleness and femaleness they possess is something which both sexes value, and gender identity continues to challenge both men and women. In a recent article in *The Times* newspaper, the playwright Zoe Lewis[6] expressed how she feels betrayed by the feminism she embraced over 20 years ago. She writes:

> I thought men would love independent, strong women, but (in general) they don't appear to. Men are programmed to like their women soft and feminine. It's not their fault – it's in the genes.

Later she writes:

> Somewhere inside lurks a woman I cannot control and she is in

---

6. Lewis, Z. (2009). I should have ditched feminism for love, children and baking. *Times 2*, February 5th. pp. 8 – 9.

the kitchen with a baby on her hip . . . It's an instinct that makes me a woman, an instinct that I can't ignore even if I wanted to.

How much of our gender identity and gender roles are due to our genes, natural instincts, and biology, and how much to the culture in which we live? The answer to this question becomes clearer as we begin to understand more about sex differences and the way in which gender identity develops. Having said that, its complexity continues to challenge us.

The work of Simon Baron-Cohen[7] is a good illustration of the progress that has been made in this area of gender differences. He has brought new insights into the heart of the debate by suggesting that the key psychological difference between men and women is between their ability to systemise and empathise. He proposes that the female brain is predominantly hard-wired for empathy and the male brain predominantly hard-wired for understanding and building systems.

Empathy is the ability to identify another person's emotions and thoughts, and respond to them with an appropriate emotion. It is not just concerned with the identification of the emotion, but it is about feeling the appropriate emotional reaction. The motive is to understand another person and anticipate their response, thereby connecting with them emotionally.[8] Baron-Cohen suggests that, on average, females spontaneously empathise more than males. Likewise males, on average, systemise more than females. Systemising is defined as the drive to analyse, explore and construct systems. Systemisers try to figure out how things work, and work out the input and output of systems. They work with the rule, 'If–then'. The evidence for this is compelling and very helpful to our understanding of gender identity and difference.[9]

7. Baron-Cohen, S. (2004). *The Essential Difference*. London: Penguin.
8. Ibid pp. 2–6.
9. Baron-Cohen, S. (2002). The extreme male brain theory of autism. *Trends in Cognitive Science 6(6)*, pp. 248–254.

Below is a sample of the evidence for the females being more empathetic:[10]

- On average girls show more concern for fairness and less rough-and-tumble play than boys.

- Girls from age of 1 year show greater concern for others. More women than men report frequently sharing the emotional distress of others and show more comforting behaviour towards others.

- Girls at the age of 3 years are ahead of boys in their ability to infer what others might be thinking or intending.

- Women have better sensitivity to facial expression and decoding nonverbal communication.

- More woman value relationships and their development than men.

- Aggression is associated with reduced empathy and men show more direct aggression than women.

- Women talk more about feelings.

There is also compelling evidence for the males being more inclined towards systemising.

- Boys are more likely to choose toy vehicles, weapons, building blocks and mechanical toys.

- Occupational choices such as metal-working, manufacturing musical instruments, boat-building etc. are dominated by males.

- Mathematics, physics, and engineering are dominated by males.

- On 3-D mechanical construction tasks men on average score higher than women. Boys show more interest in construction toys such as Lego, and are faster at copying 3-D Lego models.

- Attention to detail is superior in males.

- On average boys are better at map-reading than girls.

10. Baron-Cohen, S. (2002). The extreme male brain theory of autism. *Trends in Cognitive Science 6(6)*, pp. 249–250.

The question remains: what is the cause of these differences which shape gender identity? Are we 'hard-wired' to be this way through evolutionary processes reflected in our genes and biology, or do our culture and upbringing determine these differences?

The insights from biology

It goes without saying that men and women look different, and human beings are dimorphic. The sexual organs of the female differ from those of the male. From 7–8 weeks after conception the sex of the foetus is determined and in the majority of births there is no ambiguity concerning the sex of the baby. The sex of the foetus is determined by two things: sex chromosomes and sex hormones.

Males have one X and one Y chromosome (XY) and females have two X chromosomes (XX). Males produce testosterone from their testes and this begins rather soon after conception. Testosterone is also secreted by the adrenal glands and this explains why it is present in females. Males obviously produce more testosterone. Females produce female sex hormone, oestrogen, from their ovaries.

Chromosomes

Very occasionally the pattern of the sex chromosomes varies and this has significant effects on the development of the genitalia and the secretion of sex hormones. Turner Syndrome occurs when an individual has a missing sex chromosome. Hence instead of the 46 chromosomes, 22 pairs of autosomes and one pair of sex chromosomes, they are missing a sex chromosome (45 XO). People with this condition give us some indication of the contribution of genetics to gender difference and gender and sexual identity, and for that reason it is worth taking some time to understand the effect these differences can have.

Those with Turner Syndrome are identified as females because their external genitalia are female at birth, but these remain immature as there is no secretion of any sex hormones. Consequently, they do not menstruate, or develop breasts or pubic hair at puberty unless they are given artificial sex hormones. They are brought up as girls and even though they have do not have any sex hormones they show gender identification, i.e. they identify themselves as female. This suggests that upbringing has a significant effect on gender identity in childhood and can compensate for an absence of sex hormones resulting from a chromosomal abnormality.

Another chromosomal abnormality which has generated interest is those men who have an extra Y chromosome (47XYY). Early studies suggested that there was a higher incidence of these men in prison than in the general population. Furthermore, it was suggested that these men were more likely to be convicted of violent crime, linking violence to the extra Y chromosome. This was found not to be the case in a study[11] which compared XYY males with men with another chromosomal abnormality in men, namely XXY males who have an extra X chromosome. The study found no link between violence and the extra Y chromosome. In fact the only man in the study with a conviction for a violent crime was one with the XXY syndrome.

Sex hormones

The role played by both chromosomes and sex hormones in sexual dimorphism (differences between men and women) is indisputable. From the early stages of life, sex hormones play a crucial role in sexual development. As the human embryo develops, sex hormones continue to be secreted and the external and internal sex organs develop. After birth the levels of these hormones remain relatively stable and then at puberty their levels increase as the secondary sex characteristics develop.

The levels of testosterone have been found to follow a pattern of three peaks. The first is prenatal, between eight and twenty-four weeks into a pregnancy. Then there is another surge at approximately

11. Witkin, H. A., Mednick, S. A., Schulsinger, F., Bakkestroom, E., Christiansen, K. O., Goodenough, D. R., Hirschhorn, K., Lundsteen, C., Owen, D. R., Philip, J., Rubin, D. B. & Stocking, M. (1976). Criminality in XYY and XXY men. *Science, 193,* 547–55.

five months after birth, and then a final peak at puberty. These are coincident with the brain being most sensitive to hormonal changes and are referred to as 'activational' periods. The sex hormones are seen as having a prenatal activating effect on the brain.[12] The potential consequences of this will be discussed later in the chapter.

What other evidence is there that prenatal hormones influence subsequent behaviour when the chromosomal pattern is normal? Studies of different syndromes where hormonal disorders have occurred, have enabled the effects of hormones on behaviour to be examined. However, the various influences on human behaviour, including family context, expectations and the nature and quality of relationships, mean that any conclusions drawn need to recognise that the effect of hormones is just one of many factors influencing behaviour.

The most convincing evidence comes from the studies which have looked at children's play. The syndrome Congenital Adrenal Hyperplasia (CAH) is a genetic disorder which leads to high levels of the male sex hormones being secreted from the adrenal gland in girls. This begins whilst they are still in the womb and can be quickly diagnosed since the girls have partially masculinised genitalia. When these girls play they show a preference for the toys which are usually chosen by boys, such as cars and trains, and, compared with other girls, they are less likely to choose dolls. They also get involved more in rough-and-tumble play, which is more typical of boys.[13] It is important to note that these findings have been consistent with researchers in other countries who have used interviews, questionnaires and also watched the girls' play to establish this behavioural pattern. Baron-Cohen[14] has noted that these girls are better at spatial systemising compared with their sisters and close female members who are not

---

12. Baron-Cohen, S. (2004). *The essential difference*. London: Penguin, p. 101.
13. Hines, M. (2002). Sexual differentiation of the human brain and behaviour. In D. W. Pfaff, A. P. Arnold, A. M. Etgen, S. E. Fahrbach, R. T. Rubin. (Eds.). *Hormones, brain and behaviour*. (4th Ed., pp. 425–461), San Diego: Academic Press, & Hines. M. (2004). *Brain gender*. New York: Oxford University Press.
14. Baron-Cohen, S. (2004). *The essential difference*. London: Penguin, pp. 104–5.

exposed to the high levels of androgens (male hormones) in the womb. This suggests that testosterone plays an important part in the development of the brain and subsequent behaviours, which leads to the observed differences in empathising and systemising. It has been suggested[15] that testosterone in the womb affects the growth rate of the two hemispheres of the brain, predicting that males have faster growth in the right hemisphere. This hemisphere is associated with spatial ability, which helps systemisation become a more dominant characterisation of males.

This provides one illustration of a possible effect of prenatal sex hormones on behaviour, but what effect, in the case of CAH, might this syndrome have on girls' subsequent development and gender identity? Girls born with this syndrome and its associated ambiguous genitalia usually have surgery. Although their parents are instructed to raise their daughters like any other girl, the fact that they are born with this ambiguity might well influence both the individual's self perception in terms of gender and sexual identity and also the way in which their parents respond to them. Again both the social and biological factors inevitably interact in these cases.

The effects of testosterone

As noted earlier, testosterone is now understood to be highly significant in the prenatal stages of development, and when later the surges take place at five months and puberty. Here it has been associated with the development of the brain and the secondary sexual characteristics. However, testosterone is also associated with certain male-typical behaviours such as aggression and strong sexual desire. The association between testosterone and aggression in animals is well-documented.[16] Males tend to show more direct aggression than females e.g., pushing, hitting, thumping. The preference by boys for rough-and-tumble

---

15. Geschwind, N., & Galaburda, A. M. (1985). Cerebral laterisation, biological mechanisms, associations, and pathology: A hypothesis and programme for research. *Archive of neurology, 42*, pp. 428–59.
16. Kalat, J. W. (1992). *Biological Psychology.* Belmont, CA: Washington.

play has also been linked to testosterone. However, recent findings suggest that increasing levels of testosterone do not correspond with increased aggressive behaviour, rather there appears to be a threshold level which, when passed, causes more aggression in certain people under certain circumstances. But other factors like personality traits e.g., impulsivity, also play an important role in moderating the expression of aggressive behaviour, and these have to be taken into account. We can say then, that although testosterone influences behaviour, it is not the only factor operating. For different individuals there are different effects.[17]

The effects of oestrogen

Research into the effects of premenstrual syndrome (PMS) has led to the identification of various links between sex hormones and behaviour in women. Before the mid-1980s this focused on the effect of hormonal changes on mood. There is no doubt that the stereotype of a woman suffering from PMS has exaggerated the effects of this, but it is clear that ovarian hormones play a part in triggering mood swings.[18] However, as in all research into the effect of hormones on behaviour, the conclusions are complex. The regulation of the mood changes triggered by hormones in PMS may well be related to the context a woman finds herself in. In her work environment she is likely to show more emotional regulation than at home with her family, but there may be times when the hormonal effect in PMS might result in more extreme emotional responses becoming apparent at work.

The research into the menstrual cycle has also revealed that levels of oestrogen affect performance on spatial tests, verbal fluency or

---

17. O'Connor, D. B., Archer, J., Hair, W. M. & Wu, F. C. W. (2002). Exogenous testosterone, aggression and mood in eugonadal and hypogonadal men. *Physiology and behavior. 75*, 557–566. Quoted in Neave, N., & O'Connor, D. B. (2008). Testosterone and male behavior. *The Psychologist, 22(1)*, pp. 28–31.
18. Hampson, E., & Moffat, S. D. (2004). The psychobiology of gender: Cognitive effects of reproductive hormones in the adult nervous system. In A. H. Eagly, A. E. Beall, R. J. Sternberg (Eds.). (2004) *The psychology of gender* (2nd Edition). London: The Guildford Press, p. 43.

word generation. This is important evidence in supporting the idea that hormones influence differences in measures of verbal fluency in men and women.[19]

As our knowledge of genetics, physiology and biochemistry increases, the influence of these factors on sex differences will become better understood. How these factors interact with and are affected by our upbringing, culture and social environment is undoubtedly a significant question for our understanding of gender and sex differences. In the next section we examine the evidence that these cultural factors play a significant role in gender identity and sex differences.

Parenting, culture and social construction

We respond to people on the basis of their sex. Everyone is 'doing gender' without thinking about it.[20] This influences both our expectations and interpretations of the way people behave. The social construction theory of gender suggests that once a baby is born, they are assigned to a sex category on the basis of their genitalia and from that time on they are dressed and responded to on the basis of their sex. Once a child can talk they identify themselves according to their gender and by the time they reach puberty their sexual desires and practices have been shaped by gender norms and expectations. Parenting is also gendered with the expectations of mothers and fathers in society differing on this basis. Likewise, occupations are gendered, as we have discussed earlier. All of these produce different feelings, relationships, skills, identity or ways of being feminine or masculine. Social construction theory suggests that gender is a social institution and one of the major ways that human beings organise their lives. It contends that gender can not be equated with biological and physiological differences between human males and females, but

19. Hampson, E., & Moffat, S. D. (2004). The psychobiology of gender: Cognitive effects of reproductive hormones in the adult nervous system. In A. H. Eagly, A. E. Beall, R. J. Sternberg (Eds.). (2004) *The psychology of gender* (2nd Edition). London: The Guildford Press, p. 45.
20. Lorder, J. (1994). *Paradoxes of Gender*. Yale: Yale University Press.

that individuals are taught to be masculine or feminine. Gender is created by social relationships influenced by culture and society. Clearly much of the evidence we have considered from the biological research and also evolutionary psychology contradicts this position, but there is some evidence that parenting and culture influence gender identity.

This point is made clearly in what is known as The Baby X experiment.[21] A videotape of an upset child was shown to a group who were told the baby was a boy. They interpreted the child's response as anger, but another group who were told the same baby was a girl described the child's response as fear. Why does this happen? Is it simply the result of the stereotypes in our culture or is it that we have observed and associated these responses as typical of boys and girls?

The different expectations that we have of boys and girls are also reflected in the different parenting styles which are adopted for each. Boys are punished more, controlled more and receive more prohibitions and threats than girls. Is this because parents believe that boys are likely to get themselves into trouble, are less cautious, and more deviant than girls? Are cultural stereotypes the cause or source of this difference in the way parents treat boys and girls, or could it be, as Baron-Cohen suggests, that boys are poorer empathisers than girls, and this gives rise to a number of sex differences in social behaviour? Boys are less socially compliant; they are not as skilled as girls at picking up the social cues and predicting the effects which their behaviour has on others. Parents may be responding to this natural difference by exerting more control over them.

Another example of differences in parenting is that boys are encouraged to be less emotional and more independent than girls. Here again we have to ask if parents are socialising their children into the different gender roles of the culture or if are girls are simply

---

21. Condry, J. & Condry, S. (1976). Sex differences: a study in the eye of the beholder. *Child Development, 47,* pp. 812–819.

better at managing their emotions appropriately. Therefore we need to ask if parents are responding to a fundamental difference between boys and girls or if the parent's response causes the difference.

There are some differences that are present at a very young age, and it is these which make it difficult to see how culture can be the primary or only factor which determines sex differences. For instance, before the age of two boys mostly choose to play with cars and trucks and girls with dolls and cuddly toys. This happens at an age when they are not likely to be aware of the gender stereotypes associated with toys. Social influences are therefore unlikely to be determining the choice they make.[22] The presence of these sex differences at a very early age has led Baron-Cohen[23] to suggest that whereas culture and socialisation might partly determine if you develop a male brain (stronger interest in systems) or female brain (stronger interest in empathy), biology might also partly determine this too. There is a considerable amount of evidence for both cultural and biological determinism. The nature-nurture debate continues. Some researchers believe that the interpersonal and cultural environment we inhabit is the dominant source of influence in sex difference, whilst others believe that many of the different psychological dispositions between the sexes are due to biological make up. As we have seen, this is a complex matter and continues to challenge psychology as it struggles to fathom the way in which evolutionary, cultural and biological factors combine to influence gender differences.

It may appear that we have gone on a long journey to reach this point, however it is in fact a brief summary of a complex debate. At the risk of simplifying this debate, it is safe to say that the current state of research suggests that sex differences are due to both cultural/social and biological factors. Work still needs to be done to tease out the relationship between the two. There is however, one further influence to bear in mind; that of evolution.

22. Baron-Cohen, S. (2004). *The essential difference*, London: Penguin, pp. 92–93.
23. Baron-Cohen, S. (2002). The extreme male theory of autism. *Trends in Cognitive Sciences Vol. 6(6)*, pp. 248–254.

Evolution

We have established that sex differences appear to be the result of both social and biological factors. But how many of the sex differences have resulted from the process known as natural selection, because they improve the chances of survival and reproducing? Many of the sex differences seen in human beings are similar to those in animals, especially those concerning the different roles men and women have in reproduction and nurturing, and aggression.

A number of gender differences in sexual behaviour have been plausibly explained by evolutionary theory.[24] For example, men tend to desire more partners and more novelty than women.[25] This difference in promiscuity has been explained by evolutionary theory in terms of reproduction and the desire to pass on our genes. By having many sexual partners men can father many offspring. For women the gestation period of nine months restricts them to no more than one pregnancy a year. A promiscuous woman is limited by this too. But for women, monogamy can be seen as advantageous because passing on one's gene does not only depend on producing babies, but requires that the babies themselves should survive to reproduce themselves. A child requires care, protection and food. If, as in a monogamous relationship, there is a father present to provide for some of these needs, then a child's chances of survival increase. Ensuring that their offspring survive is also important for men, and the strategies of both monogamy and promiscuity can be seen to be advantageous. Some men have adopted both strategies. They are married but have sex with other women. Interestingly, Betzig[26] makes the point that many powerful men in history have done this; typically having a wife and many mistresses or concubines.

24. See Buss, D. M. (1994). *The evolution of desire: strategies of human mating.* New York: Basic Books, for a full description of evolutionary psychology and this approach.
25. Lawson, A., & Samson, C. (1988). Age, gender and adultery. *British Journal of Sociology, 39*, pp. 409–440.
26. Betzig, L. (1986). *Despotism and differential reproduction: A Darwinian view of history.* New York: Aldine.

It also appears that women are more likely to limit their sexual activity. This is a consistent finding across most cultures. In terms of evolutionary theory, this is a good strategy for women as it suggests that they exercise more care when choosing their sexual partners, spending more time with a man before embarking on a sexual relationship. For a woman, there is more at stake if she makes a mistake when selecting a mate, since she can only pass on her genes through pregnancy once a year. Men have less to lose by having sex when and with whom they choose.

The investment by women in nurturing and feeding babies has also been used by evolutionary theory to explain differences in gender roles, as well as some cognitive sex differences such as those proposed by Baron-Cohen. He suggests that women, with their more empathetic brain, have an evolutionary advantage in the task of nurturing and caring for a baby, since they are better able to predict and understand their baby's needs. This also equips them to make friends more easily, and set up good support networks which watch over and look after their children when other demands are made on the mother, thus increasing the survival chances of the baby.[27]

Evolutionary heritage can be seen to be expressed in behaviour through the interaction between genetic dispositions and our social environment. This is a complex process, and one which we are still a long way from understanding fully. Yet we need to acknowledge that it plays a significant part in our understanding of gender identity along with the other factors we have discussed. Biology is not necessarily destiny, but clearly sex differences arise from attributes which are more likely to be found in one sex than the other. As human beings, we can manage and regulate our behaviour in most circumstances. We are largely responsible for our actions both as men and women and for the way we relate to each other as gendered sexual human beings.

27. Baron-Cohen, S. (2004). *The essential difference.* London: Penguin, pp. 127–8.

Gender identity and disorders

Gender identity is almost always consistent with both genetic and anatomical gender. So, biological females have female gender identity and biological males have male gender identity. They are normally brought up and socialised according to their anatomical gender, which reinforces their gender identity. However, this is not the case for everyone.

There are a small number of intersexuals who have both male and female traits, including reproductive organs, secondary sexual characteristics and sexual behaviour. They are often called hermaphrodites and since the 1940s, they have been encouraged to have hormonal and surgical treatment so that they can appear fully male or female, since it is assumed that without this they would suffer from a confused gender. It is estimated that the incidence of this is 1 or 2 in 1000 births.

There have also been a few cases when boys have had severely damaged penises in infancy and then have been surgically feminised and reassigned as female with hormonal treatment. In one case reassignment happened as a result of a tragic accident eight months after birth, when a baby's penis was damaged during an operation to remove the foreskin (circumcision). The strategy was seen to be successful during childhood but by adulthood he was living as a man and reported to have been deeply unhappy when trying to live as a female. After he was told that he had been born male, the feminising hormone was reversed and he underwent a double mastectomy and an artificial penis was created for him. He married and had adopted daughters,[28] but sadly, later committed suicide.[29] In another case where the penile damage occurred much earlier, at the age of 2 months, the outcome following the adoption of a female identity

28. Colapinto, J. (2000). *As nature made him: The boy who was raised as a girl.* New York: Harper Collins quoted in Miracle, T., Miracle, A. & Baumeister, R. F. (2003). *Human sexuality: Meeting your basic needs,* New Jersey: Prentice Hall, p. 314.
29. http://www.slate.com/id/2101678/

was very different: there was no evidence of unhappiness or desire to change sex.[30]

Layers of sexual life

Our sexual lives can be described as being organised into five layers,[31] with each layer building on the previous one:

1. The first layer is sexual identity, which usually corresponds to our chromosomes

2. Sexual orientation is built on top of this. Usually men are attracted to women and vice versa, though, as we know, some people are attracted to people of the same sex or to both (bisexuality)

3. Sexual interest comes next. This refers to the types of individuals, parts of the body, or situations, which we fantasise about or which arouse us

4. The fourth layer is our sex role, which is the expression of our sexual identity and involves the ways we express and communicate to others that we are male or female

5. Finally, the fifth layer is sexual performance, which concerns our sexual desires, levels of arousal, and achievement of orgasm. This fifth layer is associated with a number of sexual dysfunctions.

We can use this model to understand better different disorders that relate to sexual and gender identity.

Gender Identity Disorder and transsexuality

From this model it is evident that in transsexualism the core level of erotic life, namely sexual identity, is disordered in some way.

Gender Identity Disorder (GID) occurs when an individual has a strong and persistent cross-gender identification or desire to be the

30. Bradley, S. J., Oliver, G. D., Chernick, A. B., & Zucker, K. J. (1998). Experiment of nurture: Ablatio penis at 2 months, sex reassignment at 7 months and a psychosexual follow up in young adulthood. *Pediatrics 102*, 91–95.
31. Seligman, M. E. P., & Rosenhan, D. L. (1997). *Abnormality.* New York, London: Norton, pp. 417–418.

other sex, and persistent discomfort with the assigned sex and its gender role (American Psychiatric Association, 2000). When this occurs in boys, they may show a preference for dressing in female clothes and be preoccupied with traditionally female activities. Girls with this disorder generally prefer playing with boys and show intense negative resistance to wearing female clothes. It is important to note, however, that there are some girls who behave as 'tomboys', who do not have a gender identity disorder. For those who have the disorder, the behaviours noted above can help in providing an accurate diagnosis. In adults there is a strong desire to live as a member of the other sex and this extends to adopting that social role and then to surgery and hormonal treatment. Often they feel they are trapped in the wrong sexed body. The extreme of this order is transsexuality.[32]

Transsexuals have a profound sense that their body is 'the wrong kind'. Many experience their bodies as disgusting and the prospect of living in their body for the rest of their lives gives rise to depression, a sense of hopelessness, and sometimes suicide. In extreme cases they will mutilate their genitals. Cross-dressing commonly occurs by their early twenties but this is not for sexual excitement, as is often the case for transvestites, rather to enable them to lead a life more compatible with their sexual identity.

The cause of this disorder is understood to be predominantly hormonal. Earlier in this chapter the role of sex hormones, in particular testosterone, in sexual development was discussed. Testosterone also has an effect on the brain. This occurs in the third month of foetal development. It is thought that one effect of testosterone is to produce the male sexual identity or, in its absence, a female identity. In transsexuals it has been suggested that there is some disruption in the sexual identity phase. So, for the male-to-female transsexual, the identity phase of masculinisation does not occur, but the masculin-

32. Miracle, T., Miracle, A. & Baumeister, R. F. (2003). *Human sexuality: Meeting your basic needs*, New Jersey: Prentice Hall, p. 316.

isation of the male sexual organs takes place as normal. For the female-to-male transsexual, masculinisation of identity occurs but the sexual organs are feminised as normal. Additional effects of parenting, pubertal hormones, sexual organs and also the stigmatisation which take place will undoubtedly contribute to the disturbance or reinforcement of the core sexual identity. This biological origin is considered by some to be the reason why medical intervention rather than psychotherapy is the only option for successful treatment.

Transsexuality occurs in more men than women, which has given rise to the suggestion that a contributing factor may be the different status which exists between males and females in most societies. The male role is over-valued compared with that of the female, and men who feel that they do not fit into this stereotype have a greater sense of role conflict which leads to gender and sexual confusion resolved through transsexuality.[33] A well-known transsexual, Jan Morris, describes in her book *Conundrum* that from her earliest childhood she was unhappy as a boy. This persistent desire to change her identity from male to female drove her to take the step of surgery even though she was married and had fathered children. She now lives comfortably with her new gender identity as a female.

Clinicians seem to agree that female-to-male sex reassignment is more successful then male-to-female even though sex-reassignment surgery, particularly with respect to an erectile penis, is very difficult to achieve.[34] The outcome of surgery is not always positive. There are some studies which suggest that some transsexuals are less well adjusted after surgery than before.[35]

Transsexuals tend to form heterosexual relationships with a partner of their birth (natal) sex. Some male-to-female transsexuals classify themselves as bisexuals, or if they have exclusively female sexual partners,

---

33. Siann, G. (1994). *Gender, sex and sexuality: Contemporary psychological perspectives.* London: Taylor & Francis p. 19.
34. Money, J. (1988). *Gay, straight, and in-between: The sexology of erotic orientation.* Oxford: Oxford University Press, p. 92.
35. Siann, G. (1994). *Gender, sex and sexuality: Contemporary psychological perspectives.* London: Taylor & Francis p. 20.

as lesbians. In cases where a male-to-female transsexual is married and stays with their spouse, they often describe themselves as sisters.

The discovery of being attracted to a preoperative or postoperative male-to-female transsexual can cause panic or even enrage some men, who fear that they might have homosexual tendencies. For the majority of transsexuals the importance of reassigning their sex enables them to live in a respected heterosexual relationship with a partner of their natal sex.[36]

It is not unusual for some transsexuals to hide their story from all but family and friends, but others are more open about their previous life. Hence, there may well be transsexuals in a congregation which the majority are unaware of. For those who are open about their transsexuality, the significance of accepting them in their present sexual identity is paramount. This is a disorder which causes psychological trauma and requires considerable medical intervention. Acceptance is a necessary aspect of the support offered.

Gender Identity Disorder in young people

The incidence in childhood of cross-gender identification has not yet been established. However, it seems that it is rare and more likely, when it occurs, to occur in boys. The disorder is associated with a number of other psychological problems including separation anxiety, depression and emotional and behavioural difficulties. The most common feature associated with the disorder is relationship difficulties with parents and peers. It seems that children with gender identity problems experience considerable isolation because of relationship issues. They are often the victims of persecution and harassment and this may be a significant contributory factor to feelings of depression. Another factor is the high percentage of mental or physical health problems in their families. The likely causes are

36. Money, J. (1988). *Gay, straight, and in-between: The sexology of erotic orientation.* Oxford: Oxford University Press, pp. 92 – 93.

the same as those considered for transsexualism in adults including hereditary factors, hormonal influences and early childhood relationships. Again it is unlikely that any one of these factors alone is sufficient to produce the disorder, rather it is a combination of a number of these at a particular time in the child's life.[37]

The outcome of this disorder in children is not easy to predict. One study found that out of 66 boys in a 'feminine boys' group only one had a transsexual outcome. Interestingly, of the 44 who were followed up, 75% of them were homosexual or bisexual in their adult lives.[38] This is a developmental disorder which involves uncertainty and requires considerable tolerance by the family and the child as they work together to foster a non-judgemental acceptance of the gender identity problem, and resist the pressure to force a solution. Guidance for the management of this disorder stresses that giving attention to emotional and developmental needs of the child or adolescent is important and any consideration of physical intervention should be cautious. It states that surgical intervention cannot be justified until adulthood.

Transvestism

This is considered in chapter 8 which looks at sexual perversions. Transvestites (or cross-dressers) are normally men who persistently dress in women's clothes (frequently lingerie) for sexual excitement. Masturbation often accompanies cross-dressing. The majority of transvestites are married heterosexuals but they are unlikely to disclose this to their wives prior to marriage, often believing the desire will leave them with marriage.[39] Wives respond in a variety of ways when their husbands reveal their secret. Some become angry and confused by this confession, whilst others show understanding. But it can be a

37. DiCeglie, D. (2000). *Advances in Psychiatric Treatment, 6*, pp. 458 – 466.
38. Green, R. (1968). Childhood cross-gender identification. *Journal of Nervous and Mental Disease, 147*, pp. 500 – 509.
39. Bullough, V. L., & Weinberg, T. S. (1988). Women married to transvestites: Problems and adjustments. *Journal of Psychology and Human Sexuality 1*:83 – 104.

major problem in a marriage and one which remains a painful secret between a couple. It is important to note that most transvestites have masculine gender identities, are masculine in their appearance and describe themselves as heterosexual, but are mistakenly often thought to be homosexual.

Sexual orientation

Sexual orientation relates to the second layer of sexual life described above, and is concerned with whether one falls in love with men, women, or both. Our sexual fantasies are indicative of our sexual orientation. Kinsey, an important researcher in the area of human sexuality,[40] suggested that sexual orientation was bipolar, with people who are entirely heterosexual at one end and those who are entirely homosexual at the other, with a range in between. He located bisexuality in the middle of his spectrum. The diversity of human sexual responsiveness suggests that such clear categories do not sufficiently describe human sexual practice and the lifelong experience of sexual orientation.

There are some people whose sexual orientation changes during the course of their adult life. A considerable number of lesbian women, for example, have had heterosexual intercourse. Quite often they have been in a heterosexual relationship before entering a lesbian relationship. During adolescence, where there is often a developmentally normal confusion regarding sexual orientation, experimentation with both homosexual and heterosexual relationships may occur before consolidation of identity.

Bisexuality

Bisexuality is a sexual, emotional and social attraction to members of both sexes, though not necessarily at the same time or to the same

---

40. Kinsey, A. C., Pomeroy, W. B. , & Martin, C. (1948). *Sexual behavior in the human male*, and Kinsey, A. C., Pomeroy, W. B., Martin, C. E., & Gebherd, P. H. (1953). *Sexual behavior in the human female*, both Philadelphia: Saunders.

degree.[41] In most cases, bisexuals engage first in a heterosexual relationship and enter into a homosexual relationship later.

There are different opinions as to whether bisexuality is a distinct sexual orientation or not. Some view it as a phase which some people experience when they are experimenting with their sexual identity or in a period of transition. Others see the heterosexual experiences as a denial of one's real orientation to be homosexual. Another theory is that we all have the potential to be bisexual and it is expressed in some of us and not others. This suggests that for some people sexual identity is more fluid and does not fit into a discrete category.

Homosexuality

A homosexual is a person who is erotically interested in someone of the same sex. They have sexual fantasies and fall in love with persons who have the same body sex – the same genital and body morphology (shape and characteristics) as themselves.[42] This attraction informs the development of a homosexual's sexual identity.

The development of a gay identity is thought to progress through four stages which are described by Troiden as follows:[43]

1. *Sensitisation* which includes feelings of marginality and perceptions of being different from same-sex peers. This usually occurs before adolescence.

2. *Identity confusion* happens during adolescence when the label of homosexual begins to be associated with feelings, thoughts and behaviours.

3. *Identity assumption* is when the individual believes that he or she is gay and begins to present him or herself as gay.

4. *Identity commitment* is the acceptance of a gay sexual identity.

41. Miracle, T., Miracle, A. & Baumeister, R. F. (2003). *Human sexuality: Meeting your basic needs.* New Jersey: Prentice Hall, p. 326.
42. Money, J. (1988). *Gay, straight and in-between: The sexology of erotic orientation.* Oxford: Oxford University Press, p. 12.
43. Troiden, R. (1989). The formation of homosexual identities. *Journal of Homosexuality, 17*: 43 – 73.

This stage model reflects some of the experiences of homosexuals, but not all. Lesbians, for example, often develop their sexual identity later than gay men. Important to this process is the context of a romantic-emotional relationship later in life. This model of development also fails to take account of the fluid nature of sexual identity for some individuals.

Research on gender identity offers a number of formulations regarding sexual orientation and sexual identity. These cover the same areas as gender identity, namely: parenting, culture, social, biological and learning theories. It is evident that the explanations of sexual orientation have been influenced by cultural assumptions and the view that heterosexuality is 'normal' and homosexuality and bisexuality 'abnormal'. Some believe that homosexuality is a matter of choice and others that it is a medical condition characterised by addictive behaviour. Hence, some people believe that it can be 'cured' whilst others believe it is the way some people are. Studies are inconclusive regarding the genetic, hormonal and environmental factors which give rise to sexual orientation, but the growing acceptance of homosexuality and gay rights has undoubtedly made a considerable difference to the experience of sexual identity for homosexuals.

Reflections on gender and sexual identity and the Church

Our sexuality and gender are important aspects of our personhood and as embodied human beings our physical, biological nature is a significant aspect of who we are. In this final section I reflect on how gender and transsexuality challenge the Church in its ministry and theology.

Gender

The Christian Churches continue to struggle with the issue of gender. For centuries women have played a significant part in the ministry of the Church, but its leadership has been overwhelmingly male. Although the Church has allowed and relied on the ministry of women, they have been largely excluded from positions of power and decision-making. The recent history of the Church has seen it grapple with the questions raised in the human and social sciences regarding gender, as has been seen in the painful and often divisive debate surrounding the ordination of women in the Church of England.

Gender is an issue which can not be separated from important perspectives on the theological and ecclesiological nature of the Church, and this has added to and exacerbated the controversy and pain caused. Questions of the nature of authority within the Church, and the effect on other churches of one church adopting such a radical change in church order and still remaining part of the global 'catholic' church, are examples of the complexity and difficulty the issue of gender raises in this context.

It is helpful at this point to examine the arguments regarding the ordination of women to serve as an example of how gender and gender identity are important factors in the current life of the Church. Opponents of the ordination of women have used several arguments to support their perspective. Two main lines have been pursued. The first is based on the understanding that gender difference is an expression of the fundamental innate difference between men and women. Accordingly it is argued and taught, we have been designed by nature to fulfill separate roles in the Church and society. This line of reasoning extends to conclude that men are intrinsically created for and suited to the ordained ministry and women are not. Another recurring argument used to support an all-male priesthood is that women and men are 'equal but different'. This difference, at its extreme, means that just as men are not best suited to nurturing children so women are not suited to the priesthood.

The second theme focuses on the representative nature of the role of priesthood and questions whether women can ever represent the male figure of Christ to the Church at the celebration of Holy Communion. This draws eucharistic theology into the debate and different understandings of the role of presidency at the Eucharist. Is the presider an icon of Christ or a representative of the worshipping community? For some, presiding is dependent on the celebrant embodying the male Christ. Since God Incarnate was a man, men are able to represent the divine in a way that the female gender is not.[44] However, others respond by asserting that women and men are both made in the image of God and therefore, in order to fully reflect the divine, an inclusive priesthood is necessary.[45]

In 1992 the motion to ordain women as priests was carried in the General Synod of the Church of England, with the first 32 women priests being ordained in 1994. At the same time 383 working priests left the Church of England and safeguards were also put in place for those who were unable to accept the professional ministry of women in the form of the Act of Synod of 1993. The Act has been seen by some as incorporating a view of women as both a different and inferior version of man, and that it represents the 'institutionalisation of sexism par excellence'.[46] The experience of operating in a male-dominated Church has undoubtedly been challenging for many ordained women as they pioneer a different way of doing things in what has been for centuries a patriarchal institution. Many clergywomen still face gender-based discrimination and have few role models to draw upon.

Recent research into the experience of ordained women has identified both gender-based expectations and some gender differences in ministerial practice (see chapter 13). Many ordained women continue to find that expectations stemming from gender stereotypes spill over into ministry, with clergywomen expected to be caring and

44. Graham, E. (1995). *Making the difference: Gender, personhood and theology.* London: Mowbray, p. 38.
45. Ibid p. 39.
46. Shaw, J. (1998). Gender and the Act of Synod. In Furlong, M. (Ed.). *Act of Synod – Act of Folly?* London: SCM Press. Quoted in Bagilhole, B. (2003). Prospects for change? Structural, cultural and action dimensions of the careers of pioneer women priests in the Church of England. *Gender, Work and Organization 10(3),* 361 – 377.

compassionate, and to function as loving mothers to their congregations. It has been suggested that many clergywomen fulfill this expectation as a means of overcoming resistance to women holding authority in the Church.[47] Evidence from an examination of the patterns of ministry of ordained women indicates that they tend to focus more on pastoral care and counselling,[48] are likely to be more approachable, emotionally vulnerable, and share their personal stories with their congregations. In this way they are seen to be adopting a relational approach to ministry.[49]

The gendered nature of human experience and the complexity of the development of gender identity takes us far beyond the straightforward issue of the differences between men and women and the gender stereotypes which are present in any society. The 'equal but different' position which has been voiced frequently in the Church is no longer satisfactory, because difference can be and is used in a manner which leads to inequality. As a Church we need to work with changes in thinking about gender in a way which does not view women as a threat to the stability of the Church, but rather as an opportunity to embody justice and enrich the life and ministry of the whole people of God.

The definition of sexual identity includes the way in which one identifies the self in terms of whom one is sexually attracted to, whether one is attracted to members of the same gender as one's own or the opposite gender. In chapter 7 on homosexuality, Ashley Wilson discusses sexual identity and sexual orientation and the Church, so I will not address this here. Instead I will examine the issue of transsexualism, which is of particular significance to the Church in the United Kingdom since the Gender Recognition Bill was passed in

47. Lawless, E. (1988). *Handmaidens of the Lord: Pentecostal women preachers and the traditional religion.* Philadelphia: University of Pennsylvania Press. Quoted in Frame, M. W., & Shehan, C. L. (2004). Care for the caregiver: Clues for the pastoral care of clergywomen. *Pastoral Psychology 52(5),* 369 – 380.
48. Perl, P. (2002). Gender and mainline Protestant pastors' allocation of time to work tasks. *Journal for the Scientific Study of Religion,* 41, 169 – 179.
49. Simon, R. J., & Nadell, P. S. (1995). In the same voice or is it different? Gender and the clergy. *Sociology of Religion,* 56, 63 – 70.

the British Parliament, giving transsexuals legal recognition, with the right to marry and claim benefits and have a new birth certificate. For the Church this raises the question of an appropriate Christian response to someone who changes their God-given gender.

In *Issues on Human Sexuality* the Church of England bishops recognise that there are some whose sexuality feels to them to be at odds with their bodies.[50] In her book *Conundrum*, Jan Morris articulates this experience very clearly:

> That my conundrum might simply be a matter of penis or vagina, testicle or womb, seems to me still a contradiction in terms, for it concerned not my apparatus, but my self. If society had allowed me to live in the gender I preferred would I have bothered to have the sex change? Male and female are sex: masculine and feminine are gender. Though conceptions obviously overlap, they are far from synonymous.[51]

For the Church this presents a far-reaching ethical dilemma which can not be addressed before addressing the issue of the gender of the individual (transsexual) in question. One author[52] suggests that three dependent questions arise from this for a Christian ethical response, namely:

- Should gender status act as an impediment to the individual's participation in the community of faith?

- Is sex reassignment surgery a morally acceptable treatment for transsexual persons?

- Should the church recognise and solemnise marriages or other unions of transsexual persons?

The traditional Christian understanding of sexuality is that it is intrinsic to God's creation and to our human nature. There is a distinction to

---

50. *Issues in Human Sexuality: A Statement by the house of Bishops of the General Synod of the Church of England (1991)*, p. 26.
51. Morris, J. (1974). *Conundrum*. London: Faber & Faber.
52. Kolakowski, V. S. (1997). *Theology and Sexuality, 6:* 10 – 31.

be made between the belief that our sexuality is part of our core identity and the belief that it is a faculty which may be used for God's intended purpose of procreation.[53] In response to the Gender Recognition Bill, a report in *The Tablet*[54] quoted Fr George Woodall, the Catholic moral theologian, as saying that:

> The notion of 'gender reassignment' runs counter to Church teaching. People are created by God male and female. The physiological indicators are the ones that would indicate what sex and gender someone is.

Changing one's gender is therefore changing something which God has created. Surgery of this kind is considered to be a form of mutilation by some in the Church.[55] Traditional Christian responses to transsexuality are based upon this notion, that the establishment of sexuality by God is an intrinsic part of the creation of a person. When this is combined with a view that human sexuality is primarily for procreation, transsexual surgery is judged by many Christians to be morally wrong.

The question of transsexuals marrying also presents challenges to the Church. For many Christians the recognition and solemnising of a marriage involving a transsexual makes a nonsense of the Christian understanding of marriage, in particular the emphasis on procreation and the upbringing of children.[56] However, the increasing tendency to recognise the value of marriage whether there are children born within a marriage or not, has persuaded some Christians to become more supportive of transsexual marriages. Whatever the ethical position adopted amongst Christians regarding transsexuals, they require support and help from the Christian community.

With the many ethical difficulties surrounding this issue what should our pastoral response be? There is considerable fear regarding

53. Kolakowski, V. S. (1997). *Theology and Sexuality, 6:* 10 – 31.
54. Curti, E. (2004). Born in the wrong body. *The Tablet.* 31 January, 2004.
55. Ibid quotation from Archbishop Smith.
56. Curti, E. (2004). Born in the wrong body. *The Tablet.* 31 January, 2004.

those who are different from ourselves, but we are all created in the image of God. The Church is a body of individuals; each unique and shaped by their personal experience of self and others. Within this diversity, the body is held together by the spirit of unity in Christ and its proclamation of the Gospel of Christ. To love, welcome, and support does not always require agreement, but it does depend upon respect for other human beings and acceptance of them as fellow children of God.

- Ignorance is a source of fear and the more information available regarding transsexuality and other sexual and gender related problems, the more appropriately church communities can respond to transsexuals and gender dysphoria in their congregations.

- Family and friends of transsexuals often require counselling as well as those with gender dysphoria.

As part of the Church we are tasked with knowing ourselves, recognising our uniqueness as well as our shared humanity, reflecting on our personal desires, convictions and sense of calling, and relating them respectfully to those of others. This can only be achieved in a community which is open to God and one another. In the complexity of gender and sexual identity, an openness of mind and heart to listen and care for our brothers and sisters in Christ who are struggling or confused by their sexual or gender identity presents a significant challenge to the Church, but one which it is called to wrestle with, both theologically and pastorally.

THIRTEEN

Sexuality in ministerial relationships

Brendan Geary and Alison Moore

Introduction

Sexuality, like ministry, is fundamentally about relationships. Wherever men and women work together there will be dynamics at play, and this will undoubtedly include our sexuality. Sexuality involves more than genital sex; it involves issues of power, our passions, attractions, sense of personal boundaries, feelings and vulnerabilities. All of us are 'embodied', and our bodies are the source of our communications. Ministry happens through interaction, and this involves our thoughts, feelings, desires, giftedness, clumsiness, inspirations and mistakes. Our bodies are also the place where we experience (or deny) our sexuality, and our sexual needs. The Churches have often ignored issues relating to sexuality, but can do so no longer.

The fall-out from sex-abuse scandals has precipitated a greater awareness of sexual issues in ministry. While these have been predominantly related to the abuse of children and adolescents, there has also been a growing recognition that many people, mostly women, have either been exploited by or become sexually involved with priests or ministers.[1] All of the Churches have had to deal with the publicity that has resulted when sexually inappropriate relationships have been made public. There have been parallel developments in other professions, such as counselling, law, psychiatry or medicine, where professionals have behaved in sexually inappropriate ways in what Peter Rutter, a psychiatrist, called, 'the forbidden zone'.[2] Our understanding of relationships in ministry has been influenced by

1. http://www.guardian.co.uk/uk/2003/jul/20/religion.world2, retrieved August 10th, 2009.
2. Rutter, P. (1989). *Sex in the forbidden zone: When men in power – therapists, doctors, clergy, teachers, and others – betray women's trust.* New York: Fawcett Crest.

the world of psychology and counselling, where careful analysis has clarified the relationship between the professional and the client, and ethical codes have been established.

In a study of sexual contact between health-care professionals and clients, a minority (10% of male and 4% of female respondents) acknowledged sexual contact with a patient. The overwhelming majority of respondents who had treated patients who had been sexually involved with other health-care professionals said that it had harmed the patient in some way. They said that their patients felt betrayed and exploited and that trust had been betrayed.[3]

Research undertaken in the United States suggested that the prevalence of sexual contact between members of the clergy and parishioners may be higher than with mental-health professionals, and that it does not appear to vary across denomination, theological orientation or gender.[4] More than two-thirds of the clergy in the study said that they knew of another member of the clergy who had had sexual intercourse with a member of their congregation. These figures are based on research that is between twenty and thirty years old. However, it is clear from the work of Margaret Kennedy in the United Kingdom and the people who manage the www.advocateweb.org website in the United States that there is still exploitation of clients, patients and members of congregations by professionals and clergy. Margaret Kennedy writes:

> This is not a relationship but an abuse of power. The women who have come forward talk of how they were usually vulnerable and at a low ebb – at crisis point in their lives. Many have a history of being sexually abused as a child or are in a difficult marriage or family situation. The woman is often depressed and suffering

---

3. Gartrell, N. K., Milliken, N., Goodson, W. H., Thiemann, S., & Lo, B. (1995). Physician-patient sexual contact: Prevalence and problems. In J. C. Gonsiorek, (Ed.). *Breach of trust: Sexual exploitation by health care professionals and clergy.* Thousand Oaks: Sage, pp. 18 – 28.
4. Fortune, M. (1995). Is nothing sacred: When sex invades the pastoral relationship. In J. C. Gonsiorek, (Ed.). *Breach of trust: Sexual exploitation by health care professionals and clergy.* Thousand Oaks: Sage, pp. 29 – 40.

from low self-esteem. They seek the clergy's counsel and support
– and never envisaged any sexual involvement.[5]

The purpose of this chapter is to present a discussion of a range of
issues related to sexual dynamics, and not simply sexual intercourse
or abuse, important as these undoubtedly are. Sexuality, present in
all encounters, can be a source of passion and life in ministry.
Equally, it can interfere with or even block effective ministry – especially
when those in ministry are unaware of or self-deceptive about their
own needs and motivations.

The starting point for any discussion of the issue of sexual dynamics
in ministry is the fact that all of us are sexual beings. We all find ourselves attracted to people, and have to use our judgement and exercise
restraint regarding the appropriate places and situations in which to
express or act on any attractions we may feel. As sexual issues to do
with children are covered elsewhere, this chapter will focus on sexual
dynamics within adult relationships.

Power

In September 1996, the Scottish Catholic Church was shaken by the
story of Bishop Roddy Wright of Argyll and the Isles, who resigned
from ministry when it was revealed that he was involved in a relationship with a married woman. It appears that Mrs Kathleen MacPhee
had approached the bishop for pastoral support at a time when her
marriage was under pressure.[6] The bishop at first denied the allegations, and then confessed. In the ensuing media coverage it emerged
that he had earlier fathered a son, who was living with his mother in
England. There were various reactions to this story. A great deal of
the press focused on the sensational aspects of the incident: a bishop
who had taken a vow of celibacy being caught in an adulterous

5. Kennedy, M. (20th July, 2003). The church must support victims. *The Observer.*
   http://www.guardian.co.uk/uk/2003/jul/20/religion.world2, retrieved August 10th, 2009.
6. *The Tablet,* 21st September, 1996. Fugitive bishop stands down. pp. 1239 – 1240

relationship, the attempts to lie to superiors and later to the press, the discovery of a previous affair, the existence of an apparently unsupported son, questions about his sense of responsibility etc. However, the real issue, as Brian Linnane wrote, was 'sexual abuse, or more precisely, professional malpractice by means of sexual abuse'.[7]

Linnane looked beyond the particular behaviour and the sensational elements of the story to focus on issues of power and responsibility. His article continued:

> The genesis of both relationships was professional; both women sought assistance in a time of crisis from a minister they presumed to have been trained and certified by the Church to offer the sort of assistance they required.[8]

Mrs MacPhee was a vulnerable member of Bishop Wright's diocese. She came to him for support and counsel, and found herself falling in love. As other authors have noted, this is not an unusual occurrence.[9] No one suggests that managing these pastoral relationships is easy. However, it is clear that the responsibility to manage the relationship, and to maintain the appropriate boundaries, belongs to the priest or minister. When Bishop Wright discovered that he was also falling in love, and chose to let his feelings be known, he carried the responsibility for crossing the boundary between minister and lover.

One of the reasons that societies have legal age limits for sexual behaviour is to protect those members of society (children) who lack the emotional maturity and freedom to give consent to a sexual relationship. Other vulnerable adults, such as those who are physically or mentally handicapped, or elderly, are protected by the law in other ways. The law recognises that there is an imbalance in the distribution of power in these relationships. Professional relationships between a psychiatrist, doctor, counsellor or lawyer and his / her client recognise

7. Linnane, B. (12th October, 1996). Playing with sore hearts. *The Tablet.* p. 1239.
8. Linnane, B. (12th October, 1996). Playing with sore hearts. *The Tablet.* p. 1239.
9. Becker, J. F., & Donovan, D. I. (1995). Sexual dynamics in ministry relationships, *Human Development, 16(3),* pp. 23 – 27.

the same power imbalance, which is articulated in codes of practice. This also extends to relationships in ministry. Ministry relationships may lack the contractual definition of a counselling agreement or legal contract, but the minister holds the power conferred by religious authority, and it is realistic to expect a non-explicit agreement to be maintained between the person ministered to and the minister.

Priests and ministers encounter many very needy people in the course of their work. Some of them can become very dependent on their pastor, or, indeed, fall in love (or have the feeling of being in love).[10] Clergy are often highly empathic individuals, whose ministry involves giving time to vulnerable people, especially at times of emotional difficulty, such as bereavements, illness, loss, or relationship difficulties. If the pastor is also emotionally needy, and is not aware of this, then the emotional space between these two people can become highly charged, or the ministerial tasks can be subordinated to having personal needs met. This can be a recipe for disaster. The following personal account was written by a priest who was later imprisoned for sexual abuse of adolescent boys:

> The needy and deprived kids received my attention the most. Since I was not relating well with my peers, I turned to the parishioners and kids for support . . . I identified with their needs and hurts . . . I think what started it was I got involved with one of the kids who was sexually precocious. I was in the swimming pool and he just started all this sexual stuff in the pool. It tripped something; it pushed all my buttons . . . I had no control. Some months later, he wanted out . . . I could not stop.[11]

This priest was acting out of his own needs and hurts. But a minister can also be drawn into a sexual relationship if he confuses the respect and adulation of a member of the congregation for love. Wise ministers

10. Becker, J. F., & Donovan, D. I. (1995). Sexual dynamics in ministry relationships, *Human Development, 16(3)*, pp. 23 – 27.
11. A priest child abuser speaks (1990). S J. Rossetti (Ed.). *Slayer of the soul.* Conneticut: Twenty-Third Publications, pp. 99 – 111.

recognise that they will probably occasionally fall in love with a member of their congregation. A study in the United States noted that a significant number of Catholic priests left ministry within the first five years, and that many of them said they had fallen in love.[12] Enlightened college staff who work with people going into ministry warn students in advance that they should expect to fall in love – and have people fall in love with them. This is not a sign of a vocational crisis, although it may be a sign of a crisis in human development, particularly if the priest or minister has never been in love before. Ministry can be a lonely and unrewarding place; experiencing appreciation or love from a parishioner or co-worker can soothe hurt feelings and raise self-esteem. It is a small step from here to falling in love or sexually inappropriate behaviour.

Boundaries

Professional relationships are 'boundaried'; that is to say, there are contractual agreements regarding what services are to be offered, where they are to be offered, how much is to be paid, and what standard of delivery can be expected. Most professions have codes of ethics and grievance procedures to establish standards of appropriate conduct and mechanisms for redress, disciplining of malpractice or expelling a member of the profession whose behaviour is not acceptable and brings the profession into disrepute.

In most denominations, clergy do not have the same clarity about professional boundaries as counsellors or other health-care professionals. A counsellor is involved in a relationship which has a clear focus: the emotional well-being of the client. Ministers occupy a variety of roles in people's lives. This involves them in 'dual relationships', i.e., playing a range of roles, and relating in a range of ways.[13]

---

12. Hoge, D. R. (2002). *The first five years of the priesthood: A study of newly ordained Catholic priests.* Minnesota: The Liturgical Press.
13. See Syme, G. (2003). *Dual relationships in counselling and psychotherapy.* London: Sage. Much of this book is relevant to ministerial as well as to therapeutic relationships.

A priest or minister will be the person who leads worship, and may be the line manager for one or more people who work in the parish. He or she may be the chairperson of the board of governors of a school and may be the person to whom members of the congregation go to for confession or pastoral support. It is likely that there will be a core group of parish workers, who see the priest or minister as a personal friend (though this may not be how things are seen from the point of view of the priest or minister). Ministers may use the doctor or dentist who attends the church, or engage members of the congregation for contractual work in the parish or at home: electricians, plumbers, builders, gardeners etc. They may also be the carriers of secrets, the ones called upon to share emotional burdens, which they cannot share with others. Clergy are expected to be competent and clear in managing these different relationships and roles.

> John is a clergyman in a rural parish. A single man, he lives far from his family and friends. Some of the parishioners have invited him for meals, and one young married woman, Kate, has become particularly close, confiding in John about her family and work concerns. She has also taken on responsibility for the newsletter, which she does efficiently. Her husband, Mike, is involved in care of the fabric of the church. Over time tensions have developed in their marriage, and John finds himself torn between the friendship which he values, the pastoral counselling relationship which is developing with Kate, and the semi-professional relationship he has with Mike, which involves contracts and advice.

The ministerial training period can help people to experience, explore and understand the complexity of dual relationships in ministry, like the ones presented above. Indeed within seminaries and theological colleges students will inevitably experience a number of dual relationships. Members of staff can be teachers, tutors, and supervisors, involved in scrutiny of candidates, as well as in varying degrees of friendliness and socialising. They will pray and eat together and possibly play sports together. From one perspective this is a recipe for relational disaster. At the same time, if handled well – which it often is – it can be the place where people training for ministry acquire the skills necessary to understand and negotiate their way through multiple relationships in ministry. The perennial problem for those involved in preparation for ministry is that students often think that things will be different once they are working in a parish.

The skills involved in managing dual relationships and multiple roles become particularly crucial when issues of attraction and sexual need enter the picture. It is important to provide a safe space during training so that students can become aware of their sexual orientation, their sexual needs, and the needs of others, and find healthy ways to have those needs met. Ministry can be a minefield of sexual temptations. When the subject is ignored in training, the message conveyed is that this cannot be talked about. This kind of attitude makes it more difficult to deal with sexual temptation when students encounter it as part of their ministry.[14]

Although the priest or minister, like any other professional, must always take responsibility for maintaining the boundary, some people will want to push the boundary to have their own needs met. This can be difficult, as ministry relationships lack the clarity of other professional relationships, and ministers are often reluctant to do anything that might cause offence.

Mark is a forty-year-old monk in a large monastery, part of whose ministry involved responsibility for the Abbey retreat house team. Simon is a twenty-two-year-old theology graduate who works as part of the team. He has recently undertaken a course in massage therapy, and, needing to complete practice

---

14. Marshall, W. (2007). A proposal for the prevention and treatment of child molestation by Catholic clergy. *Seminary Journal, 13(3)*, 20 – 36, and Meek, K. R., McMinn, M. R., Brower, C. M., Burnett, T. D., McRay, B. W., Ramey, M. L., Swanson, D. W., & Villa, D. D. (2003). Maintaining personal resiliency: Lessons learned from Evangelical Protestant clergy. *Journal of Psychology and Theology, 3* (4), 339 – 347.

hours as part of his training, he asked the team members if they would help him by letting him give them a massage. Mark and others agreed to this request. Up until this point neither Mark nor Simon had spoken of their homosexuality. The sessions started very professionally. However, they found each other attractive, and the massage setting blurred the roles of team leader and team member; in the end, each gave the other a massage, and a sexual relationship followed. Mark felt guilty and asked Simon to leave the team. Simon reported this to the Abbot and spoke about it to other staff members, leading to the situation becoming public. When Simon did eventually leave the team, he felt hurt and exploited.

Mark had many roles: he was Simon's line manager, but also his friend, confidant, colleague, source of professional support, and eventually lover. It was Mark's job to hold the boundary. He should have declined the request to help Simon with his practice, firstly because of the professional boundary and secondly because he was aware of his own sexual orientation and attraction.

Similar situations occur in parishes and other church settings, and can just as easily occur between two ministers, especially where one is in a superior position. Again, it is the person with the most power, the one who is in a position of authority, who must manage the boundary. Lamenting afterwards that 'someone came on to me', or that 'I fell in love', denies the issue of responsibility for the relationship. As Mark found, ministry relationships are fraught with complexity. He may not have wanted to appear unsupportive. He may also have felt that he valued Simon's friendship, and wanted to encourage him. However, he may also have secretly found the idea of having a massage from Simon stimulating sexually, and, in the privacy and vulnerability of the therapeutic massage, allowed himself to make choices that were inappropriate, but which helped him to have his own sexual and relationship needs met.

The Facebook generation

Richard Malloy, in an article on the Facebook generation, notes that young people today communicate in ways that were not available to previous generations.[15] They use mobile phones, texting, messenger systems and social-networking sites with ease. These systems are very different from previous ways of communication, with instant, often brief messages, and encouraging exposure of private details to a wide audience. As with every advance, these new media also have their downsides. There is now the phenomenon of cyberbullying, and there can be competition between young people regarding how many named 'friends' they have on their site (see Internet chapter). These developments have implications for ministry. Take the following two scenarios:

1. Roberto is a young religious in a South American country. He is a good teacher, is conscientious, has an attractive personality and relates well with young people. One of his 14-year-old pupils, Anna, made sexual advances to him. Shocked, he said an emphatic 'no', and made it very clear that this was inappropriate. However, she had his mobile phone number and started to send him a combination of angry messages and messages with sexual content. Roberto was advised to report the situation to the school authorities, which he did, and he subsequently had to change his mobile phone number.

2. Chris is a priest in his late twenties who is friendly with some families in his parish. The 12-year-old girl in the family sent a message to his Facebook site asking if she could be added as one of his friends. Chris felt uncomfortable about having a 12-year-old girl as a friend, but he did not want to

15. Malloy, R. G. (July 7th, 2008). Religious Life in the age of Facebook: where have all the young people gone? 14(3). Academic OneFile. Gale. Loyola Notre Dame. 2 Feb, 2009.

hurt her feelings and cause feelings of embarrassment or rejection. He decided to speak with her parents to ask them to explain that he was not rejecting her, but that this was not appropriate.

These media can be intrusive, and do not allow for the gradual building-up of relationships. There are many stages between introduction and calling someone a friend. A priest can be 'friendly' with a 12-year-old girl, in the context of relating to her family. But that does not mean that she is a friend in the same way as the adults in his life. Facebook and other Internet friendship systems do not make these distinctions. Priests and ministers are vulnerable when there are requests, communications and propositions that have no subtlety, and no room for gradations of understanding. These media open up whole new areas of opportunity, but also of concern.

Our past in the present

Margaret is a newly ordained minister in a suburban congregation. The parishioners have responded well to her appointment and have been grateful for the new energy and life that she has brought to the parish. Peter, a leading member of the parish council who supported her appointment, is particularly attentive to her. On numerous occasions he has told her what a wonderful daughter she would make. Peter's own two daughters have moved away after disagreeing with their father's advice about their career choices. In parish meetings Peter tends to be protective of Margaret, but also gently chides her when he is not comfortable with some of her initiatives. Margaret finds him supportive but also feels paralysed when trying to confront some of the ways of working in the parish which no longer serve the ministry of the church, particularly her desire to welcome more couples with young families.

How Peter relates to Margaret appears to be based on how he relates to his own daughters. We can speculate that he learned this from patterns in his own family of origin. The way that all of us tend to repeat such patterns in our lives is known as *transference*. This occurs when feelings or attitudes that belong to a previous relationship become part of a current relationship. In that sense, our past is being relived in the present.

From a therapeutic perspective transference is very important, as it gives the therapist a clue about what is happening in the world of his or her client. The client may, for example, be relating to the therapist as if he or she were their father or mother. Transference is not confined to the counselling room; it can be seen in ordinary life too. For example, how many people slow down when they see a police car in the rear-view mirror while driving – even if they are not speeding! Transference is not always negative either; therapists cannot be effective and ministers cannot be helpful unless people 'transfer' their positive experiences of being able to place their trust in people who are in positions of authority. This kind of positive transference becomes the foundation for trusting relationships in life, which is why the abuse of such trust is so damaging. We tend to relate to significant persons in our adult lives in ways that reflect patterns we learned in our childhood.

Transference in ministry is positive when it arises from healthy trust (in parents or teachers, for example) experienced earlier in life. It can become problematic, however, when it emerges from unhealthy relationships. For example, some people seem to demand that authority figures meet all their needs. They can trade adulation for care, becoming dependent on a priest or minister. Members of a congregation may look up to the priest or minister, putting them on a pedestal. They might transfer erotic feelings, looking for a lover rather than a pastor. A young man who was subservient to his father could demonstrate transference by becoming similarly subservient to the minister, or in constantly behaving in a way that seeks approval. A woman whose parents continually ridiculed her may be afraid of any criticism from the minister. Transference may be at work when someone constantly challenges decisions or undermines the leader in aggressive or passive-aggressive ways.[16] It appears that the more intense the relationship, the more intense the transference.[17] This can be particularly problematic if the member of the congregation, often a woman, experiences respect, affection and care for the first time, and experiences this as falling in love. It is clear to see how, if the minister is caught in a reciprocal emotional pattern, this can lead to inappropriate romantic or sexual involvement.

Transference can manifest itself in other ways. Margaret's experience of being 'fathered' by Peter can be mirrored by the young male curate being 'adopted' by the women in a parish, especially if he is boyish-looking, or is a bit immature or vulnerable in some way. A mutual dynamic can develop where the women enjoy being substitute mothers, and the priest enjoys the benefits of their care and generosity. The problem is that there can be an unstated contract where the priest is expected always to behave like a 'good boy', being nice, appreciative, considerate – and probably asexual. It then becomes almost impossible for him to be assertive, challenging, or to establish clear boundaries regarding time, gifts or gratitude. Of course these relationships are not sexual in a genital sense, but they involve aspects of human sexuality related to parenting and being a child. And when there is an unspoken agreement not to allow the minister's sexuality to be present, this becomes unhealthy as it leads to 'neutering' of passion and commitment, which can effectively block initiation of necessary change in a church.

Margaret's story, begun above, shows how such situations might develop.

16. see Bryan, J. (2008). Dealing with difficult people. In B. Geary & J. Bryan (Eds.). *The Christian handbook of abuse, addiction and difficult behaviour.* Suffolk: Kevin Mayhew.
17. Becker, J. F., & Donovan, D. I. (1995). Sexual dynamics in ministry relationships, *Human Development, 16(3),* pp. 23 – 27.

Margaret came from a non-church family. Her father tended to use his disappointment and displeasure to control his children's behaviour. Margaret could have become a professional musician, but instead she chose ministry. Because her father saw this choice as a waste of her talent, she had to deal with a lot of disapproval and tension at home when she asserted her desire to pursue this calling. Working with Peter was similar to her relationship with her father, and over time she became irritated at the suffocating effect of his kindness and the paralysing effect of his indirect controlling behaviour. Over time, the irritation led to avoiding him, reacting curtly to his suggestions at meetings, arguing with him over small details, to the embarrassment of other members of the parish council, and then actively trying to get people to consider voting him off the parish council. Margaret spoke about this to her supervisor who helped her to see what was happening. Once she realised it, she was able to become more assertive, without being offensive, and worked to build more support for her ideas from other members of the parish council. Eventually she had to have a difficult conversation with Peter, where she calmly explained the shared vision for the future of the church. This led to a cooling in their relationship, but freed her to be her own person, and to lead the parish in the way she wanted, which was appreciated by others.

Peter's behaviour to Margaret was 'transferred' from his past. Margaret's reaction to Peter (in turn influenced by her own past) can be described as 'counter transference', because it exists as a direct response to the original transference. However, anyone might have been irritated by Peter's behaviour, so how could Margaret spot that her reactions were unusual? It has been suggested that when someone experiences an unusually strong or exaggerated reaction to a person or situation, warning bells should ring, as this could be evidence of the presence of counter transference.[18] For example, a *strong* need to help some-one, or feeling moved to go to *extraordinary* lengths to solve a problem, or having an *intense* dislike of someone, may well indicate counter transference. This means that the minister's own unmet needs are surfacing (which is natural), and therefore she finds herself responding or strongly wanting to respond in a way that attempts to have those needs met.

Margaret's feelings of being subtly manipulated, and her need to assert her independence had the potential to interfere with her pro-fessional judgement. Peter's need to patronise and protect interfered with his ability to accept the leadership of the minister and the views of other members of the congregation.

As Margaret and Peter's story shows, transference and counter transference relate to more than sexual feelings. However, the feelings involved can sometimes lead to sexual behaviour. 'Loneliness, vul-nerability, and tenderness especially stir our sexual feelings'.[19] These feelings do not relate only to celibates. All people in ministry are vulnerable to situations where, as a result of stress or constant personal exposure, strong feelings, including sexual ones, are close to the surface, often while ministering to vulnerable people. The feelings them-selves are normal. Failure comes, not from *having* these feelings, but from dealing with them inappropriately. 'Success and failure should be measured by how well one can identify these dynamics and refrain from destructive behaviours.'[20] As Margaret found, experience suggests that ongoing training and pastoral supervision are essential to help ministers be alert to and deal with these situations. Robert Wicks recommends that ministers as well as counsellors should undertake a brief review at the end of each day, by answering the following questions:

---

18. Racker, R. (1968). *Transference and countertransference.* London: Karnac. p. 111.
19. Becker, J. F. & Donovan, D. I. (1995). Sexual dynamics in ministry relationships. *Human Development, 16(3),* p. 24.
20. Becker, J. F. & Donovan, D. I. (1995). Sexual dynamics in ministry relationships. *Human Development, 16 (3),* p. 24.

- What made me sad today?
- Did anything overwhelm me?
- Was I sexually aroused?
- Did anything make me extremely happy or confuse me?

By being 'brutally honest', the minister can get in touch with the parts of the day that have the potential to derail, and identify what needs to be discussed with a pastoral supervisor or mentor.[21]

Me – or not me?

> Tony is 40 years of age. He is a parish priest, chaplain to a boys' secondary school and involved in diocesan youth work, where he works more with the young men than the young women. He is homosexual, but has never felt at ease with his orientation, nor has he shared this with anyone who is close to him. In his work as chaplain and youth worker he often gives talks to the boys about issues related to sexual development, including masturbation and sexual orientation. He seeks to engage the boys in conversation, liking to give the impression of being knowledgeable about this topic. He tells them that many young men have confided in him over the years, and how helpful this has been for them.

It is not difficult to see that Tony is trying to sort out his own issues about sexual development and sexual orientation, through seeking to help the boys and young men with whom he works. It is too threatening for him to face these directly, so instead he puts this on to the young men to whom he is called to minister. He is behaving like a projector, where the film exists inside the machine, but is seen on the screen opposite the projector. This term, 'projection' is another from the world of psychoanalysis. Patrick Casement writes

21. Wicks, R. J. (2008). *The resilient clinician.* London: Oxford, p. 31.

that, 'It is well known that when projection is operating, the projector disowns some aspect of the self and attributes this to another.'[22] Even if the boys do talk freely with Tony, this will not actually help him with his own life and his personal struggles.

The following example shows what can happen when someone is in the grip of projection, and where other personality issues may be present:

> John, a minister in an inner-city parish, was aware that Anne was always present in church, sat in front of him during every service, and would even try to hide in the church when it was due to be locked up. On previous occasions she had stayed behind and then walked into the parish office, explaining that she had been locked in the church. However, she accused John of following her, saying that he wanted to have an affair with her. John made sure that he was never alone with her. Eventually he had to report the situation to the police, leading to a restraining order being issued against her. At that point Anne wrote to the bishop to report that John was having an affair with the parish secretary.

It is likely that Anne desired to have an affair with John, but when her desire was thwarted, rather than deal with her own feelings, which were too strong, she 'projected' them on to John, and accused him of the thing she desired, but was afraid to acknowledge. John ended up being stalked by Anne, and when this happens, sexual dynamics are experienced in a rather extreme and disturbing form.

Brian Nicol writes that stalking 'involves repeated, persistent, unsolicited communications or physical approaches to the victim', and adds that the result 'is to induce in the victim a state of alarm and distress or fear of physical violence'.[23] Many countries and States in America now have legislation related to stalking, to provide some

22. Casement, P. (1985). *On learning from the patient.* London: Routledge, p. 81.
23. Nicol, B. (2006*). Stalking.* Great Britain: Reakton Books, p. 17.

protection for victims and redress in law. Stalking can happen to anyone, ordinary people as well as celebrities, and there is a growing awareness that it can be an issue for ministers.[24]

Sometimes the stalker is someone who has become emotionally dependent on or obsessed with the priest or minister, leading to this extreme behaviour. Conversation with a number of priests, ministers and people training for ministry reveals that this is more of a problem than people might think. A Catholic priest, for example, described in an anonymous article how a woman came to the parish, started to attend Mass daily, and then asked for prayers for a relative. After that came letters which at first were effusive and complimentary, but which raised a healthy sense of caution in the priest. The letters then became bizarre, with accusations of meetings with other women and of sexual innuendo communicated to her from the pulpit. The situation deteriorated rapidly, with the priest being followed, accusations of affairs, and messages communicating anger and hatred. The priest kept key parishioners informed, sought help from the diocese and finally hired a lawyer. The priest wrote: 'The last two years have been extraordinarily difficult. To see dry words on a page makes the experience seem almost banal. The day-to-day reality of it was deeply disturbing.'[25] Other priests and ministers have had similar experiences.

What causes this behaviour? It appears to involve a delusional belief system. The stalker believes that they have a special relationship with the victim, at first pursuing and then turning on them. Unable to accept the reality that their affection and attention is not reciprocated, they constantly challenge social and personal boundaries as they do not respect the normal social signals by which others live. It has been suggested that these people have a weak sense of self and feel that they desire to 'merge' with the other person; the potential for an

---

24. Reid Melloy, J. (Ed.). (1998). *The psychology of stalking: Clinical and forensic perspectives.* New York: Academic Press.
25. Haunted by a wounded soul. (18th October, 2008). *The Tablet*, pp. 6 – 7

unhealthy sexual dynamic is clear. When they do not achieve their desire, they fall into a rage to punish their victim.

Stalking is at the extreme end of a pattern of behaviour that sees the priest as someone who exists solely to fulfil others' needs. While not all people behave in such extreme ways, priests and ministers need to guard against the satisfaction to be gained if they are idolised, seen as the source of wisdom, or are constantly praised or depended upon. Some clergy are prone to the 'Messiah' complex, and some individuals can feed this illusion, and, in extreme cases, bring grief and suffering to innocent but vulnerable clergy.

John's experience with Anne illustrates clearly how the dynamic of projection can operate in a way that gets mixed up with sexual feelings. This highlights the need for clear and transparent boundaries, so that ministers are not left alone in situations where they can become vulnerable. Does this mean that a minister should never be alone with a parishioner? Not necessarily. However, particularly in situations where the minister senses that there is something unhealthy or uncomfortable in the relationship, prudence would suggest taking appropriate precautions, including never being alone with someone like Anne. A precaution that John took was to talk to her only in parts of the church that were covered by security cameras, so that in the event of the police receiving a complaint – which they did – all his interactions could be seen.

People in groups

People do not live in isolation, we live in groups. The various groupings we belong to, family, church, work, associations, networks of friends, political parties, etc., all have their own 'rules'. These codes of understanding are usually unwritten, with the shared opinions about what are approved or unacceptable behaviours or attitudes simply developing over time. Such groupings, each of which has its own culture, can be described as 'systems'. We all live in a variety of groups or systems, in which we interact with others and are affected by their attitudes, behaviours, expectations and dynamics. A system can be defined as follows:

> A set of interrelated elements or units that respond in a predictable manner and where the nature of the interaction is consistent over time.[26]

Dioceses, parishes, presbyteries, organisations and committees are all systems. Systems exercise considerable influence as each has both stated and unstated norms, which differ from system to system. This is true for Churches too, where the same norms might be expected. For example, in the Catholic Church, Rome holds central authority, while the parish priest is seen as the leader in a range of parish roles. In the Presbyterian Church the elders have both authority and power. In the Church of England the bishops, clergy and laity share power in a tripartite structure through the General Synod. Church systems also create expectations, for example, about the behaviour and role of clergy spouses, and of the laity in general. Particularly relevant to the topic of this chapter is the way that systems need to protect the status quo and will protect their own members at all costs in order to do so. This has been seen for example in the way that Catholic bishops and Religious Superiors often protected priests who abused children, although this was clearly against the law. The Churches are at last recognising this and dealing with the consequences of such abuse in the past. An editorial in the Irish Times made the following observation about the abuse of children in residential care homes in the Republic of Ireland:

> The very scale of the violence made it impossible to keep it sealed off from either officialdom or society at large. Contemporary complaints were made to the Garda (police), to the Department

---

26. Napier, R. W., & Gershenfeld, M. K. (1993). *Groups: Theory and experiences* (5th. ed.). Boston: Houghton Mifflin. p. 297.

of Education, to health boards, to priests and to members of the public. The department, 'deferential and submissive' to the religious congregations, did not shout stop. Neither did anyone else. Indeed, perhaps the most shocking finding of the commission is that industrial school inmates were often sexually exploited by those outside the closed world of the congregations, by 'volunteer workers, visitors, work-placement employees, foster parents' and by those who took them out for holidays or to work.

The key to understanding these attitudes is surely to realise that abuse was not a failure of the system. It was the system.[27]

Ministers within a church carry power which can tip into abuse, which is why vigilance, oversight and accountability are necessary for any system to remain healthy. Organisations like churches, which outwardly reject exploitation and abuse, and indeed stand for the opposite values, can collude with such behaviours. They do so by encouraging or sanctioning structures which facilitate abuse, or by failing to create or implement procedures which can be used effectively to prevent abuse, or make perpetrators accountable when it occurs.[28]

William White, an organisational consultant, writes that every organisation or system also has a 'sexual culture'.[29] This culture is expressed in the kind of language which is used, artefacts and symbols, such as art work, calendars, furniture, posters etc., ethics and values, and the way that relationships are modelled by leaders in the organisation. There is sometimes a tension between the implicit and real cultures that exist in organisations – a tension sadly all too recognisable in many churches. White suggests that two sets of circumstances can contribute to the existence of sexual harassment and exploitation.

27. The savage reality of our darkest days. (2009, May 21). *The Irish Times.* Retrieved May 21, 2009, from http://www.irishtimes.com/newspaper/opinion/2009/0521/1224247034262.html?via=rel
28. Geary, B., & Montgomery, E. (2008). Adult bullying. In B. Geary & J. Bryan (Eds.). *The Christian handbook of abuse, addiction and difficult behaviour.* Suffolk: Kevin Mayhew.
29. White, W. L. (1995). A systems perspective on sexual exploitation of clients by professional helpers. In J. C. Gonsiorek (Ed.). *Breach of trust: Sexual exploitation by health care professionals and clergy.* Thousand Oaks: Sage.

The first is when an organisation is going through a period of transition marked by turbulence and uncertainty. Such times can lead to uncertainty and vulnerability, where personal needs come to require more attention. Rather than facing up to and dealing with the uncomfortable feelings involved in a transition, an individual can seek relief in inappropriate ways. White writes:

> Attempted sexual contact in worker-worker and worker-client relationships during such turbulent periods may have more to do with power, anger, aggression, physical depletion, loneliness, or desperate needs for self-affirmation than with sexual attraction.[30]

The second set of circumstances occurs when there is what White calls an 'incestuous' system. This is where the members seek to have most of their needs, personal, professional, social, *and sexual*, met within the boundaries of the organisation. Within a church context, places like retreat houses, monasteries, house churches, tightly focused work teams, orphanages, formation houses and boarding schools, are particularly prone to this kind of dynamic. White itemises some of the characteristics he has noticed in such groups:

- The emergence of a rigid and unchallengeable belief system
- Centralisation of power and the emergence of charismatic leaders
- Isolation from other groups
- Homogenisation of the workforce/team/community and an inability to incorporate or tolerate difference
- Over-work
- Intense focusing on interpersonal and intrapersonal dynamics
- Projection of problems onto other groups and scapegoating
- Emergence of a punitive, abusive organisational culture

---

30. White, W. L. (1995). A systems perspective on sexual exploitation of clients by professional helpers. In J. C. Gonsiorek, (Ed.). *Breach of trust: Sexual exploitation by health care professionals and clergy.* Thousand Oaks: Sage, p. 189.

The potential for abuse in such circumstances is clear. With gradual isolation from others the boundaries between personal life and work or ministry are eroded. All of us have unmet needs, but when these unmet needs emerge in an unhealthy system such as this, it is hardly surprising that the sexual dynamics involved can lead to inappropriate crossing of boundaries, with abuse and exploitation of others.

Women in ministry

A number of Churches, e.g., the Church of England and other Episcopal Churches, the Methodists and the Church of Scotland (Presbyterians), now have women in public ministry. There are also many women who work in leadership roles in the Catholic Church. This exponential growth in the number of women in ministry or in training programmes has exposed more clearly ways in which power is exercised in churches, with the continuing influence of patriarchal structures and theologies. More importantly for this chapter, it has enabled serious reflection on how dynamics related to sexuality and gender are played out in Churches, congregations and administrative structures.

While this development has been welcomed by many people, it has also brought its own strains and tensions. The Anglican Communion struggles to hold together those who welcome the change and those who believe it is theologically unacceptable or untimely. Women themselves can feel the strain in terms of work expectations and overload, and tensions within their families. Also there can be direct or subtle resistance from male (and female) members of the clergy or members of congregations. It appears that women often take on a 'mothering' role, partly as it appears to be what is expected, and partly as it helps to overcome the resistance of men who resent or object to women being in positions of authority. Research suggests that women appear more vulnerable and approachable, are more likely to hug and to be more open about themselves to their congregations.[31] The gift of relationality can turn into a burden of unrealistic expectations, from the women ministers themselves as well as from those to whom they minister. It can also lead to difficult situations involving sexual boundaries:

> Yvonne was a newly ordained minister in a church where the vicar, David, had diocesan responsibilities. They quickly established a good working relationship, and David came to value Yvonne's work ethic and the ability she had to minister to those in distress or with emotional difficulties. Over time he began to confide in her about his own marital difficulties, partly brought on by the pressures of work from his diocesan responsibilities. Yvonne was very fond of David and appreciated the trust she experienced. She also gradually found herself becoming attracted to him. David, likewise, was becoming attracted to Yvonne and was grateful to receive an invitation to her home on the second anniversary of her ministry in the parish.

David and Yvonne have reached a crucial point in their relationship. David, as the senior colleague, has particular responsibility, but both now need to exercise judgement and restraint. Crossing the boundary from superior and colleague to friend and confidant can so easily transform a work relationship into a sexual one. People who experience this often say how 'natural', 'inevitable', 'right' and 'God given' the sexual relationship feels. However, the fallout will undoubtedly lead to complications for both people involved, and their whole church community.

One of the ways in which women appear to differ from men in church leadership style is in the area of power: it has been suggested that where men are inclined to exercise power over the laity, women are more inclined to seek to empower the laity.[32] This difference will

---

31. Simon, R. J., & Nadell, P. S. (1995). In the same voice or is it different? Gender and the clergy. *Sociology of Religion, 54,* 115 – 123.

32. Frame, M. W., & Shehan, C. L. (2004). Care for the caregivers: Clues for the pastoral care of clergywomen. *Pastoral Psychology, 52*(5), 369 – 380.

of course impact on sexual dynamics in ministry. People who are empowered will become more confident and have a sense that they are growing as persons and in their relationship to God. Such empowerment may well be linked to the ability of the woman minister to share her own vulnerability. Therefore the woman minister may find herself in an emotionally vulnerable place with someone who is growing and changing, and who may want to push against pre-existent boundaries. Women ministers are also likely to have to work with people who disagree with or resent women in leadership roles, or who prefer a more hierarchical approach. Although these can be presented in a pseudo-rational argument, they may well be fundamentally due to a clash in gender dynamics. The outcome is likely to be a direct or indirect undermining of the minister, as the following story shows.

> Linda had been appointed as minister in a Presbyterian church. Although warmly welcomed, she noted that the elders, most of whom were men, were seldom enthusiastic about the plans she suggested, often responding by saying, 'That's not how we do things', or 'That might suit the women, but the men won't like it'. The elders would take responsibility for issues related to the church buildings, and it was subtly communicated to her that she was not expected to be concerned with financial matters. She came to realise that they expected her role to be confined to leading the Sunday service, the youth group, the women's group and pastoral care. The elders would even compliment her on her dress, but make patronising remarks if they felt she was showing too much of her legs or arms. These sexual digs were clearly designed to keep her in her place and remind her of who held the power in the church. When she attempted to confront the issue at the presbytery meeting there was a perplexed silence and swift footwork by the chairman to move on to the next agenda item.

It appears that single heterosexual women or lesbians can have a particularly stressful time in male-dominated church systems. Researchers have found that the main areas of stress for women ministers involve family issues, boundaries, the need for personal time and privacy, balancing work and family life, and sexuality.[33] In a healthy system people can confront these issues and talk about them, but the reality of our culture (including church culture) is that there is a continuing gender power differential due to the legacy of patriarchal structures and its ongoing benefits to men. Women are thus more vulnerable than male members of the clergy, experiencing jealousy from both male and female colleagues. Attempts to resist being set up in culturally sanctioned roles such as 'mother' or 'counsellor' can be interpreted as rudeness or aggression rather than assertiveness.

Difficult people

Louise was a minister in an inner-city parish, but also spent time as a counsellor at a women's refuge where women who had left abusive relationships could find emergency accommodation. A young woman, Claire, arrived at the refuge and very quickly formed a bond with Louise. As well as the counselling sessions, she chose to sit with her during meals and sought her out during coffee breaks. Soon she was asking Louise to meet her during her free time, to go for walks or have a coffee. Louise wanted to support Claire so she agreed to some of these requests, but as the demands increased, she began to decline invitations. One morning Claire broke down in tears and asked Louise why she would not spend time with her. She asked in an angry and plaintive tone, 'Why can't you be my friend?'

It was an intense moment. Louise was very aware of the fine line she was walking. She knew Claire was feeling that this was

33. Frame, M. W. & Shehan, C. L. (2004). Care for the caregivers: Clues for the pastoral care of clergywomen. *Pastoral Psychology, 52* (5), 369 – 380.

yet another experience of rejection. At the same time, she did not want to promise to be her friend when she knew this would be false. After a pause she said calmly, but firmly, 'Claire, I am sorry, but I cannot be everything you would like me to be.' Claire gradually stopped crying as she absorbed this information. They continued to meet after this, but the pressure for more personal contact ceased.

Churches and church personnel are often attractive for people who have problems in forming relationships, or who are in difficulty for a range of reasons. In the case described above, Claire was very vulnerable, and needed support and care. Louise, however, was not in a position to give Claire everything she wanted. By making clear what her limits were, Louise established boundaries in the relationship. This enabled her to provide a level of care and support which was within her competence and at the same time ensured that she could meet her other commitments and responsibilities. It is important for ministers to take note when they experience feelings of personal discomfort in a pastoral relationship, and seek to take the difficult step of setting boundaries. This is particularly important because in some instances professional help is needed as well as pastoral support.[34]

Mike is a priest in his thirties in a busy parish. He lives in the upstairs part of a large presbytery although the dining room and utilities are downstairs with the parish offices. He tends to throw his washing in the machine when he has time, and irons in the evening while watching TV. Debby has just moved into the parish and has begun to come around to the parish office after morning Mass to help. One morning when Mike came to retrieve his washing he found that Debby had already taken it out of the machine. Mike thanked her and thought no more about it. However from here, events developed in a way that

34. see Ciarrocchi, J. W. (1993). *A minister's handbook of mental disorders.* New York: Paulist Press.

became disturbing: first he found that Debby had ironed his washing for him. He felt a little awkward, but did not want to make a fuss so he thanked her again. Next he found that Debby had removed his dirty laundry from his bedroom and put it in the machine. This felt a bit intrusive, but as she was only being helpful he made no comment. Later for his birthday she bought him boxer shorts like the ones she had been ironing. By this point he felt things had gone too far, but he did not know how to ask her to stop, so still said nothing. Finally, Mike accepted an invitation to a 'birthday meal' at her house, where she gave him too much to drink and persuaded him to sleep on the sofa. She came into the room to 'check he was comfortable', then started to kiss him and from here they were into a full sexual encounter.

Debby was unable to see or keep to boundaries that would be obvious to most people, but was aware only of meeting her own desires and needs. Mike needed to develop the confidence to set his own boundaries, risking offence if necessary.

Not all difficult people are sexually aggressive. Many of them, however, like Debby, have problems with boundaries, and some may have problems with emotion-management and relationships. However uncomfortable, it is essential that ministers manage these boundaries; this means making it clear where they draw the line about what is acceptable with touch, attention or personal involvement. Without this, not only can there be a lot of misunderstanding and hurt, but conscientious ministers can find themselves devoting disproportionate amounts of time to people who really need help from psychotherapists or other mental-health professionals. That is not to say that clergy do not have a role in helping difficult people, but they need to take account of the different sorts of responses required, and the limits of the care they can offer.

Touch

One of the consequences of the child-abuse scandals that have affected the churches is a concern about the place of touch in ministry. Jesus often touched people as part of his healing ministry, and touch is an integral part of many liturgies, from sharing the sign of peace, to the laying on of hands in a healing service or at ordination. The Sacrament of the Sick in the Catholic Church involves touching the person receiving the sacrament with holy oils. In many pastoral situations it can appear both natural and appropriate to hold a hand, or put a hand on someone's shoulder, or possibly give a hug.

Rigid avoidance of touch may be harmful to some people, but, on the other hand, there may be people who for some reason have no desire to be touched and for whom some liturgical or social rituals may be difficult or impossible. The most important point to remember in the context of sexual dynamics is that touch is ambiguous. It may convey warm greetings, a sign of deep affection, of encouragement, gentle support or healing; equally it may convey intrusive interference, a way of exercising power, possibly in an oppressive way, or a sexual invitation. We need to understand that what we think we are conveying may be quite differently interpreted by the person we touch. We also need to be aware of our own needs. Richard Gula provides sensible guidelines regarding touch in pastoral relationships:[35]

- Always seek permission before touching
- Always respect the other person's right to refuse
- The perspective of the less powerful person must have priority.[36]

Ministers need to behave in ways that respect people, both children and adults, and which also protect themselves from being misunderstood or accused of inappropriate behaviour.

---

35. Gula, R. (1996). *Ethics in pastoral ministry.* New York: Paulist Press.
36. Gula, R. (1996). *Ethics in pastoral ministry.* New York: Paulist Press.

Conclusion

In this chapter we have explored a range of ways that sexuality and sexual desire can be present in ministry. Sexuality should be a healthy presence in ministry, as the passion, generosity, care, attentiveness, and skills in building relationships and communities, which we value and develop in pastoral ministry, come from the same source as our sexuality and sexual desires.[37] This chapter has concentrated on ways that our sexuality can be a source of difficulty, misunderstanding, inappropriate behaviour and ultimately abuse or exploitation. It has demonstrated how easily misunderstandings can occur, a minister's vulnerabilities can be exposed or exploited, ministry can be compromised and innocent people become victims. The suffering of whole communities through the public hurt or scandal that follows is well known. Certain skills are of fundamental importance to the minister: self-awareness, maintaining proper boundaries, awareness of power differences, sensitivity to the vulnerabilities and needs of others, and attention to the presence of issues of sexual dynamics in all our relationships. Attending to ethical codes, and adhering to principles of transparency and accountability, with good judgement, can help ministers to avoid finding themselves in situations where sexual dynamics become destructive. Then our sexuality will be released to be life-enhancing, one of our greatest allies in Christian ministry.

37. Rolheiser, R. (1999). A spirituality of sexuality. In *The holy longing: The search for a Christian spirituality.* New York: Doubleday.

PART IV

Theoretical perspectives

FOURTEEN

Sexuality and spirituality

Christopher C. H. Cook

Introduction

What does sexuality have to do with spirituality? Or, to put it another way, why should there be a section on spirituality in a book about sexuality? Sexuality is seen by many, at best, as having nothing to do with spirituality or, at worst, as being opposed to spirituality. Expressions of sexuality are often viewed as sinful, except when confined within marriage. Even marriage has sometimes been viewed by Christians as a way of keeping sexual sin under control, or else as primarily about providing a context in which to raise a family. Yet, marriage is also viewed by many Christians as a sacrament – an outer sign of an inner and spiritual grace. Does this suggest that marriage should be viewed as more of a spiritual than a sexual relationship? Or does it suggest that sexual union can also be the context of spiritual grace?

The relationship between sexuality and spirituality is – or should be – a matter of some practical concern, for a crude idea that sexual feelings are wrong, unspiritual and shameful, except in very limited circumstances, is the cause of much needless guilt, anxiety and misunderstanding. Not only does this limit and undermine relationships, and impair mental well-being, but it also prevents spiritual growth.

In this chapter, I will explore the nature of the relationship between sexuality and spirituality, examine some of the Christian traditions which have expressed this relationship in different ways, and consider what might be most helpful in responding to some of the sexual-spiritual challenges presented to Christians today. But first we must consider more carefully exactly what sexuality and spirituality are.

Sexuality and spirituality defined

Sexuality is such a familiar part of life that we do not usually consider the need to define it. Yet, it is not easy to define. It is about relationships, and yet single people are as sexual as those who have partners. It clearly involves our bodies, but much sexual activity takes place in people's minds. It clearly involves our affections, and yet much sexual activity (sadly) takes place in the absence of any affection between those involved. It is a deeply moral concern, and yet it is acknowledged as often in the breach as in the observance of moral codes.

Sexuality clearly has something to do with being male or female. Adrian Thatcher has suggested that:

> Human sexuality is about how men and women respond to themselves as sexual beings, and how sexually they relate to each other.[1]

In a sense, we may feel that this hardly moves us on very far in our quest to define sexuality. What does it mean to be a 'sexual being'? Is this primarily a biological, social or psychological concept? However, it is clear that Thatcher is also very close to the heart of the matter. Whatever it may be, sexuality is concerned with maleness and femaleness, and our relatedness as male and female.

Mary Kirk takes a further step in defining sexuality in terms of the different aspects of what it is to be male and female:

> Those physiological, psychological, behavioural and spiritual dimensions of being a male or female human being which may or may not be given expression in sexual feelings and activity.[2]

This definition identifies that sexuality 'may or may not be given expression', thus helpfully acknowledging that it remains present, or potentially available, for all human beings, regardless of physical,

---

1. Thatcher, A. (1993). *Liberating Sex*. London: SPCK, p. 2.
2. Carr, W., Capps, D., Gill, Obholzer, A., Page, R., van Deusen Hunsinger, D., and Williams, R. (2002). *The new dictionary of pastoral studies*. p. 335.

social or psychological factors which may determine its non-expression from time to time, or even for prolonged periods. More importantly, and perhaps surprisingly, Kirk also understands maleness and femaleness as having a spiritual, as well as physical, social and psychological, dimension. What does this imply?

We might immediately assume that the spiritual aspect of being sexual is concerned with religious tradition. Kirk does, in fact, go on to consider the way in which Judeo-Christian teaching has surrounded sexuality with moral rules, which she understands as necessary protection against the powerful potential of sexuality to cause wounds as well as to bring healing. But it is not necessarily the case that spirituality implies religion.

Spirituality is increasingly acknowledged, in a variety of contexts, as being a universal dimension of human experience which is concerned with such themes as relationship, meaning, and transcendence.[3] According to such definitions, the atheist and agnostic may be just as 'spiritual' as the religious person. Of course, some people may choose not to acknowledge spirituality as an aspect of their own experience of being human, and may even find disrespectful suggestions that spirituality is a universal human phenomenon.[4] On the other hand, there will also be those for whom spirituality and religion are inseparable. For example, we might note Sandra Schneiders' strongly Christian understanding of spirituality as:

personal participation in the mystery of Christ.[5]

Yet, elsewhere, Schneiders is able to define spirituality much more broadly:

---

3. Cook, C. C. H. (2004). Addiction and Spirituality. *Addiction*, 99, 539 – 551. Flanagan, K., and Jupp, P. C. (Eds.). *A Sociology of Spirituality*. Aldershot: Ashgate, (2007), Koenig, H. G. (2007). *Spirituality in Patient Care*. Philadelphia: Templeton.
4. Poole, R., Higgo, R., Strong, G., Kennedy, G., Ruben, S., Barnes, R., Lepping, P. & Mitchell, P. (2008). Religion, Psychiatry and Professional Boundaries. *Psychiatric Bulletin*, 32, 356 – 357.
5. Schneiders, S. M. (1996). Scripture and Spirituality, p. 2. In McGinn, B., Meyendorff, J. & Leclercq, J. (Eds.). *Christian spirituality: Origins to the twelfth century*. London: SPCK.

the experience of conscious involvement in the project of life-integration through self-transcendence toward the ultimate value one perceives.[6]

So, whilst remaining respectful of those who do not wish to see themselves as spiritual at all, it is possible to conceive of spirituality very widely – potentially even as a universal dimension of human experience – but also much more specifically within the framework of a particular faith tradition such as Christianity.

Sameness and otherness in mystical relationships

In fact, when we look more closely, we find that sexuality and spirituality have many things in common. Amongst these connections, we might note:

- Universal aspects of being human
- Relationship with another person/God
- Intimacy – knowing and being known
- Nakedness – spiritual, psychological and physical
- Desire
- Difference and sameness
- Easily linked with fear, guilt and shame
- Mystery of the forbidden
- Ineffability.

If we accept for the moment that both are universal aspects of being human,[7] what is the nature of sexual and spiritual relatedness? Sexuality, as Thatcher notes, is about relationship with oneself as well as relationship with other people. However, amongst those to whom one may relate in a sexual way, we may also (as we shall see later) include God. Sexuality and spirituality are therefore both, at least potentially,

---

6. Schneiders, S. M. (2003). Religion Vs. Spirituality: A Contemporary Conundrum. *Spiritus,* 3, 163 – 185, p. 166.
7. Notwithstanding the observations that some people do not self-identify as spiritual and a small percentage of the population deny any significant sexual interest at all.

concerned with relationship with oneself, other people and a transcendent order (God).

The nature of the relatedness with which sexuality and spirituality are both concerned is difficult to define. There certainly appears to be an empirical link between sexuality and spirituality. Retreat directors, for example, are very familiar with the way in which sexual feelings are evoked alongside, or intermingled with, spiritual processes during a silent retreat. Psychosexual therapists are similarly aware of the way in which sexual feelings may become associated with, and abused within, religious contexts.[8] However, the link is not simply one of statistical association. It is concerned with the quality and nature of relationship between self and other. It is concerned, I believe, with the self in intimate relationship to both the 'sameness' and the 'otherness' of the other; knowing and being known.

The sameness which is at the basis of our experience of spiritual and sexual relationships may be that of humanness, or personhood. But alongside this sameness there is also a significant otherness. At the simplest level, this may be the difference between male and female, or between human and divine. However, the differences may be much more subtle. There is the difference (physical, social, psychological and spiritual) that exists between any two human beings. Whilst this will not always be overtly sexualised, or perceived as spiritual, it clearly can become either or both of these. For gay or lesbian couples, there is an appreciation of difference which, alongside the sameness of being gay or lesbian, adds a sexual attraction to the other person that makes the relationship sexual. There is also the potential to reflect upon oneself as a spiritual and/or sexual human being in such a way as to recognise one's own sexuality or spirituality as 'other'. This might be in relationship to a fantasy of a partner, a virtual other, or else in a prayerful relationship of appreciation of

---

8. Birchard, T. (2000). Clergy Sexual Misconduct: Frequency and Causation. *Sexual and Relationship Therapy,* 15, 127–139.

oneself in the presence of God. However, I think that at some level we also have a self-reflective capacity for relationship with ourselves which can, at least potentially, take on sexual or spiritual significance.

It might be argued that there are examples of sexual relationships which do not include an element of sameness, but only of otherness. For example, we might consider fetishism or bestiality under this heading. Usually, however, the history of these disorders will suggest a pathology of relationship within which sexual feelings became attached to these other objects or creatures in place of other people. Examples of spirituality which do not involve an element of sameness are more difficult to identify. In fact, mystical states which are not experienced in the context of any faith tradition often still include a sense of 'oneness' with all things. A relationship with a transcendent order or being, where the transcendent object is utterly beyond anything knowable, might fall into a category of relationship with that which is other and in no sense the same. However, if there is absolutely no possibility of relationship with such an object (or God) then arguably this is not in fact a spiritual relationship at all, but rather a matter of mere dogma or philosophy. If there is a possibility of relationship, this must be built on some kind of common ground, and it is on this common ground, whatever it is, that the relationship may be said to enjoy a degree of sameness, however small.

Sexual and spiritual relationships seem to always display a degree of intimacy. This intimacy may be understood as spiritual, physical, or psychological, or any combination of these. Traditionally, it is sexuality which is associated with physical intimacy and spirituality which is associated with spiritual intimacy. But a good marriage may be experienced as an intimate relationship on each of these dimensions and, as we shall see below, spiritual relationships do not exclude physical intimacy. Within these different kinds of intimacy, we might see 'nakedness' as a helpful metaphor. Whilst at a literal level nakedness and intimacy are usually associated with sexual intercourse, nakedness can also be symbolic of spiritual or psychological experience, as when we are known 'as we are' by God, or by a good friend.

Within this world of relatedness, both sexuality and spirituality are characteristically associated with desire for the other. This desire may focus on otherness – e.g., the attraction of male for female – but it is also embedded in sameness. It may focus on particular spiritual, psychological or physical attributes, but the other person is desired not only for those attributes. They are desired for what they are, in themselves, out of love. There is a paradox here, for if the other person were to change so radically that they were no longer desirable, love might still demand that they are yet to be loved, as in Shakespeare's famous sonnet:

Let me not to the marriage of true minds
admit impediments. Love is not love
which alters when it alteration finds,
or bends with the remover to remove:
O no! it is an ever-fixed mark
that looks on tempests and is never shaken;
it is the star to every wandering bark,
whose worth's unknown, although his height be taken.
Love's not Time's fool, though rosy lips and cheeks
within his bending sickle's compass come:
Love alters not with his brief hours and weeks,
but bears it out even to the edge of doom.
If this be error and upon me proved,
I never writ, nor no man ever loved.[9]

So, sexuality and spirituality are both about desire but, at their best, are not limited by desire of a crude or sentimental kind. Love transcends this – spiritually, physically and psychologically.

---

9. Shakespeare, W. Sonnet 116.

Within the relationship of sameness and otherness that sexuality and spirituality both engage in, the otherness is also associated with a kind of mystery which gives rise to fear or arousal. This fear might be seen in the propensity, which both sexual and spiritual relationships have, to generate guilt and shame when they go wrong. But I think that it is actually, at heart, a much more positive thing than this. Perhaps it is something akin to the kind of fear associated with dangerous sports – such as sky-diving or rock-climbing. The sky-diver does not want to hurtle uncontrollably into the ground and be destroyed by gravity, but it is doubtful that sky-diving would have the same attraction if it were completely harmless and without any danger of such a possibility. Similarly, the fear associated with looking into the eyes of the one you love is not there because of some pathological desire to engage with something inherently dangerous for its own sake. It is, in any case, modified by love in such a way as to make the experience deeply attractive. But it is very similar to the fear that acknowledges the awfulness of the Divine concurrently with a deep attraction to the Divine.

Rudolf Otto wrote of the *mysterium tremendum* and the *mysterium fascinans*, which are associated with awareness of the Divine presence. The *mysterium tremendum* is characterised by the awfulness, over-powering, and energy of the experience of being in the presence of that which is 'wholly other'. This fear causes us to respect God, as we should, but it is somehow linked to a deep-seated attraction which overcomes fear out of desire for intimacy. This attraction, the *mysterium fascinans*, is alluring, seductive, even erotic, in quality.[10] It is this combination of awe and mystery with deep attraction, all of which are evoked at a very non-rational level (although they may be subject to rationalisation), that is associated with both sexual and spiritual relationships.

10. Otto, R. (1980). *The Idea of the Holy*. OUP.

Sexual and spiritual experiences have given rise to some of the most beautiful art, including prose and poetry, which human beings have created. Yet, the lover and the mystic both also acknowledge that words are inadequate. Sexual and spiritual experiences, especially at their most intense, are ultimately ineffable. Whilst words can be found to describe them, and the finding of words can produce a degree of pleasure and satisfaction, yet the most intense of such experiences always seem to go beyond anything that words can adequately convey.

Sexuality in Hebrew and Christian scripture

In Hebrew scripture, sexuality is encountered in the very earliest texts. In the creation narratives of Genesis 1–3 we find the theme emerging. In the first narrative, human beings are created in the image of God. This image manifests both sameness and radical otherness in relationship to God. They are also created as male and female, thus manifesting both sameness and otherness in their relationship with one another.[11] In the second narrative a man is created first and then a woman is created as a 'helper' or 'partner'.[12] The man and the woman are both the same ('bone of my bones and flesh of my flesh'[13]) and yet other, but they are also complementary to each other. This part of the story concludes:

> Therefore a man leaves his father and his mother and clings to his wife, and they become one flesh. And the man and his wife were both naked, and were not ashamed.[14]

Sadly, in the following chapter, everything starts to go wrong as a result of disobedience to the Divine command. Ostensibly, that disobedience has no sexual element to it, although the story of taking

11. Genesis 1:27.
12. Genesis 2:18.
13. Genesis 2:23.
14. Genesis 2:24, 25.

the apple from the tree has nonetheless been interpreted in Christian tradition as symbolic of sexual sin. Whether or not that primal act of disobedience is understood in sexual terms, it has sexual consequences. Amongst other things, the man and woman become aware of their nakedness, and this awareness is associated with fear. The woman is destined to desire her husband, and yet to be subject to him.

We have not time to dwell at length on these passages here, but they set the scene for a canon of texts which returns to sexual themes again and again. Not infrequently, this is in the context of things going badly wrong in human relationships. Thus, for example, we read of the failure of Onan to perform his sexual duty to the widow of his brother,[15] the adultery of David with Bathsheba,[16] and the abuse by Absalom of David's concubines as a means of gaining power.[17] And this recurring theme of failure and abuse in sexual relationships is used repeatedly by the prophets (notably by Jeremiah, Ezekiel and Hoseah) as an image of the failure of the relationship between God and his people. The image is one of the human–Divine relationship as marriage, with human propensities to the worship of idols being seen as adultery or prostitution.[18]

But there are positive images too. Thus, in the book of Proverbs, we find wisdom personified in female form as desirable, to be embraced.[19] Psalm 45 is a wedding song which was interpreted first by Jews as having Messianic reference, and then by Christians as having reference to Christ. And in Isaiah we find the relationship between God and human beings likened to that between a bride and bridegroom.[20] Perhaps supremely, however, we find in the Song of Songs an extended and explicitly erotic account of a relationship between a man and a woman within which some of the most beautiful

15. Genesis 38:3–10.
16. 2 Samuel 11:3–5.
17. 2 Samuel 17:21.
18. See, for example, Jeremiah 3:9, 5:7, 7:9; Ezekiel 23:37; Hosea 1:2.
19. E.g., Proverbs 4:5–13.
20. Isaiah 62:5.

and romantic verses of the Bible may arguably be found. Take, for example, this extract from Chapter 4:

> How beautiful you are, my love, how very beautiful! Your eyes are doves behind your veil. Your hair is like a flock of goats, moving down the slopes of Gilead. Your teeth are like a flock of shorn ewes that have come up from the washing, all of which bear twins, and not one among them is bereaved. Your lips are like a crimson thread, and your mouth is lovely. Your cheeks are like halves of a pomegranate behind your veil. Your neck is like the tower of David, built in courses; on it hang a thousand bucklers, all of them shields of warriors. Your two breasts are like two fawns, twins of a gazelle, that feed among the lilies. Until the day breathes and the shadows flee, I will hasten to the mountain of myrrh and the hill of frankincense. You are altogether beautiful, my love; there is no flaw in you.[21]

This book has been extensively allegorised by both Jews and Christians as being concerned with the relationship between God and the human soul, or God and the community of faith. Indeed, if this interpretation were not possible one wonders whether it could have found its way into either Hebrew or Christian scripture at all.

In the Gospels of the New Testament, Jesus takes up the familiar Hebrew use of the term 'adultery' to refer to the unfaithfulness of God's people,[22] a theme which appears again in eschatological context in the book of Revelation.[23] Adultery, in its immediate literal sense, is also a recurring theme. In his teaching about adultery, Jesus extends the concept to include lustful thoughts, as well as acted-out behaviour,[24] and he draws attention to the origin of such sin within the human heart.[25] Frustratingly, we are left without any detailed

21. 4:1–7.
22. Matthew 12:39, 16:4; Mark 8:38.
23. Revelation 2:22.
24. Matthew 5:27, 28.
25. Matthew 15:19; Mark 7:21, 22.

exegesis of this by Jesus. Somewhere between the innocence of finding a man or woman sexually attractive, and the sinfulness of allowing that attraction to express itself in adultery, is a line which Jesus urges us not to cross. But he leaves us in no doubt that sexual attraction is a spiritual matter.

Of course, Jesus is also recorded in the fourth Gospel as having attended a wedding, and thus implicitly is believed to have affirmed matrimony.[26] However, the most positive, and arguably most significant, New Testament appearances of the theme of sexuality are found in images of the relationship between Christ and the Church as one of marriage. In the epistle to the Ephesians, husbands and wives are exhorted to treat each other in accordance with this image, an image which is rooted explicitly in the Genesis narrative.[27] In the book of Revelation, the image of the Church as the bride, and Christ as the bridegroom, makes repeated appearances, with the eschatological culmination of all things being likened to a wedding banquet.[28]

There are thus very positive Hebrew and Christian scriptural associations, even identifications, of the human–Divine relationship with the sexual relationship of marriage. The Hebrew and Christian canonical texts are not unrealistic about the potential for this mystical relationship to be abused, and for it to fail through human sinfulness. But there is no doubt that in the beginning and at the end of all things sexuality is understood as holy and good, and intimately linked to spirituality.

Sexuality in Christian tradition

Even a cursory survey of Christian tradition would seem to reveal that there have been at least two approaches taken to the relationship between sexuality and spirituality. An ascetic (self-denying) tradition,

26. John 2:1–11.
27. Ephesians 5:22–33.
28. Revelation 19:7–9, 21:2, 9, 22:17.

which appears to have emerged very early on in the history of Christianity, has emphasised the dangers of sexual temptation and has sought to avoid sexual sin, usually through celibacy. A more affirmative tradition, however, emphasising the allegorical scriptural images of relationship with God as sexual, has not been shy of speaking explicitly about the possibilities for this relationship, and marriage, in sexual language.

The ascetic tradition, dating back to the Desert Fathers, has emphasised the sinfulness of sexuality, and has therefore understood sexuality as opposed to spirituality. Within this tradition, marriage is therefore more or less a compromise, necessary for the procreation of children and the limitation of sin. This understanding of the relationship between sexuality and spirituality is largely dualistic, emphasising sexuality as concerned with physicality, which is understood in this context as 'bad', and spirituality as concerned with that which is non-physical and 'good'. The scriptural themes that have been emphasised in the ascetic tradition have been those of 'the fall' in Genesis 3 (with its perceived or imagined overtones of sexual desire as the starting point of human sinfulness), and that of adultery as unfaithfulness to God, arising from sexual temptation. Here, the emphasis is upon fearful avoidance of sin, and the consequent risk is that of rejecting God's good gift of sexuality.

Examples of the ascetic tradition include Evagrius of Pontus (c.345–399), who identified eight thoughts, later to be adapted as a basis for the 'seven deadly sins', about which monks wishing to lead a life of prayer were encouraged to be informed. The emphasis of Evagrius' writings about the thoughts was not so much on the sinful behaviour towards which they might lead, although that was a concern, but rather on the progressive way in which apparently innocent thoughts might lead to worse things:

> Flee encounters with women if you want to be chaste, and never allow them familiarity to be bold with you. For in the

beginning they will have or pretend to have pious reverence, but later they will dare anything without shame. At the first encounter they keep the eyes lowered, they speak softly, cry emotionally, dress modestly, and moan bitterly; they inquire about chastity and listen earnestly. At the second meeting you notice her looking up a little bit. A third time, they look directly at you without shame, you smile, and they laugh heartily. Then they adorn themselves and make an open display of themselves for you; they look at you in a way that shows the promise of their passion. They raise their eyebrows and bat their eyelashes; they bare the neck and use the entire body in an enticing manner; they speak words that caress the passion and they practise a voice that is enchanting to hear, until they besiege the soul by every means. These are the hooks laid out to catch you in death and the entangling nets that drag you to destruction. May they not lead you astray with their nice words, for the evil poison of beasts is concealed in these women.[29]

Evagrius is not suggesting that women are all poisonous beasts, although there may be echoes here of the offering of the fruit to Adam by Eve in the Genesis narratives. Rather, he is aware of the direction in which apparently innocent and enjoyable thoughts lead. Neither does he suggest that all temptation is sexual – he has much to say about gluttony (which comes first in his list), avarice, anger, sadness, acedia (listlessness), vainglory and pride. Rather, he is aware that sexual thoughts easily distract from prayerfulness, and that they do this from seemingly harmless starting points.

Another early source of the ascetic tradition in sexuality and spirituality is Augustine of Hippo (354–430). Augustine was engaged in a monogamous relationship with a mistress which was culturally normal for Roman society at the time. But, for reasons which are beyond the scope of this chapter, Augustine saw himself as presented

29. Sinkewicz, R. E. (2003). *Evagrius of Pontus: The Greek Ascetic Corpus.* OUP, pp. 76 – 77.

with a choice other than the obvious one of that between continuing his relationship and getting married. Rather, he found conversion to Christianity inextricably linked in his own mind with a call to a life of celibacy. The choice that he perceived was, effectively, between a sexually active life and one of renouncing sexual activity. Such was the influence of Augustinian thinking on the subsequent course of Christian theology that many have perceived Christianity as having a fundamentally negative attitude towards sexuality ever since. In particular, Augustine's doctrine of the transmission of original sin from one generation to the next through sexual intercourse, has been perceived as binding sexuality and sinfulness closely together.

Returning to the connections between sexuality and spirituality that we identified above, we might note that the distinctive form that they take in the ascetic tradition is dualistic and emphasises human sinfulness:

- Universal aspects of being human – *universal human sinfulness*

- Relationship with another / the other – *broken and distorted by sin*

- Intimacy – knowing and being known – *physically (sexuality) and spiritually (spirituality)*

- Nakedness – spiritual *(in spirituality)*, psychological, and physical *(in sexuality)*

- Desire – *physical vs spiritual*

- Difference and sameness – *physical difference being bad, and spiritual sameness being good*

- Easily linked with fear, guilt and shame – *and sexuality therefore best avoided in order to focus on spirituality*

- Mystery of the forbidden (*but without the positive element of the* mysterium fascinans)

- Ineffability – *sexuality (in contrast to spirituality) best not spoken about except in terms of warning.*

The affirmative tradition, dating back at least to the early Middle Ages, has emphasised the goodness of sexuality as created by God, and has therefore understood sexuality as expressed in, and expressive of, spirituality. Within this tradition, marriage is fundamentally good in its physical and spiritual aspects. This understanding of the relationship between sexuality and spirituality finds each merging with the other as at once physical, psychological and spiritual forms of relationship. The scriptural themes that have been emphasised in the affirmative tradition have been those of the union of male and female (prior to the fall) in Genesis 3, the relationship of human beings with God at its best as marriage-like (cf. Ephesians 5), the personification of divine Wisdom as female (and therefore attractive to men, just as Jesus is potentially sexually attractive to women), and an eschatological vision of the Church as the bride of Christ. Here the emphasis is upon grateful affirmation of sexuality, and the risk is that of naturalism – an elevation of the natural order as good within itself.

Many examples of the affirmative tradition may be identified. We might note, for example, Bernard of Clairvaux (1090–1153) who left a large collection of sermons on the Song of Songs, the anonymous *Cloud of Unknowing* (fourteenth century) with its references to God as a jealous lover, or the emphasis of the Carmelites, John of the Cross and Teresa of Avila (sixteenth century) on ecstasy, betrothal and union in mystical relationship with God. As an example for somewhat more detailed study here, however, let us take the poetry of George Herbert (1593–1633) and John Donne (1572–1631).

In 'Love bade me welcome', Herbert describes the relationship of sinful human beings with a gracious and forgiving God:

> Love bade me welcome, yet my soul drew back,
> guilty of dust and sin.
> But quick-ey'd Love, observing me grow slack
> from my first entrance in,

drew nearer to me, sweetly questioning
if I lack'd anything.

'A guest,' I answer'd, 'worthy to be here';
Love said, 'You shall be he.'
'I, the unkind, the ungrateful? ah my dear,
I cannot look on thee.'
Love took my hand and smiling did reply,
'Who made the eyes but I?'
'Truth, Lord, but I have marr'd them; let my shame
go where it doth deserve.'
'And know you not,' says Love, 'who bore the blame?'
'My dear, then I will serve.'
'You must sit down,' says Love, 'and taste my meat.'
So I did sit and eat.[30]

The poem portrays the remorse of the human creature in relationship with forgiveness offered graciously by the Divine Creator. It is a deeply spiritual poem. But, on more careful examination, there is a deeply physical aspect to it. In fact, in the concluding verse, where the poem reaches the climax of Divine love, it emphasises most the physicality of partaking in the Divine, in terms which are easily understandable as references to the Eucharist. But is there not also a sexual edge to this poem? It is almost erotic in its charting of the Divine love affair.[31]

A poem by John Donne, 'To his Mistress going to Bed', provides a contrasting example. Here, the theme is explicitly sexual, but it is as though Donne cannot express himself adequately without repeatedly returning to the language of spirituality. As he exhorts his wife to undress, her girdle is 'like heaven's zone glittering, but a far fairer world encompassing'. The bed is 'love's hallowed temple', his wife is

---

30. This poem can be found in many sources, including Tobin, J (1991). *George Herbert: The complete English poems.* London, Penguin, p. 178.
31. See, for example, the commentary by Alan Bartlett (Bartlett, A. (2007). *A passionate balance: The Anglican tradition.* London: DLT, p. 189).

dressed like an angel, and the effect that she has on him (again described in explicit terms) is affirmed as good. He continues:

> How am I blest in thus discovering thee!
> To enter in these bonds, is to be free;
> then, where my hand is set, my soul shall be.
> Full nakedness! All joys are due to thee;
> as souls unbodied, bodies unclothed must be
> to taste whole joys.[32]

The sexual relationship between man and woman in marriage is here affirmed – but not merely affirmed. The only language adequate to describe the spiritual and emotional aspects of intimacy – alongside the physical – is that of the joy of the human soul. Just as the joy of sexual intimacy is found in the shedding of clothes from the body, so the joy of the soul (implicitly to be attained in union with God in death) will be found when the soul sheds its body. Further on, the beauty of the clothed female body is compared with that of a mystical book. Each must be 'revealed', the one through undressing and the other through opening and reading, in order that the grace within may be known. At first, this is simply a sexual poem written by a man as an appreciation of his wife. But, on closer inspection, it reveals an interweaving of sexual and spiritual themes as inextricably linked, and each in need of the other for its full expression.

Returning again to the connections between sexuality and spirituality that we identified above, we might note that the distinctive form that they take in the affirmative tradition is of a merging of the physical and spiritual domains, and an emphasis on sexuality as a good gift of God:

- Universal aspects of being human – *both created as good*
- Relationship with another/the other – *expressed in ways given by God*

32. Coffin, C. M. (1994). *The complete poetry and selected prose of John Donne.* New York: Modern Library, p. 83.

- Intimacy – knowing and being known – *physically and spiritually (in sexuality and spirituality alike)*

- Nakedness – spiritual, psychological, and physical *(in sexuality and spirituality alike)*

- Desire – *physical and spiritual, overlapping and intermingling*

- Difference and sameness – *physical and spiritual alike being good*

- Easily linked with fear, guilt and shame – *but only when misused and abused*

- Mystery of the forbidden – *embracing fully the positive element of the* mysterium fascinans

- Ineffability – *sexuality and spirituality each needing the other in order that it may be more adequately appreciated.*

It is not clear that Christians have ever been very good at embracing the strengths of both of these traditions at the same time. We might note that writers such as Bernard of Clairvaux and Teresa of Avila were celibate and so had, in one sense, embraced aspects of both traditions. We might note also that George Herbert and John Donne expressed their sexuality each in marital commitment to one woman, thus renouncing other relationships with women. In a sense they also therefore demonstrated both ascetic and affirmative aspects to their sexuality. But this does not entirely undo the legacy of the ascetic tradition in bestowing a sense of sinfulness upon sexuality that other good gifts of God have generally not suffered. This is clearly not the fault of Evagrius, who listed gluttony before fornication as one of the eight thoughts of which Christians should be wary. We do not tend to see food as sinful in the way that we see sex as sinful – even though both can be used or misused, for good or ill respectively.

It is also interesting that today's Church has become obsessed with a debate about human sexuality which focuses on a minority who find themselves sexually attracted to people of the same sex, whilst the heterosexual majority (within and outside our Churches) engage in sexual activity outside of marriage more than ever before. It is hard to avoid the conclusion that many people find it easier to affirm their own sexual activity and deny that of others than they do to follow the ascetic path themselves. This is not to offer any comment either way on sexual ethics (which have deliberately not been explored here) but rather to note that we have a novel contemporary way of avoiding the real issue for Christian spirituality. How can we affirm all that is good in both Christian traditions of sexuality and spirituality, whilst avoiding their potential pitfalls?

Sexuality and spirituality – finding a helpful way forward

Perhaps it is in the nature of the *mysterium fascinans* that human beings will always feel ambivalent about sexuality and spirituality. With the powerfulness of sexual attraction comes great responsibility. Sometimes, it is easier to avoid this powerful force than to risk a sense of guilt at expressing it. Sometimes it is easier to suppress the guilt rather than to risk the powerful sense of loss associated with not being able to express it. The answer, it would seem, is not to be found in denial or pretence, but rather in a better integration of sexuality and spirituality in the Christian life. If these are things that we struggle with, they can also be things that we talk and pray about. Sometimes, it might be necessary to confront the fear of giving up something which we deeply desire. Sometimes it might be necessary to take the risk of getting it wrong and needing to ask forgiveness. But always it will be necessary to ask ourselves what we most desire and to be willing to discover, if need be, that it is not what we thought it was.

Sexuality and spirituality, as we have already considered, both represent deep-seated, yet also transcendent, human desires. If there has been a tendency in the past to deny one of these desires in preference for the other, or to see them as being mutually exclusive, does this need to be the case? One tradition of Christian spirituality which offers a way of exploring desire is to be found in the teachings of Ignatius of Loyola. Whilst it is not suggested here that this is the only Christian tradition within which sexuality and spirituality can be mutually affirmed without either excessive licence or inhibition, it is a currently popular form of spirituality which does lend itself to this task. It is therefore worthy of further exploration here, by way of example of what might be helpful as the basis for a more affirming and balanced expression of Christian sexuality and spirituality.

Ignatian spirituality

The question of what we most desire is a distinctively Ignatian one. Ignatius of Loyola (1491–1566) devised a set of spiritual exercises which were designed to assist in exploring vocation. Most of the exercises involve meditation on scripture, in such a way as to facilitate a subjective engagement with the text that makes full use of the imagination and of feelings as aids to prayer. To undertake the full exercises requires either a fairly lengthy residential retreat (usually of 30 days) or else a longer period of commitment to working through the exercises alongside the commitments of daily life. However, it is possible to undertake shorter retreats using similar principles and selectively drawing upon the full programme of exercises that Ignatius devised.

Almost all of the Ignatian exercises, after a preparatory prayer and one or more other preludes, begin with a request that God will give us what we desire. This is rarely left completely unspecified for the retreatant and Ignatius not infrequently expects us to pray for things that we may well feel we don't desire at all. Thus, for example, near the beginning of the third week, in preparation for meditation on Christ in the garden at Gethsemane, Ignatius provides this prelude to the exercise:

. . . to ask for what I desire. Here it is what is proper for the Passion: sorrow with Christ in sorrow; a broken spirit with Christ so broken; tears; and interior suffering because of the great suffering which Christ endured for me.[33]

What does all of this have to do with our theme of sexuality and spirituality?

Firstly, I think that both sexuality and spirituality confront us with the question of what we most desire. Spirituality, as we have seen, can be treated as a positive choice for something more important than fulfilment of physical sexuality but, even then, it will not be healthy to deny that we have any sexual desires. Healthy spirituality confronts us with sexual desires and encourages us to integrate them into our relationship with God. Sexuality can be affirmed by Christians as something which is given by God – as something which it is legitimate and proper to desire. But, even then, it will not be either healthy or fulfilling to pursue that desire at the expense of all others. As Christians, we are called to place this gift alongside others that we have been given and to seek the best way of using all of these gifts for a higher purpose. A fundamental starting point in the Ignatian exercises is to explore exactly what that higher purpose must be. To cut a long story short, it is to be found in following Christ, not in pursuing our own sexual fulfilment above all else.

Secondly, however, the exercises enable us to explore our humanity and, as a part of that humanity, our sexuality. Although they are always referred to as 'spiritual' exercises, they encourage us to engage fully as human beings with the scriptural text, in particular the Gospel narratives. When we find ourselves encouraged to imagine ourselves present when Christ is engaging as a human being with other human beings, we find ourselves, as human beings, encountering

---

33. Ganss, G. E., Divarkar, P. R., Malatesta, E. J., Palmer, M. E. & Padberg, J. W. (1991). *Ignatius of Loyola: Spiritual exercises and selected works.* New York: Paulist, p. 169.

him. And these encounters engage us as whole people, body, mind and spirit in all aspects of our being, including our sexuality.

Many men are surprised to discover that Christian women sometimes struggle with a sense of being attracted sexually to Jesus, as a man. But in the Ignatian exercises, we all engage as sexual beings with whatever encounter they bring us to, whether we are male or female. A man might, therefore, find himself attracted to a female character in the narrative, or might imagine himself as one of the women in the story, attracted to Jesus. Whatever the dynamics that are elicited, and these are obviously by no means always concerned with sexual themes, Ignatius encourages us to bring these thoughts and feelings into our prayers. They may therefore be safely acknowledged and examined, recognising that they are a part of the people that we are, in the context of exploring our vocation as Christians – whatever that might specifically be.

Thirdly, the exercises enable us to engage with the full humanity of Jesus. Whatever our own sexual identity, we are confronted with a Christ who is fully human – including his sexual identity as a man. The exercises will not address historical critical questions surrounding that identity, so we cannot know exactly whom Jesus was historically attracted to or exactly how he handled those feelings as a matter of historical record. But they do address the subjective question of our own thoughts and feelings about that reality, and how it affects our own sexual self-understanding.

It is not suggested here that every Christian must go on an Ignatian retreat in order to explore their sexuality and spirituality. Rather, this very brief examination of how sexuality may be explored within one Christian spiritual tradition today is offered as an example of what may be undertaken in different ways in most, if not all, of the living Christian spiritual traditions. However, what is affirmed here, is the need to acknowledge our sexuality, rather than to deny it, and to make it a part of our prayers. Although this will always be challenging, it will also always be better than either of the extremes of denying our sexuality in order to pray, or denying our spirituality in order to pursue sexual fulfilment.

Finding solutions to problems

The focus of this chapter has been a very broad one. It has been concerned with the connections between sexuality and spirituality, and how different Christian traditions have understood the relationship between them. It has been suggested that there is a need to bring together the best aspects of the ascetic and affirmative traditions to inform a more balanced, creative and guilt-free state of sexual and spiritual well-being. However, it is also necessary to find practical solutions to the problems that people face. Ignatian spirituality provides one example of how this may be explored. But what are the specific problems to which solutions must be applied?

The problems are many and, in a sense, they are explored in more depth in every other chapter of this book. On the one hand, they include a range of problems which are often approached at a purely ethical or psychological level. They include the sense of guilt or compulsion that may be felt about masturbation. They include the difficult feelings encountered by married people who continue to find others sexually attractive. They include the tensions associated with different levels of desire between a husband and wife. But, on the other hand, they also include more explicitly 'spiritual' matters. They include the sense of guilt and confusion that might be associated with finding Jesus sexually attractive, or feeling aroused when receiving the sacraments. Because human beings are biological, psychological, social and spiritual creatures, all of these problems need to be addressed in a multi-faceted way. But a part of an overall strategy to helping will need to include much more attention than has previously been given to exploring individual tendencies towards excessively ascetic, or excessively affirmative, relationships between sexuality and spirituality, with a view to achieving greater balance. This might be achieved by greater awareness of psycho-sexual therapists about the need to address spiritual issues, or it might be achieved by a greater readiness to recommend that clients engage in spiritual direction alongside psychological and other therapies.

Sometimes, the problem may be more with the helper than with the person being helped. Weingarten[34] describes the experiences of a spiritual director who noted that sexuality never seemed to emerge as a theme with her directees until she found herself more able to integrate her own sexuality and spirituality. As she addressed these issues in her own spiritual direction, her directees all seemed to start talking to her about their sexuality too. As with all aspects of spiritual direction, no director or directee will ever achieve perfect understanding and integration of their sexuality and spirituality in this world. But being on a journey towards fuller understanding and integration would appear to be an important part of helping others.

What principles might guide the spiritual director, the therapist, or the person who is struggling with particular issues at the interface of sexuality and spirituality? The following are proposed as a provisional working framework to guide practice, and as a starting point for discussion:

1. Sexuality and spirituality are universal and interrelated aspects of human beings. Both may fundamentally be affirmed. Both can become disordered.

2. Sexuality and spirituality are both about mutual relationship and will always need evaluation in the context of relationships with oneself, other people and God. Does any particular expression or withholding of sexuality or spirituality build or undermine these relationships?

34. Weingarten, T (2005). Sacred fire. *Spirituality and Health,* March – April, pp. 60 – 63, 69.

3. Sexual and spiritual intimacy may each be developed on physical, psychological and spiritual levels. Expression or denial of sexuality or spirituality at any of these levels may foster or hinder intimacy.

4. Sexuality and spirituality involve nakedness with another – a vulnerability which must always be treated tenderly.

5. Sexuality and spirituality are concerned with our deepest desires. Sometimes sexual desire may be misplaced (e.g., in fetishism) or disproportionate (whether by greater or lesser degree). In such cases, the individual will need affirmation. Such disordered desires are not chosen, and do not disappear at will, any more than do emotions of depression or anger. But they do present opportunities to grow in knowledge of ourselves and others.

6. Sameness and otherness both offer opportunities to develop sexual and spiritual intimacy.

7. Sexuality and spirituality are easily associated with misplaced fears, regrets and attributions of blame. Spiritual direction and psychological therapies provide opportunities to explore and allay these sources of dysphoria.

8. Sexuality and spirituality are associated with a paradox of fear and attraction towards the other. This paradox may potentially be undermined by imbalances of either fear without intimacy or unalloyed familiarity.

9. Sexuality and spirituality operate at levels which often defy adequate verbal expression. Non-verbal expressions of relation-ship, such as eye contact, caress, music and silence may all assist in deepening relationship.

Conclusions

Sexuality and spirituality, far from being opposed to each other, are connected at many levels. Each has the capacity to evoke – or inhibit – the other. Traditions of Christian spirituality have each, in different ways, sought to manage this complex relationship. An excessively ascetic response runs the risk of the denial of that which is fundamentally good and of inducing guilt and fear. Physicality is sacrificed in favour of spirituality. But an excessively affirmative response runs the risk of breaching ethical boundaries and focusing on the physical at the expense of the spiritual. A balanced Christian approach to sexuality and spirituality would appear to need an affirmative and an ascetic element in order to avoid these dangers. A recognition of the delicate and complex balance that is required, and an affirmation of the ways in which sexuality and spirituality may be mutually supportive, would appear to have important implications for addressing a wide range of sexual and spiritual problems.

Bibliography

Bartlett, A. (2007). *A passionate balance: The Anglican tradition.* London: DLT.

Birchard, T. (2000). Clergy Sexual Misconduct: Frequency and Causation. *Sexual and Relationship Therapy,* 15, 127–139.

Carr, W., Capps, D., Gill, R., Obholzer, A., Page, R., Van Deusen Hunsinger, D. & Williams, R. (2002). *The new dictionary of pastoral studies.* London: SPCK.

Coffin, C. M. (1994). *The complete poetry and selected prose of John Donne.* New York: Modern Library.

Cook, C. C. H. (2004). Addiction and Spirituality. *Addiction,* 99, 539–551.

Flanagan, K. & Jupp, P. C. (Eds.). (2007). *A sociology of spirituality.* Aldershot: Ashgate.

Ganss, G. E., Divarkar, P. R., Malatesta, E. J., Palmer, M. E. & Padberg, J. W. (1991). *Ignatius of Loyola: Spiritual exercises and selected works.* New York: Paulist.

Koenig, H. G. (2007). *Spirituality in patient care.* Philadelphia: Templeton.

Otto, R. (1980). *The idea of the Holy.* OUP.

Poole, R., Higgo, R., Strong, G., Kennedy, G., Ruben, S., Barnes, R., Lepping, P. & Mitchell, P. (2008). Religion, Psychiatry and Professional Boundaries. *Psychiatric Bulletin, 32,* 356–357.

Schneiders, S. M. (1996). Scripture and Spirituality. In McGinn, B., Meyendorff, J. & Leclercq, J. (Eds.). *Christian spirituality: Origins to the twelfth century.* London: SCM.

Schneiders, S. M. (2003). Religion Vs. Spirituality: A Contemporary Conundrum. *Spiritus, 3,* 163–185.

Sinkewicz, R. E. (2003). *Evagrius of Pontus: The Greek ascetic corpus.* OUP.

Thatcher, A. (1993). *Liberating sex.* London: SPCK.

Tobin, J. (1991). *George Herbert: The complete English poems.* London, Penguin.

Weingarten, T. (2005). Sacred fire. *Spirituality and Health,* March – April, pp. 60 – 63, 69.

FIFTEEN

Theology and sexuality

Charles Gay

Introduction

Has sin changed? Does morality change? What happened to sin? These questions are the titles of three books by the Irish moral theologian, Sean Fagan, published in 1977, 1997 and 2008 respectively.[1] Whatever the response of the author to each of these questions, it is clear that the questions reflect a sense of unease, of uncertainty and the thoughts of the ordinary man and woman in the pews. A cursory glance at news headlines and commentaries and even more so, at the correspondence columns, will reinforce in the reader the perception that something has changed. We read increasing reports of violence, be it knife-crime among young people, rape, murder or domestic violence. The present situation in the financial markets does nothing to dispel the gloom; rather it further adds to perceptions of widespread greed at individual and corporate levels. There appears to be a breakdown in standards and values in private and public life. But what perhaps is of greater concern to the ordinary person in the pew is that members of faith communities seem unable to agree on standards and values. The correspondence columns in the religious press demonstrate the same variety of responses and strongly held views as those of the secular press. Perhaps more than in any other area of life, it is in sexual mores and interpersonal relationships such as contraception, cohabitation, homosexuality, same-sex civil partnerships that the conflicting views of different faith communities and of members within these communities create most confusion. How can

---

1. Fagan, S. (1977). *Has sin changed?* Ireland: Gill & Macmillan. Fagan, S. (1997). *Has morality changed?* Delaware: Michael Glazier. Fagan, S. (2008). *What happened to sin?* Dublin: Columba Press.

we understand such apparent change, the conflicting views and the confusion they bring?

In this chapter I hope to show that there have been a number of significant shifts in the way that theologians (and Churches) reflect on human sexuality. In the first place there has been a shift from focusing on a static conception of human nature, to a dynamic understanding of the human person. Secondly, the earlier approach based on evaluating the status of moral acts has given way to a more complex reflection on the meaning of individual acts in the context of the lives and realities of unique persons, each of whose lives and particular circumstances are different. In recent years there has been a notable increase in writers (particularly women) who reflect on sexuality in terms of justice and human rights, rather than behaviours in the abstract. Lastly, a significant shift has happened in Western culture in terms of valuing human experience as a source of knowledge in moral decision-making. This was well expressed by Pat Collins CM in an address to Irish priests when he said that, 'The centre of gravity in modern Catholicism is shifting from the experience of religious authority to the authority of religious experience'.[2] The various Christian Churches all approach the issue of authority in different ways, but, I would argue, all now have to take the human experience of members of their Churches into account as they provide guidance and statements in the area of human sexuality.

Models and paradigms

I would like to begin this chapter by providing an outline of the idea of paradigms. This way of thinking has had a significant impact on all areas of knowledge, as it helps to explain how ideas and ways of understanding become dominant, and how, over time, they tend to give way to new understandings. As the chapter progresses it should

---

2. Collins, P. (29th September, 1990). Address to the National Conference of Priests of Ireland, quoted in *The Tablet*, p. 1242.

become clearer how this insight helps us to understand some of the changes that have taken place in the different Christian Churches and how the process of change often generates resistance, and, in some Churches, fundamental splits in communion. I will write mostly from the perspective of the Catholic tradition, which I know best, having watched the changes unfold over nearly 50 years since the convening of the Second Vatican Council (1962–65). I hope, however, that readers from other Churches will be able to make connections with the processes of theological reflection on sexuality that are taking place in their own Churches with the tensions and difficulties that this reflection poses.

It was Thomas Kuhn who, in the context of the history and philosophy of science, with the publication in 1962 of *The Structure of Scientific Revolutions*,[3] began to develop and popularise the concept of the *paradigm* and *paradigm shift*. It is reckoned that by the year 2000 his work had been translated into 25 languages and that the English language editions had sold one million copies. It is hardly surprising that the concept has been taken up and used in many other fields and disciplines, including theology. Avery Dulles, in his opening chapter of *Models of the Church*,[4] looks at the relationship between images, models and paradigms. Images, he tells us, function as symbols: they speak not so much to the mind as to the heart, the imagination, the whole person. They have evocative power. In order to be effective and be accepted by people, images (symbols) must resonate with the experience of the people. Religious images must be deeply rooted in the corporate experience of the faithful. In times of rapid cultural change some images lose their effectiveness and others need time to take root. In some cases, in order to preserve the 'story' of the people, some symbols require that the people be given instruction e.g., in Liturgical catechesis.

3. Kuhn, T. S. (1962). *The structure of scientific revolutions*. Chicago University Press.
4. Dulles, Avery SJ. (1976). *Models of the Church: A critical assessment of the Church in all its aspects*. Ireland: Gill and Macmillan.

When theologians use an image they do so for the purpose of gaining a better understanding of the mysteries of faith. They employ images in a reflective and discriminate way, recognising which aspects of the image are applicable and which are not. When an image is used in a reflective and critical way to deepen our understanding of a reality it becomes a *model*. When a particular model becomes dominant over time it becomes a *paradigm*. It is clear that for centuries the dominant model of Church was the institutional model, an institution which Bellarmine referred to as 'a perfect society'. (It should be noted that the word 'perfect' in this context is not a moral judgement but a reference to the institutional structure.)

As such, this model had the power of a paradigm. In *Models of the Church,* Dulles suggests further models e.g., The Church as Sacrament, The Church as Herald, The Church as Servant.

In terms of their use Dulles tells us that models in theology can be explanatory or exploratory. On the explanatory level, models serve to synthesise what we already know and are inclined to believe. A model (of the Church for example) is accepted if it accounts for a large number of biblical and traditional data which accord with what history and experience tell us about the Christian life. The more applications a model has the more it suggests a real relationship between (in this case) the Church and the reality being used as an analogue. The exploratory (heuristic) use of models on the other hand, is their capacity to lead to new theological insights. This is not new revelation in the strict sense, but thanks to the ongoing experience of the Christian community, theology can discover aspects of the Gospel of which Christians were not previously aware or rediscover aspects which had been lost.

Dulles makes two further useful points we do well to bear in mind when considering change within theology. Whereas in the field of science, models and their application can be verified or falsified; in theology they must be judged by their fruits. So, Dulles reminds us, where the result is inner turbulence, anger, discord, disgust, distraction and the like, the Church (the people of God) can judge that the Spirit is not at work. In theology we assess models by living out the consequences to which they point. A model that leads to abuses is a bad model. His second point is that models in theology and religion have only partial correspondence with the reality they seek to explore. They are therefore inadequate and do not tell the whole story or present the full picture. Pursued alone any single model will lead to distortion.

Diarmuid O'Murchu[5] in his three-part article, before looking at five new paradigms in theology, answers the question *What is a paradigm?* 'A paradigm,' he tells us, 'is a framework of thought, a scheme for understanding certain aspects of a reality. A paradigm may be described as a "set of assumptions" whereby I understand reality in a certain way, and I respond (and act) in the light of that understanding.' By way of example he illustrates how the car mechanic who, faced with a car which has a fault, goes through a 'conceptual script'. He examines the car part by part to find the fault. Having found the part which is faulty, he replaces or repairs it and everything is back in working order. The assumption behind this approach is that the whole is equal to the sum of its parts. For a car, this mechanistic approach, model or paradigm is generally successful in finding the fault. For years this mechanistic paradigm was also used in medicine and, indeed, is still used in medicine today. However, it fails to solve many medical problems. As the findings of Freud, Jung and other schools of psychology and psychiatry came into vogue a new approach emerged which takes into account psychosomatic illness. This approach is an example of a *shift* from a mechanistic to a holistic view of reality. Here the underlying assumption is that the whole is greater than the sum of its parts. It was this shift which concerned Kuhn. O'Murchu goes on to describe the five stages in a paradigm shift identified by Kuhn:

5. O'Murchu, D. (1990). New Paradigms in Theology. *Priests and People, 4(10),* 388 – 396.

1. This first stage is noting anomalous findings that cannot be explained in terms of the current paradigm. At this early stage the paradigm itself is not questioned.

2. But in the second stage these findings appear so often that they cannot be ignored and at this stage the paradigm itself is questioned. Our way of viewing or understanding a reality no longer fits in with our experience of that reality.

3. This gives way to a third stage where a new paradigm is formulated to explain the anomalous findings. Behind the new paradigm are new experiences which lead to the new ways of thinking – the new conceptual and perceptual models.

4. In the fourth stage conflict emerges. Orthodoxy has been challenged with the introduction of the new paradigm. The guardians of orthodoxy, the establishment, in turn, challenge the new paradigm and will try to suppress it. A long, bruising battle may ensue between the promoters of the old and those of the new.

5. The final stage of the shift is generally the wide acceptance of the new paradigm as it gains credibility in explaining the new experiences.

In the light of these five stages O'Murchu goes on to define a paradigm shift as 'a distinctly *new* way of thinking about old problems. It is not figured out,' he tells us, 'but suddenly seen. It is not a discovery based on deductive reasoning. It arises as a type of quantum leap in human understanding.'

Those of us in the Roman Catholic Church, who lived through the optimism and hope of the Second Vatican Council and the years following, will surely recognise the stages identified above. I believe we are still at stage four. Within the Church we have experienced in the last forty years a struggle for the acceptance of new ways of thinking about old problems. How we interpret the Council Documents themselves is a case in point. There is the conflict between continuity and discontinuity: is it continuity and development? continuity and rupture? continuity and reform?[6] Several new ways of thinking have gained modest to widespread acceptance in the Church over these years. I would suggest that the shift from *contract* to *covenant* in the way we speak of marriage is an example. It is well illustrated in the language of The Document of Vatican II entitled *The Church in the Modern World,* which is known by its Latin title, *Gaudium et Spes* (Nos 47–54)[7] as an 'intimate partnership of life and love' and found its way into the opening Canon (1055) on marriage in the 1983 Code of Canon Law.[8] We note the important words in brackets in O'Murchu's definition above of a paradigm shift. It is not simply that we have a new understanding of a reality, but that 'we act' on this new understanding. In the area of moral theology, and in sexual morality in particular, this is important. It is in the area of sexual morality in particular that we experience stage four of the paradigm shift.

Those in other denominations will perhaps be more familiar with debates and struggles over the issue of the place of women in ministry. The Church of Scotland, the Church of England and the Methodists, for example, now ordain women to positions in ministry. Is this an example of theological and ministerial development, or, as some would argue, a rupture in the nature of the Church? Some would say that a change such as this should not take place in one Church in isolation from the rest of the Churches. Has the women's movement led to new ways of understanding the human person which are now reflected in expanding the place of women in ministry? Or has this change in the theology and structure been an example of 'bending to the latest fashion', which has no place in the Church? This issue has

---

6. For a discussion on this see O'Malley, J. W. et al. (2008). *Vatican II: Did anything happen?* New York: Continuum.

7. Flannery A. (Ed.). (1975). *Vatican II: The conciliar and post conciliar documents.* Dublin: Dominican Publications.

8. The Canon Law Society of Great Britain and Ireland (1983). *The Code of Canon Law in English translation.* London: Collins.

become more acute for some members of the Church of England who have been able to tolerate women priests, but who draw the line at the thought of women bishops. The movement from women being involved in ministry, to women being eligible for ordination represents a paradigm shift in the way that Kuhn and O'Murchu have outlined.

The traditional model or paradigm

The traditional model for sexual morality in the Catholic Church and which remains the official teaching of the magisterium is based on several principles, namely that the purpose of sexual activity is both procreative and unitive; that these two purposes must not be separated; that sexual activity belongs within marriage and the married relationship is to be exclusive, permanent and open to new life. In effect traditional sexual morality is marital morality. In recent years when these principles have been listed the statement has been added that marriage is between a man and a woman. Until recently, this traditional model has been shared by most Christian communities.

The architect of this teaching on marriage and sexuality is St Augustine (354–430). He is described by Jack Dominian as 'a theological giant whose influence remains to this day and a Christian sexual catastrophe whose shadow also remains to this day'.[9] Much of his thinking on sexuality came from his own experience – Dominian refers to him as 'addicted to sex' and says that he later came to deal with this as many addicts do, 'by repudiating, rejecting, rationalising and blackening their addiction'. It was Augustine who attached sexuality to original sin and particularly to Eve. He shared with the earlier Fathers of the Church a deep suspicion of sex and of women, aswell as the preference for virginity, continence and celibacy over marriage. Sexuality was a necessary evil. The Anglican theologian Bailey suggests,

---

9. Dominian, J. (2004). *The Evolution of Sexual Morality from Biology to Love,* Catholics for a Changing Church pamphlet. Chapel-en-le-Frith, High Peak: Blackfriars Publications.

'Augustine must bear no small measure of responsibility for the insinuation into our culture of the idea that Christianity regards sexuality as something particularly tainted with evil'.[10]

The influence of Augustinian teaching is found in the reformers. Luther was an Augustinian monk who shared the view that God had created men and women to marry for pleasurable procreation and companionship. The Fall, however, put an end to this by corrupting them. For Luther then, sex is not intrinsically good but basically corrupt and is redeemed by marriage. Sex outside of marriage is 'coarse, filthy, defiling, demonic'.[11] For Calvin, as Jordan quotes, 'the conjugal union itself is ordered to be a remedy for necessity, that we not break out into unrestrained lust . . . if the decency of marriage veils the shamefulness of incontinence, it ought not necessarily be made a provocation for it'. The reformers did not follow the superiority of virginity and celibacy over the married state, but while they defended marriage, gave it a dignity missing from previous medieval texts and insisted that it was perfectly compatible with ministry, this positive teaching on marriage did not include marital sex, something which was permitted but with cautions against abuse. As Jordan comments, 'good' sex is defined, not by its own characteristics, but by the absence of 'bad' sex. Calvin's veil covers the 'sordid'.

The 1917 Code of Canon Law (c.1013) in the Catholic Church distinguishes between primary and secondary ends, 'The primary end of marriage is the procreation and education of children: its secondary end is mutual help and the allaying of concupiscence'. That procreation should have been judged to be the primary end of marriage is enmeshed in the Church's understanding of sexuality throughout its history. But this is not an isolated history: rather, the Church's understanding has been shaped and influenced throughout the last 2000 years by the societies, cultures and philosophies within

10. Bailey, D. S. (1959). *The man-woman relationship in Christian thought.* London: Longman, p. 59.
11. Jordan, Mark D. (2002). *The ethics of sex.* Oxford: Blackwell, p. 120.

which she has grown. Like other religious and cultural traditions, the teachings within the Christian tradition regarding human sexuality are complex, subject to multiple outside influences and expressive of change and development through succeeding generations. In some instances the Churches' reaction to the influences is assimilation, adoption and acceptance: in others, it is a fiercely contested counter-cultural claim in which the Churches have sought to defend their own values and remain faithful to their sacred tradition and the teachings of Christ. This can be seen, for example, in the responses of different Churches to the topics of contraception, masturbation, homosexuality, and divorce and re-marriage.

The major influences on the nascent Christian Church were her Jewish origins and the Hellenistic-Roman influence of the empire to which she quickly spread. Although the latter influence eventually overwhelmed Jewish custom, nevertheless, the Jewish vision of marriage left its effect on the early Christian consciousness.

In the Old Testament there is a high regard for children, particularly boys. So of Rebecca in Genesis 24:60 we read, 'O sister of ours become the mother of thousands of ten thousands', and in Psalm 128 sons are 'olive plants around the table', and in Psalm 127 they are 'a reward like arrows in the hand of a warrior; happy the man who has his quiver full of them'. Sterility was considered an evil (Genesis 16:2, 30:2) or a punishment from God (Genesis 20:18) or as a disgrace from which, for example, Sarah, Rachel and Leah all tried to clear themselves by adopting the child which their maids bore their husbands.

In the New Testament, marriage was regarded as obligatory. An 18-year-old male could be compelled by a court to marry and the principal (primary) motive for marriage was procreation: to provide children, as Mackin tells us, 'so as to preserve the husband's family, to keep his and his father's name from dying and to keep the tribe, the nation itself, as the people of God in existence, withal to honour the ancient covenant commitment with Yahweh to be a light to the nations'.[12] Here already, at the birth of Christianity, the importance of procreation is linked to the major twin themes of Israel's vocation, covenant and election. Again, because of the demographic situation in the Judaism of Palestine at the time of Jesus with its high infant mortality and low life-expectancy, it was important for the child-bearer to marry as early as possible, that is, at the onset of puberty, so as to bear as many children as possible. Mackin concludes that if one were to ask about the essence of marriage among the Jews of Jesus' time, 'no more exact answer could be given than that it was an abiding relationship between a man and a woman intended mainly (primarily), although not exclusively for children'.[13]

The Old and New Testament scriptures are one source, the primary source indeed, among many in moral discernment, in deciding what is right and wrong. As in other disciplines there has been development in biblical scholarship. This has come about as a result of taking on broad findings from associated disciplines such as archaeology, Semitic languages, comparative literature and others. A traditional literal understanding and interpretation of scripture began in the middle of the nineteenth century to give way to a broader understanding of how 'the Bible came to be written' and led to 'the historical critical approach'. In terms of sexual morality these developments have given rise to new questions about, for example, how we are to understand 'homosexuality' in the Bible. An earlier understanding of masturbation in males was based on a particular interpretation of the story of Onan in Genesis 38:4–10 and indeed it was often referred to as onanism. No consideration whatsoever was given to masturbation in females. The use of the Bible as offering proof texts for particular moral condemnations is fraught with difficulty. There

12. Mackin, T. (2006). The Primitive Christian Understanding of Marriage. In K. Scott & M. Warren. (Eds.). *Perspectives on Marriage: A Reader.* OUP, p. 25.
13. Ibid p. 25.

is little agreement on what the particular language of the texts means. In discussing this issue Jordan[14] points out that there is a problem of always receiving scripture already categorised under some scheme of moral topics. We already know which verses are supposed to answer which moral question, so much so that he suggests when someone in discussion says, 'the Bible says', 'it is not so much a statement of interpretation but more a declaration of one's denomination'.[15] So the conflict in biblical interpretation and the use of the Bible, particularly in relation to issues of sexuality, is widespread throughout the denominations. It is clear from the ongoing debate within the Anglican Communion, which resulted from the Episcopal ordination in New Hampshire of Gene Robinson, and more recently within the Scottish Presbyterian Churches as a result of the induction of an openly gay minister into a parish in Aberdeen. We shall see later that developments in the other sources of moral discernment lead to new questions and provide new answers to old questions.

When we examine the Hellenistic and Roman influence on early Church thinking and experience we again see a society which daily faces immanent death, where infant mortality is very high and life expectancy equally low. It is understandable that procreation should feature more prominently than other aspects of sex. It is into such a society that the early Church was born and grew. Peter Brown described the Roman society of the early Church as a population, 'grazed thin with death'.[16] Citizens in the Roman Empire, he tells us, were born with a life expectancy of 25 years. Only four out of every hundred men and fewer women lived beyond the age of fifty. But beyond any personal desire for some form of immortality, as in Horace's great ode (I have built a monument)[17] these demographic circumstances highlighted a great social need. For the population of Rome to remain even stationary it would appear that every woman

14. Mark D. Jordan. (2002). *The ethics of sex.* Oxford: Blackwell, p. 36.
15. Ibid p. 20.
16. Brown, P. (1988). *The body and society.* London: Faber and Faber, p. 6.
17. Horace, *The Odes,* 3.30. See http://bafooz.livejournal.com/352381.html, retrieved August 7, 2009.

would have to have produced an average of five children.[18] There was great pressure on young men to use their bodies for procreation. The ancient city expected its citizens to expend a proportion of their energies begetting and rearing children to replace the dead. The emperor Augustus introduced legislation, which penalised bachelors and rewarded families for producing children. While virgin women had been part of the religious world of classical antiquity, the virgin priestesses, such as the Vestals, were free to marry later in life. By not marrying till they were thirty the Vestal Virgins stood out as an anomaly. They were, so to speak, the exception which proved the rule. The presence of such people in the cities heightened the awareness that marriage and childbirth were the unquestioned destiny of all other women.

The Church and the Natural Law paradigm

A key concept in the history of moral discernment (how we decide in specific cases what is right and what is wrong) in the Catholic Church has been that of *Natural Law*. It would be true to say that until the time of Thomas Aquinas there was no coherent, cohesive underlying philosophical system supporting the Natural Law. Nevertheless, the Natural Law theory can be traced back to our Greek and Roman philosophical heritage.

The basis of the theory is that we can arrive at a *general* norm of 'law' through the use of right reason applied to the human person and creation. For Catholics this has been a major source of moral discernment alongside Divine Revelation. Indeed, some descriptions of Natural Law would say that it is divinely inspired e.g., 'Deep within his conscience man [sic] discovers a law which he has not laid upon himself but which he must obey'.[19]

18. Horace, *The Odes*, 3.30. See http://bafooz.livejournal.com/352381.html, retrieved August 7, 2009. p. 6.
19. Gaudium et Spes 16, in Flannery A. (Ed.). (1975). *Vatican II: The conciliar and post conciliar documents.* Dublin: Dominican Publications.

For Aristotle, every living organism has its own nature which is teleological (i.e. it has an end or purpose or goal) dynamic and specific. However, for humans, Aristotle did not accept any *intrinsic* dynamism which propels the human towards this end, purpose or goal. There is the desire to reach this goal, but it depends more on favourable *extrinsic* circumstances, such as health, wealth, family, friends and so on. The general norm deriving from this understanding of nature is 'to do good and avoid evil'. We can note the universality but the lack of particularity – i.e. it applies always and everywhere but gives no guidance as to what to do in specific cases.

The Stoics also used the term Natural Law, sharing with Aristotle a rational view of reality but not stressing the individual organism as Aristotle did, but rather regarding the universe as the unit of intelligibility. So for the Stoics, happiness (the end or purpose or goal) consisted in having a right relationship to the universe or cosmos. Nevertheless, although there is general agreement among the Stoics, again it does not extend to the morality of particular actions. And this we shall see is the basic conflict and weakness in Natural Law Theory, how to translate the universal into the particular.

Roman law also adopted the notion of Natural Law, but as with the Greeks before them, there were different ways of understanding this Natural Law, e.g., Gaius, Cicero, Ulpian. The most influential view which has come down to us is that of Ulpian. While Gaius and others proposed a twofold law, namely, *Ius Civile* (the law proper to each country – determined by the legislature, custom and culture) and the *Ius Gentium* (the common heritage of all humanity), Ulpian proposed a threefold division of the Law in which he held to the *Ius Civile* but for him the *Ius Gentium*, while being universal as Gaius and others held, referred only to that part of the common heritage of all which could be arrived at through the use of reason. His third category of Law is *Ius Naturale*, Natural Law, also universal but defined as that which is common to man [sic] and the animals and is arrived at apart from any intervention of reason. In effect this turns out to be reproduction and nurture and has been extremely influential in the Catholic Church's teachings on matters of sexuality, while the *Ius Gentium* has influenced other aspects of morality e.g., the social teaching of the Catholic Church.

While Albert the Great rejected the Ulpian view of Natural Law, Thomas Aquinas accepted it and it has been the works of Thomas Aquinas which have found favour in the teaching of the Catholic Church for the last five hundred years and more. The great danger in the Ulpian view of Natural Law is to identify the human action with the physical or biological structure of the act which becomes a mere animal or biological process. So for example, in the approach to marriage and sexuality, traditional Natural Law moralists concentrated on the biological components of sexual intercourse. The personal aspects of the sexual union received little, if any, attention in spite of the official teaching of the Church from the time of Augustine about the goods of marriage. Ulpian's influence made it easier for Catholic Natural Law thinking to identify the human act with the physical structure of the act. This weakness of the traditional Natural Law was not confined to matters of sexuality but applied also to truth telling. The other major weakness of the traditional Natural Law theory as received through Ulpian is that of the *Classicist world view* (with its emphasis on the static, the immutable, the eternal and unchangeable and a methodology that is abstract, a priori and deductive) as distinct from the view of *historical consciousness* (with its recognition of dynamism, progress, change, growth and development and a methodology that is concrete, a posteriori and inductive). The first stresses the universal and the other the particular. In his treatment of Natural Law in relation to sexual activity, Aquinas distinguished between sins 'against nature' (*contra naturam*) and 'sins according to nature' (*ad naturam*). The first include those sexual activities where the purpose or finality of the act (procreation) can not be achieved e.g., masturbation, homosexuality, sexual intercourse using artificial contraception, bestiality and so on. The latter include those activities which are sinful even though they do not frustrate the purpose of the act, e.g., rape, fornication, adultery. Sins against nature according to Thomas are more serious than sins according to nature. This leads to the conclusion that masturbation is more serious than rape. Such a counter-intuitive conclusion demands a re-examination of the premises and indeed of the whole Natural Law argument.

New Natural Law Theory (NLLT)

A modern approach to *Natural Law Theory* from a traditionalist perspective, which seeks to revise the Natural Law Theory of Aquinas, has been proposed by Grisez, Finnis and Boyle and most fully explained in Grisez, *The Way of the Lord Jesus*.[20] It is summed up well by Todd A. Salzman.[21] The NNLT, also known as Basic Goods Theory (BGT) is based on the First Principle of Practical Reason (FPPR) or the First Principle of Morality (FPM) articulated by Aquinas as 'do good and avoid evil'. This principle 'articulates the necessary relationship between human goods and appropriate actions bearing upon them'. The basic goods (fundamental universal values) are divided into two sub-divisions. The first sub-division is a set of three, namely human life (including health, physical integrity, safety); knowledge and aesthetic appreciation; skilled performances of all kinds. These three goods are 'non-reflexive' or 'substantive' i.e. they exist prior to action and are therefore not defined in terms of choosing but indeed, provide reasons for choosing. The second sub-division of four basic goods includes self-integration; practical reasonableness or authenticity; justice and friendship; religion and holiness. These basic goods are 'reflexive' since 'they are both reasons

---

20. Grisez, G. (1993). *The way of the Lord Jesus.* Quincy, Illinois: Franciscan Press.
21. Salzman, Todd A. (2004). Natural law and basic goods: Particular to someone everywhere. In J. Keating (Ed.). *Moral theology; New directions and fundamental issues.* Paulist: New York.

for choosing and are in part defined in terms of choosing'. More recently an eighth basic good has been added, namely marriage and parenthood. In total these basic goods indicate what human beings are capable of becoming both as individuals and in community. Since these goods are aspects of personhood to which all beings have a natural inclination, they are universal. In 'doing good and avoiding evil' one ought to choose and will only those possibilities where willing and action are compatible with integral human fulfilment. Therefore, any actions, according to NNLT, that work against integral human fulfilment are unnatural and therefore morally wrong. Two other aspects of the NNLT must be mentioned, namely one is to respect every basic good and never choose against a basic good. Moreover, all basic goods are equal i.e. they are incommensurable.

Several criticisms can be made of this theory. We note immediately the deductive and universalist approach of the first principle of morality and the first principle of practical reason. The general principles need content and this is what the BGT proposes to offer. Salzman suggests the theory does not in fact do that. He criticises the theory because its 'lack of consideration for the particularity of basic goods is evident in the underlying world view, anthropology and ethical reasoning.' Salzman also criticises the theory on the grounds of inconsistency, particularly where the theory deals with aspects of basic human goods. Some aspects of a basic good are open to further understanding and others are not. In the case of slavery (an aspect of the basic good of justice) developments in understanding first allowed slavery, but future developments now forbid slavery. This is accepted as an authentic development. Yet other norms grounded in an aspect of a good do not allow development. There has been development in slavery and usury (aspects of the basic good of justice) but not in areas of sexuality. Salzman further asks what are the criteria for a solution where there is conflict among goods such that there is a development in one good which has repercussions on other goods or aspects of goods where development is not allowed? This is particularly problematic since the BGT, as we noted above, regards all goods as 'incommensurable', i.e. there is no hierarchy among them. From the perspective of the BGT the Magisterium is the definitive judge of whether an aspect of a basic good and the norm deduced from it can be revised. But this solution is unsatisfactory since it is based on authority and not on the particularity of the basic good. While the theory appears to participate in the paradigm shift from human nature to human person (see below), in as much as the basic goods are aspects of personhood, its underlying world view, anthropology and ethical reasoning as critiqued by Salzman, demonstrate that it is really a matter of 'new wine in old wineskins'.

From human nature to human person

In our consideration of the influence of both our Jewish and Hellenistic background on the priority of procreation we saw that demographics played a substantial role. But we can look at a different and much later demographic picture; this one offered by Pohier.[22] I quote the section in full.

> For many centuries half the human beings who were born did not reach the age of fifteen, and half of those who reached this age did not reach the age of thirty-five. That means that only a quarter of the babies who were born would be concerned with problems that might be posed by life after the age of thirty-five and only half of them by the problems of life between fifteen and thirty-five. Half the baby girls would die too young ever to achieve marriage or motherhood, and less than a quarter would have the experience of the menopause.
>
> In the middle of the nineteenth century, well after longevity had already begun to increase slowly, essentially for social and

22. Pohier, J. (1985). *God in fragments*. London: SCM, pp. 194–195.

economic reasons, a marriage would last on average for thirty-four years. The first third of it would be taken up by pregnancy and breastfeeding six children (on average); the husband would die before the last child got married. However, for numerous centuries the average length of a marriage was no more than twelve years, a period which was taken up with the pregnancies and breastfeeding of six children. French women who married in 1900 had a 15% chance of celebrating their golden wedding; for those who married in 1980 the chances (divorce apart) are 54%. The considerable increase in longevity, combined with the fact that thanks to a decrease in child mortality, two or three pregnancies (instead of seven) are enough for at least two children of a couple to reach adulthood, means that the life of a Western woman is divided into a different number of stages of a different kind from those which marked the life of her forebears.

Four years elapse between her wedding and her last pregnancy; then there is a much longer period in the marriage when the education of her children gives her a chance of working again much sooner, whether by necessity or by choice; then there is a long period in the marriage when the children have left home, but she, and certainly her husband, will both be retired and alone at home; finally there will be a period of widowhood which in France will be on average between seven and ten years.

So, over the centuries, the sexual life of a woman will on average have lasted less than twenty years, almost all of which will have coincided with the years taken up with her six pregnancies. However, the sexual life of a married Western woman at the end of the twentieth century will last on average over fifty years, only six or eight of which will have been taken up with two or three pregnancies.

Such changes, even if they are not those which most attract the attention of ideologists, have a considerable effect on sexual experience; quite apart from any theory, any choice or any reflection, the function of reproduction moves into the background, while the forefront is occupied by personal relationships and personal development.

It is to a consideration of a major shift in moral methodology in the last 40 to 50 years that we now turn. This shift is one away from human nature as the key concept in moral discourse to that of the human person. Using the language of Thomas Kuhn and those who follow him this is a major *paradigm shift* where we can trace the stages outlined by O'Murchu in the early part of this chapter.

Morality

In an introductory course on Moral Theology I would begin by suggesting to students that 'morality is a human endeavour'. By this I am suggesting that those of us who call ourselves Christian do not have a monopoly on morality. Other believers and non-believers can be, and of course are, moral. When we say it is a human endeavour we are also saying that humans only can be moral or immoral. We sometimes see people out walking with their pet dog and scolding it for being 'naughty' and telling it to 'behave'. No matter what language they might use they are not imputing moral guilt. Cats and dogs cannot be moral or immoral. We have all seen people, and perhaps have done it ourselves, go out to their car on a cold and frosty morning and find that the engine won't start. They begin by being 'nice' to it and try to cajole the thing into starting in the same way as they might cajole children into accepting their wishes, until finally in a fit of anger and frustration they kick the car, lock it up and start out on the long, slow, freezing walk to the bus stop. Again, no matter what language they might use, they do not impute moral guilt on the car. No, only people can be moral. Actions can't be moral – any morality assigned to actions is derivative: that is to say, derived from their human quality, derived from the fact that they are actions placed by humans and so become human actions. When we say, therefore, that morality is a human endeavour we are also saying that 'the human person is the foundational concept in morality'. Ethics, or the study of morality, like the study of economics, only exists because human beings live together and share the world's resources. Morality is about being human: it is about human interaction, the human interacting with self, other selves, with the world and with the transcendent, the last one from a faith perspective, with God. This understanding of morality as a human endeavour can be summed up in three quotations – and notice I keep using the word endeavour. Morality is something we have to work at; being fully human is something we have to work at: and when I say 'morality is a human endeavour', I am also saying morality is the endeavour to be fully human. The first of my three quotations is from an Anglican source, from the Anglican Board for Social Responsibility 1987 Report No 56:

> Morality is essentially a matter of respect for persons and the necessary conditions for their flourishing.[23]

We find the same emphasis on the human person in the Second Vatican Council Document on the Church in the Modern World, *Gaudium et Spes* (Paragraphs 3, 12, 35 and 76). My second quotation is from a Roman Catholic Source, from the drafting committee of that document, *Gaudium et Spes,* and states:

> Human activity must be judged in so far as it refers to the human person integrally and adequately considered.[24]

The third of my three quotations is from a secular source, from the Universal Declaration on Human Rights which recognises,

> These rights derive from the inherent dignity of the human person.[25]

23. Changing Britain: Social Diversity and Moral Unity n. 56, (1987). Produced by the Church of England Board for Social Responsibility (BSR), quoted in Kelly, Kevin T. (1992). *New directions in moral theology: The challenge of being human.* London: Chapman, p. 27.
24. Acta Synodalia Concilii Vaticani II, vol IV, part 7, p. 502, n. 37, quoted in Kelly, Kevin T. (1992). *New Directions in moral theology: The challenge of being human.* London: Chapman, p. 30.
25. http://www.un.org/en/documents/udhr/, retrieved August 7, 2009.

This shift is one from the act to the person placing the act, a shift from an act-centred morality to a person-centred morality. A major consequence of this shift is to look again at such traditional ideas as 'intrinsic evil' and 'objective and subjective morality' and 'exceptionless norms', an understanding that certain actions are always and everywhere wrong. This is the language of act-centred morality. It seems to me that the judgement of an action only becomes a moral judgement when we consider the person placing the act and in the context within which the person places the act. This idea of the three-font principle, the material act, the person placing the act and the circumstances is not new. Certainly we can suggest universal norms such as do good and avoid evil. Certainly we can promote universal values such as honesty, fidelity and many others. These are characteristics of human persons which find expression in the actions of persons. But the traditional act-centred morality is an inadequate instrument for determining morality in particular cases.

The concept of 'the human person integrally and adequately considered' has been developed in recent years by a number of writers and opens up a wider Christian anthropology than the Natural Law arguments. One of these writers is the Flemish moral theologian Louis Janssens. He developed his ideas in an oft-quoted article in *Louvain Studies*[26] where he looks at eight 'Fundamental and Constant Dimensions of the Human Person'. In the same year Richard McBrien[27] in his chapter on Spirituality explores the same subject matter with twelve 'theological criteria to evaluate a spirituality consistent with the Catholic tradition'.

An example of a paradigm shift described above which has taken place in the last 50 years or so is to be found in the report of the Catholic Theological Society of America in 1977.[28] In this report the

26. Janssens, L. (1980). Artificial Insemination: Ethical Considerations, *Louvain Studies*, 5, pp. 3 – 29.
27. McBrien, R. (1980). Spirituality. In *Catholicism, Vol. 2.* London: Geoffrey Chapman. pp. 1090ff.
28. Kosnik, A., Carroll, W., Cunningham, A., Modras, R., & Schulte, R. (Eds.). (1997). *Human sexuality: New directions in American Catholic thought.* New York: Paulist.

authors suggest a broadening of the traditional purpose of sexuality from *procreative and unitive* to *creative and integrative*. They formulate their basic principle as follows:

> Wholesome human sexuality is that which fosters a creative growth towards integration. Destructive sexuality results in personal frustration and interpersonal alienation.

How then do we morally evaluate sexual activity? They suggest:

> We maintain that it is appropriate to ask whether a specific sexual behaviour realises certain values that are conducive to creative growth and integration of the human person. Among these values we would single out the following as particularly significant; they are those which are: self-liberating, other-enriching, honest, faithful, socially responsible, life-serving, joyous. Where such qualities prevail, one can be reasonably sure that the sexual behaviour that has brought them forth is wholesome and moral. On the contrary, where sexual conduct becomes personally frustrating and self-destructive, manipulative and enslaving of others, deceitful and dishonest, inconsistent and unstable, indiscriminate and promiscuous, irresponsible and non-life serving, burdensome and repugnant, ungenerous and un-Christ-like, it is clear that God's ingenious gift for calling us to creative and integrative growth has been seriously abused. (pp. 78–79)

The reception of this report was rather mixed. Here are some of the comments made by reviewers at the time. Among the unfavourable reviews we have:

1. New York Diocese (Chancellor): 'tips the balance between objective law and subjective conscience and gives a purely subjective definition of sexuality.'

2. William B. Smith (Theologian): 'the book deserves an X rating, not for pornography, but for violence – the extreme

violence done to sources of Sacred theology, Sacred Scripture, Sacred Tradition and the Magisterium of the Church.'

3. Six members of the CTSA (Catholic Theological Society of America) under whose auspices the report was published view the work as 'partisan in outlook, poor in scholarship, weak in argumentation and fallacious in conclusions'.

Among the favourable reviews are the following:

1. Rosemary Ruether (Theologian): 'a major effort to shift the basis of sexual ethics from act-oriented to person-oriented principles . . . traditional moralists will be acutely discomfited by these principles.'

2. Giles Milhaven (Theologian): 'the result of listening to that large segment of the Catholic people, growing larger each year, that live sexual lives in ways different from what the Church sanctions.'

3. Joseph Cuneen (Theologian): 'a courageous and long-overdue achievement. Any fair reading of the text will make clear that its authors are moderates in their approach to theological ethics and that they are concerned to preserve continuity in Catholic teaching while presenting a more contemporary person-oriented rather than an act-oriented approach to sexuality.'

Several things stand out in these comments: firstly, they are sharply divided and secondly, they seem to reveal as much about the perspectives of the respondents as they do about the book itself. They lay bare what the respondents expect and desire to find in a theological study of sexuality. These expectations demonstrate certain attitudes towards human nature, Church authority, moral norms, the maturity of people etc. They represent those who are called the 'traditionalists' (the unfavourable comments) and those who are called 'revisionists' (the favourable comments). These terms are not intended to be pejorative but simply to identify two contrasting approaches or, in the language of the beginning of this chapter, 'paradigms' in sexual ethics. It is clear from the language of the comments, sometimes quite intemperate, that in 1977 we were still at stage four in the development of a paradigm shift. The situation over 30 years later is little different.

This paradigm from the Catholic Theological Society of America is only one of a number which have emerged in recent decades from within faith communities. Insights from various forms of liberation theology, be they from a gay and lesbian perspective, the perspective of women, from the poor, or some other perspective, have challenged the orthodoxies of the various faith communities in relation to sexual and marital morality. What the various insights have in common is that they highlight the needs, concerns and realities of the disadvantaged and the marginalised. From outside organised faith communities also, for example the various manifestations of the 'New Age Movement', further paradigms have been emerging which likewise challenge the traditional orthodoxies.

More recently, theological discourse in the area of marital and sexual morality has highlighted the meaning (of the sexual act) and the understanding of complementarity. We see this in the writings of Pope John Paul II and those who adopt the Natural Law approach. Salzman and Lawler[29] develop their understanding of complementarity in their person-centred Natural Law approach, an approach which seeks to develop the person-centred paradigm within the Natural Law tradition. This approach considers a holistic complementarity based on a relationship model where the authors consider personal complementarity of greater importance than a reproductive complementarity emphasised in John Paul II's 'Theology of the Body'. In this person-centred complementarity we see the relationship between

29. Salzman, Todd A. & Lawler, Michael G. (2009). *The sexual person: toward a renewed Catholic anthropology.* Washington DC: Georgetown University Press.

the two traditional purposes of sexuality and marriage, the unitive and the procreative, come once again under scrutiny. The traditional hierarchy of purposes of sex and marriage (primary and secondary) which had been enshrined in the 1917 Code of Canon Law and omitted from the 1983 Code reappears reversed. This relationship approach to complementarity allows a more liberal interpretation of many of the moral issues surrounding marriage and sexuality such as the use of artificial contraception, cohabitation, divorce and re-marriage and homosexuality. A reviewer of the book notes that 'the book will be noticed because of its controversial positions . . . but they (the authors) have begun exactly the right kind of dialogue about how sexual actions affect real people's lives'. She adds, as if alluding to stage 4 in the development of a paradigm shift, 'May it continue in peace'.[30]

Beyond sexuality

We mentioned above that there are a number of sources for moral discernment and that developments have taken place over the years in those disciplines which have been used as tools in moral discernment. One such development has been to make a distinction between sexuality and gender. This is a distinction recognised by people of all faith communities as well as by those who have no religious affiliation. This development has important implications for ethics and morality. It creates a whole new arena within which to look at 'the human person integrally and adequately considered' and gives rise to different questions. The moral and ethical issues surrounding gender are much broader than the sexual; they are issues of justice, equality, rights, individual freedoms, inclusion, empowerment and others. They give rise to debates on public accountability and public policy. Activities, which in the past would have been considered sexual and

30. Hanlon Rubio, J. (6th February, 2009). Winter books: Sex that contributes. (Review of the book *The sexual person: Toward a renewed Catholic anthropology.*) *National Catholic Reporter.*

moral judgements about which would have come under the umbrella of sexual ethics, are now seen to have much wider ramifications. In the Canon Law of the Catholic Church, for example, the sexual abuse of minors by a cleric is treated in canon 1395 §2 as 'an offence against the sixth commandment of the Decalogue'.[31] It was the Council of Trent (1545–1563)[32] which put all matters of sexuality under the umbrella of the commandment, 'Thou shalt not commit adultery'. Such offences whether committed by clerics or others are now seen and experienced as much more than that. Rape is recognised and experienced as an act of violence and power; aspects of pornography are seen and experienced as essentially expressing certain attitudes towards women.

Allied to this distinction between sexuality and gender is the growing understanding of the importance of the experience of 'ordinary people' as a source of moral discernment. We saw hints of this when looking at the process of a paradigm shift. This experience of 'ordinary people' highlights within faith communities the importance of the 'reception of doctrine'.[33] This recognition of the importance of the experience of the faith community is too serious to be dismissed by an argument which says the Church is not a democracy or moral decisions are not arrived at through opinion polls. Rather, the experience of the faith community is an aspect of the 'sensus fidelium', a recognition that the Holy Spirit blows where she wills and cannot be confined to authority structures of an institution.

Conclusion

In this chapter I have sought to demonstrate that once we are able to appreciate the value of the paradigm shift as a tool for understanding change we become more open to change. Within any faith community

---

31. *The Code of Canon Law.* (1983). Eerdmans.
32. http://history.hanover.edu/texts/trent.html, retrieved August 7, 2009.
33. For examples of acceptance of change see Hoose, B. (1994). Received Wisdom? Reviewing the Role of Tradition. In *Christian ethics.* London: Geoffrey Chapman.

change can be experienced in a whole variety of areas, in the structure and governance of the community, in its prayer and worship, in its attitudes to women, to the environment or to issues of justice and many more. In the context of this book this chapter looked at the paradigms in relation to sexual morality. The paradigms we have looked at have laid bare various anthropologies on the basis of which individuals, theologians and faith communities make their moral judgements on sexual behaviour. Thus I have looked at the traditional Natural Law paradigm, the Person-Centred paradigm and two approaches which seek to combine the two paradigms, the traditionalist Basic Goods Theory of Grisez, Finnis and Boyle and the more recent revisionist approach of Salzman and Lawler. The paradigm shift from the traditionalist to the revisionist is in the first instance a shift in perception or world view, brought about by unexplained experiences, from the *classicist* world view with its emphasis on the static, the immutable, the eternal and unchangeable to the *historical consciousness* world view with its recognition of dynamism, progress, change, growth and development. This change in world view leads to a change in methodology in theology, in this case in theology of sexuality. It is a change from a methodology that stresses the abstract, the a priori and the deductive to one which favours the concrete, the a posteriori and the inductive. We stressed that as our perception changes so we act upon it. So, finally, in the application of the theology to issues in sexuality there is a shift in moral judgement from the universal and general to the specific and the particular. The reader must decide which of the various approaches speaks more clearly to the experience of men and women today and realises more fully those values which support human flourishing.

SIXTEEN

In conclusion:
Sexual continence, sexual sublimation and fidelity to the Gospel

Joanne Marie Greer and Brendan Geary

This book has been written for Christians who find themselves dealing with a range of sexual issues and feel the need for up-to-date research, reflection and guidance. All of us are sexual beings, and all of us try to live Gospel values of Jesus faithfully, as well as provide help and guidance to people who also look for help in the area of sexuality.

All of the authors are involved in pastoral work in some capacity, as priests, chaplains, teachers, counsellors, psychiatrists, or psychologists. Dermot Lane, President of Mater Dei Catechetical Institute in Dublin, asked recently, 'How does theology keep pace with the extraordinary developments in other disciplines, especially the social sciences, the hard sciences and cosmology?'[1] This book is an attempt to bring insights and knowledge in the area of psychology and psychotherapy to people who are actively involved in or who are in training for ministry. Research and knowledge in the social sciences continually develops. Christians need to keep one eye on the tradition and another eye open to developments that can improve pastoral practice. As Charles Gay mentioned in his chapter on Sexuality and theology, theological models must be evaluated according to their fruits: does this way of understanding promote the values of the Gospel? Does it promote fidelity, foster compassion, ease unnecessary suffering, promote well-being, and enhance our humanity? In opening

---

1. Lane, D. A. (2009). Fifty years of theology. *The Furrow, 60*, (7 /8), 399 – 403.

up sexual topics for exploration and discussion, are we enabling people to live better Christian lives?

Sexual continence

It is a given of the Christian faith, with its central focus on incarnation, that both Jesus and ourselves are embodied beings. Historically, this doctrine stood in opposition to many early Christian-era heresies that saw the body as evil and only the soul as potentially good, and Jesus as possessing only a sort of pseudo-body. In a Gospel-based practice of Christianity, we must perforce see both body and soul as good and as united inseparably as a '*psyche-soma*'. The natural interplay of each unique *psyche-soma* originates at the creation of each human being, but is further shaped by that person's everyday struggles. Someone once compared each Christian community to a vessel full of rough-shaped rocks. In rubbing up against each other and in the 'shake-ups' that life brings, each rock is gradually transformed into a smooth stone. This metaphor implies some pain, some sacrifice, some 'chipping-off of rough edges' in our interactions. There is pain and sacrifice in being sexual *and* Christian, just as there is integrating any other aspect of human relations with our faith.

While embracing sexuality as a natural, normal, and beautiful aspect of humanness, Christians must integrate it into the one necessary goal of a Christian life, the following of Christ. This implies some conscious, purposeful choices about sexual expression and sexual enjoyment. Some examples have been mentioned in the preceding chapters, for example the married man who must abstain from intercourse for a period of weeks after the birth of his child, in order to protect his wife's sexual health. This requires an attitude of Christian love and justice toward the wife's bodily needs, and a deliberate inhibition of a natural impulse that is morally neutral *per se*, but morally wrong (un-Christlike) in this specific context. This type of temporary, purposeful sexual abstinence has been termed 'sexual continence'. One does not completely abjure sexual acts, as a vowed celibate might, but one's choices of when and how to be sexually active are modified by more important considerations. In this case, the man modifies his attitude toward his sexual object (here, the wife) and his inward sexual impulse (the wish to enjoy intercourse).

If the following of Christ is the one necessary thing in our lives, sexual choices must be approached as one aspect of who we aspire to be as a Christian, rather than blindly driven by hormones and obsessions. However, this does not imply that Christians lack either hormones or obsessions, but simply that we are aware of and apply ourselves to the task of maintaining sexual continence. We guide our sexual acts and sexual impulses in a direction commensurate with our overarching life goal. This might mean less sex, but on the other hand it might mean more sex. For example, if a man (typically) has more intense and frequent sexual needs, his wife might, in Christian charity, offer him her body when she herself would rather just go to sleep. This is not patriarchy or sexual slavery – it is a generous act of Christian love between equals before God. And if she cannot offer herself generously and lovingly on this particular night, it is best for the marriage that she simply go to sleep, and her husband practise sexual continence.

Sexual sublimation

Sublimation is a psychoanalytic term that refers to the redirecting of a bodily drive to a higher end. Because sexual examples are always 'hot potatoes' in a classroom, one of us (Joanne) usually began teaching this concept from the perspective of eating. One can sublimate the animal drive to eat by good table manners, nice crystal and china, attention to the needs of other diners, pleasant conversation, taking only one's share, etc. In this way an animal-level act becomes a social grace and perhaps even an act of loving concern toward fellow-diners.

Sexual sublimation is one way of living out the Christian calling. It is a conscious choice of those Christians who pursue a celibate lifestyle in order to put themselves completely at the service of the Christian community. Having no spouse, they choose God for their special object of intimacy. Having no children, all children in need become their children.

Sexual sublimation may be forced upon a Christian when the only sexual object desired by the 'natural man' is incompatible with justice and charity. For example, the paedophile cannot satisfy his natural sexual desires without a grave injury to another human being. In this case, the Christian paedophile must either abstain sexually, or choose an unexciting object for his sexual needs. For example, he might choose a woman with whom he shares other bases of intimacy (it should be remembered that many paedophiles are also able to be attracted to adult, usually female, partners), and with whom he would like to start a family, even though sexual intercourse will not be as exciting for him as it would be with the forbidden child. In this situation, his sexuality must be consciously sublimated into an unselfish devotion to his marriage partner, including seeking her sexual satisfaction.

The current obsession of Christians with sex: is it Gospel-based?

The reader was perhaps surprised by the reference above to the 'Christian paedophile'. In the current excessive chatter surrounding sexual sins of prominent Christians, especially in the USA, we must beware of elevating sexual purity to a litmus test of Christian faith. None of us is perfect; each of us is capable of serious sin, including serious sexual sin. Both of us shared a similar story related to elder members of religious orders. Joanne writes:

> In my college days I frequently passed through a door tended by a nun in her late eighties. Although she was retired and fragile, this was her way of continuing to contribute to the community. It was an object of hilarity to me and the other young women studying there that she would always greet us thus: 'Good

morning, dear. Pray for my perseverance.' 'After sixty-five years as a nun, what evil was she anticipating that she would get into?' we giggled to each other. As I slowly approach her age, I now understand very well that we are all, at every moment of our lives, capable of losing our way.

In Brendan's order (the Marist Brothers) a similar story is told of an older Australian Brother who had been in positions of leadership in the congregation for over thirty years. In his later years he often asked the younger men to pray for his perseverance.

In this book, which assumes a Christian but ecumenical audience, the one thing the writers and readers certainly hold in common is Jesus, the Christ, as his words and acts are presented to us in the four Gospels. So the question suggests itself, 'What did Jesus say about sexual problems and misdeeds, and how much did he emphasise them?'

Looking at the four Gospels, Jesus uses the word 'God' 395 times, 'man' 117 times, 'woman' 113 times, and 'child' 105 times (see Table 1). In contrast, words related to sexuality are almost never found in the Gospels. This is all the more striking since, by consulting the Epistles as well as secular historical sources, we find that the world of Jesus' time was rife with all sorts of repugnant sexual excesses, even including infanticide of newborn babies. But evidently Jesus simply had nothing direct to say about all of this! Instead, his preoccupations were faith, hope, and loving relationships of men, women, and children to God and to each other. He was also concerned with hypocrisy, living in a way that rejected violence and exploitation of others, and calling people to repentance. Implied in Jesus' teaching, of course, is the assumption that human beings would treat each other kindly and fairly, including in the sexual sphere. But we do not find the *emphasis* on sexual acts that is present in many Western Christian churches today. Jesus appears to assume that if people tend seriously to the business of seeking God, other things will fall into place, and do not need enumeration item by item.

Making the rounds of the 'talking heads' on television at present is a recent quip of a nutrition writer: 'Eat food, not too much, mostly plants'. His laconic understatement was meant to reprove the greedy abuse of food, resulting in myriad health problems and an excess consumption of the world's resources. It is not food that is killing people; rather, it is excessive preoccupation with food. Similarly, it is not sex that will take Christians away from Gospel values; rather, it is excessive preoccupation with sex. So, one might analogously conclude 'Be sexual, not too much, in ways that don't harm you or others'. Then we can all get on with the real business of the Gospel message: love of God and our fellow human beings. This supports Karl Hanson's observation that it would be strange if human beings had learned that healthy living involved exercising restraint in all areas of life except sexuality.[2]

That said, the existence of this book is still justified. Many earnest Christians have difficulty surmounting the obstacles that sexual issues throw in the path of their journey toward union with God. When Joanne, as a sixteen-year-old, first encountered the Gospels seriously, a teacher[3] commented, 'Remember, feelings don't count. What counts are your intentions'. This is certainly true; 'Love is in the will', according to St Augustine. This doesn't mean that feelings are not important; it does mean that they are not always the best guide to personal behaviour, especially in the sexual area where passions can often run high. But we must also recognise how difficult it is when a person's spontaneous sexual feelings create a sense of shame, degradation, or unworthiness. Sexual feelings are inescapable; they are part of being human. Many Christians live/worship in religious settings where a specific sexual protocol is equated with Godliness. They suffer immeasurably, sometimes to the point of despair.

---

2. Långström, N., & Hanson, R. K. (2006). Population correlates are relevant to understanding hypersexuality: A response to Giles. *Archives of Sexual Behavior, 35*: 643 – 644.

3. Sister Beverly Lartigue, C.S.J., St. Joseph Academy, New Orleans, La. 1954.

In this book, we offer useful resources for those clergy, vowed religious, or lay church workers to whom Christians may turn when they feel confusion or shame concerning their sexual lives. It may be that the book will be useful for those who suffer to read directly as well. However, we hope we have not implied that sexual issues are at the core of the Christian journey. Nothing could be further from our intentions.

Table 1
Some word counts from the four Gospels

God	395
Man (*excluding* 'Son of Man')	117
Woman	113
Child	105
Wife	45
Body	40
Marriage	23
Adultery	15
Husband	13
Sodom(y)* (used as a proxy for homosexuality)	5
Masturbation	0
Rape	0
Onanism (used as a proxy for masturbation)	0
Abortion	0
Lay with	0
Intercourse	0
Prostitute	0
Fornication, Fornicator	0
all 5 instances occur in the context of 'your situation will be worse than that of Sodom'	

Source: New American Bible Intratext: http://www.vatican.va/archive/ENG0839/_FA.HTM.
Counts are certainly approximately correct. Any small errors are due to Greer's computer manipulations of the text.

About the contributors

Jocelyn Bryan is Postgraduate Director at St John's College, Durham. She is a Methodist local preacher and has worked in ministerial formation for the past 10 years. Her PhD is in psychology and she teaches in practical theology, pastoral care, and psychology and Christian ministry. She has published chapters on adolescence and dealing with difficult people. She co-edited *The Christian handbook of abuse, addiction and difficult behaviour* with Brendan Geary.

Christopher C. H. Cook is a Professorial Research Fellow in the Department of Theology and Religion at Durham University. He trained at St George's Hospital Medical School, London, and has worked in the psychiatry of substance misuse for 24 years. He was ordained as an Anglican priest in 2001. He worked as Professor of the Psychiatry of Alcohol Misuse at the University of Kent from 1997 to 2003. He is interested in spirituality, theology and health, and has recently edited (with Andrew Powell and Andrew Sims) a book entitled *Spirituality and psychiatry* (Royal College of Psychiatrists Press, 2009).

Gerard Fieldhouse-Byrne is a priest of Salford Diocese in England, and is currently the Director of the St Luke's Centre, Manchester. He has a Masters in Clinical Social Work and a Doctorate in Counselling from Boston University, USA. After two years on the staff at the Saint Luke Institute in Maryland, he returned to Manchester where he had a private clinical practice and established support structures for priests within the diocese. He has been assigned to two parishes recovering from clergy sexual abuse and has worked with perpetrators and victims of clergy sexual abuse. Currently assigned to the St Luke's Centre in Manchester he is involved in assessment, treatment and education work for clergy and members of religious orders.

Charles Gay FMS, a Marist Brother from Scotland, has recently retired after 40 years in education during which time he was a secondary RE teacher, head of an RE department, an RE adviser and inspector and, in the last five years, a lecturer in Religious Studies at a university college in Nairobi, Kenya. Brother Charles is a graduate in Economics and German of the University of Glasgow, in Religious Education of the Mater Dei Institute, Dublin, and holds the post-graduate degrees of MTh (Christian Ethics) and MA (Canon Law) from Heythrop College, University of London.

Brendan Geary FMS is a Marist Brother and Provincial of the West Central Europe Province of Marist Brothers, based in the Netherlands. He has worked as a teacher, spiritual director and psychotherapist, and specialised in work with victims and perpetrators of sexual abuse. He has worked in the United Kingdom, Africa and the United States, and has published papers on sex offenders, counselling, and spirituality. He contributed chapters on Child Sexual Abuse and Adult Bullying to *The Christian handbook of abuse, addiction and difficult behaviour*, which he co-edited with Jocelyn Bryan.

Joanne Marie Greer, PhD, is Professor Emerita of Pastoral Counselling at Loyola University Maryland, USA, where she formerly directed the research component of the pastoral counselling doctoral programme. She is also a retired psychoanalyst. She has edited two books on sexual abuse victims and sexual abusers. She also edited the professional journal *Research in the Social Scientific Study of Religion* until retirement. She has written a number of journal articles on public health, mental health, and religion or spirituality.

Ed Hone CSsR is a Redemptorist priest who is currently doing post-graduate study at Durham University. He is a graduate in Theology from Durham and Kent universities. He has a wide experience in mission and evangelisation as a pastor, writer, preacher of parish missions, retreat-giver, lecturer and broadcaster. He is co-author with Dr Roisìn Coll, a lecturer in education at Glasgow University, of 'All Together – Creative Prayer with Children'.

Kevin Kelly is a retired Catholic priest of Liverpool Archdiocese. As well as serving as parish priest in inner-city Liverpool, Skelmersdale New Town and Widnes (a shared Catholic/Anglican church), he taught moral theology at Heythrop College and at Liverpool Hope University, where he is now an emeritus research fellow. He has written numerous articles on moral and pastoral theology. He is author of 'Divorce and Second Marriage', 'New Directions in Moral Theology', 'New Directions in Sexual Ethics', and 'From a Parish Base', and is a member of CAFOD's HIV Advisory Group.

Alison Moore currently works as Adviser in Pastoral Care and Counselling for the Diocese of Durham, Church of England. She trained in counselling in the 1980s, for many years specialising in relationship counselling, which has led to an ongoing interest in conflict transformation. She now oversees the diocesan counselling service in Durham and also offers training and consultancy in pastoral care for parish groups and ministers. Convinced of the importance of lay theological education, she holds a Cambridge theology diploma. Previous writing includes an autobiographical chapter in *My Journey Your Journey*, a collection of faith stories commissioned by the previous Archbishop of Canterbury, George Carey, and the chapter on 'Care of Self' in *The Christian handbook of abuse, addiction and difficult behaviour*. Having found that therapeutic and theological language can be incomprehensible and disempowering for ordinary readers, Alison is committed to being a good 'translator' of technical language.

Andrew Peden is a clinical psychologist at St Luke's Centre, Manchester, where he coordinates psychological assessments of candidates for the priesthood and religious life. He has 30 years' experience in mental health. For many years, he worked within the National Health Service, at one point as the head of a child and adolescent psychology service, in which capacity he sat on the Area Child Protection Committee, and the Child Abuse Prevention Sub-Committee. He also acted as an independent expert in providing assessment of adults seeking compensation through the Redress Board arising from experiences of abuse in the Irish Industrial Schools.

Tony Robinson is a clinical psychologist who works in private practice. He has worked in Australia and the USA, and was a consultant at St Luke's Centre in Manchester, England, along with some of his co-authors. Dr Robinson has over 20 years' experience in mental health. He has presented papers at a variety of national and inter-national conferences and has published professional articles.

Mary Ross SND is a Sister of Notre Dame and an Educational Psychologist. In 2008 she retired as Director of the Notre Dame Centre in Glasgow, which offers professional assessment and therapeutic support to children, young people and their families from all back-grounds and many parts of Scotland. Recently Mary has opened a Parental Advice Shop in a shop front store in the West End of Glasgow, which is free of charge, with flexible opening hours. Mary was awarded an MBE in the 2008 Honours list for her services to children.

Gerardine Taylor-Robinson is a clinical psychologist and consultant who works in private practice in Sydney, Australia. She has over 20 years' experience in mental health both in the USA and Australia. For over 11 years, she was the Clinical Director of Encompass Australasia. Under her direction, this service gained an international reputation as a multi-disciplinary team which delivered best-practice treatment approaches in an encouraging and non-judgemental environment. She has published professional articles and has presented papers at a variety of national and international conferences.

Ashley Wilson is Chaplain to St Chad's College in Durham. Before ordination he worked as a veterinary surgeon in general practice for fifteen years. He is a graduate in Theology from Durham University and prior to taking up his current post he was a parish priest in North Yorkshire, as well as a Children & Youth Officer in York diocese. His PhD (also from Durham University) is in Ethics and Theology. He is a member of Changing Attitude and is married with two grown-up children.

Indexes

Index of subjects

Index of authors